Popular Music of Vietnam

Routledge Studies in Ethnomusicology

Popular Music of Vietnam

The Politics of Remembering, the Economics of Forgetting

Dale A. Olsen

Routledge
Taylor & Francis Group
New York   London

First published 2008
by Routledge
270 Madison Ave, New York, NY 10016

Simultaneously published in the UK
by Routledge
2 Park Square, Milton Park, Abingdon, Oxon OX14 4RN

Routledge is an imprint of the Taylor & Francis Group, an informa business

© 2008 Taylor & Francis

Typeset in Sabon by IBT Global.
Printed and bound in the United States of America on acid-free paper by IBT Global.

Library of Congress Cataloging in Publication Data

Olsen, Dale A. (Dale Alan)
  Popular music of Vietnam : the politics of remembering, the economics of forgetting /
By Dale A. Olsen.
    p. cm.—(Routledge studies in ethnomusicology ; 1)
  Includes bibliographical references (p. 269) and index.
  ISBN 978-0-415-98886-5
  1. Popular music—Vietnam—1991–2000—History and criticism. 2. Popular music—Vietnam—2001–2010—History and criticism. 3. Musicians—Vietnam. I Title.
    ML3502.V5O57 2009
    781.6309597—dc22
    2008005453

Trịnh Công Sơn song lyrics, from Hue-Tam, ed. 2001. "Faces of Remembrance and Forgetting." In *The Country of Memory: Remaking the Past in Late Socialist Vietnam*, edited by Hue-Tam Ho Tai, (p. 167–195). Printed by permission of the University of California Press, Berkeley.

Trịnh Công Sơn song lyrics, from Jamieson, Neil L. 1993. *Understanding Vietnam* (p. 326–329). Printed by permission of the University of California Press, Berkeley.

Phạm Duy song lyrics, from Phạm Duy. 1975. *Musics of Vietnam*. Edited by Dale R. Whiteside, with an Introduction by Stephen Addiss. Printed by permission of the Southern Illinois University Press, Carbondale, from the "Introduction" by Stephen Addiss (p. xvii), from the song "Heart Song—Our Foe" by Phạm Duy.

Three illustrations (cartoons) printed by permission from the *Việt Nam News Agency*. (1) Cartoon from the *Việt Nam News*, February 5, 1996 (Figure 6.1). (2) Cartoon from the *Việt Nam News*, February 9, 1996 (Figure 9.1). (3) Cartoon from the *Việt Nam News*, March 14, 2004 (Figure 9.3).

ISBN10: 0-415-98886-1 (hbk)
ISBN10: 0-203-89279-8 (ebk)

ISBN13: 978-0-415-98886-5 (hbk)
ISBN13: 978-0-203-89279-4 (ebk)

Dedicated to Diane and our shared memories of Vietnam

Contents

List of Figures

Foreword

Saigon rocks! The Dana Leong Band's tour of Vietnam, sponsored by the U. S. Department of State's Bureau of Educational and Cultural Affairs, arrived in Vietnam in December 2007, and "Vietnamese audiences were spurred to dance, sing, and try out rapping" (http://hochiminh.usconsulate. gov/). Packed Vietnamese concerts given by American duo Bob and Tucker Livingston took "Vietnamese audiences 'down country roads'" in 2008 (op. cit.). In January 2008, the biggest "Tiger Unite 08" concert extravaganza to date drew in 25,000 people (as noted by major national newspapers) for a joint concert by the American Grammy Award-nominated band My Chemical Romance (MCR) and Vietnam's Rock Your Passion Award-winning bands Unlimited and *Ngũ Cung*. It was sponsored by the Tiger Beer Company. MCR sang in English without Vietnamese translations, which is not so unusual in this striving-to-become-globalized country of Vietnam. These and other phenomenal pop culture events may surprise outsiders who think of my Socialist Republic of Vietnam as a backward and sheltered communist country. It emphatically is not, as this book, *Popular Music of Vietnam: The Politics of Remembering, the Economics of Forgetting*, makes so very clear. Relevant to the aforementioned American and Vietnamese musical events and performers, a contextualization and interpretation of current popular music in Vietnam will be found in this book by distinguished ethnomusicologist Dale A. Olsen.

Dr. Olsen rightly points out that modern Vietnamese popular musical forms and their often quieter antecedents since Vietnam's entry into the market economy in the 1990s cannot be expressed by a single term; in fact, a multitude of musical expressions exists for which a single Vietnamese word does not suffice. After exploring the Vietnamese media's use of adjectives and metaphors, and assessing a large number of terms that translate as "pre-war music," "renovated music," "modern music," "lyrical music," "youth music," "light music," "yellow music," "red music," "market music," "cheesy music," and others, Olsen decides on a general term, "contemporary popular music," which is subsumed by an even more general term in the title of this book, "popular music." Popular music, rarely given serious attention by Vietnamese scholars, plays a crucial role in the contemporary history of Vietnam. For over a century, for example, popular music of one kind or another was played by French colonial bands, heard on the anti-French revolutionary front, on the Ho Chi Minh Trail during Vietnam's war against the "American imperialists," in the training camps of communists, during students' political movements, in television commercials, at ballroom dances, and on many other occasions. Eventually, popular music became a prominent part of the curriculum of Vietnam's national conservatories. This institutionalization of popular culture helped create the formation of a class of musicians and composers who were the well-known creators of Vietnam's revolutionary music of the past and the sources of inspiration for much commercial and entertainment music of the present. Many of the songs of Vietnam's former times were a part of the historical soundscape during the country's military/political upheavals and victories, and today their composers have been rewarded and accorded with titles such as People's Artist and National Meritorious Artist. Some of this older music, which Olsen calls "traditional popular music," often expresses the pain as well as the pride of the past, whereas the more recent "contemporary popular music" occasionally addresses current social issues but more often expresses complacent sentimentality and puppy love. Readers will find in Olsen's extraordinary accounts of both "traditional popular music" and "contemporary popular music" a variety of attitudes, responses, interpretations, and conflicts from Vietnamese authors, composers, performers, and people of many ages and walks of life, within and outside of Vietnam.

Age-old traditional or classical music of Vietnam has been researched by many scholars for decades; in contrast, in this comprehensive book, Olsen explores, for the first time, the contemporary popular music of today's Vietnam, expressed mostly through its dissemination by the most prominent vocalists of Vietnam's idols since the beginning of the second millennium. Leaving aside the academic approach of compositional analysis, Olsen instead spent many hours in Ho Chi Minh City (Saigon) and Hanoi with Vietnam's most celebrated singers and musicians in numerous informal locales (private homes, restaurants, coffee houses, and hotel lounges) to interview and talk and in performance venues (public stages, dance halls, karaoke bars, nightclubs, youth centers, bowling alleys, and water parks) to listen and observe. In the process, he collected an astonishing amount of data, not only on how popular musicians experience their professional lives but also about how music drives, guides, and ultimately gives them and many of the youth in Vietnam a purpose in life. Cultural settings and political influences, songwriters and pop stars, rock and pop bands, recording industry production and newspaper coverage, and popular music competitions and dissemination are all discussed in this single volume. Olsen uses a variety of ethnomusicological and historical musicological research methodologies, and his critical discussions about Vietnam's contemporary popular music and its role in Vietnamese culture are insightful.

Although not all of the popular music surveyed in this book has its roots in Vietnam, its impact on and importance in Vietnam's society are, indisputably, enormous. Olsen's study mirrors Vietnam's aching past and expresses some of the concern about the government's censorship policies which, as one writer suggests, can "inhibit [one's] ability to be fully human" (Nuzum 2004:153). Olsen also presents his own perspectives, as he writes: "Beyond the aspirations and successes of a few pop stars and bands in Vietnam, the youth in general make a connection between contemporary popular music, globalization, making money, learning English, and *not* thinking about the past," and "[Vietnam] is not an isolationistic country that lives in the past, but . . . is a forgiving and hopeful one that looks toward the future." These insights by the author, and his syntheses of many data and ideas from other scholars, journalists, laypeople, and the musicians themselves, provide an important view and interpretation of popular music making and thinking in Vietnam between 1990 and 2005.

I have carefully read *Popular Music of Vietnam: The Politics of Remembering, the Economics of Forgetting* while being mindful of Vietnam's past and present. Dale A. Olsen's book elicits my most sincere appreciation.

Phong T. Nguyen, Ph.D.
Visiting Professor of Music
University of Michigan

Acknowledgments

I have many organizations and people to thank for making this book a reality. First, my thanks go to the Florida State University's Council for Research, International Programs (Dr. James Pitts, Director) and the College of Music (Dr. Jon Piersol, former Dean) for providing financial assistance that enabled me to go to Vietnam for extended periods of time between 2002 and 2005. I am also extremely appreciative of and honored by research funding awarded to me by the Guggenheim Memorial Fellowship Foundation (2005–2006) which allowed me to travel to Vietnam in the summer of 2005 and establish my writing retreat space on St. George Island, Florida, during the winter of 2006. I am additionally very grateful to Dr. Terry Miller and Dr. Ricardo Trimillos, for their encouragement and letters of recommendation.

I wish to thank my American study abroad students in Vietnam and doctoral seminar students in Tallahassee for their shared enthusiasm for my research. From the former I gained youthful perspectives as we experienced fieldwork together in Ho Chi Minh City, and from the former I learned about popular music scholarship as we explored a number of theoretical concepts, such as memory politics, censorship, identity, and many others. I am particularly grateful to Robbie Fry, Jeff Jones, Francisco Lara, and Stephanie Stallings for their thoughtful readings and critiques of an early draft of this book. I am also grateful to Dr. Frank Gunderson and Dr. M. Diane Olsen for their critical readings of my manuscript. I am especially indebted to Dr. Nguyen T. Phong for his enthusiasm for my research, his assistance with the Vietnamese language diacritics in this book, his reading of several "final" versions of the manuscript, and his tremendous help as my Vietnam liaison during the book's final stages (helping me obtain permissions, making translations, and writing the forward).

I have many people and organizations in Vietnam to thank for making my 2002, 2004, and 2005 research possible. I thank the staff at the head offices of the Việt Nam News Agency in Ho Chi Minh City for allowing me to work in their newspaper archives. I thank "Mr. Anonymous 1" for introducing me to so many musicians and entrepreneurs in Ho Chi Minh City and "Mr. Anonymous 2" for his extraordinary assistance with translations during interviews—they remain anonymous at their own requests. I also thank all of the anonymous Vietnamese musicians and others in the music industry for their willingness to work with me in this study of their music. Also at their requests, they shall remain anonymous, except in particular statements that they approved for inclusion in this book. Finally, I thank all those artists in Vietnam who were so helpful during my research. I thank you especially for what you continue to do to make this world a better place through your music.

1 Prelude

The female pop singers are almost all young and sexy. The lighting effects match the songs: subtle changes, circles moving about, fade-outs, flashes, colored gels, etc. "I'll miss you like crazy," sings "Miss Blue" in English. At one point she walks out on the dais projecting into the audience and somebody gives her flowers.

—Fieldnotes while attending the M&Tôi popular music
listening club in Ho Chi Minh City in 2004

The last performer is a well-known young female market music singer, who is singing to a canned musical accompaniment. The bass is so incredibly loud, however, that even with earplugs it is unbearable. One of my Vietnamese rock musician friends told me that "market music singers can't sing." Maybe she can, but I can't hear her because the bass is so loud. I think Vietnam is suffering from (or making up for) thousands of years without bass parts. I would say that the pre-dominant American popular music influence is not percussion, harmony, or melody—it's the unbearably loud booming bass!

—Fieldnotes while attending the Đồng Dao popular music
listening club in 2005

This book is about Vietnam's popular music at the end of the twentieth century and beginning of the twenty-first century. It is based on my research in Ho Chi Minh City, Hanoi, and elsewhere throughout the country during the summers of 2002, 2004, and 2005. As the above epigraphs suggest, the Vietnamese popular music scene in 2005 was, as it is today, colorful, loud, diverse, vibrant, and intertwined with many hidden and often complex issues. In the twenty-first century, many of the young people of Vietnam (i.e. those under 30), all of whom were born after the American War (what the Vietnam War is often called in Vietnam; the terms may be used interchangeably), have been greatly affected by the economic changes in Vietnam, as the country, and especially Ho Chi Minh City (formerly Saigon), embraces the current world market economy and experiences globalization in its many forms.

In this book I argue that (a) memory politics and its many facets in Vietnam since the end of the American War and reunification in 1975, (b) Vietnam's *đổi mới* (literally, "changing for the new," "new way," or "renovation") policy in 1985 and the country's consequent embracing of capitalism, and (c) President Clinton's 1994 lifting of the trade embargo with Vietnam all subconsciously influence, affect, and drive the musical expressions and preferences of Vietnam's young people and the Vietnamese music industry. Consequently, the musical expressions and preferences of Vietnam's youth affect and often clash with the communist government's attitudes about music, aesthetics, and morals. To support my argument, I look at the ways market economics and globalization since *đổi mới* have affected and influenced the music and musical lives of the Vietnamese youth in Hanoi, Ho Chi Minh City, and other Vietnamese urban areas, specifically within the time period from 1990 to 2005. In this book I focus on Vietnamese contemporary popular music, the performers, the consumers, the music industry, and the government during those approximate fifteen years and place that information within a theoretical framework that pertains to memory politics (i.e. the politics of remembering, nurtured by the desires and actions of the Vietnamese communist government, and the economics of forgetting, driven by the capitalistic interests of Vietnam's youth subcultures), globalization versus glocalization, and social issues.

Vietnam has an estimated population of over 82 million people, of which less than thirty percent lives in urban areas (Taylor 2004:54). Thus, the majority of Vietnam is rural. The present book on Vietnam's popular music, however, will relate only to urban areas between 1990 and 2005. The year 1992 (www.davang.com gives the year as 1991) is important in Vietnamese popular music history because in early March the first Pop-Rock Festival, which featured only Vietnamese bands and singers (rather than foreign musicians), took place in Ho Chi Minh City at Ky Hoa Park (*VNN*, March 4, 1992).[1] Analogous to the Woodstock Festival in the United States, because it "ushered in the big business/mass music culture of the contemporary era" (Garofalo 1992:15) in Vietnam, the first Pop-Rock Festival attracted dozens of bands and singers, and tens of thousands of Vietnamese youth. I end my survey in 2005 because of certain technological and political developments in Vietnam that year, such as sophisticated digital recording technology in Ho Chi Minh City and the enforcing of international copyright laws.

This survey is the first book-length study of the contemporary popular music of Vietnam's youth at the end of the twentieth century and beginning of the twenty-first century. Peter Manuel's section on Vietnamese popular music in *Popular Musics of the Non-Western World* (1988:198–204), for example, only includes discussions of *cải lương* (renovated theater) and the song "*Vọng Cổ*" (Nostalgia for the Past); this popular old musical song and genre have wide public appeal among certain middle-aged populations of Vietnam, by virtue of the numerous theaters and television shows devoted to them in southern Vietnam. His study, however, does not include the Vietnamese popular music that is sung, performed, listened to, and danced to by Vietnam's youth. That latter popular music is known in Vietnam as *nhạc trẻ* (youth music), *nhạc thị trường* (market music), *nhạc nhẹ* (light music), *tình ca* (love songs), *vina pop* (from *Viet Nam* pop), or any of the myriad American- and British-derived genres, such as pop, hip-hop, and rock (terms used by Vietnam's youth). Likewise, although Philip Blackburn and Jan Dodd are more inclusive of recent popular music trends in *World Music, The Rough Guide* (2000:262–269), they only mention three pop singers who are still active in Vietnam in 2005 (Hong Nhung, Thanh Lam, and My Linh). Finally, Jason Gibbs, in his entry on Vietnam in the *Continuum Encyclopedia of Popular Music of the World (Volume V: Asia and Oceania)*, does not discuss popular music past 1990, except to list several names of pop singers (2005:221–229). Two excellent studies that include popular music among the Việt kiều or overseas Vietnamese have been made by Adelaida Reyes Schramm (1991) and Deborah Wong (1994; 2004). The first looks at Vietnamese popular music in terms of history and politics; the latter publications deal with karaoke among the Vietnamese and Vietnamese Americans and the music of the Vietnamese diaspora in California.

I use the term *popular music* in a general sense to incorporate all of the music genres loved by Vietnam's youth between 1990 and 2005; however, I also specifically refer to particular genres with the terms used by the Vietnamese youth and/or the music industry themselves. A study of recent popular music in Vietnam is timely, as Vietnamese youth at the dusk of the old and dawn of the new millennium (1990–2005) are influenced by the challenges generated by a number of seemingly opposite ideologies and realities, such as the past versus the present, socialism versus capitalism, cultural traditionalism versus globalization, and old guard versus youth. How the Vietnamese cope with these opposing and contrasting forces is often expressed in their active and passive music making, that is, by the music they make or dance to, and the music they listen to, respectively.

During my research in Vietnam, a title that occasionally appeared in my bibliographic sources was "Farewell to the Past" ("Giã Từ Dĩ Vãng") a 1998 hit song by the Vietnamese pop music diva Phương Thanh. It is also the name of a film featuring the same singer. Moreover, "Farewell to the Past" was the first compact disc (CD) recorded and produced in Vietnam. That title has an important meaning for my book because, as I argue, it metaphorically represents a technological and philosophical leap into the future and a break with the past for many adherents of Vietnamese contemporary popular culture. As we shall see, however, the popular music of Vietnam between 1990 and 2005 does not always include a complete break with the past, because nothing in Vietnam can be explained that easily. However, breaking with the past and moving forward often appears to be the case during public popular music concerts and festivals.

For that reason, I have chosen as the subtitle of this book "The Politics of Remembering, the Economics of Forgetting," which is inspired by Arjun Appaduri who expressed the following:

> A question that particularly interests me now apropos the nation-state is the shifting relationship between the politics of remembering and the politics of forgetting. Some people stress the business of remembering and that's quite justified for a lot of these groups, but not enough attention has been paid to the economy of forgetting and remembering in any given place or situation or in any given national space. (2001b:36–37)

I have dichotomized these ideas into the politics of remembering and economics of forgetting, because such a conceptual play of opposites seems to be apparent when applied to Vietnam's contemporary popular music. However, as with the problem already explained regarding the concept "farewell to the past," nothing in expressive culture is that simple, and contemporary popular music in Vietnam cannot be completely explained or understood through a simple dichotomy. Yet, the dichotomy exists, and because of that, the "the politics of remembering, the economics of forgetting" will serve as a starting point for exploring contemporary popular music in Vietnam between 1990 and 2005.

RESEARCH METHODS

In this book I attempt to sort out all of the facts, feelings, ideas, and opinions about the contemporary popular music of Vietnam between 1990 and 2005 and to present a view of musical phenomena relating to the youth subculture of Vietnam during that time period. In my attempt to clarify the concept of popular music in Vietnam, I will make broad categorical distinctions between traditional popular music and contemporary popular music. However, beyond my use of those two designations in this chapter (for clarification only), I will endeavor to use the terms employed by the Vietnamese in Vietnam for their specific genres.

By the term *Vietnamese traditional popular music* I refer in general to music that is appreciated by a large number of Vietnam's people, who have given it the test of time. Vietnamese traditional popular music includes at least the following categories, which are often performed daily on radio and television, and are additionally listened to via audio and video cassette tapes and CDs: (a) *nhạc cải lương* or music (i.e. songs) derived from *hát cải lương* (renovated theater) and other theatrical genres; (b) *hát ru* and *hò* or lullabies and work songs; (c) *nhạc trữ tình* (lyrical music), including romantic music and love songs; (d) *nhạc tiền chiến*, prewar music or nationalistic songs that refer to Vietnam's people, history, geography, and other nonpolitical (at least not directly political) aspects (see also Gibbs 1998); and (e) *nhạc đỏ* (red music), a folk revival movement that includes the performance of revolutionary music having to do with all aspects of Vietnam's struggles against outside forces (mostly French and American) and with the country itself (civil war), including prewar, wartime, reconstruction, and other songs of pre- and post-revolutionary times. The first two broad categories are not studied in this book because I do not consider them to be genres appreciated by the majority of Vietnam's youth.

By the term *Vietnamese contemporary popular music*, on the other hand, I refer to the music that is popular among the Vietnamese youth and which could be called simply music of the youth. This Vietnamese popular music includes broad categories termed (a) *nhạc trẻ*, literally youth music; (b) *nhạc thị trường* and *nhạc sến*, market music and cheesy music; (c) *nhạc nhẹ*, light music; and (d) North American and British genres such as rock and metal music; pop-rock; vina pop; disco and techno (electronica) music; hip-hop; and other mixtures of foreign styles such as Cantopop (Hong Kong-derived pop sung in Cantonese; Witzleben 1999, called *nhạc hoa* in Vietnam), and other terms used by the press and outsiders.

The first category of music, *nhạc trẻ* (youth music), is the largest; therefore, I will dicuss it in some detail. As an outsider, I see the term as having two applications. First, and perhaps foremost, it is a particular kind of sentimental, ballad-like Vietnamese music that is sung in a crooner style (i.e. in a soft and intimate manner) by a solo female or male singer/idol or idol wannabe. I am tempted to call this generic *nhạc trẻ* (i.e. *nhạc trẻ* as a genre) or perhaps proper *nhạc trẻ* or original *nhạc trẻ*; however, I will not use any adjectives for its use in this book—I will just call it *nhạc trẻ*. This kind of music is usually performed at popular music listening clubs (see Chapter 6) and sung and recorded by Vietnam's young female (starlets) and male (stars) pop singers (see Chapter 3). In my second understanding of the term *nhạc trẻ* (which I will translate as "music of the youth," to give it a broader usage), I mean *all* music pertaining to Vietnam's youth. To clarify this and always keep it apart from the other use of the term, I will call this "collective *nhạc trẻ*" because it includes all the music that is listened and danced to and performed by Vietnam's youth, from local to foreign musics, from rock to rap, from karaoke songs to trance music, and including generic *nhạc trẻ*. Everything in this book, then, it could be argued, is collective *nhạc trẻ*, but it is important to understand that newsprint and Internet authors (who have contributed the only publications on Vietnamese contemporary popular music to date) often confuse the terms by using the one to mean the other. Therefore, I will most often use the terms *rock, rap,* and other foreign terms that the Vietnamese also use, for the genres in collective *nhạc trẻ*.

Nhạc trẻ (the first usage explained above) has musical vestiges of the French past and was probably inspired by the French *chanson* during colonial days. It is inspired by the term *duyên* (Hồng Nhung, personal interview 2005), a word meaning charm.

Because the term means youth music, its usage expanded to include soft [or light] rock styles as well, and in 1981 *nhạc trẻ* was used for rock 'n' roll, which was also called *yellow music* (generally, however yellow music or *nhạc vàng*, is the term ascribed to southern Vietnamese sentimental songs from the period before the reunification of Vietnam in 1975). Philip Taylor explains that Vo Van Kiet, a Communist Party leader, delivered a speech in 1981 in which he condemned *nhạc trẻ* (by which he was referring to Western rock, pop, and Vietnamese compositions inspired by those foreign styles) because "it dissipated youths' revolutionary activity" (2001:42). In the same speech, Vo Van Kiet (1981:133) said:

> We have also seen more clearly the deep marks left on many of our youth by the old way of life. This 'yellow' and 'wandering' music with its persistent resonance was part of the enemy's 'cultural pacification process'. The whole society must be made aware of the seriousness of the question.

The "old way of life" he refers to is from the period or focus of Americanization during the American (Vietnam) War, when rock 'n' roll, rhythm and blues, and other American popular musics were introduced into Vietnam. Indeed, as Reebee Garofalo writes, "Rock . . . was not only the soundtrack of domestic opposition to the war [within the United States]; it was the soundtrack of the war itself [within Vietnam]" (2007:3).

Nhạc trẻ (the first usage), in addition to French influence, also reveals Japanese (*enka* music) and Chinese (Cantonese) popular music influences with its heavy use of pentatonic scales and sentimentality. Thailand has also influenced *nhạc trẻ* with its love song style: "Thai pop ballad is gentle and melodious, and like the Chinese music that was once very popular here, is music that Vietnamese youth can easily relate to, said [Vietnamese] musician Nguyễn Hà" (*VNN*, July 4, 2001). The Thai love song style is more common in Ho Chi Minh City than anywhere else in Vietnam. Several Thai ballads have been recorded and performed in Vietnam with song titles that reveal their sentimentality, unrequited love, and loneliness (in English they are "Discreet Love," "Sincerely Sorry!," "Love Will Not Easily Fade Away," "Heart of Spring," and "Dove-Eyed"). Often, Vietnamese singers write their own Vietnamese words to the songs, suggesting that it is the musicality (i.e. melody and rhythm) of the songs that the singers find appealing, as explained by Vietnamese musician Nguyễn Ngọc Thiện: "One . . . reason for the success of the trend is that modern Thai melodies permit bands to use the entire range of notes simultaneously and their rhythms lend easily to bustling dances" (ibid.) Nguyễn Ngọc Thiện continues to be pragmatic about the Thai melodies as he explains: "[The] Vietnamese attraction for Thai music and other Asian pop is just a temporary trend. What domestic music (musicians, singers, CD producers and show organizers) should do is welcome the progressive trend and learn whatever is positive from it" (ibid.)

Nhạc trẻ as sentimental music also exhibits American and British influences. The American artists most revered by the Vietnamese *nhạc trẻ* fans are mostly crooners, such as Elvis Presley, Marc Anthony, and others who are known for their ballad singing. The favored British music is by the Beatles, especially their slow songs, such as "Let it Be." Ballads, especially those in minor keys, are held in high esteem by Vietnamese *nhạc trẻ* aficionados.

In spite of these heavy foreign influences found in *nhạc trẻ*, however, there are occasional uses of traditional Vietnamese tone systems and dynamic nuances, as well as some original compositional and expressive ideas. These are especially noticeable in the sentimental songs of Trịnh Công Sơn (see Chapter 5). Fast songs are not very popular in *nhạc trẻ*, and it is rare to hear fast Vietnamese pop music at all unless it's somewhere within the broader category of collective *nhạc trẻ*, such as in rock and its many variants.

A generation after the reunification of Vietnam in 1975 (i.e. the fall of Saigon), contemporary popular music in Vietnam has been heavily influenced by outside forces since the country's embrace of capitalism beginning with its 1985–1986 *đổi mới* policy, the 1994 lifting of the U. S. trade embargo by President Clinton, and the massive global influences of popular culture at the end of the twentieth century and beginning of the twenty-first. However, although capitalism and globalization have affected and influenced the music and musical lives of much of the urbanized Vietnamese youth, particularly in Ho Chi Minh City and Hanoi, some popular music songwriters and singers express themselves with a kind of pre-globalized soundscape based upon or influenced by a song style highly approved of by the communist government. This creates a kind of musical dichotomy of the past versus the present or traditional popular music versus contemporary popular music. Additionally, governmental control versus freedom of expression creates another kind of musical dichotomy. The Vietnamese government's Ministry of Information and Culture, Performing Arts Department, for example, is in charge of determining what music can and cannot be performed publicly and recorded for publication. Adding to the complexity of the musical and social construction of Vietnam's popular music (both traditional and contemporary) is the attempt by some singers and songwriters to create a more original and nationalistic popular music. I call this process *culturation,* which I define as *the concept of a culture or a person developing, expanding, or growing in a self actualization or self-fulfilling process that includes a kind of unconscious or intentional glorification and continual (re)creation of its or one's own culture* (Olsen 2000).

With regard to contemporary popular music (because this is the main focus of my book, I will henceforth refer to it simply as popular music, unless I feel the need to clarify it with the adjective contemporary), culturation is driven by a creative effort that Plomana Kourtova calls "indigenizing the global" (n.d.). Borrowing from Marshall Sahlins's concept of indigenizing the modern, Kourtvoa writes, "the process of negotiating

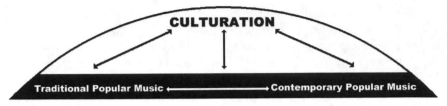

Figure 1.1   Popular Music Continuum (and Arc of Culturation). © Dale A. Olsen.

the *local* and the *global* becomes a continuity in itself, an indigenization of modernity in which 'the innovations follow logically from the people's own principles of existence, a traditionalism without archaism' (Sahlins [2000], 492)." This creative concept can also be called *Vietnamization* (but not to be confused with Nixon's political use of the term), which I define as *the process of bringing local musical colors into an otherwise Western-influenced palette*. It can also be explained through the concept of "glocalization" (see Robertson 1995), which includes a combination of global and local elements.

Given this complex musical soundscape in Vietnam, I will argue that popular music in Vietnam is built upon the above dichotomous processes that exist within a dynamic continuum from traditional popular music to contemporary popular music. Within this continuum, culturation and Vietnamization often exist like the swing of a pendulum, sometimes occurring and sometimes not, depending upon the creativity of the musicians. I present these concepts graphically in Figure 1.1, "Popular Music Continuum (and Arc of Culturation)." The three double-headed arrows leading to and from "Culturation" can also be seen as subcontinua, representing various dynamic degrees or levels between the various concepts. I consider this way of looking at (and listening to) Vietnam's popular music to be logical, clear, and important, because as an ethnomusicologist I enjoy popular musical creations that attempt to be nationalistic, personal, and even clever. This interest is evidenced by one of the major questions I asked Vietnamese musicians during interviews: *What is Vietnamese about Vietnamese rock and pop music?*

Research Source Materials

I have derived my resource data for this book from the following general sources: American, Australian, British, and Vietnamese books and journals published in English; Vietnamese English language newspapers; Internet sources in English; personal interviews with numerous popular musicians in Vietnam, conducted either in English or in Vietnamese with a translator; my personal participant observations of and fieldnotes from public music events; ethnographic fieldnote studies by my American students in Vietnam; my analysis of audio and video materials (cassette tapes,

CDs, VCDs, DVDs, etc.); and analysis of Vietnamese song texts translated into English.

Considered secondary resource materials, books and journal articles about Vietnam since the fall of Saigon in 1975 are abundant. Most of these are published in the United States and Australia by scholars, journalists, former Vietnam War correspondants, overseas Vietnamese (Việt kiều or former refugees), and others. Most of the theoretical books and journal articles about popular music and popular culture are published in England. Specific journal articles and books in English about Vietnamese music are published both in Vietnam and the United States. Three American publications, *New Perspectives on Vietnamese Music: Six Essays*, edited by Phong T. Nguyễn (1991); *Nhac Viet: The Journal of Vietnamese Music*; and "Vietnam" by Phong T. Nguyễn (1998) in the *Garland Encyclopedia of World Music, Vol. 4, Southeast Asia*, are most valuable.

A major part of my research has been derived from newspaper articles in the *Việt Nam News*, the official English language newspaper in Vietnam, and other English language newspapers in Vietnam such as *The Saigon Times Daily* and *Thanhnien News*. During the summers of 2002, 2003, and 2005, I researched every issue of the *Việt Nam News* from its beginnings in 1991 (June 17) to the present (2005). As the official government-approved English language newspaper, the *Việt Nam News* is not without its bias, as is the case, perhaps, with any newspaper. To what extent can the veracity of the *Việt Nam News* be trusted? Outsiders may assume that the topic of Vietnam's popular music would not be subject to editorial distortion. Is that, however, a safe assumption? Although it is tempting to use the articles in the *Việt Nam News* and other English language newspapers as the truthful voices of the people of Vietnam, I am constantly reminded of the words of an important and influential Vietnamese musician who told me: "When they talk in the newspaper, it's not the truth" (pers. com., July 13, 2002, Ho Chi Minh City; the musician has requested anonymity). Though one could expect this to be at least partially true with the official English language newspaper in Vietnam, the hundreds of lengthy and informative articles published in the *Việt Nam News* and other newsprint, I feel, are better than no views at all. When they are apparent to me, editorial biases will be pointed out, and I will always attempt to present my perspectives and analyses, which are based on information gleaned from dozens of interviews, personal observations, and musical analyses.

Another important question arises from my use of the published critiques and reporting of others: Why did I not use newsprint articles in Vietnam that are not associated with the communist government? The answers are simple. There are none, as Benedict Kerkvliet explains:

All newspapers, publishing houses, and printing presses are owned and operated by government ministries, the Communist Party, and official organizations. Authorities in the Ministry of Culture and Information [*sic*] and the Communist Party's Department for Culture and Ideology scrutinize and often intervene to determine the content of publications. . . . (2003:37)

Moreover, the *BBC News* wrote that Reporters Without Borders, a media watchdog group, determined that out of 167 countries, "a survey of journalists and human rights activists" placed Vietnam seventh among the ten worst countries (October 26, 2004). The group reported that those countries "lack an independent media or journalists are 'persecuted and censored'."[2] Secondly, I neither read nor speak the Vietnamese language.

I have also consulted the Internet at length, and numerous English language essays and blogs have been useful for their recent opinions and views about popular music in Vietnam. Unfortunately, however, many of them have since gone out of service. That is the nature of the Internet. Nevertheless, when I have used Internet sources, I have provided the URL addresses, whether available or not. Numerous Vietnamese language Internet Web sites exist in Vietnam, and Vietnam Brewery Limited sponsors one of the best, known as *Tiger Translate* (2007–2008), providing links to information about artists, performances, recordings, visuals, and more, including a search engine for locating links to individuals (http://www.tigermusic.com.vn/home.php). Mandy Thomas and Lisa Drummond have written the following about the Internet and censorship in Vietnam: "While it is still too early to see what impact the net may have on consumption patterns and upon political change, the state has tried to censor its use and limit circulation of some kinds of information through nation-wide firewalls (electronic filters)" (2003:5). Whether such censorship has reached into the communication efforts of popular music fans is not known.

During the four-year timespan when I conducted research in Vietnam, I purchased and subsequently listened to, viewed, and analyzed songs in over 150 CDs, VCDs, and DVDs of Vietnamese contemporary popular music. My analyses of many of these include their audio and visual aspects, including the translation of particular song texts into English by Vietnamese translators.

Vietnamese music languages (i.e. the musical sounds) can neither be adequately expressed in English speech language nor in Western graphic languages, such as musical staff notation. English words can express some ideas about compositional and performance styles, but musical staff notations can only provide a vague idea, at best, about the subtleties and nuances of individual pop singers, rock guitarists, or other popular musicians (this is true for most cultures, not only for Vietnam). Therefore, musical transcriptions will not be found in this study. A common way to give readers an idea of how a particular music sounds is to provide an accompanying CD; that, however, is also not feasible here because of copyright infractions, even though the majority of CDs purchased in

Vietnam are pirated copies for which copyright issues are either vague or nonexistent.

I conducted many interviews with Vietnamese popular singers and musicians, songwriters, nightclub owners, jazz musicians, and others who are knowledgeable about Vietnam's youth subcultures and Vietnamese popular music and have added their knowledge (and further biases, perhaps) to the mix. The majority of my interviews are with Vietnam's best-known popular musicians of the twenty-first century. All interviews took place in Ho Chi Minh City and were conducted either in English or in Vietnamese with a Vietnamese–English translator.

Throughout this book I have tried to counteract the possible newspaper biases with my own views and those of my American students, through participant observations captured in fieldnotes. Either together or individually, my students and I attended numerous popular music performances, from rock concerts to disco clubs, competitions in parks to benefit concerts, karaoke bars to lounge rooms, and much more.

THE CONTENTS

This book consists of ten chapters. In this present Chapter 1, "Prelude," I discuss background issues, my research design, and other introductory matters. Chapter 2, "Cultural and Political Settings for Vietnam's Popular Music," also serves as a kind of introduction in that I contextualize the popular music of Vietnam with regard to its historical, cultural, and political bases. In Chapter 3, "Vietnamese Pop Music Stars and the Bumpy Road to Stardom," I address the questions of who becomes a pop music star and why, how ethnicity and gender play important roles, how stars and wannabes market and disseminate their music, the influence of Việt kiều (overseas Vietnamese) singers who have returned to Vietnam, and how much money can be earned by singers. In Chapter 4, "Vietnamese Rock, Pop-Rock, and Pop Music Bands," I describe several kinds of popular music ensembles and analyze why they exist, who plays or sings in them, and how they are viewed by youth and the government. In Chapter 5, "Vietnamese Songwriters, Social Issues, and Government Persuasion," I introduce the best-known songwriters in Vietnam, discuss the importance of song lyrics, and study how Vietnamese popular music interacts with social issues such as drug use, the handicapped, HIV/AIDS, and others. Chapter 6, "Performance Venues for (Mostly) Live Popular Music," is a study of musical performance places, such as youth community halls, cultural houses, dance clubs, nightclubs, music clubs, coffee houses, bowling alleys, and other venues. In Chapter 7, "Disseminating Popular Music: Pop and Rock Music Concerts, Festivals, and Shows," I discuss large-scale popular music performance events, which constitute live forms of music delivery. In Chapter 8, "Disseminating Popular Music:

Audio and Video Recordings," I discuss the history and development of mediated popular music in Vietnam, including issues of piracy and copyright. In Chapter 9, "Vietnamese Karaoke: Place, Pleasure, Politics, and Profit," I study karaoke establishments, public and governmental attitudes about the format, and the law. Finally, in Chapter 10, "Conclusion: The Politics and Economics of Popular Music in Vietnam," I summarize the book, synthesize the material presented in the earlier chapters, and provide further comparative information in an attempt to speculate about the future of popular music in Vietnam.

ORTHOGRAPHY

I have attempted with utmost care to include correct Vietnamese language diacritical markings throughout this book, except where I have quoted materials that do not use them (such as early and late issues of the *Việt Nam News* and particular books by American scholars). I am greatly indebted to Dr. Phong T. Nguyễn, who has thoroughly edited the final draft of the manuscript for proper Vietnamese orthography.

My above writing of Dr. Nguyễn's name raises another orthographic concern: the arrangement of given name, middle name, and surname. In Vietnam, his name would be written Nguyễn Thuyết Phong, and he would be formally referred to as Phong (or Dr. Phong), whereas in the United States he would be called Dr. Nguyễn. I have attempted to include the proper Vietnamese name order throughout this book.

Certain place names in Vietnam are written with their proper diacritics and separation of syllables when they appear that way in publications. For example, Hanoi is sometimes written Hà Nội, Saigon is Sài Gòn, and Vietnam is Việt Nam. Throughout the book I use English spellings for place names, except when I quote materials and sources.

It is interesting how the globalized use of English has led many authors and publications not to use Vietnamese diacritical markings. While this is perhaps understandable when English authors publish in the English language (and it is much easier), it is incorrect. However, even the *Việt Nam News* did not use diacritics in its early issues and stopped using them in 2004. Moreover, very few Internet sources use diacritics, and Internet bloggers almost never do. Therefore, occasional orthographic inconsistencies in this book are caused by my desire to quote my sources correctly (i.e. I follow the usage in the original secondary sources). Sometimes inconsistencies are inadvertent because I could not decipher my digital photographs of the original sources. I alone am responsible for those inconsistencies, for which I apologize.

To conclude this Prelude I borrow some words from Keith Negus, whose *Popular Music in Theory: An Introduction* (1996) has greatly influenced the final direction of my book. His words explain an important reason I have for researching and writing this book about popular music in Vietnam (one I had not thought of until I read his text). By writing this book I hope to "contribute to a web of knowledge, critical dialogue and intercultural conversation that is doing more than simply offering proposals to governments and making contributions to the well-being of national music industries" (Negus 1996:223). Over the years I have grown to love Vietnam, its people, their incredible tenacity and will to survive, their hope for the future, and their love of life as they express it through their popular music. By putting together my words and ideas, many derived from the words of Vietnamese musicians, critics, and common people, into a book that is the first study of Vietnamese popular music between 1990 and 2005, I hope indeed to "contribute to a web of knowledge" that will also contribute to the understanding of Vietnam and especially of its young people. The world of Vietnamese popular music is complex, exciting, expressive, and in many ways charming (to elaborate upon pop diva Hồng Nhung's explanation that it has *duyên* or charm), because it is made in Vietnam by complex, exciting, expressive, and often charming musicians who are passionate about what they do.

2 Cultural and Political Settings for Vietnam's Popular Music

Vietnam has experienced contrasts, conflicts, foreign occupation, and disunity for millennia, perhaps because of its geographic position as a crossroads between North and South Asia, East and West Asia, and Asia and Oceania. The crossroads metaphor implies a brief meeting place of disparate factions coming from many directions, and decision-making about what direction to take. The crossroads metaphor also refers to factors that led to the Vietnam War, because the United States feared that if Vietnam went communist, so would the rest of Southeast Asia and beyond. Thus, the crossroads had to be turned into a dead end, according to Presidents Eisenhower, Kennedy, Johnson, Nixon, and their chiefs of staff. The political crossroads turned into a dead end for the United States with the loss of the Vietnam War and the deaths of thousands of American soldiers (and the deaths of more than a million Vietnamese). But a musical crossroads developed and it led to an *Americanization* of Vietnam's popular music culture for several decades.

VIETNAM'S WAR MEMORIES AND THE CONSUMPTION OF AMERICAN MUSIC

One of the largest bodies of music consumed (i.e. danced to, listened to, performed, and enjoyed) in Vietnam since the end of the American War has been American popular music. A surge of interest in American popular music took place in 1994, shortly after President Bill Clinton removed a thirty-year economic embargo against Vietnam, and normal relations began on July 11. Shortly after the lifting of the trade embargo by the United States, and somewhat ironically it seems, in 1995, the Vietnamese government sponsored the twentieth anniversary of the liberation of Saigon.

It surprised me that mementos of the American War are found in the commercial districts of Saigon, as the downtown region (District 1) of Ho Chi Minh City is still called, where hundreds of war trinkets are sold, some authentic, others copies. In addition, folk art is made from Coca-Cola cans and other American materials, some nightclubs have American names, and other kinds of American War memorabilia can be seen:

> On the streets of Ho Chi Minh City, reminders of the "American War" abound. Toy jet fighters and helicopters made out of Coca-Cola cans are big sellers in downtown stalls. Tourists snap up "Good Morning, Vietnam" T-shirts named after a U.S. film set in wartime Vietnam. A downtown bar was named "Apocalypse Now" after another war film. Market stalls sell U.S. identification dog-tags, engraved Zippo lighters, flak jackets, uniforms and other paraphernalia which supposedly date back to the war. (*VNN*, February 4, 1995)

There is virtually no animosity towards Americans in Ho Chi Minh City, and "little resentment is evident in Vietnam. 'Vietnam now wants to close the past and look forward to the future', said Nguyễn Sơn, a spokesman for city authorities here. 'We want to have normal relations with the United States'" (*VNN*, February 4, 1995).

Normal relations with the United States can be seen in many places in Ho Chi Minh City, and in the many ways that American-influenced musical activities proliferate, including the performance/presence of American popular music and jazz, musical performances by Vietnamese youth that imitate American singers and bands, piracy of CDs and DVDs recorded by American pop singers and their purchase by youth, the karaoke-ing (karaoking) of American tunes, and others. These musical activities reveal much about how youth subcultures have succeeded in (re)creating a new imagined identity. Theirs is a complacency towards or unawareness about the American War, and the music they acquire and use negotiates and helps define their imagined identities. Two processes are at work as youth (re)create their imagined identities: globalization and Vietnamization (and anything in between). But first, who are the youth of Vietnam?

VIETNAMESE YOUTH SUBCULTURES

At the beginning of the twenty-first century in Vietnam, David Lamb wrote that approximately 60 percent of the population is under 30 years of age and 80 percent is under age 40 (2002:152), or, as Nguyễn Xuân Phong explains, 50 percent are under the age of 25 and 80 percent are under age 45 (2006:20). However put, this means that the majority of Vietnamese were either not born by the end of the American War in 1975, or they were in their infancy. Lamb wrote the following in 2002:

> I asked my standard question about the young one day when I went to interview a Vietnamese business man about the new economic order. Nguyễn Tran Bat was fifty-five, a former North Vietnamese soldier

who had started studying Marxism as a teenager. . . . [He said,] "The young today love their country no less, I think, than my generation, but they love it in different ways. We wanted peace, unity, security. This generation wants Vietnam to be football [soccer] champion of South Asia. It wants its singers to perform like Michael Jackson. It's materialistic. It complains about the pace of reform. The kids are restless, impatient. If they live in the Highlands, they probably want to go to Hanoi for action and opportunity. If they live in Hanoi, they want to go to Ho Chi Minh City. And if they live in Ho Chi Minh, they want to go to California. . . . You can't prevent the young from doing their own thing. They have their own values and principles and whatever you think of them, those values are going to be the values of this nation ten years from now." (152–153)

I refer to these Vietnamese youth of the postwar era not as a subculture, but as subcultures, in the plural for intergenerational purposes, that is, to identify subdivisions within a generation. This is a useful way to look at any generational categorization of people, because age, class, education, location, and many other factors inform the characteristics of any particular group, especially those between the ages of 10 and 30, that is, between preteen and young adult. Therefore, there is not homogeneity among the youth of Vietnam that one would expect. The term *youth* throughout the globalized world, in fact, is a slippery concept. In spite of the British Centre for Contemporary Cultural Studies' meganarratives deriving from youth culture theory, politics of youth, and youth subculture analysis (see Redhead 1990:89 and Paul Willis 1988, cited in Redhead), and other scholars who refute the idea of youth as "a monolithic cultural construct, cutting across class, and ethnic and regional boundaries" (Hamm 1995:22), I wonder if youth can be considered a theoretical concept at all in Vietnam. Or is it merely a loosely defined age category that includes teenagers, collage-agers, and young adults? Roy Shuker argues that "The blanket term 'youth' conceals more than simple age divisions, as a social category it embraces a wide variety of taste groups, subcultures, and fandom; all audience segments themselves differentiated by class, ethnicity, age, and gender" (2003:195). I agree with Shuker's argument and will use the term youth subcultures in Vietnam to mean not only all people (mostly) under age 30, but others who constitute a social category which shares a passion for popular music.

Marr and Rosen write, "most younger Vietnamese are tired of war stories, convinced that these have little relevance to present conditions, and eager to look to the future" (1998:166). Vietnam's economic and globalized realities encourage the unconscious erasure of the past among Vietnam's youth, as former ambassador Pete Peterson told me regarding the Vietnamese youth's understanding of the past, and in particular, the American War: "It's not that they don't remember it, they just don't know about it" (pers. com., 2003). Given this fact, coupled with youth interest in making money in Vietnam, one could argue for an economics of not knowing. However, all concepts should be viewed as being broad enough to include all nuances and permutations. Therefore, my use of the concept I call economics of forgetting includes not knowing as well as complacency.

Nevertheless, it is unwise to generalize, because there are about 50 million young people under 30 years of age in Vietnam. In addition, youth in Hanoi are different from youth in Ho Chi Minh City, and youth in smaller cities and in rural areas are again different from their large city peers. Alexander Soucy states,

> Youth in Hanoi have not turned their backs on Vietnamese tradition. They recognize certain elements as being essentially Vietnamese, and ratify them through their speech and their actions. . . . They are not, [however], simply receivers of the state's version of tradition, but are active in the process of its creation. (2003:134)

Moreover, the government (especially in southern Vietnam) is also heavily involved in a political process of forgetting particular inconvenient aspects of the past, including aspects of the musical past. Conversely, some youth, the music industry, and many Vietnamese associated with Vietnam's market economy are also substantially involved in remembering the past. The dichotomy of the politics of remembering and economics of forgetting is a complex ontological construct, but one that it is worthwhile to consider for a complex society like Vietnam.

POLITICS AND THE ARTS IN VIETNAM SINCE 1975

Vietnam's history suggests that governmental policies and political events have influenced musical expressions in the region for millennia. Under the thousand-year Chinese rule, for example, the region's music was at least affected, if not regulated, by mandarins, royal courts, and Confucian doctrine, the latter considering "'good' music, properly performed, necessary to maintain a stable society" (Perris 1985:104). Confucian ideology, if not the actual doctrine, continued after the defeat of and independence from the Chinese in 939 A.D. into the present day. Perhaps the most important and engrained Confucian (or neo-Confucian) ideal in Vietnam is the focus on "proper relationships between categories and groups of people [which] produce social harmony, creating happy and prosperous families, villages, and nations" (Jamieson 1993:12).

Another ideological influence on music in Vietnam was a socialist realism movement (originating in Stalinist Russia) that inspired the founding of an Artists' Association (*Hoi Nghe Si Tao Hinh*) in 1957, whose goal was to "produce art to serve the propaganda needs of the government" (Nora

A. Taylor 2001:110). Then-president Hồ Chí Minh advocated a concept he called *dân tộc* (nationality, nation, or national) and its variants *tính dân tộc* and *văn hoá dân tộc* (respectively, national character and national culture), through which he wanted his people to be characterized and portrayed in the arts (especially painting): "The term was first used by Hồ Chí Minh around the time of the August Revolution in 1945 to define the goals of the cultural policies established by the Democratic Republic of Vietnam" (ibid.:113). This had an important effect on the development of popular music in Vietnam.

Moving ahead to the period after the American War, a similar ideal existed within Vietnam's Communist Party (CPV). In 1976, for example, Secretary General Le Duan revealed the Communist Party's attitude towards music, which Stephen B. Young describes as being inspired by Confucius, as he writes:

> And as Confucius was contemptuous of contemporary music as licentious and self-indulgent, so Le Duan considered the culture of South Vietnam under his opponents to be "mongrel" and "decadent." He wrote that "It induced a considerable number of people, especially city dwellers, to indulge in living at a fast tempo an individualistic, egoistic life of depravation, and gave stimulation and encouragement to the basest instincts and the most vulgar tastes." (1979:778, citing Le Duan 1976:190)

This kind of attitude towards Saigon (later to be known as Ho Chi Minh City) by the socialist leaders in Hanoi continued after 1975 and still exists in the 2000s. Influenced by the overwhelming cultural and economic changes that were taking place as a result of *đổi mới* and the new economic freedom after the lifting of the U.S. trade embargo, the Vietnamese government felt an urgent need to deal with the myriad foreign cultural influences that began to accompany Vietnam's economic globalization.

The Official View of the Communist Party

In 1996, the Central Committee published several lengthy reports to the Eighth National Congress of the CPV. In them they addressed their particular concerns about the many changes taking place in Vietnam, including their impact on arts and culture.[1]

The first, the "Political Report of the Central Committee (VIIth Tenure) to the VIIIth National Congress of the Communist Party of Vietnam," includes a section (V in Part III) subtitled "To Build an Advanced Culture with Profound National Identity." As the subtitle suggests, the items that are emphasized relate to national identity (including the arts, but not necessarily popular culture). The Central Committee believes these are essential for the stability, growth, and well being of Vietnam in its confrontation with market economics (*VNN*, Supplement, April 10, 1996):

The central task in the fields of culture, literature and arts is to help shape the Vietnamese person in terms of thinking, behavior, morality, feelings, and lifestyle. . . . Given conditions of a market economy and expanded international exchanges, particular attention should be given to preserving and enhancing national cultural identity, inheriting and promoting the people's ethical traditions, fine customs and practices, attachment to the nation's origin and national pride; to overcome money worship, defiance of morality and insensibility to human values. . . . To build plentiful, cultured and happy Vietnamese families, making the family the sweet home of each and everyone. . . . To encourage literary and artistic creations reflecting new elements in society, stimulating the good and the beautiful in relations between man and man, man and society, man and nature, criticizing the wrong, condemning the bad and the evil, reaching out to the true, the good and the beautiful. . . . To prevent tendencies toward alien and profane cultures, to combat the intrusion of noxious cultures.

Moreover, the Report states that it will accomplish these goals in a number of ways, including the following: "To develop along with administering properly the networks of information flow, press, publication, radio broadcasting, television, cinematography and other forms of artistic [endeavors, with] . . . which to improve the knowledge and cultural enjoyment level of the people in all regions of the country, and to guide them towards a lifestyle conformable to fine customs and habits, social order and State laws."

The second report, "The Communist Party of Vietnam, The VIIIth National Congress (An unofficial translation of the main body of the address made by General Secretary Do Muoi at the opening of the Congress)," elaborates on the government's desire to solve several problems that have occurred because of at least two factors, as the Report states: "A series of social problems are unfolding before us, either as a result of the serious consequences of the years of war and the poorly developed economy or newly emerging from the transition to market mechanism and broadened international exchange" (*VNN*, Extra, June 29, 1996). The frankness with which the Communist Party writes is noteworthy, as it openly shares with its readers the difficulties in finding solutions to the problems, as the Report continues: "It is impossible to solve all these problems at one time, given our still low social productivity, restrained budget revenues and the need to accumulate for national industrialization and modernization." The most important issue in the Report for popular music, however, has to do with Vietnam's national identity and culture (referred to as the "spiritual foundation of society" that creates "happiness in the people"):

Culture is the spiritual foundation of society, being both the objective and the driving force for socio-economic development. Together with science and technology, and education and training, cultural and artistic activities have an important position in developing personality and in the spiritual life of the Vietnamese.

The "spiritual life of the Vietnamese" is not explained, but the first Report refers to "humanism" as an important pillar of the individual, school, and family.

After five years, in April 2001, the Central Committee submitted another political report; this one to the Ninth National Congress of the Communist Party. Titled "CPV [Communist Party of Vietnam] Central Committee's Political Report," it explains the reasons for the report and the objectives of the CPV:

> The Ninth Congress is to review and evaluate past achievements and shortcomings, make decisions for the coming period, serve to raise the leadership capacity and combativeness of the Party, motivate and promote the strength of the whole nation, continue with the renovation process, step up industrialization and modernization, build and safeguard the socialist Vietnamese Homeland, and advance assuredly into the new century.

In the subsection, "To Build an Advanced Culture with Profound National Identity," the Central Committee identifies the following as detrimental influences of outside cultures:

> [It will be the task of the Vietnamese government] to help culture infuse deeply into each and every community, family and individual, further complete the new set of values of the Vietnamese man, inherit the nation's traditional cultural values while acquiring the humankind's cultural quintessence, increase resistance against pornographic and noxious cultures. (*VNN*, Supplement, April 20, 2001:1–15)

Finally, the 2001 Report states that it will accomplish its goals with the following strategies: "To develop and modernize the mass media network, and improve the quality of radio, television, press and publishing products and services. . . . To strive for the basic popularization of radio and television receivers to all families by 2010."

In both the 1996 and 2001 Reports, the term *culture* was used over forty times.[2] This emphasis upon, fascination with, or paranoia about culture is a kind of reverse cultural domination on the part of the CPV. In the words of Hue-Tam Ho Tai, it represents *hyper-mnemosis*, "the intense, even obsessive, effort to keep [the past, that is, traditional Vietnamese culture] at the forefront of consciousness, to shape it and to exploit it for a variety of purposes" (2001b:7).

The biggest changes in the 2001 Report, when compared with those from 1996, are the down play of what I call *Internationalism* and the addition of a category I label *Sports and Culture*. While international interest is still present, it is now taken for granted as an aspect of tourism, cultural exchanges, sports events, and other aspects that accompany economic globalization. In the early twenty-first century, for example, Vietnam has taken a very active role in several international sporting events, such as the SEA Games and the ASEAN Paragames for which Vietnamese popular music composers have written the opening songs (see Chapter 5).

The directives of the Communist Party, as expressed in 1996 and 2001, have had a considerable effect on the continued development of Vietnamese classical music, including *nhạc dân tộc cải biên* (reformed/improved/renovated national music; see Arana 1994; 1999) and perhaps have contributed to the popularity (or revival) of revolutionary and war songs (see Gibbs 1998). They have had little effect, however, on the development of popular music in Vietnam. Vietnam's youth and the music industry that caters to the desires of youth have paid little heed to the memory politics of the government. The youth subcultures' views are different from the State's view, and the former's somewhat collective lack of concern about the past usually clashes with the memory politics of the Communist Party and with the attitudes about life and values of older Vietnamese.

A Concern for Values

Throughout the 1996 and 2001 Reports are many statements about the preservation of values. Although not expressed directly, concerns for family, loyalty, national identity, and many other aspects having to do with values may derive from the innate infusion of Confucian ideals that have been a part of Vietnamese culture for well over a thousand years, even though Confucianism was considered bourgeois by the communists. Arana writes that "Confucian morality was subject to intense scrutiny" (1999:27) during the period leading up to the 1945 Revolution. Of particular concern to the CVP is the loss of what they consider cultural patrimony, as stated in the second 1996 Report:

> As we enter into the market economy and broaden international exchanges for national industrialization and modernization, if we absorb cultural values of other nations while distancing ourselves from our traditional values and national identity, we will lose our own identity and become a weak reflection or a copy of others.

By 2001, the concern had become more specific with a statement about the influx of pessimism, sex, and violence into music, as transmitted via films, music videos, and karaoke, an influx that has troubled many traditional Vietnamese adults. As Mai Hong writes:

> There are many youngsters who now only have "alien" music to influence them, full of pessimism, sex and violence. Disturbing videos,

films and books add to this cultural deterioration, as does the proliferation of karaoke bars and "bia om" [beer and hugging, i.e., sex]
bars. Unfortunately they are all gaining in popularity. The growth
of such commercial forms of entertainment is bringing with it many
social ills. (1995)

Kim Thinh refers to these types of entertainment as "cultural media," and
warns about their dangers to Vietnam's youth and how they can undermine
traditional values (1995:5). Popular music, through the media of CDs,
music videos, VCDs, DVDs, and particular performances in Vietnam's
cities (especially in Ho Chi Minh City), can be included in Kim Thinh's
description and analysis of "cultural media," although he is specifically
speaking about the visual arts and printed word. The printed media he
refers to include imports from the West, Taiwan, and Hong Kong, as well
as materials printed in Vietnam. He blames "higher living standards [that]
have created demands for a greater quantity and variety of entertainment
[and have caused] the boom in violent or pornographic films and books
which bring nothing but harm." As solutions to the problem, Kim Thinh
advocates censorship or "firm control by the state over the content of publishing, [the content of] audio-visual products such as video films, and the
import and export of cultural matter in general. . . ." Indeed, censorship of
the popular arts is a reality in Vietnam.

Government Censorship of Musical Programming

The censoring power of the Ministry of Information and Culture, Performing Arts Department, is especially felt by foreign groups on tour that want
to include Vietnam in their itineraries. All foreign individual artists and
troupes, including musicians, dancers, and others who want to perform in
Vietnam must obtain a permit, which requires approval by the Department
of Culture and Information. The governmental scrutiny is thorough—song
by song and act by act. Months in advance of their proposed engagements,
foreign artists must submit performance videos, provide the lyrics of all
songs performed, and allow government officials to attend and review all
dress rehearsals. Furthermore, each solo artist or performance group must
partner with a Vietnamese artist or group, an act that often catapults the
latter to fame within Vietnam.

Vietnamese artists and performance groups are not required to go
through the same process, although they must provide the Ministry of
Information and Culture with a recording of and lyrics to the songs they
will sing when the musical occasion is a large show; the Ministry tries to
maintain the Vietnamese language as the primary linguistic vehicle and to
insure that the content of the music is wholesome and nonpolitical, according to its standards. An anonymous consultant told me in 2005 that a
famous pop singer (whose name will also remain anonymous) said during a

concert in [anonymous city]: "I wanted to sing [song title], but I couldn't get it approved." If a singer performs an unacceptable song during a concert, or releases such an unapproved song on a CD or other medium, the artist risks being fined VNĐ 10 million (about US$650) per song.

American reporter Ben Stocking, writing for the *San Jose* [California] *Mercury News* in 2003, briefly discusses censorship in Vietnam as he sees it:

> Vietnam's communist government, whose musical preferences tend toward the wholesome, still exerts close control over what music can be played here. But lately it has eased its grip a bit, allowing a few officially sanctioned rock shows that drew thousands of passionate fans. There is no Top 40 machinery here, no all-powerful recording industry catapulting its artists to stardom. The censors permit only a few carefully chosen MTV clips on Vietnamese television.

More of Stocking's views, especially about rock music, gender issues, and the role of electronically produced mediation as transmitted in Vietnam, are presented in later chapters. I also present more analysis of censorship and values in later chapters about Vietnamese pop and rock artists and their performances, the recording industry, and the Internet.

CONCLUSION: FROM GLOBALIZATION TO VIETNAMIZATION

Many factors have influenced the palette of contemporary popular music in Vietnam between 1990 and 2005. With regard to the soundscapes of the music composed, arranged, performed, and recorded during those years, a subcontinuum that I call *globalization/Vietnamization* is apparent within the right side of the Arc of Culturation, as indicated by the double-headed arrow in the right-hand side of the Popular Music Continuum (and Arc of Culturation) diagram in Figure 1.1.

Globalization

This broad term, introduced in the 1980s to explain economic flows around the world, has been applied to popular music studies since the 1990s. Negus insightfully describes the concept with regard to popular culture:

> [T]he appearance of the same cultural forms around the world is not due to the activities of imperial powers (whether nations or corporations) but is a consequence of processes of 'globalization' in which various patterns of difference and the convergence of cultural practices and social activities are making it difficult to identify any power that might

be directing such movements. The globalization argument, in its various forms, tends not to identify any forms of overt exploitation or imposition, but is employed to emphasize processes of 'transculturation' whereby various forms of musical expression are continually interacting with one another, in the process generating a variety of musical styles that might be leading to a 'transnational music' or a converging 'nationless culture'. (ibid.:176–177)

Regarding music and other cultural attributes, critics of globalization are concerned with what they interpret as "the devastating destruction of local traditions, the continued subordination of poorer nations and regions by richer ones, environmental destruction, and a homogenization of culture and everyday life," whereas proponents claim that globalization "produces hybridity and multiplicity, arguing that global culture makes possible unique appropriations and developments all over the world with new forms of hybrid syntheses of the global and the local, thus proliferating difference and heterogeneity" (Kellner n.d). Regardless, and "no matter how inspiring the musical creation," writes Steven Feld, success is driven by "more and more markets and market niches." Globalization is, therefore, mostly market driven (2001:213).

In Vietnam's contemporary popular music, however, globalization also includes a kind of Western homogenization of Vietnam's popular culture, with self-styled imitators of Britney Spears, Michael Jackson, 'N Synch, and Kurt Cobain (respectively, Mỹ Tâm, Kasim, MTV, and Trần Hà, among others). As we shall see, globalization affects much of the popular music in Vietnam, although aspects of hybridity and/or multiplicity are evident when the music is carefully listened to. Perhaps these types of complexities can be seen as "unique appropriations and developments," as Kellner writes, even though they appear on the surface to be imitations. Feld's take on globalization concerns world music, which is indeed a product of globalization. Within Vietnam, however, I include one aspect of this (globalization-produced/world-music-inspired) product within the category I call Vietnamization, which goes far beyond globalization.

Vietnamization

I was inspired to use this term with regard to Vietnam's popular music when I listened to two recent (2005) CDs by Vietnam's two most popular divas, *Khu Vuon Yen Tinh* (Tranquil Garden) by Hồng Nhung and *Này Em Có Nhớ* by Tranh Lam. Vietnamization is a result in Vietnam of what I refer to as *culturation*. Koji Onishi captures the essence of the concept and its relationship to globalization when he writes, "As globalization proceeds, repertoires become unified and people need something new. Thus local music culture is a good spice with which to revitalize the global music scene" (1998:483). More specifically, however, and more than simply "good spice" or an attempt to "symbolize 'authenticity' to many in the Western 'world music' audience" (Witzleben 1998:469), Vietnamization is the process of making Vietnam's popular music sound Vietnamese because it *is* Vietnamese (i.e. made in Vietnam by Vietnamese). The other terms I have used to explain this overall process, as I discussed in the Prelude—*indigenizing the global* and *glocalization*—will be used interchangeably with culturation and Vietnamization.

In the next chapter I explore the music and musical lives of perhaps Vietnam's largest institution of popular music, that of the solo singers who are a part of the country's star system.

3   Vietnamese Pop Music Stars and the Bumpy Road to Stardom

Vietnam's popular music scene is based on the star system, and to become a pop music star is the dream of many Vietnamese teenagers and young adults. It is often a pipe dream, however, because the road to fame is bumpy, and there are many difficulties involved in becoming a pop music star. To make it as a pop star in Vietnam requires charisma, good looks, talent, and luck. In this chapter I assess the bumpy road of the pop singer's profession, relative to issues of memory politics and market economics, by making biographical sketches or profiles of Vietnam's best-known pop singers during the 1990s and early 2000s, rising stars or wannabes, established singers or local returnees, and Việt kiều singers who routinely return to their homeland to perform. Gender and age issues are important factors that are discussed. I also describe several strategies undertaken to become a pop singer in Vietnam, such as lessons, talent shows and singing contests, personal marketing and the Internet, and the role played by the film industry. I conclude by examining personal earnings in the pop singing profession. Therefore, this chapter mostly pertains to the pop singers themselves and their profession; I discuss other musical topics, such as compositions, songwriters, and fusion, in later chapters.

BASIC TRAINING

Few pop singers in Vietnam have been born into families and situations that have made it easy or natural for them to achieve success in popular music. Most have had to devote years of study to reach their goals. For example, numerous young pop singers study music and singing at the national conservatories in Hanoi and Ho Chi Minh City; others study privately in a more traditional one-to-one relationship. Some pop star wannabes spend millions of VNĐ—the equivalent of hundreds of dollars (in 2001, there were approximately 15,000 VNĐ to US$1)—to study with pop singers who have chosen to pursue more stable careers as private teachers, so competitive and insecure is the professional route. Nguyễn Thu Huyền, a student at

Ho Chi Minh City Open University who attends a vocal training class run by one of the city's best-known singers, explains:

> To become a pop star is a dream of many young people like me. . . . I learn vocal music, dance and practice my voice in the class. The fee is more than VNĐ 1 million for a three month course. I often lose study time at the university but I don't mind. . . . I hope I will become one of the top singers in the future. I believe in the teacher's ability because he is a famous singer. He can teach me how to become the best singer. (*VNN*, April 23, 2001)

Neither is it enough just to have a beautiful voice to become a pop singer; those who desire to become pop stars must also be able to dance. In the 2000s, many professional pop singers employ numerous dancers during their performances, and many singers are also excellent dancers. Dance was not always as important as it has become in 2005. During the 1990s and even the early 2000s, for example, the addition of dance to a show was considered a concession to the purity of solo singing and was said to be resorting to gimmicks with little success, according to the Vietnamese press and the musicians interviewed by music critics. The songwriter Trần Thanh Tùng, for example, explained the use of dancers: "To attract audiences, [pop singers] have asked dancers to perform in their shows. Sometimes, [performances] look like amateur night club acts. . . . It's wrong to think that good looks and some nifty dance moves are enough" (*VNN*, December 16, 2001).

Another technique that is part of a pop singer's basic training in the 2000s is lip-synching, primarily so the dancing pop star can dance with vigor and still appear to be singing with a full voice. Like dancing, however, lip-synching was also frowned upon during large shows, as explained by a music critic from Ho Chi Minh City: "Young singers know they face many challenges in performing live. They must be highly skilled in terms of the level of their performance and their musical ability. To deal with these challenges, some of them turn traitorous to their fans by lip-synching like robots" (*VNN*, July 26, 2002). Nevertheless, both dancing and, to a lesser extent, lip-synching, have become standard performance requirements in live musical shows, because of the interest in emulating American and other non-Vietnamese kinds of musical extravaganzas. Thus, singing, dancing, and lip-synching have to be practiced diligently.

ISSUES OF ETHNICITY, GENDER, AND AGE

Popular music in Vietnam is not classified or marginalized by ethnicity and gender, as it is in the United States and Britain. There are no hyphenated musical metagenres[1] (such as Afro-American or Native-American musics in the United States); there are neither riot grrrl bands, gay/lesbian heavy metal groups (although there are boy and girl bands, as discussed in the next chapter), nor other ensembles that developed because of anger, difference, marginalization, oppression, or political dissatisfaction. Nevertheless, ethnic and gender issues *do* play a role in Vietnam's music industry, as they do everywhere. Age is also a factor, as choice of musical genres and singing styles seem to be determined by the age of the singer, at least to a certain degree.

Ethnicity

The majority of the pop singers in Vietnam belongs to the Việt ethnic group, which is the largest and most dominant ethnicity in Vietnam, constituting about 90 percent of the country's population. There are fifty-three ethnic minority subgroups in Vietnam, however, including the Hoa or people of (mostly) Han Chinese heritage, the Khmer or people of Cambodian ancestry, the Chăm or people of Indian heritage, and numerous hill people (mostly people of Austro-Polynesian descent) referred to as Montagnards during the French colonial period. While I use the term *heritage*, it is important to keep in mind that Vietnam's crossroads past began millennia ago. Therefore, most of Vietnam's diverse heritages do not consist of recent outsiders, although many ethnic minorities are marginalized by the dominant Việt.

A few Vietnamese composers/songwriters of popular music have recognized the uniqueness and value of incorporating folk song materials into their songs and other compositions—most notable are Nguyễn Cường and Lê Minh Sơn (see Chapter 5). Nguyễn Cường, known as the Tây Nguyên Rock King because of his use of Ê Đê ethnic minority musical materials from Tây Nguyên (Central Highlands) in his songs, sees his approach to songwriting as important because ethnic minority musical materials are "in their own way a bridge between Western and Eastern music" (*VNN*, March 31, 2002). It is even more evident, however, that the ethnic minority pop singers themselves constitute that bridge, at times moving completely into a Western rock music style.

The ethnic minority popular musicians discussed in this chapter include female singers Siu Black and Bonneur Trinh, and male singers Lam Trường, Kpa Y Lăng (also spelled Kpa Ylang), Y Moan, and Y'Zak. Occasionally Vietnamese singers of ethnic minority heritage appropriate their ethnicities to a degree by wearing either traditional dress or clothing fabricated with ethnic patterns. Most often, however, popular music singers from ethnic minority backgrounds perform without external ethnic accouterments, except when they make music videos where visuals are of particular importance. The several ethnic minority singers discussed in this chapter are organized first by gender and then alphabetically, along with everyone else.

Gender

A 1997 *Việt Nam News* article titled "Women rule music scene" reported on the dominance of female pop singers in Ho Chi Minh City:

> Male singers appear to be getting crowded off the stage as young starlets continue to dominate the music scene here. . . . There are also only a handful of males over 45 still performing and [of the] many singers who were popular in the 1980s. . . . [o]nly a few male singers under 30 are well-known in HCM City. (June 3)

In 2005, the trend was the same, as the article "Women singers overshadow men" makes clear:

> Women singers continue to dominate Việt Nam's music scene, while male singers struggle in the background. . . . [T]he female singers are the big sellers. . . . Most of the female vocalists have won top prizes in national singing contests organised in Hà Nội and HCM City in recent years. They can be seen regularly at concerts in the country's big cities. (*VNN*, March 12, 2005)

There are literally hundreds if not thousands of female pop singers in Ho Chi Minh City and Hanoi, and in 1999 music critic Đức Ngọc offered his view in an article titled "Việt Nam's pop queens crown music scene":

> The question on the lips of every music fan and critic in Vietnam is: Who is the Queen of Vietnamese Pop? Mỹ Linh, Thanh Lam, Hồng Nhung, or Trần Thu Hà? The four singers from Hà Nội are winning millions of new fans in the South and are adding a new and interesting dimension to the pop scene. Each singer has a unique performance style and way of expressing the essence of a song. (*VNN*, December 3)

By 2005 the names of the top female pop singers has not changed much, except for the addition of younger stars such as Mỹ Tâm and Thanh Thảo. In addition, several new male pop singers have raised the public's eyebrows and opened their ears to more fashionable music, such as hip-hop (ibid.), while other new idols continue as romantic crooners.

It is perhaps not unusual that young and beautiful female pop singers are the majority of the stars in Vietnam's pop music world, because the phenomenon is common throughout the pop music world, particularly in the United States, the United Kingdom, and Japan, as Whiteley explains: "As musicians, women have traditionally been viewed as singers, positioned in front of a band, the focus of audience attention not simply for what they sing, but for how they look" (2000:52). In Japan, especially, the concept of *kawaii* or "cuteness" is very prevalent, and it exists on a scale from female innocence to graphic sexuality. Brian McVeigh captures the breadth and depth of the concept in Japan in his book *Wearing Ideology: State, Schooling, and Self-Presentation in Japan*:

> Cuteness is an expression of a sociopolitical theory visible in the commodities of everyday life and touches upon the relations between the powerful and the less powerful: family structure, the ubiquitous hierarchical junior-senior relations and, in particular, male/female relations. Being cute toward those above is often a way of obtaining favors and attention, while displaying cuteness to one's subordinates is a method of appearing non-threatening, thereby gaining their confidence, and perhaps more cynically, control over them. (2000:143)

Although perhaps seen as female appropriation by outsiders, acquiring the confidence of male subordinates and ultimately control over them by female pop singers are examples of female empowerment, according to McVeigh. In Japan, the term *girl-pop* has been in vogue for some time to identify the pop music phenomenon sung (and often performed instrumentally) by young females (Milioto 1998:485).

In Vietnam, such outward female appropriation or inward female empowerment has not reached the levels that it has in Japan (there is no girl-pop concept, for example), although Vietnam's tourism industry often portrays Vietnamese women according to

> the Western ideal of obeisant Asian beauty, diminishing the significance of the roles played by Vietnamese women throughout history. . . . [I]mages of women . . . are ornamental and sexual; their faces are round, smiling, unconcealing. A Vietnam characterized by such harmless creatures is safe and unthreatening" (Kennedy and Williams 2001:159).

The similarity between Vietnam's tourism industry and its music industry is striking in this regard, perhaps because feminine beauty (what I call the *cuteness factor*) as portrayed on travel posters and CD covers sells products (see chapter 10).

Vietnamese attitudes towards women (i.e. including both their appropriation and empowerment) are thought to be rooted in Vietnam's folklore and history. For example, kinship practices at one time stressed patrilocal residence, meaning that "descent was traced mainly through men; . . . a newlywed couple [resided] with the husband's parents after marriage . . . ; and authority, both domestic and public, rested with men" (Luong 2003:203). In addition, Confucian ideology emphasized the concept of "'the three submissions' whereby [a woman's] life was divided into the stages of childhood, marriage and widowhood in which she was expected to obey successively three masters: her father, husband and eldest son" (Fahey 1998:246, fn. 4).

The Confucian moral code for women "was guided by the 'four virtues': to work hard, remain beautiful, and to speak and behave demurely" (ibid.). On the other hand, it is believed that prior to Confucianism (which was introduced into Vietnam in the second century B.C.) the region known today as Vietnam was matriarchal and women had predominant power. "Vietnam has an official matriarchal heritage," writes Fahey (233), citing Vietnamese scholars (Mai Thi Tu and Le Thi Nham Tuyet 1978), and "[Vietnamese] women commonly occupied the rank of goddess presiding over the cultivation of rice and other food crops." In spite of, or perhaps on account of, these traditional and Confucian beliefs, women have always been major contributors to Vietnam's economic development because of their roles in trade, production of crafts, and agriculture. During the French colonial period, the status of women became slightly elevated, as educational and occupational opportunities developed (inspired by the European system), and during the period after the defeat of the French, the "communist ideal for women was equality with men [a concept that] directly confronted Confucian views of the position and role of women" (ibid.:234). After the liberation of Vietnam in 1975 the status of women rose even more. Luong explains that by 1989 "the gender gap had virtually been eliminated" in some areas and that the "percentage of women in the state bureaucracy of unified Vietnam reached 51.4 percent" (2003:204–205). Into the 1990s, with the development of Vietnam's market economy, the status of women continued to rise.

At the same time, however, the 1994 lifting of the trade embargo by the United States and the influx of foreign investors from many regions in Asia, Europe, and America led to "the commodification of women's bodies through the significant growth of the sex industry and mistress arrangements" (Luong 2003:211). The Western ideals of feminine beauty, cuteness, and purity not only sell tourism and pop music in Vietnam; in 2001 official sources estimated that there were 40,000 female prostitutes in Vietnam, not counting the innumerable hostesses in places of entertainment such as bars, dance halls, and karaoke clubs.

For some teenage girls in Vietnam, becoming a pop music singer is a respectable way out of poverty, and indeed, some female singers, such as Ánh Tuyết, Siu Black, Phương Thảo, and Phương Thanh, have true rags to riches stories. A few female pop singers, Thanh Lam, Hồng Nhung, Mỹ Linh, Hà Trần, and Mỹ Tâm, seem to have been born into music. Exceptional musical talent is, of course, a major requirement, and though some singers rely on their natural musical talents, many study vocal music at any of the several national conservatories of music in Hanoi and Ho Chi Minh City or in smaller cities. Other major requirements for becoming a successful female pop singer, however, are physical beauty, cuteness, and neatness, all expected to be portrayed on stage during musical performances. I argue that although these last requirements may appear to be an appropriation of feminine sexuality in Vietnam's pop music industry, they are actually forms of female empowerment related to and perhaps derived from a kind of goddess cult that exists in Vietnam.

Philip Taylor explains that seventy-five goddesses have been identified in Vietnam, mostly in rural areas. He writes the following about goddess worship:

> Vietnamese ethnologists and folklorists have found in the popularity of goddess worship clear signs of the endurance of the nation's traditions and of its cultural integrity. . . . The selection of feminine images to symbolize such qualities as regeneration, nurturance, purity, continuity, sacrifice, duty, and constancy, which are held to sustain the nation, draws on this familial metaphor reflection the expectations placed upon women in Vietnam to reproduce and sustain families and embody their family's honor. (2004:49–50)

Indeed, motherhood and/or daughterhood are common forms of female empowerment among female pop singers, and both are frequent images evoked through their album covers, live shows, and song lyrics.

Female empowerment as expressed in motherhood is strengthened in Vietnam by the following three cultural foundations: (1) an innate Confucian belief that *yin* is the Great Mother and *yang* is the Primal Father; (2) the feeling, nurtured by centuries of war, that the mother is the cultural embodiment of grief, memory, and nostalgia; and (3) a subconscious adherence to a female goddess cult as evidenced by the veneration of and reverence for a multitude of female religious icons, of which two especially stand out in Ho Chi Minh City.

Although the *yin* side of Confucian thought represents female attributes and the *yang*, male, they are not in conflict, as Tai suggests

> [D]espite the Confucian emphasis on the continuity of the male lineage, it is the image of the mother that represents the nostalgic days of childhood and the sense of connectedness with one's personal past. Idealized pictures of young mothers rocking infants in hammocks form a recurrent motif in the visual arts. Countless odes to motherhood have been penned by poets, while popular music, both traditional and modern, abounds in songs with titles such as "Mother's Love," "Mother's Lullaby," and "Mother's Song." (2001a:169)

The songs cited by Tai were composed by Trịnh Công Sơn and/or Phạm Duy and are tributes to Vietnamese mothers who lost sons in the several wars of decolonialization. They are also symbolic of Vietnam, the motherland, and her (Vietnam's) loses during war (see Chapter 5).

Goddesses can also be seen as symbols, not of, but *for* Vietnam, as representatives of "protective nationalism" (Taylor 2004:52). The majority are rural goddesses seen as "border guards" of Vietnam's identity (ibid.:51), but in the huge urban sprawl of Ho Chi Minh City it is the dual popularity of Quan Thế Âm (the Goddess of Mercy in Buddhism, sometimes written as Quan Âm or Kuan Yin, the latter her Chinese transliteration) and the Virgin Mary (the Mother of Jesus in Roman Catholicism) who symbolize fertility, gentleness, purity, motherhood, and perhaps protection. Their youthful and gentle feminine attributes are represented in statues that look very similar

Figure 3.1   A statue of Quan Thế Âm, Goddess of Mercy, on a hilltop within the grounds of the Linh Phong Buddhist convent and pagoda in Dalat, Vietnam. Photograph by Dale A. Olsen, 2004.

when seen from a distance, as they adorn upper balconies of homes, watch over courtyards or street intersections, or stand in front of or within places of worship throughout Vietnam (see Figures 3.1 and 3.2).

Notwithstanding (the essence of) motherhood, beauty, purity, cuteness, neatness, and other ideological attributes (and national symbols) that are the

Figure 3.2   A statue of the Virgin Mary, in the public square in front of the Notre Dame Cathedral in downtown Saigon (Ho Chi Minh City). Photograph by Dale A. Olsen, 2002.

apparent requirements of young female pop singers in Vietnam, singing ability is also important, as suggested above and supported here by folklore. A proper balance of visual and aural beauty are necessary for musical success, as has always been the case in Vietnam, judging from this line in the folk tale "Nguyễn Kỳ and the Songstress": "She was not only beautiful; she also sang admirably. When her lips parted, the notes came forth like precious gems" (*Vietnamese Legends and Folk Tales* 2001, Folk Tale #18:145).

Age

Age is an important factor in Vietnam's pop music profession. Ethnicity and gender never change, age does (an obvious truism for which we should be thankful, given the alternative). Although Quan Thế Âm and the Virgin Mary are ageless, few pop singers can ever hope to be so enshrined (however, Carlos Gardel of Argentina, Elvis Presley and Frank Sinatra of the United States, and a few others come to mind). More important is the following question: *does age affect and/or determine a singer's style, choice of music, and/or popularity?* The quick answer is, "of course," because human bodies change. The question, however, requires lengthier answers; therefore, age issues are woven throughout this book, and a short analysis appears in the conclusion to this chapter.

STAR PROFILES: FEMALE POP SINGERS

In the following survey of female pop music starlets, I present brief biographical sketches of the ten most famous female pop singers (divas) in Vietnam during the early 2000s, in ascending chronological order according to their dates of birth: Ánh Tuyết, Siu Black, Phương Thảo, Thanh Lam, Hồng Nhung, Phương Thanh, Mỹ Linh, Mỹ Tâm, and Thanh Thảo. Through their encapsulated life stories, we can understand something about that bumpy road to professionalism by looking at how they became famous, how they define their careers, how they sell their product, how they are empowered, and what typifies their style.

Ánh Tuyết

Born in 1961 and raised in Hoi An, "from rags to riches" could be the motto of Ánh Tuyết, as suggested by music critic Anh Thư:

> Born into a large family in Quang Tri Province, Tuyết was a small and thin child. When she was only four years old she had to take to the streets selling *banh u* (small glutinous rice cakes). Tuyết sang as she sold her wares and learnt many songs at local snack shops, her first music schools. (2000)

Both her parents are musical: her mother was a folk singer from the province, and her father played music on guitar and spoons.

Ánh Tuyết made her singing debut by winning the top prize in a singing contest in her hometown in 1976 when she was only in seventh grade. Later she studied with Lô Thanh, a vocal teacher in Hue, and then attended the Hue School of Music and sang several years with a group of professional musicians from Quang Nam Province. She was once criticized by a panel of judges from the Hanoi Conservatory of Music for having a "limited" voice (*VNN*, February 27, 1998). She overcame the criticism by winning a gold medal in 1983 at the National Professional Singers Festival singing contest for her rendition of the song "Waiting for You Forever" and winning the same prize again in 1985 with the song "Visiting Uncle Ho's Mausoleum" (*VNN*, January 23–30, 2000).

Ánh Tuyết moved to Ho Chi Minh City in 1990 and won acclaim in a 1993 concert by singing Văn Cao's nationalistic songs, which had not been heard for a long time. She won yet another gold medal in 1998 at an international festival in Korea when she sang "Singing from the City Named Uncle Ho," composed by Cao Việt Bách (*VNN*, February 27, 1998).

Ánh Tuyết (Figure 3.3) is popular among middle-aged Vietnamese who remember the past, as well as among some young Vietnamese for whom the past is an aspect of their identity. Although she became successful in Ho Chi Minh City, it was not without difficulty, as she explained to Anh Thư:

> In 1990, I traveled to Saigon to look for a job but was refused by many art troupes. My hands trembled from fatigue and hunger when I sang at cabarets and bars, but that was the time I sang the most beautifully. I sang as if I never had a chance to sing. I sang with all my passion and love for life. . . . I did not surrender [to the tough life in Saigon] because I loved music. (ibid.)

She eventually landed a job as a vocalist with the official government-sponsored Bông Sen (Lotus) Music and Dance Troupe, and has toured throughout Vietnam with them (*VNN*, February 27, 1998).

Meeting Văn Cao (see Chapter 5) and singing his music changed Ánh Tuyết's life forever; he gave her confidence and a purpose for singing, as she explained to Anh Thư: "With Văn Cao, I found my favorite musician after half my life" (ibid.) It became her goal to disseminate his songs of remembrance. To make her dream of singing a commercial success, Ánh Tuyết opened her own popular music listening club in Ho Chi Minh City in 2000. The building she chose for her newly created ATB club was formerly used for *hat boi* traditional theater and music, and it retains a characteristic Vietnamese appearance (see Figure 6.6). The interior of the club features numerous lanterns from Hoi An, large urns, a miniature waterfall, and a Buddhist shrine, all meant to memorialize the past. She also has formed a band (including backup singers) named ATB (Ánh Tuyết Band), with whom she concertizes throughout Vietnam, often giving benefit concerts. On November 1 and 2, 2001, for example, she and the ATB band performed a benefit to help the flood victims in the Mekong Delta, raising millions of Vietnamese đong (*VNN*, October 29, 2001).

Critics say that Ánh Tuyết has "a special silken voice and skillful way of treating rhythm."[2] Because of her pleasing and even soothing style of singing, and the fact that she specializes in singing songs of remembrance composed before 1975, especially those of Văn Cao, I place her at the traditional popular music end of the Popular Music Continuum. About her particular style and choice of repertoire she explained, "I sing songs composed before 1970, mostly love songs. The songs of today are songs for the common people. They hear them and then they forget them. But the songs I sing will last

Figure 3.3 Ánh Tuyết performing at her club, ATB, in Ho Chi Minh City, August 4, 2005. Photograph by Dale A. Olsen.

Figure 3.4   A poster of Ánh Tuyết "playing" (holding) the *tỳ bà*, displayed in the foyer of her club, ATB, in Ho Chi Minh City. Photograph by Dale A. Olsen, 2005.

forever" (personal interview, August 4, 2005). To further her desired image of representing Vietnam's past and its traditional culture, several years ago she posed with a *tỳ bà* (a traditional Vietnamese lute, similar to the Chinese *pipa*) in her hands (as if playing it) for the creation of a colorful poster (Figure 3.4). It now hangs in the foyer of the ATB club, and when I asked her if she plays *tỳ bà* she laughed and said "no, it's just a prop." Ánh Tuyết makes use of other visual props throughout the ATB club (lanterns, projections of landscapes, Buddhist statues, etc.) and occasional audio props, when, for example, a synthesizer imitates a traditional Vietnamese musical instrument. Yet, I see and hear these not as attempts at culturation, but as visual and musical reminders of the not-too-distant past, perhaps inspired by the 1996 Vietnamese Communist Party *Report*'s (see Chapter 2) emphasis on the importance of "preserving and enhancing national cultural identity" and, of course, by Hồ Chí Minh's (Uncle Ho's) teachings about nationalism, especially that of *tính dân tộc* (national character).

Siu Black

Born in the Central Highlands province of Dac Lac in 1967, Siu Black (also spelled Blak) is a member of the Bahnar ethnic minority group. Although she was raised in a poor area of Vietnam, "[h]er remote native land is a common source for her songs, which she belts out in a wild but loving voice that has grabbed national attention" (*VNN*, April 19, 1997).

Siu Black was discovered by songwriter Nguyễn Cường in 1984, who essentially got her a job with a musical ensemble in the area. He wrote the following about his impression of her from that time: "Her voice will surpass the Central Highlands. This land won't have a better voice even in 10 or 20 years" (*VNN*, April 19, 1997). In 1985 she studied music at the Dac Lac Music School. In 1995 Siu Black sang "Nhịp Chiêng Buôn K'siar" (Rhythm of the Gongs from K'siar Mountain Village), by Nguyễn Cường, at the Asia Pacific Pop Rock Festival in Japan, which brought her a standing ovation. She was also the only Vietnamese singer invited to the festival (ibid.).

In 2004 she was further described as being "famed for her puissant and savage voice" (*VNN*, May 15, 2004). Her family did not approve of her departure and breakaway from her traditional Bahnar village and lifestyle. Her grandmother told her: "If you go, all you'll take with you are the clothes on your back" (*VNN*, April 19, 1997). Musically, however, she never left her Bahnar heritage behind, and it is one of her biggest trademarks as she blends Bahnar musical instruments and sentiment with modern pop music and rock expressions, as she explained (*VNN*, May 15, 2004):

> Ethnic minority music is like a river that forever flows into my soul. . . . My voice becomes stronger and more powerful when I breathe, eat and drink in the highlands. I love my country. I love my compatriots and love trees, springs, mountains in the highlands. I don't care about money and glory. I sing by my soul, my blood and my passion (*VNN*, March 26, 2004).

Traditional Bahnar music utilizes a number of single gongs, each played by an individual in interlocking fashion with the other gong players. Siu Black has captured the vibrancy and rhythmical pulses of Bahnar gongs in her rhythmical rock style, "her own brand of vibrant rock . . . steeped in the highlands" (April 19, 1997). Moreover, she expresses Bahnar feelings through the lyrics of her songs, many composed by Nguyễn Cường, which are steeped in cultural and personal memory; most notable are "Nín Nín Đi Em" (Please, Don't Cry Any More) and "Em Muốn Sống Bên Anh Trọn Dơi" (I Want to Live with You Forever).

Figure 3.5   Siu Black performing at the M&Tôi popular music listening club, Ho Chi Minh City, July 23, 2005. Photograph by Dale A. Olsen.

A live show captured on DVD (*Những Bài Tình Ca Tây Nguyên*) is representative of the wide diversity of Siu Black's musical style and her varied approaches to stage presence and performance technique. In several songs she is accompanied by Tây Nguyên ethnic minority musicians playing traditional gongs, and in one song she enters the stage on the back of an elephant. I heard Siu Black live several times in Ho Chi Minh City during the summer of 2005, and in one outdoor show her entire accompaniment was mediated, allowing her to make sonic use of her trademark Central Highland gongs and rhythms in certain songs. They were used sparingly, however, and her basic style was rock. Likewise, when I heard her at the M&Tôi popular music listening club (Figure 3.5), her style was totally rock and ballad, with some songs accompanied by prerecorded sound tracks and some live with the house band. On both occasions, the audience was very enthusiastic. Indeed, Siu Black is highly appreciated during her live performances, and her rapport with her audience, young and middle-aged, is outstanding.

Because of her heavy use of rock and other popular musical characteristics, Siu Black is highly influenced by globalized soundscapes, and with her adherence to and appropriation of her own ethnic minority aesthetics and roots, she is in synch with the government's desire to glorify Vietnam's minority cultures (see Chapter 2). Siu Black has not rediscovered her rural and ethnic minority roots, however; she has merely taken them with her to Ho Chi Minh City, the entertainment capital of Vietnam. She has indigenized the global or turned to culturation not so much through a self-realization process as much as always remaining herself, although many of her songs have been composed by Nguyễn Cường, adding to the exoticism of many of her recordings and live presentations.

Phương Thảo

Born in 1968 in what was then South Vietnam, and raised in Sa Dec, now Dong Thap, Province, Phương Thảo is unique because she is Amerasian (*my lai* in Vietnamese, and more rarely, *hapa*); her father was an American soldier in the Vietnam War. Most members of this hybrid subculture were highly discriminated against for more than a decade after the end of the War (in colloquial Vietnamese they were called *bụi đời*, dust of life). Phương Thảo, however, has been a big hit as a pop singer in Vietnam since the early 1990s, after winning a gold medal in a singing contest in 1987 and moving to Ho Chi Minh City (*VNN*, July 28, 1999). In 2000, the on-line *Asian Week Archives* published the following story, by Edith M. Lederer of the Associated Press, about Phương Thảo's ambitions, memories, and reunion with her father (May 4, 2000, Volume 21, No. 36, "Hapa Singer Overcomes Discrimination"):[3]

Growing up during the Vietnam War, Phương Thảo knew she was different. She was bigger than her classmates, and she had hair on her arms and white skin, all thanks to an American father she never had met. She also could sing. Years later, her deep-throated voice put her at the top of the country's pop charts and has helped her conquer the discrimination that children of U.S. servicemen often face in Vietnam. . . .

Phương Thảo's stage success is tempered by her private struggle to find out more about herself and her roots. Raised by her grandparents in the Mekong Delta province of Sa Dec, now called Dong Thap, she never had enough to eat. Children on the street made fun of her because she was half-American. She didn't have a close relationship with her mother, and they never discussed her father. "It was very delicate," she explained. "I did not want to make her sad." In 1983, the U.S. government offered the children of American GIs—"Amerasians"—the opportunity to move to the United States. But Phương Thảo said she couldn't bring her grandparents "who [sic] I love very much, so I decided not to go." Years later, her mother applied to go under that program, but Phương Thảo again chose to stay, to pursue a singing career. Besides, she didn't know if she could find her father in America. In 1988, she moved to Ho Chi Minh City, the former Saigon, to see if she could make it. She joined a group and a year later was on her way to stardom.

An American writer doing a story on Amerasians interviewed her in 1990 and asked whether she wanted help finding her father. She said yes. "I wanted to know if he was alive or dead," Phương Thảo said. Her mother provided a name and the base near Sa Dec where her father had worked. Three years later, the writer reported success. . . ."[Her father] was at first surprised he had a daughter in Vietnam," Phương Thảo said. "He did not know." But she said there was never any doubt they were related. Her mother said she looked like her father, and when he saw her picture, he agreed: "It's my daughter." For three years, they wrote letters and chatted by phone. Finally, in November 1996, when she was 28, he came to Vietnam to visit. "The first time I saw him, I cried like a child—like a child," Phương Thảo said, her voice breaking with emotion.

Phương Thảo's story and her success as a pop singer in Vietnam are remarkable, considering her background and the discrimination that Vietnamese Amerasians have faced since the end of the American War. It is perhaps proof of the powers of pop music, of a market society desiring to be modern, and the economics of forgetting among the Vietnamese youth.

Timothy P. Maga makes a similar conclusion about Phương Thảo's achievements:

In 2000, 32-year-old Phương Thảo was labeled the "Mariah Carey of Vietnam" by her adoring Vietnamese fans. Her success as Vietnam's pop diva would have been impossible only a decade before. As the out-of-wedlock daughter of a South Vietnamese typist and an American serviceman, she was considered a social outcast when she was younger. Some 50,000 mixed-race children were left behind by American troops. Viewed as symbols of America's pollution of Vietnamese culture, many of these children were herded into crowded, poorly funded orphanages. Phương Thảo was lucky to be brought up by her mother, but destitution and derision was their fate. Thanks to her singing ability, well-publicized singing contest victories, and the changing attitudes among young Vietnamese who never experienced the Vietnam War, Phương Thảo's career took off in the mid-1990's. (2000:301)

Her success was the result of a farewell to the past attitude by the public, in addition to her musical talent and tremendous luck.

Moreover, she sang the right songs at the right time. Phương Thảo's musical preference has been to sing romantic songs, which have great appeal among young people. She performed several songs composed by Ngọc Lễ for the first time in 1990, as she explained to Trần Minh Phi: "It seemed that I had found my music partner the day I sang Lễ's song. We both have similar tastes in music" (199). Shortly thereafter, Phương Thảo and Ngọc Lễ formed the Đen Trắng (Black and White) band, and they married in 1996. Trần Minh Phi writes, "Since their marriage, Thao has only performed [songs] written by Lễ. This makes them different from the other duos, especially when Lễ plays guitar and Thảo plays mandolin during their performances."

Their first CD album, *Cafe Một Mình Mot Minh* (Coffee Alone), released in 1996, sold about 100,000 copies (Click2VietArtists, 2000). Their second CD, *Ru Cho Con Và Em* (A Lullaby For Our Child And You), was released in 2000 and dedicated to their first daughter—NaNa. Because of its emphasis on the couple's first-born child and family values, the CD is popular among young Vietnamese families.[4]

Phương Thảo's veneration of motherhood and, through it, the glorification of her daughter, establishes her as one of the most important voices of memory cum mother goddess figures among Vietnamese pop stars. Recalling Tai's analysis of the empowerment of women in Vietnam and "how women can symbolize so many conflicting aspects of Vietnamese society and culture and, above all, how they can be made to represent both the power of memory and the fickleness of oblivion" (2001a:168), Phương Thảo's memory is not the memory of the past espoused by the Vietnamese government. It is the memory of her Amerasian roots and the gentleness of her motherhood as expressed in song.

Thanh Lam

Born in 1969 into a very musical family in Hanoi (her father is composer Thuận Yến and her mother is Thanh Phương, a traditional instrumentalist),

Thanh Lam began her vocal and piano training at age 3 with her parents and entered the National Conservatory of Music when she was 9 years old to study *tỳ bà*.[5] In 1986, at age 17, she won first prize at the Berlin International Song Festival, and in 1989 she won first prize in the Cuban Favorite Young Singer Festival. In addition, she has participated in over a dozen international music festivals in Canada, England, Germany, Japan, Switzerland, and the United States. Thanh Lam was formerly married to composer and keyboardist Quoc Trung, founder of the Phương Dong (Orient) jazz band, who often accompanied her during her concerts.

Although Thanh Lam is an accomplished *tỳ bà* player and performer of traditional Vietnamese music, critics and writers characterize her pop music singing style as Western. She also describes her style that way, as she explains to Thu Thủy, reporter with *The Thao & Van Hoa* (Sports & Culture) magazine:

> [M]y voice has a western sound . . . my style seems strong and passionate and doesn't follow any rules. . . . I cannot pander to the common denominator of music fans by changing my style. Keeping my own style is most important . . . my style is like 'the more you listen, the more beautiful the song is'. . . . When I performed in Japan last year [1996], many were surprised because my performance had an American style. I do not want to be a copy of Whitney Houston or Toni Braxton, but I find singing in an oriental style difficult. (cited in *VNN*, April 1, 1997)

It is indicative of Americanization through globalization that Thanh Lam chooses to sing, perform, and record in what she herself calls an American pop music style, even though she was raised in a household that treasured traditional music, and she received excellent musical training in traditional *tỳ bà* performance practice at the nation's most prestigious music conservatory for eleven years.

Thanh Lam always receives "warm welcomes from fans throughout the country," perhaps because she caters to a style that youth prefers: "Many people say you over-use some musical techniques and many times you almost 'scream' into the microphone," commented a reporter for *Tuoi Tre* (Youth) magazine during an interview with Thanh Lam. She replied, "I don't intend to do so. Truly, whenever I'm on stage, I devote my all to the songs and sometimes I cannot hold back my feelings. My husband also tells me: 'Your shows are always as rocky as your character'" (cited in *VNN*, January 13, 1999).

Perhaps because of a desire to do something more original, the importance of cultural and family memory, or simply maturity, in 2000 Thanh Lam's style began to incorporate traditional Vietnamese music into an otherwise American sound, as explained by Trần Minh Phi, who describes her new CD, *Tự Sự* (Talking to One's Self): "Thanh Lam, 30, sings confidently

on, in a career which is perhaps more western-infuenced, blending traditional Vietnamese music with standard pop music. For Lam, the album
is special because in it she performs songs written by her musician father,
Thuận Yến" (*VNN*, May 28, 2000). In fact, "Lam gained the highest Vietnamese honour of Diva of Light Music when she sang the song *Chia Tay
Hoang Hon* (Say Good-bye under the Sunset), written by her father, musician Thuận Yến" (*VNN*, July 19, 2004).

In 2004 Thanh Lam released a CD containing six songs by Trịnh Công
Sơn, considered by some as her greatest accomplishment at the time because
of the nature of the song material. The album received very high praise
(*Visualqui*, October 27, 2004):[6]

> Beside Thanh Lam, I could not imagine any other singers in Vietnam
> would have the confidence to release a Trịnh Công Sơn album with
> only 6 tracks. Since Trinh had more than 600 works and at least a hun-
> dred of them are extraordinary, I wonder why only 6 at first but once I
> listen to Thanh Lam's Ru Mãi Ngàn Năm, the answer is in every track.
> Each piece is carefully crafted in an intimate atmosphere . . . to offer
> listeners a pure appreciation for Trinh's work. . . . Thanh Lam and her
> musicians lull Trinh's magnum opuses to an exquisite level with her
> exotic voice, mellowing piano, soothing violin, and grooving guitar.
> Together they breathe everlasting life into Trinh's work of art. [Thanh
> Lam] also shows her innovative stylishness with Opera experimenta-
> tion. . . . She sounds as mature, fresh, and full of passion as ever. . . .
> If Trịnh Công Sơn were still alive, he would be enchanted to witness
> [how] his works have finally flourished into their full potential. It's a
> joy to see an artist like Thanh Lam constantly elevating her crafts and
> pushing herself. She takes Trinh's music to a place where no other art-
> ists have taken us before. Thanks Lam for bringing us "real" music
> we're all thirsting for.

Ru Mãi Ngàn Năm (Sing a Lullaby to Your Love Forever), released July 7,
2004, by Việt Tân recording company, is indeed a new approach to *nhạc
trẻ* music in Vietnam. Thanh Lam sings eight songs by Trịnh Công Sơn
to the accompaniment of a chamber music ensemble consisting of violin,
viola, 'cello, piano, and guitar. A number of Vietnamese pop singers have
found the maturity of their expression in the songs of Trịnh Công Sơn
(e.g., Hồng Nhung, Phương Thanh, Mỹ Tâm, Mỹ Linh), and Thanh Lam's
approach is perhaps the most Western of them all because of her use of
symphonic instruments.

Thanh Lam takes on an even more obvious Vietnamese stylistic per-
sona in 2005 with her CD *Này Em Có Nhớ*, in which traditional Vietnamese musical instruments are featured in several songs. In addition to
piano, guitar, violins, viola, and 'cello, she features melodies and fillers
performed on *đàn dáy* (lute), *đàn tranh* (zither), *sáo trúc* (horizontal flute),

and other Vietnamese instruments. The colors are a stark contrast to the usual Western orchestration of *nhạc trẻ* ballads. Like Hồng Nhung's, her style is becoming more culturated as she tastefully appropriates her traditional musical background. She explained her new style to the Culture Vulture (CV) interviewer for the *Việt Nam News*

> CV: Why were you absent from the music stage for so long?
>
> TL: I was not passionate for a long time because I could not find any suitable music. The other reason was that there was no encouragement for my work. What I needed was something new, like new songs. From my point of view, in recent years there has been almost no development in song writing. Older experienced musicians have composed none, while younger ones are not as talented. The songs of the young writers were not attractive to me. I'd always been strict with myself in the profession, which is why I only work with professional musicians.
>
> CV: You are considered Việt Nam's number one diva. A diva is one who influences other singers and creates trends. Have you done that?
>
> TL: It's true that I have been doing that, so I am always conscious about that. My name is recorded in Việt Nam's modern music history. I know I'm an idol to some young singers. In the domestic singing contest, I heard the judges ask candidates "why do you sing like Thanh Lam so much?" I've indirectly created a trend in singing.
>
> CV: Which musicians inspire you the most?
>
> TL: Recently, I am singing songs of Lê Minh Sơn. I think Sơn is a young talented musician. I co-operated with him to produce some albums in which I employ a different style. It is the way to renew my image as well as to confirm my diversified styles in performing and singing.
>
> CV: You used to sing Vietnamese songs, even ballads, in rock style. But you recently sing less "rock" and more "Vietnamese". What has made you change?
>
> TL: At present, young composers tend to write about love whereas Lê Minh Sơn writes about the countryside and ordinary life. His songs are therefore like folk songs. When singing Sơn's songs I have to use up 100 percent of my capacity. I also have chances to utilize all my knowledge about folk music, which I learnt when I was a little girl. That gives me reason to try harder, which makes me happy. Moreover, I have to change my style to match my age. (November 26, 2000)

Thanh Lam's use of traditional Vietnamese musical instruments is an example of culturation, as she moves forward in a self-fulfilling process towards a (re)creation of her own culture, which she knew as a child and a

Figure 3.6 Thanh Lam performing at the M&Tôi popular music listening club, Ho Chi Minh City, July 23, 2005. Photograph by Dale A. Olsen.

student in Hanoi. In addition to using traditional musical instruments, she often sings in a decidedly traditional Vietnamese style in those songs with traditional character. When I heard Thanh Lam perform at the M&Tôi popular music listening club in Ho Chi Minh City on July 23, 2005 (Figure 3.6), she performed several of her new-styled songs with prerecorded sound tracks. However, she displayed little usage of traditional vocal colors and techniques, unlike her interpretations of the same songs on her new CD, *Này Em Có Nhớ*.

Whereas in her early interpretations Thanh Lam was heavily influenced by American rock, she has indigenized that global expression in her latest creations. Her skill and success as a diva of Vietnamese pop music can be attributed to her diversity of vocal style and overall musical awareness. Hers is a nationalistically glocalized style that represents her culturation.

Hồng Nhung

Born in 1970 in Hanoi, Hồng Nhung is referred to as "A lark from Hà Nội" by her fans in Ho Chi Minh City, where she moved in 1993 (Figure

3.7). She began singing as a child, performing in programs for children at age 11, and singing on an overseas tour when she was only age 14 (pers. com., 2005). She told Minh Hiển, "I love singing. My father said I learned to speak when I was just a baby and that by 3, I could already sing several children's songs" (1997). In her late teens she competed in music contests and even toured outside of Vietnam to participate in international song festivals, as she continued to explain to Minh Hien: "I remember the 1989 International Pop Music Festival in Germany most of all. . . . It was the first time I'd taken part in such a big festival, and I was only 19 years old" (ibid.). Her professional career as a pop music star began in 1991, when she won the top prize in a national singing contest for professional singers, and by 1997, she had toured and presented concerts in fifteen countries.

Although she currently lives in Ho Chi Minh City, Hồng Nhung is still recognized as a Hanoi singer who braved the metropolis of Ho Chi Minh City, according to Da Ly:

> The large and raucous audiences at live music shows in HCM City have attracted singers from Hà Nội to the southern city's numerous theaters and night clubs. Pop singer Hồng Nhung is typical of the talent that is flowing from north to south. Taking a break during a performance at the Tiếng Tơ Đồng club on Đồng Khởi Street, she says her move had been risky but rewarding. "I didn't know if I'd succeed here," she says. "I decided to sing as I always had, so people would accept me and not consider me strange." (2001)

Hồng Nhung has been accepted in Ho Chi Minh City, and she continues to give concerts and record CDs (she had twenty by 2005), music videos, and DVDs. She has performed and recorded many love songs and other sentimental pop songs by such Vietnamese composers as Trịnh Công Sơn, Duong Thu, and other writers of ballads, and is considered especially suited to the repertoire of Trịnh Công Sơn, who spoke highly of her:

> [Trịnh Công] Sơn said, "For years I thought only Khánh Ly (a famous Saigon singer before 1975), with her low and warm voice, could perform my songs. Now Hồng Nhung has brought a new soul to my lyrics." Last year, Hồng Nhung and Trịnh Công Sơn organized concerts of Sơn's songs in Tokyo, which were warmly welcomed by the Japanese audiences. (ibid.)

These praises of Hồng Nhung by Trịnh Công Sơn are the exact words with which he apparently later praised Cẩm Vân (*VNN*, June 25, 1998). Whether this is plagiarism by the press or a stock response by the songwriter is not known. The May 15, 1997, source goes into more detail, as Trịnh Công Sơn and other musicians and critics describe Hồng Nhung's voice and style in a variety of ways, such as "a low and warm voice," "a strong and impressive voice," and "a free performance style" (ibid.). An Internet reviewer writes that she has "a frail emotionalism in her voice," and is characterized by a "romantic sensitivity and . . . emotionalism."[7]

One of her most notable achievements has been her role as featured singer in the soundtrack to the movie, *The Quiet American*, with music composed by Craig Armstrong in a highly Western style: [8] "[T]here is nothing Vietnamese about the melodic lines Hồng Nhung sings, but her vocal technique that uses a piercing nasally sounds, [*sic*] to a powerful end is entirely Vietnamese." She also had a short visual role in the film.

Hồng Nhung has also been described on the Internet as having an American jazz style, as written in *Vietnam Passage. Journeys from War to Peace* (The Perspectives):

> Nhung herself sings in Vietnamese with Western-style rhythms, influenced by the likes of Motown great Aretha Franklin. Jazz themes predominate, and Nhung's vibrato-free vocals soar. The signature tune from her most recent album Nhung album [*sic*] features a moody duet with a sax player—just one hint of the sophistication some of Vietnam's top artists have attained. ("Popular Music in Vietnam," see endnote 9)

However, when I asked her about this quote and the suggested American jazz influence, she responded: "I am influenced by many things, not only jazz. People write that, but there are many influences on my style" (personal interview, 2005). She explained that as one of the major interpreters of the music of Trịnh Công Sơn, as discussed above, she and many others find that his style of sentimental songs lend themselves very nicely to jazz improvisation. Nevertheless, Hồng Nhung has performed and recorded with Vietnam's most famous jazz musician, saxophonist Tran Manh Tuan. Her rendition of "Em hay ngu di" displays her soulful nature in a moody, soft jazz way (Tran Manh Tuan, however, does all the improvising).

Based on her recorded CD album, *Ngày Không Mưa*, I initially analyzed Hồng Nhung's musical style as unique and very Vietnamese, from a melodic point of view, and I thought that this style could be called a "Hanoi style," perhaps because of the northern Vietnamese genre of *ca trù* singing, captured by one or more of her songwriters. This was also suggested by an anonymous writer on the Internet: "Hồng Nhung makes us revisit furtively Hanoi with all its tree-lined streets and its special scents and makes us feel the freshness and the gentleness of the air blown by the wind of autumn" (see endnote 1). The songs on this album, for example, feature the open fifth and open fourth disjunctive melodic patterns typical of *ca trù* singing and *đàn bầu* playing, both traditional musical traditions from Hanoi. Moreover, from a rhythmic point of view, her style in this album is also unique, featuring much use of free meter, which creates an improvisatory feeling, as found in Vietnam's traditional music, for the opening portions of water puppet theater, also a northern tradition, and in the music from

Hue in central Vietnam. In the summer of 2005 I specifically asked Hồng Nhung about my analysis of her style:

> *DO:* Are you influenced by *ca trù, đàn bầu,* the improvisatory instrumental style of water puppet theater, or other northern Vietnamese traditional musical styles?
>
> *HN:* It is true. I do modern music, but I find beauty in our own authentic Vietnamese music as performed on *sáo* and *đàn bầu*; [authentic Vietnamese music] is very sweet. In Vietnam we have mostly melody and not much rhythm. The sounds are very unique. My composers and I do modern music that is blended with the traditional colors of Vietnamese music. (personal interview, July 19, 2005)

More than that, however, she continued to explain that she considers her style to be global as well, although it is more suited for Vietnamese audiences than for the world market.

> *HN:* In my last CD, titled Khu Vườn Yên Tĩnh [Tranquil Garden], however, I don't limit myself to a particular region. In one way it's Vietnamese because it carries a lot of unique melody and tunefulness, and in another way it's quite global. I have traveled all over Vietnam since age 11, touring around, and at the age of 14 my country sent me out to perform, so I have had a lot of chances to see the world a bit, to know that the world is not that big. If you can reach something, it is not that big. I am not doing just the northern thing [i.e. from Hanoi]. Music is freedom, and if it is what you like, what you think about the world, what you believe, [then it] is really [about] yourself.

She continued to explain her most recent CD, when I asked her a question about remembering the past:

> *DO:* In your music and with you personally, do you choose to sing songs that are concerned with remembering the past? Is the past important to your career, your life, your singing?
>
> *HN:* As a typical Vietnamese I must say that the past is very important; however, I tend to sing more about the present and hope for tomorrow. I think that the Tranquil Garden CD is very different from other CDs here in Vietnam in that the whole CD is about something in the garden. One song is about the rain, another about the stones, another about the birds hopping around in the garden, another just about the sunrise. We Vietnamese are like that; sometimes we don't speak directly about what we are really seeing, but we say it in a more poetic way. Just to tell about what I want, I want peace, I mean peace of mind, I want happiness.

So like an Asian person, like you see in my house [she has a beautiful tranquil garden that opens into her living room], it's very tranquil and is like a wish for peace. This doesn't mean that everything stays still. I want to go home to peace, so I can go out there and have a lively life. So, although the past is very important, we now tend to sing more about the present and hope for the future.

Khu Vườn Yên Tĩnh is filled with elaborate melodies and improvisations performed on traditional Vietnamese instruments, including various flutes

Figure 3.7 Hồng Nhung performing at the M&Tôi popular music listening club, Ho Chi Minh City, July 9, 2005. Photograph by Dale A. Olsen.

(*sáo* and *tieu*) and stringed instruments (neither the instruments nor their performers are identified) that create a very Vietnamese soundscape. Hồng Nhung's singing style moves from using traditional intervals and scales to Middle Eastern arabesques to sexy Western-style crooning, often in a decidedly improvisatory manner. Yet the music is modern because of its use of Western instruments in a sometimes sparse, sometimes rich orchestration. This album is unlike any other recorded in Vietnam, and while I don't wish to sound like a record reviewer, I believe it places Hồng Nhung in a category all of her own. Because of her use of traditional Vietnamese musical characteristics and soundscapes within her pop music style, her feelings about the importance of the Vietnamese past, and yet her desire to give more emphasis on the present and hope for the future, Hồng Nhung widely travels along a globalization/Vietnamization subcontinuum. On the one hand she recognizes the value of projecting traditional Vietnamese musical characteristics in her otherwise modern style, and on the other hand she reveals an interest in globalization and her own kind of world music fusion, as she called it, which is her own brand of glocalization, because it is a global palette blended with Vietnamese colors. Like Thranh Lam, Hồng Nhung also epitomizes the characteristic of indigenizing the global and the concept of culturation whereby she has moved forward as a part of her self-fulfilling process to (re)create her cultural past within a soundscape. As Vietnam (and Ho Chi Minh City in particular) continues to move toward a globalized market economy, Hồng Nhung's culturation is in a way a metaphor of Vietnam's own culturation.

Phương Thanh

Born in 1973 into a large and very poor family in Thanh Hoa Province in northern Vietnam, Phương Thanh is a natural talent. She has never had formal professional singing lessons, as she explained to music critic, Đức Ngọc: "I decided to sing as I always have so that the audiences would accept me and wouldn't think that I've tried to imitate other singers" (1998). In 1979, when she was age 6, her family moved to Ho Chi Minh City,[10] and Thanh herself moved there when she was 15, where her life continued to be difficult (*VNN*, June 1, 2003). While attending high school, Phương Thanh became interested in acting, music, and fashion, entering as many amateur singing contests as possible. In 1991, at age 18, she began to work for the Vietnamese youth movement and joined a club for amateur singers called Labor Theater House. Because of her naturally beautiful voice, according to an Internet article, "she soon found herself singing at wedding parties and restaurants. She wasn't a star, but her family's economic situation improved" (see endnote 10).

Just two years later, in 1993, Phương Thanh became a professional when she joined the trio Tam Ca Sao Đêm (The Night Star Trio). They performed at school and university concerts, where she received great acclaim:

The singer shot to fame in 1996 when she began singing Vietnamese songs at school and college music concerts. 'I received good responses from young audiences, and since then my singing career has sky-rocketed', Thanh says. 'I feel confident singing amid exuberant youngsters'. She has a strong voice and always chooses songs to suit the sentiments of the country's youth." (*VNN*, December 26, 1998)

She owes much of her success to Bảo Phúc, who "trained her to be a successful singer. They started with music techniques and continued with fashion classes. Shortly after, she found her own style: hard rock combined with a formidable and whole-hearted voice" (see endnote 10). Phương Thanh's fame continued to grow; in 1996, for example, she "was selected as one of the top 10 singers in Vietnam by *Đại Đoàn Kết* (Great Unity) magazine," writes Duc Ngoc, and in 1998 she was "among the top 10 singers in the country selected by *Phu Nu* (Women) magazine and listeners to the Làn Sóng Xanh (Blue Wave) FM radio music program" (*VNN*, December 26, 1998).

In 1998, at age 25, Phương Thanh began a career in film by obtaining a leading role in Trái Tim Không Ngủ Yên (A Restless Heart) as a beggar-busker who sings on the streets to earn money to support her father. It was not easy for her to break into film, as she explains: Six years ago I entered a competition to select screen actors, but I was eliminated in the first round because my appearance is not attractive. . . . Last year, film director Chau Hue refused to give me a role in the film *Nguoi Hat Rong* (A Street Singer). This time, . . . Chau Hue chose me to play in *Trai Tim Khong Ngu Yen*, but Fafilm still showed reluctance, saying that I am short and do not have a bright complexion. (ibid.)

Another film, *Giã Từ Dĩ Vãng* (Farewell to the Past), however, secured her reputation as a household name with a hit song by the same name (*VNN*, May 28, 2000). She became known as the "unrequited love song queen," according to Phạm Thị Thu Thủy (2003). Phương Thanh's "voice is acclaimed as strong but sad, appealing to the more sentimental," writes Trần Minh Phi (2000). Her hit songs, such as "Xa Rời Mùa Dong" (The Winter's Gone), "Trống Vắng" (Loneliness), and "Giã Từ Dĩ Vãng" (Farewell to the Past), the latter from the film of the same name, are filled with memory and nostalgia. Rather than looking forward to a bright future, textually, her songs from this period in her life draw strength from an unhappy past, which she tries to forget.

Phương Thanh dropped out of the pop music and film scene for about three years, claiming to be burned out and "feeling meaningless" from her difficult performance schedule. "I fell into a huge vacuum," she explained to Phạm Thị Thu Thủy. "I sang with less feeling because I had to sing too much." The writer continues:

Worn out by years of back-to-back shows, Thanh says one day she realised that her underlying passion and personal connection to each of her songs was gone. Another lesson she learnt quickly was the price of fame—the lack of privacy and control over her public life. "I was threatened for a whole year by a band of drug addicts. Police accompanied me to all of my shows. I was too scared to accept fans' flowers and gifts," she recalls. "On top of that, my younger brother gave in to the appeal of heroin." "I don't want to rise to the top any more," she says. "I now have my own position and spend more time studying new songs with a different message." (2003)

Thanh made a comeback in May of 2003, with a new attitude, a new look, and a new style:

[By wearing] traditional dress, she ditched her trademark rock chick look. Gone were the hipster jeans, wide belts and tight tank tops that made the husky-voiced songbird a provocative pioneer of Vietnamese pop. Alongside other Saigonese stars Hồng Nhung and Siu Black, Thanh looked postcard-perfect dressed in a delicate, pale yellow áo dài and traditional head band.

But after three years of virtual silence and self-reflection, Thanh's changed more than just her duds: Back on the show circuit, the 31-year-old says she is through with the highwire celebrity life—the public image and endless touring that left her feeling meaningless—and just wants to get back to her heart.

. . . "I now have my own position and spend more time studying new songs with a different message." . . . Phương Thanh is now embracing a different style of music. The new tune she's whistling is about a future with a husband and children and an idea of love that extends to her country. "I may not sing these songs as well as other established artists," Thanh confides, admitting that a good deal of her fans would likely agree. "But it is a step up in my career, a step up for me personally." It's a natural progression, with her career intertwined with her personal growth. (ibid.)

Part of Phương Thanh's "new" direction includes the singing of sentimental songs that have to do with Vietnam's past struggles (*VNN*, August 9, 2003). In 2003 she startled her fans at the M&Tôi club when she sang a romantic song titled "Giữa Mạc Tư Khoa Nghe Câu Hô Nghệ Tĩnh" (Hearing the Nghe Tinh Song in Moscow), written by Trần Hoàn, instead of her usual pop and rock songs. The song made many of her fans teary-eyed with its beauty and her new approach. She explained the following about the performance and the reaction by her fans:

I had to summon up a soldier's courage when I first performed the song, but I managed to win the hearts of my fans. . . . I believe that singers like me, and concert organizers, are wrong to think that young people are only interested in hearing songs about the pain of love and rebellion. . . . The song encourages my fans and I [*sic*] to dedicate our lives to a more noble purpose. (ibid.)

Phương Thanh's recent approach to *nhạc trẻ*, in which she recalls the *nhạc tiền chiến* or *nhạc vàng* nostalgic and sentimental songs of the past, are a sea change for her. In a 2004 interview with *Inner Sanctum*, the interviewer wrote: "Late at night, I met Phương Thanh at a café in HCM City. Contrary to the effervescent and rebellious singer on stage, in front of me was a different Phương Thanh—gentle and equable. After a long period without performance, Phương Thanh seems to have many feelings to release" (*VNN*, April 4, 2004). One of the interviewer's questions in particular addressed Phương Thanh's past: "What do you think about the past with so much bitterness and suffering, with so much happiness and so many sorrows and even losses?" In spite of the obscure question, Phương Thanh responded with hope for the future:

I perceive that when happiness and sorrows come, life will be colorful. We should not avoid them, but we should embrace them, in order to have [a] valuable experience. At present, life has made me think about many things. At times, we should be silent and calm in order to have a deeper look into things. I have gone through crises concerning my career, feelings and money. As I look back to see that I did not falter during the storm, I think that in the future I will remain strong. The professional life of a singer is [her] own obsession. Money doesn't matter, but one's spirit is very important. We should have a soul to perceive ideas and feelings, so that we can carry them in song. A singer who sings without a soul is regarded as a failure. (ibid.)

Whether money matters or not is debatable, because of the high costs of performing shows and recording albums. What is not debatable, however, is Phương Thanh's emphasis on having "a soul." As a part of that philosophical concept, which for her is like a personal quest, the songs of Trịnh Công Sơn have become important to her. The *Inner Sanctum* interviewer asked her : "When you took part in two [of] Việt Nam's *Grace* programs, both times you surprised the audience by choosing Trịnh Công Sơn's songs. What are your feelings about Trịnh Công Sơn's music?" She responded:

I think I am compatible with Trịnh Công Sơn's music. What is needed is simplicity and a soul. There is no need for technique. Through Việt Nam's *Grace* the audience could perceive that. When I was young, I did not have the life experience to understand the lyrics of Trịnh Công Sơn's music. But now as I have gone through the storms of life I have a deeper perception of it. That perception innervated me, and I wanted to express it.

I never had the opportunity to hear or see Phương Thanh live in Vietnam. As the singer of "Farewell to the Past," which inspired many portions of this book, her reversal from being the rebellious pop singer to the mature interpreter of Trịnh Công Sơn's songs and others from the past are perhaps relevant, as it reveals the complexities of Vietnam itself, as the nation strives to reach its own maturity as a socialist/capitalist country and a model of national unity.

Mỹ Linh

Born in 1975 in Hanoi, Mỹ Linh studied music at the National Conservatory of Music and English at the Language Link School in the capital city. She became a pop singer sensation after ranking very highly in a number of contests and winning several prizes between 1993 and 1997 (*VNN*, December 29, 1998). Mỹ Linh was also heavily influenced by *à đào* traditional Vietnamese music as interpreted through the songs composed by Pho Duc Phương (*Việt Nam Help*, December 3, 2002):[11] "She has been a leading performer in A Dao style music with her fluid, confident, and unique style. Mỹ Linh's direct approach and singing style express intense emotion from the heart, touching Vietnamese audiences all over the world." It is significant for Mỹ Linh's approach to popular music that she studied and performed music in the traditional *à đào* style during her formative years,[12] because it has contributed to her interest in an expanded sound base and rich sonic palette. As she developed into the early 2000s, that interest developed further as she learned more about Western musical styles, from soul to Mozart. She has strived to become famous in the United States, and perhaps because of her broad musical interests and desire to make a unique contribution, she may succeed.

In 1997, Mỹ Linh married fellow musician Anh Quân, the leader of Anh Em (Brothers), a Vietnamese soul and funk band. With music all around her, and with her husband as her newest songwriter, Mỹ Linh landed a recording contract with an American label and released a CD during the summer of 2003, as explained in *Nhân Dân online*:[13]

> Singer Mỹ Linh is hopeful of success in America with her album scheduled to be released this summer in the largest music market. On the album, Linh's songs are almost all in English and written by her husband, Anh Quan, and some musicians in Nashville of Tennessee state which is known as the capital of music in America. Two songs in Vietnamese will be included in the album. A company from the state of California has helped Mỹ Linh have access to the US music market. Mỹ Linh's new impresario, Michael McKenzie, said that the company has worked out a plan for Mỹ Linh to perform with American singers. It has also helped Mỹ Linh touch not just the overseas Vietnamese community but the American public in general. Linh will be singing in

English, and her sound will be a fusion of Vina-pop, with jazz and rap touches. "The natural voice of Linh ensures her a further future," said McKenzie. . . . A video film introducing Mỹ Linh and Vietnam . . . will be also produced. (February 5, 2003)

The publisher of this article, *Nhân Dân online*, is "The Central Organ of the Communist Party of Vietnam [and] The Voice of the Party, State, and People of Vietnam." As the official voice of the CPV, the above article is also a communist endorsement of Mỹ Linh's dissemination of vina pop to Americans, including the Việt kiều. Her video about the country of Vietnam adds an interesting element of Vietnamese memory politics, as well as nationalistic marketing, to the complete package. The *Việt Nam News* also carried a story, "Prized songbird hopes to spread wings in America", which included the following information: "'The music is the same [as sung in Vietnam] but the English words give the songs a slightly new style', said Linh. Some of the English songs are direct translations of some of her most popular Vietnamese songs. . . ." (January 8, 2003). Nevertheless, unlike Tranh Lam and Hồng Nhung's musical styles, Mỹ Linh's style is very American. Aside from the Vietnamese language and the song texts that occasionally portray Vietnamese life, neither the music itself nor her delivery reveals traditional Vietnamese characteristics.

Whereas some female pop stars have turned to the songs of Trịnh Công Sơn in their maturity (e.g., Hồng Nhung, Phương Thanh, Mỹ Tâm, and Thanh Lam), perhaps as a way to prove to the Vietnamese public that their singing style is profoundly Vietnamese, Mỹ Linh has turned to Western Europe to express her mature style. Her most recent CD album, for example, *Chat Với Mozart* (Chat with Mozart), features her vocal interpretations (in Vietnamese) of instrumental music by Schubert, Tchaikovsky, and Vivaldi. Oddly enough, Mozart is not included. She explains the logic and rationale of the album in an interview with the Culture Vulture:

> It's a [play on words], expressing my interaction with composers through the music, and also [it's] an integration between two civilizations, as informatics and digital technology mingle with the music of the 17th and 18th centuries. On the album I'm trying articulate a dialogue between generations, by representing young people while performing old music. Huy Tuấn and Anh Quận selected and recorded classical pieces suitable for my voice, and Duong Thu wrote new words for them. Despite the name, there actually aren't any Mozart pieces on the album, but he was chosen as a symbol of the genre. The record includes selections by Vivaldi, Schubert and Tchaikovsky. (*VNN*, July 7, 2005)

The interviewer prodded her with this important question: "Classical audiences can be very particular. Do you think the album will sell well?" This was Mỹ Linh's response:

We made the record because of our love for classical music, and we want to share that passion with other music lovers, especially young people. We've tried to revive these immortal pieces with modern orchestration and arrangements—to "chat" with the past. We didn't want to make a purist classical record, and Chat With Mozart blends several contemporary genres including pop, jazz and R&B. Of course, we can't be sure how audiences will receive it, but the most important thing for me is that I'm still making music. I made the album to satisfy myself, and I don't choose the music I make according to the demands of audiences. Still, I think that if the record is of high quality, it will do well. (ibid.)

Mỹ Linh's interest in the musical fusion of East and West, the past (meaning Western Europe to her, which is Vietnam's colonial past!) and the present (meaning the youth of Vietnam), and classical (meaning European classical, but not the Classical Period) and contemporary styles (meaning pop, jazz, and R&B) represents a departure for Vietnamese pop singers. It is an original endeavor, indeed, but one that makes me yearn for a deeper response to the question of *why bother?* As she stated, she made the album to satisfy herself, and that confirms my interpretation that this is how she wants to present her musical maturity. She also states, however, that "We hope to improve the popularity of classical music in Vietnam," which also leads me to ask: *why Western European classical music and not Vietnamese classical music?* The answer is that Mỹ Linh represents one of the most Westernized of the female *nhạc trẻ* singers. Whether she will ever fall back on her past experience with *à đào* is a valid question that cannot be answered for years to come. I do not necessarily support the use of Vietnamese traditional music in contemporary popular music because it is "authentic," "exotic," or to use my term, "culturated," but I am nevertheless of the opinion that appropriating European classical music is definitely not the way to create a unique Vietnamese style.

Mỹ Tâm

Born in 1981 in Danang, Mỹ Tâm left her hometown in 1997, moved to Ho Chi Minh City, and studied at and graduated after four years from the HCM City Conservatory of Music. Her family was not musical, and she paid her way through the conservatory by singing at bars, clubs, and restaurants. Mỹ Tâm's early singing career in Ho Chi Minh City was not spectacular, but she became a household word and perhaps "government approved" in 2002 when she performed a national solo concert tour for students, featuring singer/audience interaction and a simple stage setting:

Enveloping audiences with her sultry and powerful voice, pop singer Mỹ Tâm kicks off her first national solo tour for students today. The two-week tour, titled Sunsilk Cung Mỹ Tâm Toa Sang Uoc Mo (Sunsilk together with Mỹ Tâm Brightening Your Dreams), will not be an over-the-top glitzarama a la Britney, according to organizers, but will have an unadorned stage and atmosphere so that students and singer can interact. "Singing for students has been my long-nurtured dream. And now I can realize it," Mỹ Tâm said. (*VNN*, November 19, 2002)

Since those unpretentious concerts in 2002, she has had a very successful career that includes singing and making commercials for Pepsi Company with Britney Spears, Beyonce Knowles, Julio Iglesias, and others in 2004 (*VNN*, January 30, 2004). She has also won several prestigious pop music awards, such as Vietnam Television's (VTV's) *Bài Hát Tôi Yêu* (The Song I Like) and others (*VNN*, November 19, 2002; January 20, 2004), and she placed third in the female pop category in the 2000 Asian Music Awards in Shanghai. Mỹ Tâm is Vietnam's most famous pop singer in the first decade of the twenty-first century (Figure 3.8).

Mỹ Tâm has made many CDs and music videos (VCDs and DVDs), and they have been top sellers:

> The Sai Gon Giai Phong Thu Bay [Liberated Sai Gon, Saturday edition], reported that all 10,000 VCDs of female singer Mỹ Tâm's Yesterday and Now [her 2004 CD hit song, "Yesterday and Now," was composed by Canadian songwriter Lara Fabian] were sold after they hit the streets in mid-June last year. More than 80,000 copies have been sold, the highest sale of any music VCD in Việt Nam to date. (*VNN*, March 12, 2005)

In addition to her audio and video recordings, Mỹ Tâm also performs in her own live shows, which since 2004 have been the most expensive live shows ever produced in Vietnam. Her 2004 performances in Hanoi and Ho Chi Minh City, for example, cost approximately US$190,000 (*VNN*, March 31, 2004). "It is worth spending that much on a quality show, even though some say it could result in a loss," explained the director, Huỳnh Phúc Diêm (ibid.). Her show in Ho Chi Minh City, complete with a stage in the shape of Mỹ Tâm's initials, sold out and was a financial and musical success. Gone are the days of the simple stage setting.

Mỹ Tâm's reversal from live shows with a government-approved approach to live shows with a more globalized approach in such a short period is probably because of the times. Not only had she performed with and been influenced by top American pop stars, but as the twenty-first century ensued, much more freedom of expression and endorsement of huge commercial ventures have occurred in Vietnam than during the 1990s. Yet Mỹ Tâm tries to keep her youthful audience in mind when she performs live shows, as she explained in an interview with Thúy Hường (TH):

TH: What do you think is the most important aspect of your career?

MT: The most important part of my job is understanding my audience. If a singer is successful, she must sustain her connection with the audience. She should also never rest on her laurels.

TH: Audiences often want musicians to sample different genres. Will you try different styles or choose one?

MT: I always enjoy creating new styles from slight adaptations, although I think it's important to stick to a genre. Right now, I am balancing two styles: rock and ballads.

TH: Even though you can sing patriotic songs, you often stick to popular styles that are easy to remember but also easy to forget. Why?

MT: I often follow my instinct. Yes, I can sing any musical genre but I choose to sing for my audience. I don't really distinguish between serious songs and marketable music. I sing for my fans and they like ballads about love and other simple pleasures. (*VNN*, February 15, 2004)

As if remembering her humble background and the financial and musical help she received during her student years at the HCM City Conservatory of Music, Mỹ Tâm explains in the interview that she attempts to understand and please her youthful audiences. Not taking the interviewer's highly politicized bait about singing patriotic songs, she suggests that even "marketable music" will be remembered if her fans like it.

Not everyone in the audience was pleased with her extravagant concert in Ho Chi Minh City in March 2004, however:

[A]fter the poor response to her HCM City concert on March 25, music lovers have challenged Mỹ Tâm and her promoters to improve the show or pay their money back. Speaking at a press conference on Monday, Mỹ Tâm promised her fans that there would be a big difference [with her concert] in Hà Nội. Audience members at her HCM City show reported being let down by the lack of organization that saw them squeezing into a human matrix to find their seat. The audio system was also a problem, and her fans complained that they could only see their idol on a big screen but not in person. (*VNN*, March 31, 2004)

An anonymous Internet blogger, nevertheless, praised her and could not understand the criticism, as the following excerpts reveal:

The media needs to back off Mỹ Tâm. She deserves all the praises for her hard work because she rocked her concert [which was] beautifully executed . . . I don't know what the negative criticisms were about. She is young, talented, beautiful, and creative. . . . Vocally, Mỹ Tâm did a fantastic job and she was able to perform 18 plus songs without a short[ness] of breath [and] she impressed me with her English pronunciation. . . .

Choreographically, Mỹ Tâm has . . . great stage charisma. . . . . It's jaw dropping to see [how] Mỹ Tâm leaped high, rolled on the floor, and did a split at the end. The best part was that she was being herself out there and trying to have fun. She got [as] hype and wild as she pleased . . . the crowd loved it and I surely adored it.

Mỹ Tâm definitely has a fine taste in style. She looked elegant whether in a sophisticated evening gown or simple jeans and shirt. Unlike the hoochies on Paris By Night, she still appeared hot and sexy without bearing [sic] her skin. She proved talent has way more class than sex, and I respect her for that.

Although [the concert] was a huge investment for Mỹ Tâm, it was worthwhile. She did everything she could, and gave one of the best live concerts ever made in Vietnam. She should not allow the media to influence her work. She should spend her energy . . . pushing herself to the limit and expanding her artistic vision. (November 10, 2004; see endnote 6)

Of all the divas I have seen and interviewed in Vietnam in 2005, Mỹ Tâm is the biggest draw, perhaps because she is the most similar to her American idol counterparts, Britney Spears and Jennifer Lopez, whom she considers to be her role models (personal interview, August 2, 2005). From her years studying Western opera at the HCM City Conservatory of Music, to her legsplitting antics on stage, Mỹ Tâm has mastered all the requirements to be a successful pop star—beautiful singing, exuberant dancing, and excellent rapport with the audience. Moreover, she composes many of her songs and produces her own shows and recordings, as revealed through Thúy Hường's (TH) interview with her for *Inner Sanctum:*

TH: Recently, you have gotten involved in production—translating foreign lyrics, cover-design and sound editing. Do you enjoy this technical work?

MT: I've gotten involved in production as a hobby, not to polish or advance my image. I began to translate foreign songs because I think they have very beautiful lyrics that disappear in translation; I want to convey their art in Vietnamese.

TH: Many singers are crossing over into film. Do you have acting aspirations?

MT: It's an interesting prospect. Some directors have sent me scripts, but so far, I've declined because I want to devote all my time to music. But if I find an exciting role and it fits into my schedule, I will definitely accept the challenges. (*VNN*, February 15, 2004)

Mỹ Tâm's involvement with translating, performing, and recording foreign songs has made her a leader in copyright issues, and her acting aspirations are somewhat fulfilled with her story line music videos (see Chapter 8).

A description of Mỹ Tâm's attraction as a pop singer, written in 2002 by Nguyễn Hùng and Mai Phương, sums up the feelings of many of her fans: "Whenever she sings, people find it hard to ignore her or turn away, and her voice takes them to a world of happiness and peace" (2002). When I interviewed Mỹ Tâm in 2005, among my questions were several relating to her popularity with Vietnam's youth:

> *DO:* To what extent have you been influenced by what the youth market wants?
>
> *MT:* I don't know why but the youth love [also means respect] me. Maybe it is because the kind of music I sing is happy and that is why they love me. I have a staff to help me with such marketing.
>
> *DO:* Do you feel pop music has power? What is powerful about your music?
>
> *MT:* Pop music expresses the emotion of the people—you can understand together. You can hear about everyday situations and it is simple to listen to. Within the whole world we make modern types of music, and through those types we are able to bring different songs and feelings to the audience. But with pop, I just sing about simple things.
>
> *DO:* When I observe the audiences at clubs like Đồng Dao and M&Tôi, many of them seem enraptured by the music. What do you suppose they are thinking and feeling?
>
> *MT:* When they are like that, I can tell that they really love me. When I look at the audience I have strong feelings and I want to sing all night. They feel interested because they can tell what I want and that I know what to do [i.e. they can feel my confidence]. (personal interview, August 2, 2005)

Mỹ Tâm has great rapport with her young fans, perhaps because in everything that she does as a musical professional, she represents one of the most Westernized of Vietnam's female pop singers. She is the supreme pop star idol in Vietnam.

Mỹ Tâm has neither ventured into the realm of culturation like Thanh Lam and Hồng Nhung, nor has she delved into Western classical music like Mỹ Linh. I asked her how she feels about rock, heavy metal, hip-hop, and world music, and this was her response (personal interview, August 2, 2005):

> I love rock, I don't know why, but I feel it is so strong, and I feel I have something in my heart. I do not have a favorite Vietnamese rock group, and cannot really even name any. Rhapsody, a Swedish rock band, is my favorite. I also like hip-hop and I can feel it is a part of my expression. Stylistically, I am mixed between hip-hop, rhythm and blues, and

pop. In the future I would like to do acoustic music, but with different songs. I sometimes think about a world music approach, but sometimes if there is something I want to do, I choose not to do it because I have to follow what my audience—my fans—want. Perhaps at another time I will do things like that for myself and for another audience. Maybe I will bring my country's instruments into my modern music. For example, with hip-hop, if it has melody I may use sáo, or another Vietnamese instrument—like in world music. Or I could sing real Vietnamese folk songs and arrange them like world music.

Figure 3.8   Mỹ Tâm performing at the Đồng Dao popular music listening club in Ho Chi Minh City, July 3, 2005. Photograph by Dale A. Olsen.

Mỹ Tâm has made a superficial attempt to produce world music, however, with her show performance of "Giac mo muon mua," a song composed by Lê Quang. Her live show performance of it features "exotic" dancers using stereotypical Egyptian body movements and arm gestures. At one point a large Chinese or Japanese type barrel drum is brought out and played by Mỹ Tâm for a few seconds, in a style reminiscent of Japanese taiko (ô-*daiko*, "large drum") drumming. Meanwhile, the dancers beat double-headed cylindrical drums suspended from their necks, which they soon remove, place upright on the floor, and beat while kneeling. During this dance interlude, the instrumental music emphasizes a melody exploiting the augmented second interval, the most common musical stereotype of some Jewish and other Middle Eastern musics. Mỹ Tâm's staging of Lê Quang's beautiful songs is, in my opinion, an appropriation of Middle Eastern music and North African dance characteristics, similar to the music performed in the original *King Kong* movie.

"What are your goals for the next five to ten years?" I asked her. "I hope to be more of a world figure in the future," she responded. As a kind of (early) Britney Spears figure of Vietnam, she has achieved her place in the country's pop music history, and as a dancer/singer she is brilliant. As one of Vietnam's youngest stars, her future has not yet been speculated about, and she herself has not yet decided precisely what to do. So far she won't do anything differently because, as she continues to win awards and travel the world as Vietnam's pop princess, she is happy.

Thanh Thảo

Thanh Thảo was born in the mid 1980s in Danang. In the early 2000s, she is one of Vietnam's newest female pop singers (Figure 3.9). As a young singer, Thanh Thảo is noted for her soft, beautiful voice and very childlike appearance and demeanor. Thảo epitomizes pop music's cuteness cult, and because of her talent and on-stage purity and innocence, she has made numerous music videos (see Chapter 8). Several of them are of her live shows, which range from childlike innocence to the latest in hip-hop styles. Because of her relative newness to Vietnam's musical scene, very little has been written about her.

STAR PROFILES: MALE POP SINGERS

In the following pages I present short profiles of four of the best-known male pop singers in Vietnam in the early 2000s. Organized chronologically by their birth dates in ascending order, they are Lam Trường, Duy Mạnh, Quang Dũng, and Kasim Hoàng Vũ. As previously mentioned, female pop singers greatly outnumber male pop singers in Vietnam. In 1997, for example, there were very few well-known male singers under 30 in Ho Chi Minh

Figure 3.9 Thanh Thảo performing at the Đồng Dao popular music listening club in Ho Chi Minh City, July 30, 2005. Photograph by Dale A. Olsen.

City, and even fewer could be referred to as pop music idols. It was estimated that male singers accounted for about 20 percent of Vietnam's total number of contempory popular music singers in 1998 (*VNN*, October 17, 1998). Perhaps somewhat known because of exoticism and tokenism, several of the best-known male pop singers of the 1990s, such as Y Moan, and Izak Arul, and Lam Trường, belong to several Vietnamese ethnic minority groups. Some of Vietnam's male pop stars sing only Western songs, some imitate popular Việt kiều singers, most sing love songs, and all compete with their female pop music counterparts for recognition and fame among the youth of Vietnam. Omitted from this list are solo rock and boy band singers who perform exclusively with their own bands and strictly market music singers.

Lam Trường

Born in 1974 in Cholon (Chinatown, District 5) in Ho Chi Minh City, Lam Trường is a member of the Hoa minority group (Chinese-born Vietnamese). In the late 1990s he was Vietnam's most popular male singer, and in 2005 he retains his popularity, although no longer as the heartthrob of young girls. Referred to as "a current pin-up boy of Vietnamese pop music" (*VNN*, July 4, 2001) and the "Pop Prince" (*VNN*, December 23, 2003), Lam Trường maintains a busy schedule that includes recording CDs, performing live shows, and touring.

Lam Trường's popularity began when he was a member of the Friends boy band (originally a trio) from 1997 to 1999 (see Chapter 4), after which he embarked on a solo career. In 2001 he studied for five weeks at the Berklee College of Music in Boston, where he acquired "knowledge relating to music including the history of the world's major musical genres and voice skills" (*VNN*, July 4, 2001). Also in 2001, he made a television commercial with Britney Spears for the Pepsi Company, and in 2002 he performed in a Japanese NHK television show about Vietnamese pop music (*VNN*, December 23, 2003).

Lam Trường is a male crooner, with a "soft voice and passionate singing style [that] attract large audiences to his performances" (*VNN*, October 17, 1998). Because of his sentimental style, I see him firmly entrenched along the flat plane and in the middle of the Popular Music Continuum, appealing to the young generation with his youth, good looks, and passion, and to the establishment with the memory-evoking nostalgia and sentimentality of his songs. In one of the selections he performed during his live show in 2004, however, he created a Chinese setting, perhaps reminiscent of his Hoa background and suggesting culturation. Other than that creation, however, his performance style is strictly status-quo-crooning of sentimental love songs, often called *nhạc hoa*.

I heard Lam Trường live at the M&Tôi club in Ho Chi Minh City on May 28, 2004, after several hours of listening to young female and male singers perform three to four songs each. Lam Trường (who was listed on the marquee as the top attraction for that evening) made his entrance at nearly midnight. In 2005, Lam Trường is seldom heard or seen on the stages of Ho Chi Minh City. He is now busy managing his own restaurant on the edge of the Saigon River in downtown Saigon.

Duy Mạnh

Born in 1975 in Hai Phong on the western shore of Halong Bay, Duy Mạnh moved to Ho Chi Minh City in 1978 (personal interview, August 10, 2005).

He grew up with three brothers who all played saxophone. His parents who were nonmusical but professional—his father works in medicine and his mother is a photographer. As a teenager Duy Mạnh studied piano and began playing professionally in bars and restaurants in 1990. In 1995 he entered the Ho Chi Minh City National Conservatory of Music, studying piano for three years before he dropped out. He studied flute from 1996 to 1998 and learned how to play soprano saxophone from one of his brothers in 2003—Kenny G is his favorite soprano saxophonist. Duy Mạnh's singing career began in 1998, when he was playing piano in a bar on Đồng Khởi street in downtown Saigon and was asked to sing a song. He had never sung in public before, although he loved to sing as a child. From that point on, he decided he wanted to become a pop singer, specifically singing the kinds of music people wanted to hear—love songs that bring people to tears (Figure 3.10).

Duy Mạnh is a songwriter/singer who writes all of his own songs and records only his own music, often playing soprano saxophone on some of the tracks and video clips. He made his first CD album in 2003 and published it in 2004, thanks to some royalties he earned from one of his other songs. Duy Mạnh is one of the most successful pop singers in 2005, largely because he sings and records music about and for Vietnamese people from all walks of life, but mostly the lower classes. Because of his great appeal to the working class of Vietnam, his music has been called *nhạc thị trường* or market music, and even *nhạc sến* or weepy music or cheesy music, appellations he does not agree with. He wants to be known as a pop singer rather than as a market music singer, and he has strong ideas about why he is tagged as the latter. I asked him, "Who chooses those terms anyway?", and he responded:

> The public doesn't understand much about the categories of popular music when they classify singers. Some people call my music *nhạc sến* because my melodies and slow rhythms are similar to those in *cải lương* (renovated theater or opera). It's also called *nhạc thị trường* because it is liked by all types of people. However, I want it to be regarded as pop music.

The common adage for market music, "easy to sing, easy to forget," does not hold true for all of his songs.

One of his most famous songs, "Hãy Về Đây Bên Anh" (Come with Me, Close to Me), for example, addresses an important social issue in Vietnam—gambling. Originally recorded in a Chinese (Cantonese) style (another criticism of market music by other musicians), he had to visually set it in a similar style when he made a music video of it. He chose a royal court music setting from Hue, replete with colorful robes and Chinese sounding music with bowed fiddle, zither, and gong. The theme is still gambling, played out by several aristocratic-looking elders playing a traditional Vietnamese board game, but there is a great deal of flirting and love relationships between a handsome young man (Duy Mạnh) and beautiful girls (this song is discussed in Chapter 5, under social issues). I asked him why he has such a reliance on a Chinese musical soundscape:

> The reason for this is because Vietnamese music is greatly influenced by Chinese music, and most of the Vietnamese audience knows a lot about Chinese style and melodies. In the song just mentioned about gambling: people don't like the topic of gambling; they prefer the topic of love. In order to make this song and its message more acceptable, I needed to compose the melody in a Chinese style because that style is most familiar to my Vietnamese audience. That way, it is easier for the song to be accepted by them.

Although Cantopop music from Hong Kong was very popular in Vietnam in the 1980s, I asked him if he didn't think the domination of Vietnam by the Chinese for over 1000 years, the imprisonment of Ho Chi Minh by Chiang Kai-Chek in the 1940s, and general Chinese hegemony throughout Vietnam's history were still somewhat sensitive issues among the Vietnamese people. He explained that in spite of Chinese domination in Vietnam's past, it is a fact that the Vietnamese people have been influenced by Chinese culture and music. He also explained that not very many of his songs and arrangements are in a Chinese style, stressing the point that he is not trying to remember the past with his use of Chinese melodies and musical instruments but that they just match the contexts of several of his songs. Besides, he explained, the people like this kind of song genre, referring to it as *nhạc hoa*.

Duy Mạnh has hopes of becoming known internationally as well as throughout Vietnam. His album was highly accepted by audiences in Singapore and Thailand, and his songs were liked; he explained. "I would also love to get my songs translated into English for others to understand." During the next five to ten years he wants to continue to sing on stage to entertain and "serve" domestic and international audiences. "I would love to publish one CD per year." In spite of what I consider to be an oversentimentality of expression in Duy Mạnh's CDs and especially his music videos (VCDs and DVDs), the latter are among the technologically best made and videographically the most attractive I have seen coming out of Vietnam. This is perhaps a sign of the economic success of a market music approach, or perhaps it is simply the approach of Duy Mạnh. In any case, there is no doubt that he is one of the most successful pop singers in Vietnam in the early 2000s.

Because of the sentimental love themes woven throughout the majority of his songs and music videos, Duy Mạnh's approach to pop music is near the contemporary end of the Popular Music Continuum, and because of his occasional use of Chinese musical and visual characteristics, his style reveals culturation. Such Chinese elements are not acculturation (outside influence), however, as some may consider it, because Chinese characteristics are

Figure 3.10 Duy Mạnh performing at the Đồng Dao popular music listening club, Ho Chi Minh City, August 7, 2005. Photograph by Dale A. Olsen.

engrained into Vietnamese culture and are a part of the people's Vietnameseness (as Duy Mạnh explained and as history certainly proves). Culturation in Vietnam does not have to be based only on the music of Vietnam's ethnic minorities and folk music; it can also be derived from Vietnam's "mandarin period" of past Chinese cultural domination.

Quang Dũng

Born in 1975 in Quy Nhon, a city on the central coast of Vietnam, Quang Dũng comes from a musically illiterate family (personal interview, August

3, 2005). He learned how to sing in primary school, and also studied a little guitar, which he admits he does not play well. Quang Dũng never attended a music conservatory, but he was the vocalist in a music ensemble between 1995 and 1997, when he performed the love songs of Trịnh Công Sơn and other Vietnamese sentimental songs. Since his youth he has had a passion for sentimental songs, and decided early in his life that he was going to be a crooner. In 1997, at age 22, he won second prize in a television singing contest, which enabled him to move to Ho Chi Minh City in 1998, where he began singing professionally. By 2005 he was one of Vietnam's biggest male pop music idols (Figure 3.11).

In a preconcert interview in 2005, Quang Dũng said the following about his repertoire, which includes love songs composed by Trịnh Công Sơn and some of his own songs:

> I'm undertaking intensive preparations for [my] shows. . . . At each concert, I'll sing 18 or 20 songs, including those that helped me to achieve recognition after I moved to HCM City. I'll also perform some new songs. . . . including Coi Yeu Nguoi (A World of Love), which I wrote, as well as The Hien's Em Khong Biet (I Don't Know), a song about a young Agent Orange victim. (*VNN*, May 10, 2005)

Quang Dũng does not often sing songs about social issues such as the one about a victim of Agent Orange; he prefers romantic and sentimental songs. His smooth and velvety crooning voice led the *Việt Nam News* to label him "The Voice of Romance" (ibid.).

In the future, Quang Dũng hopes to experiment by making musical arrangements that would join hip-hop with Vietnamese folk music (personal interview, August 3, 2005). He explained that the folk music he wishes to work with would most likely be northern Vietnamese, and it would have to be sarcastic, funny, and nonserious, otherwise it would not work to join it with hip-hop. He also explained: "When and if I do hip-hop style arrangements in the future, it doesn't mean that I will perform hip-hop style, but I will incorporate dancers. I, myself, will not rap." The closest he has come to such experimentation with culturation is in his 2004 CD, *Nguyệt* (Moon), in which he performs several Vietnamese folk songs. He chose the album's title because the moon is symbolic of his home town and of Vietnam.

Quang Dũng has performed in several foreign countries, including Canada, France, Germany, Russia, Switzerland, and the United States. He wants to be thought of as a Vietnamese pop singer rather than an international pop star, and his goal with international tours is to introduce Vietnamese pop music to non-Vietnamese audiences. He explained:

> I don't dream a lot about being world famous, but I will be satisfied if I am recognized throughout Vietnam and people enjoy my performances.

Every singer wants to be famous in the world, not just in Vietnam. But, the important thing is that the audience, no matter where they are, sincerely recognize and applaud a specific singer's talent and success. (ibid.)

In addition to performing in large shows in Vietnam, Quang Dũng performs regularly at the popular music listening clubs in Ho Chi Minh City and elsewhere. Of all the male singers I have heard live at such clubs, Quang Dũng best keeps his audience spellbound. "Most of the songs I perform are Vietnamese love songs, and most have won the hearts of the

Figure 3.11 Quang Dũng performing at the Đồng Dao popular music listening club, Ho Chi Minh City, July 16, 2005. Photograph by Dale A. Olsen.

audience. So when the audience listens to the songs they are very attentive, both to the lyrics and the flow of the music" (personal interview, August 3, 2005). Quang Dũng's style comes very close to that of market music, and only some slight nuances of the song texts and his nonreliance on Chinese musical elements separate his musical style from that of market music singers. Most of his songs are slow, sentimental, and almost weepy. Likewise, his music videos portray overly emotional romantic and unreal situations between young lovers.

Kasim Hoàng Vũ

Born in Danang in 1980, the son of an Egyptian father and a Vietnamese mother, Kasim Hoàng Vũ (Kasim, as he is known professionally) was a 2005 winner of the Sao Mai–Điểm Hẹn (Morning Star–Rendezvous or Rendezvous with the Stars) star search music contest. In 2005, Kasim was one of the biggest new idols in Ho Chi Minh City (Figure 3.12).

Both his parents are musical. His father, a guitarist, moved to Vietnam from Egypt in the early 1960s, and his mother, Bích Phượng, a vocalist and keyboardist, was a well-known rock star in the 1970s and 1980s (personal interview, August 5, 2005). His parents divorced when Kasim was a child, and he received much encouragement and early musical training from his mother and during primary school. Also during his formative years, he studied music with Meritorious Artist (a governmental distinction) Dương Minh Đức, his first official music teacher. When he was in sixth grade, Kasim began to perform with his mother on stage, and that was when he first realized that he wanted to be a professional singer. After high school he went to Hanoi, where he studied at the Vietnamese Army's Culture and Art College, receiving the top honor in the entrance exam and graduating in 2002. He moved to Ho Chi Minh City in 2003, and two years later he won first prize in the prestigious Sao Mai–Điểm Hẹn star search contest.

Kasim explained to me that he was pretty much on his own from age 11. Devoted to his teachers who, like his mother, played such important roles in his musical upbringing, Kasim performed in a special television program in honor of National Teacher's Day (November 20) in 2004, which was broadcast on both HTV and VTV. He explained his devotion to his teachers in an interview:

> Thanks to the organizers, we can sing for our teachers, who are like second parents to students. . . . We learn valuable lessons from teachers. Even though they receive low salaries, they overcome many obstacles to provide students with knowledge and experience, and they help them to develop emotionally. (*VNN*, November 19, 2004)

He also traveled to Danang and Hanoi with other pop singers to perform for teachers and their students.

Kasim is a talented singer and showman who, as a crooner, can hold his audience spellbound. As a contemporary singer, he often adds rock and hip-hop rhythms, movements, and occasional composed rap sections interspersed between melodies. Moreover, as an adept interpreter of jazz, Kasim can make more complex songs, such as those by Trịnh Công Sơn, sparkle with stylistic improvised melodic twists. It was a hip-hop tune that won him the top prize in the Sao Mai–Điểm Hẹn star search music show on national television: "Singer Kasim Hoàng Vũ was a hit with his hip-hop song Chuyện Nhỏ (The Small Story) written by musician Tuấn Khanh, . . . one of the busiest hip-hop producers and arrangers" (*VNN*, February 28, 2005). It was again his greatest teacher, his mother, whom he honored with his win by telling her first: "I [could] feel my mother's happiness at her son's miracle. We cried with joy and happiness" (*VNN*, September 16, 2004).

I heard Kasim several times at the M&Tôi and Đồng Dao popular music listening clubs in Ho Chi Minh City during the summer of 2005. One of the songs he performed at the latter club on July 30 was in a hip-hop style, with dancers, in which he rapped for a few seconds. I asked him to explain what he was rapping about, and whether it was composed or improvised:

> In Vietnam I compose all of my rap lyrics, and at the Đồng Dao I was rapping about the bright side of some small problems in daily life, like when someone gets wet, I was saying something like "When we get wet we can go home and change clothes and everything will be alright." I was rapping about how so many people make small problems into something bigger than they really are, and how that is not a good idea. Some singers rap composed lyrics about love, but I rap about logical things. Some rappers talk about things that don't make sense with the rhythm, but when I rap I always talk about something significant. (personal interview, August 5, 2005)

I asked him then if he ever composed rap lyrics about local, national, or world social problems, like the environment, AIDS, and so on. He said "Most of the rap songs I compose are for the youth. If I were to rap about social issues it would be boring for them. Therefore, I don't sing or rap about social issues." This is a type of self censorship, and although Kasim raps, he raps carefully.

Kasim is the final male vocalist in this study, and as the youngest of the lot, he represents the next generation of youthful singers. There is no culturation in his music, and if he continues in the same direction, there probably won't be any. He explained that he wants to say farewell to the past because Vietnam is moving forward. He would like the people of Vietnam and the world to know him as a great Vietnamese pop singer, and in the near future he would like to partner with Thai and Singaporean pop singers for MTV. Kasim has performed nine times in the United States as of December 2006 (*VNN*, December 17, 2006), and is acquiring a reputation

Figure 3.12 Kasim Hoàng Vũ performing at the M&Tôi popular music listening club, Ho Chi Minh City, July 9, 2005. Photograph by Dale A. Olsen.

in MTV Thailand. As a representative of *nhạc trẻ* pop music, Kasim is at the very contemporary end of the Popular Music Continuum. In the following fieldnotes I capture some of Kasim's charm:

> It's interesting how Kasim is smaller and younger in real life, compared to how he seems on stage. The Terrace Café was in sort of a mild frenzy to have Kasim there—all the young people kept watching him. He apologized for having his cap on, explaining that it was a bad hair day for him. Several girls came up and asked him, "are you Kasim?" Then they asked for his autograph. (August 5, 2005)

ETHNIC MINORITY POP SINGERS

Several ethnic minority singers have already been discussed in this chapter (Siu Black and Lam Trường), and others have also attained popularity and fame but have since dropped out of the public eye. Nevertheless, their stories are important because they describe other musical journeys to stardom (however short-lived). Moreover, the ethnic minority singers represent further examples of artistry in Vietnam, and their stories inspire us to think about issues of marginality in a socialist country. Vietnam, for example, takes official pride in its ethnic minorities, and in 1999 a news story, "Singers Voice Ethnic Pride," opened with these words: "Ethnic minority singers are starting to make their voices heard throughout Việt Nam. These singers have begun traveling away from their tribes and villages in the Tây Nguyên (Central Highlands), popularizing the unique music of the highlands" (*VNN*, April 14, 1999).

Female pop singer Bonneur Trinh is from the Lạch ethnic minority in the Central Highlands of Vietnam. Unlike Siu Black, however, who is still popular and performing widely in 2005, the younger Bonneur Trinh is not as well known. Born in 1980, Bonneur Trinh has been characterized as a natural singer whose family was not particularly musical. At college she majored in journalism, graduating from Dalat University, and one of her first jobs was broadcasting the news in the K'Ho language on the local television station. Throughout her school years, however, she often sang for festivals, parties, and other local events; her voice kept improving, and she had a big following as an amateur singer. In 2002 she entered a singing contest sponsored by the television station and won, as Song Ngan writes:

> No one in her family knew anything about her decision [to enter the contest], as she had only told a few close friends. When she was named the winner out of more than 2,000 contestants from HCM City and nearby provinces, she was astounded. "There were so many competitors who had so much more potential and experience than me. I didn't think for a moment that I had a hope of beating them. When I heard I had won I simply couldn't believe my ears. I guess I'm just lucky," she says. (2003)

It is her unique natural ability—her innate talent and soul—that seems to inspire her audience, fans, and critics. As she suggests, it is as if she is in a trance when she sings:

> At the competition finals I did everything I could to sing beautifully and uniquely. While I was singing I completely forgot where I was and when I finished I felt as if I was regaining consciousness', she says. Audiences cite the vitality and natural, unforced quality of Trinh's voice as the secret to her success. Many say it sounds as if it rises up directly from her soul. (ibid.)

Because Bonneur Trinh is from the Tây Nguyên region, she is often compared to Siu Black, a comparison she does not like: "The comparison between the two of us helps remind me that [I have] to set up my own unique style" (ibid.). Bonneur Trinh's style is different from the rock style of Siu Black, although like her colleague, Bonneur Trinh occasionally draws upon the traditional idioms and influences from her ethnic minority heritage. In her song "Hoa Langbiang" on the music video *Đà Lạt Mộng Mơ*, for example, she sings in traditional attire to the visual accompaniment of a gong ensemble and a *khén* mouth organ player. While the ethnic minority musicians move about as they play their instruments, without an ethnic musical note being heard, other villagers dance. As the wind gently blows across the mountain where the video was filmed in the Central Highlands, the only musical accompaniment that is heard on the video was made in a studio on Western instruments, mostly synthesizers. Such visual appropriation is unfortunate but very common. It is, however, in complete contrast to Siu Black, who has included gong ensembles on the stage with her during her live shows.

Male pop singer Y Moan, born ca. 1975, is a member of the Ê Đê ethnic minority from Tây Nguyên. In 1997 he first drew attention when he performed with other pop singers in Ho Chi Minh City:

> Ethnic minority singer Y Moan . . . opened some eyes with his fresh style, winning over audiences at the Meeting '97 concert series last week. Moan seemed to be a token male at the packed concerts at Bến Thành Theater. Young starlets like Mỹ Linh and Mai Hoa were who the audience came to see. (*VNN*, June 3, 1997)

He was also certainly the token ethnic minority singer at that concert. In 1999 Y Moan again made an impression in Ho Chi Minh City: "Ê Đê minority singer Y Moan received a standing ovation at a recent HCMC City concert. . . . Y Moan has toured many countries in Eastern Europe, as well as Thailand, Malaysia, China and Japan" (*VNN*, April 14, 1999). In the early 2000s, Y Moan teamed up with Bahnar-Chăm singer and songwriter Kpa Y Lăng (see Chapter 5), and together they sang "their way down the mountain, bringing ethnic minority arts to the city" (*VNN*, January 14, 2003). In the process, they brought much of their individual musical cultures with them to Ho Chi Minh City, as the story continues to suggest:

> The singer-composer duo has been making a name for Tây Nguyên (Central Highlands) with *Suoi Hat Ayrey* (Ayrey, a Singing Stream). The song recently won the top prize of the 2002 annual Việt Nam Association of Musicians Award, and Moan received a standing ovation for his performance. . . . The music combines sonorous gongs and drums and melodious flutes. Kpa Y Lăng wrote the modern take on the traditional song especially for Moan. (ibid.)

In spite of Y Moan's fairly recent popularity, he seems to have dropped out of the limelight in Ho Chi Minh City by 2004. I found no recordings by him other than two songs on an album. Nevertheless, for his contribution to Vietnam's national identity, his performances, and inspiration for younger musicians,[14] Y Moan was honored by the Vietnamese government with the title "Meritorious Artist" (*VNN*, May 2004).

Male pop singer Izak (also written Y'Zak or Y Zak) Arul, born ca. 1975, is another member of the Ê Đê minority group from the Dac Lac Province in Tây Nguyên. Nobody in his family is musical, but that has not kept him from singing since childhood. He explained in an interview that

> Singing and dancing are daily activities of all ethnic minority people in the Central Highlands. I sing at our tribal festivals, at my school and at artistic festivals in Dac Lac Province. I sing to express to the audience my love of my homeland. I like songs written by Trần Tien and Nguyễn Cường, songs rich with Ê Đê characteristics, which the composers combined with modern music. (*VNN*, November 26, 1997)

In 1997 Izak Arul won second and third places (out of several thousand contestants) in two singing contests in Hanoi and Ho Chi Minh City, giving him the incentive and opportunities to study music at the Ho Chi Minh City Conservatory of Music. During the Hanoi contest, he was the only ethnic minority singer among the twelve finalists, and he was characterized as having a "wild yet charming voice" (ibid.). Nevertheless, Izak Arul himself explains that he prefers soft music, including the love songs of Trịnh Công Sơn and the quiet songs of his own culture: "Our Tây Nguyên music includes many gentle songs which are a type of folk music" (*VNN*, April 14, 1999).

Like Y Moan and Kpa Y Lăng, Y'Zak Arul has also disappeared from the pop music scene in Vietnam, raising questions about marginality and popularity. Is the former a deterrent to the latter? Does the success of ethnic minority pop singers depend on their heritage (i.e. exoticism) and exist as a flash in the pan situation? Are they mentioned in the English newsprint because of Ho Chi Minh's nationalistic concepts of *dân tộc*, *tính dân tộc*, and *văn hoá dân tộc* and the official desire to bring ethnic minorities into the realm of the Vietnamese nation? In other words, has their short-lived success been the result of a kind of propaganda? Ultimately, the Vietnamese music industry (like all music industries) is not about music as art, but about money. Musical shows, tours, and ultimately recording contracts are difficult to obtain for economic reasons; they are expensive and out of reach for most Vietnamese pop singers. Even if they do happen, marketing and publicity can make or break a career, regardless of the pop singer's ethnicity.

POP STAR WANNABES AND RETURNEES

On any Friday through Sunday evening at the popular music listening clubs in Ho Chi Minh City, relatively wealthy Vietnamese music lovers (or just lovers) will be entertained by new or returning up-and-coming wannabe pop singers, plus a star or two. On a typical evening between five and eight singers come on stage and sing three or four songs, usually with the house band unless they have been able to afford to make their own recorded soundtracks to which they sing along, karaoke style. Often, as previously noted, a striving young singer will make the rounds of the popular music listening clubs, singing four songs during a 15-minute time period at each venue. On July 30, 2005, I wrote fieldnotes to document a complete evening's event that featured two well-known pop singers. The following paragraphs give an idea of the activities before the arrival of the stars, and they include my comments that perhaps set me apart as an "older" fellow from a different culture:

8:50   I'm in the Đồng Dao popular music listening club now, and I decided to get here before it starts, just to see what goes on during an entire evening. There are not many people here yet, and I had the pick of where I could sit, but I chose the place I'm most used to—the back row, stage left. That way all my photos will be from the same angle and hopefully I won't have lots of people in front of me, walking, talking, smoking, etc. There is a martial arts demonstration on the large screen to my right. Canned music (instrumental ballads) is being played, and some musicians are checking their amps. I have already been pestered about buying a drink, but I said I would at 9:00 when the show begins. The two featured stars this evening are young Thanh Thảo and Kasim. Tonight I will know for sure how many acts will take place and their lengths; I'll keep a timed tally of the events.

8:59   The band is coming out now and the canned music has stopped. Their music is increasing in loudness and the lights are flashing—it's an overture of sorts, and it's time for my earplugs.

9:02   A young female singer, Lê Vy, begins the evening with a fast tune. A videographer is set up in the center of the back of the auditorium, and his shots are projected on the large screen stage left. There have not been any subtitles projected yet (these include the names of the performers, the titles of the songs, and the names of the composers). There is too much bass for my taste. I have my earplugs in so I cannot hear any applause. There are only several dozen people here at this time. Lê Vy begins her second song slowly and then it becomes up-beat. The bass is so loud it goes right into my stomach; I can hear no tones, just the awful rumble of the pitchless bass. The singer wears blue jeans, a wide black belt, white sweater with long beads, and a black silk short coat. She has a long pony tail. This is certainly not the black dress and sexy look of the super stars I've seen on stage. She begins her third song, a medium ballad with relentless bass. The spotlight is only waist up—no lower torso visible. I just removed my earplugs and still there is no pitch to the bass. The guitarist plays a wonderful rock solo (he is a fantastic player). Lê Vy finishes and introduces the next singer.

9:15   Another young female singer, Ngoc Xuan, wears a short sleeveless velvet blouse, blue jeans, cool glasses, a cap, very long necklace and long huge earrings—kind of a hippy look. She also has a ponytail. Her first song is in rock style, accompanied by flashing lights, two backup singers, and another excellent rock guitar solo. Her second piece is a cover, "Zombie," which begins as a ballad and then becomes upbeat. Likewise, her third song also begins slowly and then becomes fast.

Tonight there are a number of families here with their children—probably families and friends of one or more of the singers. A fellow just in front of me (who just arrived with a crowd) acts like he is drunk. He has been standing and dancing in place, hip-hop style, with his arms waving—obnoxious behavior I feel, for this type of listening club. His wife (girlfriend?) made him stop. They seem to be very noisy, but I can't hear because of my earplugs. They look like they are yelling.

9:30   Song Giang, another female pop singer, wears an elegant orange-red dress. Her first song is a ballad. Her second song, "Mua bao trong long" (nhạc hoa), is another medium to slow tune with a Latin beat—the second percussionist plays congas and bongos.

Now the fellow in front of me is standing and teasing the children—I guess they all know each other. The kids are also noisy—this must be kid's night—friends of the singers? The singer just received a note (request?) at the end of the song, but she didn't look at it. Her third song is another ballad, "Dắng Cay" by Lương Bằng Vinh.

About fifteen people including the children are having a party. I would think this would be a rather expensive party, with a VNĐ 60,000 cover and the cheapest drinks at VNĐ 50,000 each.

Her third tune is another ballad, "Dắng Cay" by Luong Bang Vinh (well, that's the same name as the last song; there must be a problem with the projection). I'm wondering if the nhạc trẻ (i.e., sentimental ballad) singers dress more elegantly than the pop-rock-hip-hop singers dress? I'm sure form (i.e. dress) follows function. Song Giang now introduces the next singer, a young man.

9:45   Thụy Long, a male pop singer, wears a nice sporty suit with a colored shirt. He has long hair like Kasim, and I wonder if Kasim is setting some trends about hairstyle. Thụy Long's first song is a ballad, "Bài không tên sô 8" by Vũ Thành An. (The smoke is starting to bother me now. The men in the gang of fifteen are all puffing away.) His second song is upbeat, but [it] is still a crooning tune because the melody is slow while the rhythm in the accompaniment is fast. Titled "Thu hát cho người" by Vũ Đức Sao Biển, it is a fast minor ballad. Next he does a bluesy ballad titled "Du am" by Nguyễn Văn Tỷ. He now introduces the next singer, another young man.

10:00   Khang Việt is kind of a cool dude wearing a white shirt and jacket. He wears white shoes, giving sort of an early Elvis Presley look. His shirt has a low neckline and he wears lots of jewelry. His collar is outside his jacket and his shirt is not tucked in. His unbuttoned long sleeves stick out about six inches from his coat sleeves. His hair sticks straight up on top, but is not long in back or on the sides. Like I said, he's a cool dude! His first song, "Lỡ một cuộc tính" by Thái Thịnh, is a ballad. He has two backup singers. His second tune is also a ballad. The band left and Thanh Thảo is introduced.

10:15   Thanh Thảo, one of the featured stars for the evening (Figure 3.9), enters the stage to the recorded sound track of a ballad. She wears a very short dress with black boots. The children are getting rambunctious now, and I can hear them yelling even with my earplugs in. Now they begin to run around. I will try to keep a tally of Thanh Thảo's songs (all performed to prerecorded accompaniment), although none of the titles are projected on the video screen. This is the first club performance I've been to where the people in front of me are so noisy, and none of them are paying attention to the singer. Many of them even have their backs to her. Normally at these popular music listening clubs the audience is extremely attentive and absorbed in the music—not so this evening! Thanh Thảo just ended her fifth song now, and the noisy children just brought her a bouquet of flowers. Many of the audience members in front of me continue to be noisy. Even so, the singer received three large floral bouquets during the evening. Thanh Thảo sang nine songs, including ballads, hip-hop pieces with dancers, rock tunes, and a fast Latin-sounding song. Now she has finished her set, which lasted 45 minutes.

11:00   Kasim begins his show now, and he commands much more respect from the audience with his combination of ballads, hip-hop, and rock tunes, all performed to prerecorded accompaniment.

11:30   The entire show has ended now, and it seems early for a Saturday night. Only about thirty people stayed until the end.

What I have called "disrespect for the singers" at the Đồng Dao popular music listening club on this particular evening was probably based more on the excitement of the children and families in attendance. The noisy people were probably relatives of Thanh Thảo, because of their presentations of floral bouquets to the singer. Thus, the evening was probably not typical, at least when compared to my other experiences at popular music listening clubs in Ho Chi Minh City. However, the evening performance did accurately portray the energy that popular music generates and creates among its audience members, from the very young to the not-quite-so young, even though the restrained listening atmosphere of the Đồng Dao was interrupted by it on this particular evening. I am also aware that both Thanh Thảo and Kasim are the two most popular pop idols in Vietnam in 2005, and that fact also probably contributed to the energy of the evening. While I have also experienced similar energy at youth concerts at many outdoor venues, however, I would call the energy this particular evening at the Đồng Dao club simply expensive goofing off. It was adverse to the high quality of the music by the artists. This subsection, however, is about the lesser-known singers that I call the "pop star wannabes" and the "musical returnees."

Basically, young singers perform at the popular music listening clubs for experience and to reach a few people that wouldn't normally know about them. There is also adequate money to be made for multiple 15-minute performances per week (see below). Many of the singers are repeat performers or returnees, and all are hired to perform by the clubs' management staff. Through a singer's manager, new singers will be hired. I have never heard a poor performance at any of the clubs I've attended (I am willing to accept the loud bass as something that comes with the territory and, while I do not like it, I will not cast judgment), and I have never seen any young singer who did not appear exquisitely attired in the latest Western fashions.

Rehearsals for the wannabes and returnees take place in the afternoons, usually on Thursday and Friday for Đồng Dao and M&Tôi clubs, and Monday through Friday for the ATB club. Occasionally the young pop singer will have produced a CD or two, and the club circuit is just one of the steps in the process of reaching stardom.

Often interspersed among the pop star wannabes are musical returnees, crooners that the people know and love. A recurring male pop singer at the popular music listening clubs in the early twenty-first century is Trung Kiên, who was formerly the lead singer in the original Friends boy band. Currently he is on the piano faculty of the Ho Chi Minh City Conservatory of Music. A Moscow-educated pianist specializing in the music of Rachmaninoff, People's Artist Trung Kiên is an example of the "Sovietization" of Vietnamese popular music. He is also just as confident singing jazz with the Trần Mạnh Tuấn jazz combo at the Sax and Art Jazz Club in downtown Saigon as he is singing pop music on the well-known stages of Ho Chi Minh City and Hanoi. Neither a pop star wannabe nor a superstar, but rather a solid fixture in the pop music scene in Vietnam, Trung Kiên is one of the most highly respected voices in Vietnamese music scholarship and performance. He is also a member of the government's Ministry of Information and Culture—Vice-Minister, according to Stock (2003:222)—and as such he is a knowledgeable advocate for popular music in Vietnam, in addition to other types of music and dance.

There are literally hundreds of Vietnamese pop singers in these two catch-all categories. Some will become the superstars and idols of the next ten years, others will disappear altogether, and still others will do their 15-minute performances every other week as Ho Chi Minh City's permanent musical fixtures. What is noteworthy is that the audiences at the popular music listening clubs, the stadiums, the benefit concerts, and other performance venues and occasions love them all. It is as if they are doing what probably every Vietnamese person would love to be able to do—be a pop music star.

MUSIC MARKETING, MANAGERS, FAN CLUBS, AND THE INTERNET

To become a household name as a pop singer in the United States (and probably in any country) requires marketing; very little can be done by the singers themselves. Successful marketing necessitates a personal manager, an attorney, and an agent: "The personal manager is the most important member of the three because if you get a good one, a record company is going to feel comfortable that there is someone keeping an eye on your music business life for you" (Naggar 2000–2004:13).

Exactly when Vietnamese pop singers first realized the importance of having a manager has not been documented. In the twenty-first century, however, with globalization luring Vietnamese pop singers into the world market, the need for managers became ever more apparent because of competition, copyright issues, marketing and many other factors, as Mỹ Tâm explained to Anh Thư:

> "My manager helps me organize concerts and work with VCD and CD producers. He encourages me to improve my vocal technique and dance skills, and also create stage costumes," songstress Mỹ Tâm said. Her manager, musician Thai Huan, has been a key factor in the Danang-based girl's rise to a musical phenomenon. Tâm's album Ngay Ay Va Bay Gio (Yesterday and Now), was released two months ago and has sold a record 20,000 copies. Her tours around the country, sponsored by foreign companies, often draw large audiences. Managers and

promoters now pay Tâm at least VNĐ 20 million (US$1,300) per show and even higher rates for sponsored concerts. "I believe in my bright future," said the singer, who also happens to be the face of Japanese Baby-G watches in Việt Nam. (2004a)

Thus, a typical pop singer's manager in Vietnam organizes concerts, works with recording producers, serves as song and dance mentor, functions as advisor for costuming, manages tours, mediates advertising opportunities, secures contracts for all of the above, and controls the money flow. Another function of a pop singer's manager is to locate and secure the rights to songs for her or his client.

In Vietnam, after the one-night gigging circuit (mostly at the popular music listening clubs), shows (usually with many other singers), competitions (only with a win, however), tours, and charity concerts, a record contract is the ultimate goal of pop singers. Sponsorship is vital at this stage because of the relatively high costs of studio time and record production. A successful recording also depends on distribution, sales, and especially a fan base, for without the latter there would be no record sales.

As of 2005, Vietnam did not have hard copy "fanzines" (fan magazines), although a number of fashion and other youth-oriented magazines occasionally include information about pop singers. There are also a number of small songbooks published in Ho Chi Minh City that contain lyrics of covers and some Vietnamese pop songs. These publications, however, are not part of the fan base concept, even though certain pop singers may be occasionally featured on a cover page. Since approximately 1999 in Vietnam, much of a pop singer's interaction with her/his fan base has taken place on the Internet, either by the pop singer directly or via fan clubs.

Information in the *Việt Nam News* about the Internet's role in the dissemination of pop music recordings in Vietnam first appeared in 1999, when it wrote that by downloading the American RealPlayer software, Internet users can open the webpage "Phuong Nam Net" at www.tlnet.com.vn/music and listen to over ten thousand pop songs by famous and lesser-known Vietnamese pop singers (*VNN*, May 13, 1999). The webpage includes a "music mailbox" service and a "Music World" feature, which are explained as follows:

> The [Phương Nam] Net's "music mailbox" service . . . is receiving a warm welcome from subscribers. By clicking on the name of a song, you can hear it as though it were a gift presented to you by someone special, along with some kind words. The music page also features "Music World," with biographies and photos of the 10 musicians, 21 singers and 10 bands most popular in Việt Nam. . . ."The page is beautiful and gives customers a relatively sufficient amount of information about Việt Nam's music," said one Internet subscriber. "The music information on 'Music World' is updated every day, as the competition

among companies providing Internet services is increasing," said the head of Phương Nam Net. (ibid.)

Other Internet-based pop music pages also existed in Vietnam in the late 1990s, such as those by Hanoi's Vietnam Culture and Fashion Club and Ho Chi Minh City's service provider, Financing and Promoting Technology (ibid.). More recently, in 2001, a Web site was developed by a former computer science student, Hoàng Du, in Ho Chi Minh City for the purpose of providing Vietnamese pop music to Internet users and fans worldwide (*VNN*, March 3, 2001). Now defunct, the Web site featured more than 2,500 pop songs from Vietnam, all used with permission from Vietnamese recording companies. These efforts provide Vietnamese pop music to fans locally and around the world, but they do little to help market products and make money for the pop singers.

Beginning in 2001, individualized efforts by pop musicians in Vietnam to create their own Web sites for the promotion of their CDs also gave them the opportunity to post personal biographical information, photographs, and news items about concerts. Other sites were created by fans. One of the first Web sites was about Ho Chi Minh City's star, Lam Trường, which was created by one of his fans, Xuan Nguyễn, a high school student (*VNN*, October 3, 2001). In 2008, there are literally hundreds of Web sites created by or for Vietnam's pop singers, pop bands, rock bands, and wannabes, for the purposes of selling themselves and marketing their products. In addition, several fan club Web sites function as Internet fanzines. The Rock Fan Club, for example, operates a very good web site with links to bands, news, recordings, and other information of interest to popular music fans (http://www.rockfanclub.org). Another is nhacso. net, which features links to dozens of Vietnam's pop singers, with photo galleries and current information about their recordings (http://nhạcsố. net/Music/).

Payola, the paying of a fee for the promotion of an audio or visual recording over the broadcast media, is not documented in Vietnam. This is most likely because it is not allowed, as the various media are owned by the communist government. The situation is similar to that in the People's Republic of China, where "the government regulates exposure of visual images and messages that might cause negative sentiments toward communist ideology" (Sekine 2007: 199).

VIETNAMESE POP MUSICIANS AND THE FILM INDUSTRY

Perhaps the next level, after producing successful CDs, VCDs, and DVDs, is success in the film industry: "Like Madonna, Mick Jagger and Mark Wahlberg before them, Vietnamese singers are making their move from the concert hall to the silver screen" (*VNN*, October 12, 2003). The effort on the part of the film industry is to make money by featuring a pop singer in a major role. Rarely is the coin reversed, when a former film star becomes a pop music star, although occasionally a singer may jump directly into the film industry before achieving greatness on the musical stage. That was the case with Thanh Thúy who, at the age of 17 in 1994, won first prize in a singing contest and began her film career almost immediately after that, as she and her film director explained:

> "I started my film career unexpectedly. I like singing and I only in-tended to test my vocal music ability," Thúy says. Film director Lê Dân was among [the] audience at the contest. "She sings naturally, full of purity and innocence, and I decided to choose her for the lead role in my film Người Con Gái Dất Dỏ (The Heroine of the Red Soil Region)," Dân said. The film features the active, although short, life of the brave heroine Võ Thị Sáu, who was exiled to Còn Đảo and sentenced to death by French colonialists when she was just 16 years old. Thúy gained audiences' admiration as they followed her efforts as a special force member, attacking enemy posts and killing French officers. (*VNN*, May 20, 1999)

Obviously inspired by the propaganda ballets and operas (and films) from the People's Republic of China and the Soviet Union decades earlier, Thanh Thúy sings only red or revolutionary songs. In the contest she sang "Biết Ơn Chị Võ Thị Sáu" (Gratitude to Heroine Võ Thị Sáu). Like her music, all her roles in films have been similarly inspired by revolutionary themes:

> [Thanh Thúy's films include] Những Năm Tháng Da Quã (The Past Years), Ráng Chiều (Yellow Cloud), Giai Điệu Quê Hương (Rhythm of Motherland), and Người Từ Cung Trăng (Coming from the Moon). Thúy portrays a sincere, innocent and devoted Young Volunteer named Na in The Past Years. "My mother was a former Young Volunteer in the war against the US, so when film director Cảnh Đôn invited me to play Na, I approved immediately. I wanted to do something to bring happiness to my mother," Thúy said. In the film, Na runs into lots of bad luck, but, through her will and earnest love, she still manages to devote her life to the country's struggle for peace. (ibid.)

Thanh Thúy also sings with the Seventh Military Zone's Art Troupe, which she credits for giving her many musical opportunities and providing her with experience, as she explained: "It's thanks to my singing that I can take part in films. The military art troupe has trained and encouraged me since the first steps of my singing career. I will never leave the troupe" (ibid.). In addition to her film and military art troupe career, however, Thanh Thúy has also musically concertized in regions of Vietnam with Lam Trường and the Friends band out of Ho Chi Minh City.

Although Thanh Thúy's story deviates somewhat from the topic of this book, she was one of the first of Vietnam's popular singers (not of contemporary popular music, but of traditional popular music from the far left end of the continuum) to explore film to disseminate her art form. The singing of revolutionary or red songs and the military connection has been to Thanh Thúy's advantage; however, few pop singers in Vietnam have chosen to take that route to such a great extent as she has. Whether or not her entrance into the film industry has been solely based on her enthusiasm for the revolutionary musical past, her musical talent, or a combination of the two is open to discussion. For a few other pop singers, however, silver screen opportunities have come after successes in the normal avenues of pop music stardom, especially after having recorded a song that was chosen for a film's soundtrack, or having produced successful music videos.

Pop singer Phương Thanh had the opportunity to go into film after her recording of "Giã Từ Dĩ Vãng" (Farewell to the Past) was chosen as the title song for the film by the same name. Although she did not physically appear in the film, she was later chosen for roles because of her powerful voice, but not her appearance, as explained in her brief biography above. Nevertheless, Phương Thanh starred as the leading actress in *Trái Tim Không Ngủ Yen* (A Restless Heart), in which she played the part of Ha Nhung, "a girl who sings on the streets to earn money to support her father. With help from music lovers and with her own efforts she becomes a well-known singer" (*VNN*, December 26, 1998). This uplifting theme of Cinderella-like success probably inspired many young pop singer wannabes, although such a route to stardom is nearly impossible except in folktales and the movies.

Because of her success in music videos, Mỹ Tâm has been asked several times about her interest in the film industry and has even been offered roles:

> The head of the Giải Phong (Liberation) Film Studio, Lê Đức Tiến, said the studio asked Mỹ Tâm to play the lead in the *Họa Mi Tóc Nâu* (Brown-Haired Nightingale) musical, because of her popularity with young music fans. "Young singers such as Mỹ Tâm have demonstrated their flair for acting in music videos," Tien said. (*VNN*, October 12, 2003)

Yet, she wishes to continue as a singing star and not take on a new career, as she explained in an interview with Thúy Hường: "Some directors have sent me scripts, but so far, I've declined because I want to devote all my time to music. But if I find an exciting role and it fits into my schedule, I will definitely accept the challenges" (*VNN*, February 15, 2004).

Pop star Hồng Nhung is another diva who is not ready to give up her music career for the screen, although she did have a successful role as a singer in the acclaimed film *The Quiet American*, based on Graham Greene's novel:

> Hồng Nhung, who recently had a cameo role in The Quiet American, has been slated to play the lead in Họa Mi Hót Trong Mưa (Nightingale Singing in the Rain), named after a song by Dương Thụ. The singer has performed many of the songwriter's works, and said it would be interesting to participate in a film linked to his much-loved songs. "I need to see the screenplay before I accept the role, because I'm a singer and not an actress," Nhung said. "Although I got used to film sets with The Quiet American, in which I played a singer, I think it's dangerous to give up my main occupation and take on cinema." (*VNN*, October 12, 2003)

One of the reasons for the reluctance among Vietnam's pop singers to enter the film industry is the fear of failure: "nothing good will come if the singers' performances on screen pale in comparison to their efforts on stage," explained film critic Dang Trần Kôn (ibid.).

Several male pop stars have entered into the film industry with success. Most notable is Quang Dũng, who was invited in 2003 to play the leading role in *Hàn Mạc Tử*, a film about a Vietnamese poet. Dũng explains, "I grew up in Quy Nhơn, where the poet died of leprosy, and I'm interested in his poems. I hope I can play the role well, due to my sympathy for him" (*VNN*, October 12, 2003). Another role for him is an appearance in *Gái Nhảy 2* (Bar Girls 2), in which the director Lê Hoàng hopes to attract a wider audience by featuring a real pop singer, crooner Quang Dũng (ibid.).

One of the great advantages for any pop singer who enters the film industry, in spite of the possibility for failure, is economic. Whereas performing on stage and making audio recordings usually requires upfront funds, promise to repay expenses, or a wealthy sponsor, starring in a film is free to the singer. It is employment, and the size of the contract determines the salary of the performer.

THE TWO-WAY POP MUSIC STREET OF THE VIỆT KIỀU

I title this subsection "The Two-Way Pop Music Street" rather than "The One-Way Pop Music Street" of the Việt kiều (overseas Vietnamese) because I will only discuss the role the returning overseas Vietnamese (i.e. those who have come back to their motherland) play in Vietnam. The major part of the Việt kiều pop music industry takes place in California for the overseas Vietnamese in California (hence, theirs is a one-way pop music street, because they never want to return to Vietnam as long as it remains communist). Some of their songs, however, do reach the Vietnamese homeland, although the sale of American-made Việt kiều recordings of *nhạc vàng* (yellow music or blue music) in Vietnam is against the law, and even to own them is forbidden. Nevertheless, there are many CD shops throughout southern Vietnam (especially in Dalat and Ho Chi Minh City) where pirated *nhạc vàng* CDs are sold, and are actually the preferred commodity by many young Vietnamese. The recordings are cheap, forbidden, and big sellers, not only because they are cheap and forbidden, but also because they are excellent recordings of a kind of music from an era that symbolizes the prewar past, rather than the future, of Vietnam.

Some Việt kiều singers often return to Vietnam to give concerts, a sign that *đổi mới* means forgiveness from the point of view of the Vietnamese government (but not often the internal politics of the Việt kiều themselves). By 2005 nearly one-hundred Việt kiều singers had returned to perform in their homeland:

> Overseas Vietnamese (Việt kiều) singers, some of whom were once famous before the end of the American War, are starting to return to Việt Nam, and are once again experiencing the thrill of performing in front of audiences who appreciate their music. More than 70 Việt kiều singers have been allowed to perform in the country since 1991, said Lê Nam, head of the Department for Arts and Performance Arts Management Office. More than ten Việt kiều are expected receive a license to restart singing in the country within this year, Nam added. All Việt kiều artists are allowed to work in the country if they don't join or participate in any organizations that are against Việt Nam, he said. (*VNN*, April 19, 2005)

One of the most famous singers who returned to Vietnam after more than thirty years is Phạm Duy, who was one of the best-known singers during the American War (see Chapter 5).

The first Việt kiều pop singer invited by the Vietnamese government (specifically by the Culture and Information Ministry) to return to his homeland to perform was Jimmii J.C. Nguyễn, as he is known in the United States (*VNN*, January 15, 1997). Born in central Vietnam in 1970, he was among the throngs who left Vietnam after the War, eventually arriving in California when he was age 9 or 10. Jimmii Nguyễn's concerts in Vietnam in 1997 were well received:

> Việt Kiều crooner Jimmii J.C. Nguyễn presented "The Age of 20—the Love Songs of Jimmii J.C. Nguyễn" at the [Hanoi] Việt Xô Cultural Hall last night. Nguyễn, 26, sang about his Vietnamese motherland, the environment, and young love. Touched by the heartthrob's soulful numbers, some young women in the audience took to the stage and showed their appreciation with flowers and kisses. The show also featured some well known local singers [Thùy Dung, Mỹ Linh, and Thu Phương] and the Youth Music Band. Proceeds from his national

[tour] will go to orphans, lonely elderly, the disabled and flood victims. Nguyễn will perform at the Hà Nội Youth Theater tomorrow night, and then leaves the capital for gigs in HCM City and other major cities. (*VNN*, January 22, 1997, photo caption)

Jimmii Nguyễn's *nhạc vang* sentimental songs are his own compositions and, though coming from a different continent (i.e. North America), they are similar to the *nhạc trẻ* sentimental love songs so popular with Vietnam's youth.

Another highly popular Việt kiều pop singer who spent much time in Vietnam during the late 1990s and early 2000s is Elvis Phương: "He goes under the splendid name of Elvis Phương, a definite blend of West meets East. And it's a mix that has delighted audiences on both sides of the world. For Elvis is a hit in both his adopted America and his native Vietnam in a career that has spanned 40 years now" (*VNN*, June 18, 2000). Older than Jimmii J. C. Nguyễn, Elvis Phương was born in the 1950s in Saigon and spent his youth there, leaving in the exodus of 1975. He has returned to Vietnam numerous times, producing recordings and two music videos— *Giọt Nắng Bên Thềm* (Sunlight on the Veranda) and *Quê Hương* (Motherland)—in his homeland. In 2000 he gave his first concert in Ho Chi Minh City, which was a moving experience for him, as he explains:

> I've traveled to many countries but for me none is as beautiful as my homeland. . . . I've been lucky enough to have opportunities to work with many musicians and singers here. Their kindness is very encouraging. . . . Having grown up in the then Sài Gòn, it was very moving to sing for the people of my city. (ibid.)

Both Jimmii J. C. Nguyễn and Elvis Phương have performed with a number of Vietnamese pop singers, and "are considered as much a part of the country's music scene, as equally popular resident-singers" (*VNN*, June 18, 2000). Another Việt kiều pop singer, Huong Lan, explained that "it's sheer nostalgia that brings them back." Many other visiting Việt kiều pop singers combine performing with touring in Vietnam, like any other American tourists. However, their primary motivation or desire is "to sing in our homeland before the gift that God has given us—our voice[s—are] lost," explained one of the Việt kiều musical sojourners.

MONEY MATTERS: EARNINGS, TAXES, AND GOVERNMENTAL CONTROL

"Some 30 prizes, worth VNĐ 110 million, were presented to the best singers, songwriters, directors and cameramen in Việt Nam's pop music industry" (*VNN*, January 19, 2004). That sum, translated into American dollars, equals approximately $6928.70, and when divided by thirty people is roughly $230 for each performer. Although this sounds like a lot of money initially, it does not equal the earnings of some of Vietnam's pop singers; Mỹ Tâm, for example, earns more than VNĐ 20 million (US$1,300) per show. She and other superstars are, of course, anomalies in Vietnam. Normally, singers' and other musicians' earnings are equivalent to subsistence living for an urban area.

In the following article by Đỗ Quốc Bảo, an amateur night or open mic idea is described from the point of view of Nguyễn Tiến Huy, who earns a living by providing live accompaniment for audience member singers at urban and rural cafés in northern Vietnam:

> The growing market economy in Việt Nam has created a lot of business opportunities in the entertainment industry. Amateur musicians have taken advantage of this, playing shows at cafes in villages across the country. Nguyễn Tiến Huy, [from] Phúc Thọ District, Hày Tây Province, is one such musician. A keyboard player, Huy says there's always plenty of work. The only concern is playing better and drawing larger crowds. Restaurants and cafés are more likely to hire musicians with a good reputation, he says. Huy says he is taking an intensive course to improve his skills at the Hà Nội Conservatory. He performs in Hà Nội and his village to support his studies. . . . There is a lot of competition among musicians to gain a restaurant's trust. A musician in Hà Nội can earn up to VNĐ 6 million monthly for playing shows at cafés, restaurants and weddings, he says. Money is harder to come by in rural Việt Nam, Huy says. A musician can earn up to VNĐ 2 million [US$400] monthly playing rural cafés. Weddings and other parties can boost that figure to VNĐ 3 million [US$600]. It's a good salary compared to that earned by the average rural resident, he says. Huy says he sometimes shows up at cafes with his keyboard to back up singers from the audience. The musician has to try to follow the tone and length the singer chooses. The audience is usually concerned more about enjoying themselves than the accuracy of the performance, he says. Occasionally, café and restaurant owners hire professional singers to perform, Huy says. Musicians usually ask the names of the songs and the appropriate tone in advance. It's a good chance for a musician to improve his skills and his reputation, he says. (*VNN*, February 15, 2004)

Though this article is not about pop singers, but about backup instrumentalists, it is a glimpse into the earnings of some successful musicians. In 2005 I asked a young singer and member of the chorus that backs up Ánh Tuyết at the ATB club in Ho Chi Minh City how much he and the other 10 vocalists are paid per performance. He explained that they receive VNĐ 60,000 (US$3.84) each, times four nights per week, which equals US$15.36

per week per performer. I also asked a jazz bassist friend how much musicians get paid for backing up pop singers during recording sessions. "Not much," he said. "In Việt Nam the cost of living is very low, however, and it doesn't take much money to raise a family." "Is a studio musician's salary established by a musicians' association or union?" I asked. "No. The musicians' association is not involved with that, and it doesn't matter to them what the musicians get paid," he added (personal interview with anonymous, July 28, 2005).

These earnings are extremely meager compared to those of successful pop stars, but they are probably more than those of their colleagues who perform *nhạc dân tộc cải biên* on traditional and renovated instruments in fancy Vietnamese restaurants and other tourist venues. Pop singer wannabes and stars are paid well when they perform at any of the popular music listening clubs in Ho Chi Minh City, such as M&Tôi or Đồng Dao. Mr. Nguyen Nga Son, the owner of the Đồng Dao popular music listening club, for example, told me that pop star wannabes are paid about VNĐ 2 million (US$126) for one three- or four-song set that takes 15 minutes to perform, and that a star would earn about VNĐ 5 million (US$315) for a 30 to 45-minute performance (personal interview, July 1, 2005). Philip Blackburn described the performers' routines at popular music listening clubs in 1993: "One by one the singers take turns to come on stage, sing two songs, one slow, one fast, before getting on their bikes and going to the next location to repeat the routine" (1993). Making the rounds to three or four performances per night would add up to a substantial income, providing it were steady, which it probably is not.

In theory, in a communist society there should be salary equity; in practice, however, there never is. In today's modern communist countries with massive market economies, such as the People's Republic of China and the Socialist Republic of Vietnam, there are people of great wealth and those without. Reporter To Phan (TP) questioned the Minister of Culture and Information, Pham Quang Nghi (PQN) about the high earnings of Vietnamese pop singers in 2003:

TP: Is the disparity between the money now paid 'star' singers and the majority a contradiction that is the inevitable result of socializing music, theater and the cinema?

PQN: The market economy has promoted the potential of art and met people's demands for diversified entertainment. But it has a flip side. This includes the unreasonable high payment for movie and music stars. The ministry needs to coordinate with the Finance Ministry to promulgate regulations about ticket prices and the income tax paid by high-income singers and actors. The Government can also control income of impresarios and singers. We should not all be paid the same. Talent deserves high payment, but it should not be as iniquitous as now. (*VNN*, July 10, 2003)

Beyond this short interview, there is very little published about salary inequities in Vietnam with regard to pop musicians. A handful of pop music stars do very well, financially, because of a combination of foreign tours, local concerts, recording contracts, and commercials. The majority, however, barely survive on subsistence salaries.

Personal income taxes on these rather meager earnings are not required under Vietnamese law, but in March 2005 a new personal income tax law went into effect which requires that "any singer earning more than VNĐ 80 million [US$5039] per year must pay income tax equal to one quarter of his or her earnings" (*VNN*, March 4, 2005). The first pop singer in Vietnam to pay a personal income tax was Đan Trường, who "paid VNĐ 15 million [US$945], half of the total sum he should pay based on his total income of VNĐ 261 million [US$16,440] last year, and will pay the other half later" (ibid.). That adds up to one-eighth of his yearly earnings rather than one-fourth (explained below), but it is much more than he had paid before the new law was put into effect.

The government of Vietnam knows the earned amounts of its top popular music stars and enforces the tax laws that apply to them, as Nguyễn Thai Son, head of the Ho Chi Minh City Tax Department, explains: "We have asked the city's Culture and Information Department to revoke artists' performing licenses if they don't pay their taxes. . . . We will also audit the incomes of these celebrities to ensure they are being honest about their income" (ibid.). Although there are only about twenty super star singers for the government to keep track of in Ho Chi Minh City, the system is not as straightforward as it would seem because there are several legal loopholes or deductions that may explain why Đan Trường was required to pay less than one-quarter of his earnings in 2005:

> [The head] of the Income Tax Department of the Tax General Department in Hà Nội, said the tax sector had taken into account artists' special expenses like make-up and costumes. "A singer with [a] total income of VNĐ 100 million a year will not have to really pay taxes on 25 per cent of the income," she explained. "Of the VNĐ 75 million, 60 million will not be taxed according to the decision. The artist has only to pay taxes for the remaining VNĐ 15 million." (ibid.)

In spite of the deductions, some performers are unhappy with the ruling, as pop singer Trọng Tấn explained: "After each show, if I get at least VNĐ 500,000, I have to pay immediately a sum of 10 per cent (VNĐ 50,000). . . . Then, it is my duty to keep all my receipts throughout the year to check with the tax department" (ibid.).

As Vietnam's economy continues to grow and its music industry reaches the level of Vietnam's other big businesses, issues of taxation will undoubtedly be improved. In 2005 it appears that pop music superstars are feeling the brunt of the tax system within the music industry, rather than the "gatekeepers," such as agents, managers, promoters, and other middlemen (Bayton 1998:2).

CONCLUSION: LOVE FOR SINGING
AND SINGING ABOUT LOVE

Frith, Straw, and Street write, "The history of pop music is a history of pop stars" (2001:74). The pop music scene in Vietnam, as perpetuated by its many pop singers and the masses of Vietnamese young people that make up their fan base, is vibrant and representative of a great cross section of Vietnam's people. What we learn from the music makers is that some pop singers come from musical families, others do not; some are from Hanoi or Ho Chi Minh City, the cultural capitals of Vietnam, and others are from the provinces; some have ethnic minority heritage, but most are Việt; some are born poor, others are wealthy or at least financially solvent; some are married and raise families, others are single. This all seems truistic and applicable to pop stars anywhere, and it is! That is the strength of Vietnam's popular music. Additionally, what they all have in common is talent, good looks, charisma on stage, the tenacity and will to succeed in the profession, a love for singing, and the singing about love. "Love songs have always been at the core of pop; the music is used to declare love, to chronicle love, to complain about love. Pop takes the private desires and longings of love, and makes them public" (Street 1986:177). These characteristics are also truisms and applicable almost anywhere, and, Vietnam's public loves their popular singers for for those very reasons, especially their abilities to sing about love.

Musically, Vietnamese pop singers pertain to both extremes and all points in between on the Popular Music Continuum, and some have ventured into the Arc of Culturation by singing (and sometimes composing) original scores. A singer's age affects the type of music Vietnam's pop stars sing, the particular styles they use, and the musical schedules they maintain. We have seen, for example, that the younger stars often prefer the energy of hip-hop, whereas the older stars like the sentimental songs of Trịnh Công Sơn and others. Some older singers sing rock (and sing it well), but they don't sing *only* rock as many of the younger singers do. Tranh Lam said in 2002, "I have to change my style to match my age." (*VNN*, November 26), Finally, many pop singers enter other professions when their age either slows them down, makes it more difficult for them to physically sing as they used to, or other career choices entice them out of the performing profession. The age at which a pop star receives musical training also seems to have an effect on the success of pop singers; those who take music lessons early in life (usually from musical parents), for example, often capture the hearts of critics and the public when they perform as children. Although this is also the cuteness factor, it is a truism that musicians who begin young usually have a better chance to succeed.

As I reflect on some of the personal bumps in the Vietnamese road to stardom, I feel that the Ho Chi Minh Trail to pop music success is no bumpier than Hollywood and Vine or Broadway, because all musical stardom is based on talent and tenacity, charisma and courage, good looks and good fortune. The Western world, however, has some major dips in the road, such as recording companies and other agencies in the music industry. Vietnam has not needed those gatekeepers yet, but as globalization and transculturation continue, Vietnam's pop stars may have to pay the tolls before long.

The next chapter looks at popular music ensembles, such as pop, rock, and pop-rock bands in particular. It also includes the many substyles within those broad categories, such as duos, trios, heavy metal, progressive metal, and many others. I discuss only those ensembles that have made it by virtue of concerts, festivals, recordings, television appearances, and other routes of dissemination, rather than the many commercial club bands that often play covers all night for noisy and often inebriated audiences.

4 Vietnamese Rock, Pop-Rock, and Pop Music Bands

In Vietnam's English language newsprint, the term "band" is used for any group of individuals performing popular music, including the usual loud rock bands, mellow pop-rock bands, vocal duos and trios, vocal ensembles of four and more, and boy and girl bands, which are often other words for vocal trios and quartets. Moreover, categories often merge and boundaries become blurred. The terms "professional" and "student" are also used as adjectives to distinguish bands of many types. I follow that tradition and use the term "band" in the context of this book to mean any Western-influenced popular music ensemble, but not traditional or neotraditional music ensembles, nor concert, dance, jazz, marching, or military bands.

I do not discuss the history of popular music bands in Vietnam before their occurrence in the early 1990s, except to briefly mention that during the French colonial period dance bands were common in urban areas, as they provided entertainment for the French and Vietnamese elite, and American-style Vietnamese rock bands were popular during the American War as entertainment for American soldiers. After đổi mới, Cantonese, Japanese, Thai, and Western popular music ensemble influences (re)developed and have continued in Vietnam because of global media imperialism. Of all the popular music ensembles in Vietnam, rock, pop-rock, and pop music bands (and their variants) fit mostly into the contemporary popular music end of the Popular Music Continuum. In this chapter I survey the development of those types of bands after 1990, and I discuss such issues as individual and group behaviors as musicians, vis-à-vis the communist government's attitudes and behaviors towards them and their music. I also discuss how the bands fit into the Popular Music Continuum; how they deal with status quo, originality, culturation, professionalism, power, image, and other factors that contribute to their highly visible roles in Vietnam's society; and what roles the student and amateur bands play.

Bands are made up of musical personalities (i.e. musicians) who individually and collectively create somatic and sonic images that are their trademarks. As such, bands are not much different from pop music star singers when it comes to being physical icons. In the next section I discuss some of physicality of individual musicians that make up a band, and in some instances, of solo singers as well, since many individual pop singers get their start as lead singers with a band.

PHYSICAL APPEARANCE, BODY LANGUAGE, AND THE LAW

Rock musicians and pop singers throughout the world (like some jazz musicians during the bebop era in the United States) make maximum use of their physical appearances and body language, often to the dismay of parents, elders, and governments. Vietnam has not been an exception to this phenomenon, and such use can be perhaps interpreted as political (it certainly was during the American bebop era), or it can be perhaps interpreted as modern (i.e. keeping up with the Joneses of popular culture). We have already read the official statements regarding proper social behavior in the arts (see Chapter 2), so it is not surprising that physical appearance and behavior on the performance stage are also open to critique, if not out-and-out censorship. The phenomenon in Vietnam during the early twenty-first century, however, is a late development in the history of world rock and pop music. It includes choice of clothing, facial makeup, hair color, length of hair, head shaving, and a number of other characteristics that occurred in the West in the 1980s and 1990s. Most of these characteristics have become more prevalent in Vietnam with the rising popularity of hip-hop, than with the earlier popularity of rock, heavy metal, and other popular music forms.

Anh Thư writes the following about new governmental regulations affecting dress and appearance codes, issued by the Ministry of Information and Culture in 2004:

> Under the ministry's new regulations, performance artists, including singers, dancers and music players, will be banned from wearing dyed hair and sexy costumes when they perform on stage. Artists who shave their heads or have long, untidy hair will be also banned from performing. The Ministry's regulation states that such public displays are not suitable for Viet Nam's culture or national identity. (2004b)

The government's actions have been met with approval by members of the hegemonic status quo, as Anh Thư continues:

> "I agree with the Ministry officials. We need to put a ban on young artists who abuse their career to create strange tastes that are not suitable for Vietnamese culture and lifestyle," said Nguyễn Hoang Huong, teacher at Truong Vinh Ky high school in Tan Binh District. He said that young singers had become much freer in their attitude and style on and off stage. "Their lifestyle has affected young fans, creating bad trends among youth," he said. . . . Educator Nguyễn

Lo, former lecturer at the HCM City College of Social Sciences and Humanities, said, "Our youngsters cannot have a healthy lifestyle if they often see and follow bad attitudes every day. Looking at culture and each aspect of it, like arts, literature and performance activities, we can see a mixed picture of achievement, progress and weaknesses." (ibid.)

Government censorship and control are at the crux of the proclamation. Nguyễn Lo wholeheartedly approves of this, as he continued to explain: "'Artists are first citizens, so they have the duty to observe and preserve the nation's traditional values. I give support to the Ministry's regulations', he said"(ibid.).

In what appears to be one of the first published articles about protest, Anh Thư offers the opposing view of several pop musicians themselves (ibid.):

> But many people, mostly young artists, music producers and impresarios think differently from Huong, Lo and their peers. "I don't think the Ministry is right in its ban on artists' performance styles," said Le Trinh, director of Babi Entertainment Company, in HCM City. "Dyeing hair and shaving the head are very popular among youngsters around the world. Asking our young artists in modern society to stop or limit their masquerade on stage is very unjust," she said, adding that the regulations are not suitable for Viet Nam's development.
>
> Thanh Thảo, a blonde long-haired pop singer, said, "I'm now confused when I select clothes for my show. My friends and I don't clearly know how sexy the costume is." While Thảo is worried about her colorful hair, her peer, young singer Trung Tùng of MTV Band, faces a more serious problem. "I have no hair because I was sick. If the regulations apply, I will have no way to perform for my fans," said Tùng, whose bald head is popular among fans. "I think the cultural authorities' duty is to find ways to help our young artists perform well, instead of giving us strange limitations," he said.

Anh Thư concludes with the following wise words of a theater director whom he interviewed:

> Truong Nhuan, deputy director of the Hà Nội Youth Theatre, said, "Culture and performance activities in particular are sensitive fields. Creating opportunities to help artists, especially young performers, work in a fair and free environment is our most important mission. We should be careful before applying any regulation on artists' activities" (ibid.)

Thus, Anh Thư presents several points of view about a potential censorship/protest situation regarding the politics of neatness in Vietnam that have not been resolved, although it is also neither challenged nor discussed. As a nonparticipant observer at many musical events between 2002 and 2005, I saw many dimensions of physical appearance among performers, some of them very mod, beat, hippie (to use terms from my generation), others quite conservative, and many very sexy. As I mentioned in Chapter 3, young pop stars such as Mỹ Tâm and Kasim are among the biggest fashion icons and trendsetters in Vietnam, and the communist government has no desire to lose the money such well-known pop singers contribute to Vietnam's growing market economy. Also, contrary to a section of Anh Thư's discussion about female hair color and male baldness, Thanh Thảo did not have blonde hair when I attended her concert in 2005 (see Figure 3.9); rather, it was black. Trung Tùng, meanwhile, now performs on stage and television wearing a stocking cap, a sacrifice in the heat of Ho Chi Minh City, especially under the dozens of stage lights during a performance, but also a hip-hop symbol in America.

In the following sections I discuss the types of bands (rock, pop-rock, and pop) found in Vietnam beginning in 1990, with the goal of understanding their styles and the energies that have made them successful, always with one eye on their politics or the political reactions towards them, and the other on my favorite question: What is Vietnamese about them?

ROCK BANDS

In this category I include rock, hard rock, and metal bands; pop-rock bands are discussed later. The differences are sometimes slight, although choice of repertoire is a basic determining factor. Some bands mix their styles; others choose to maintain a strict line between hard rock and metal styles. A further categorization I will make is between arena or stadium bands and club bands. However, the latter will not be discussed in this book because they are neither the trendsetters nor are they mentioned in the Vietnamese English-language newspapers. The arena or stadium bands play outdoor concerts for thousands of cheering teenagers, and the club rock bands in Vietnam are the working bands, which mostly play covers and provide loud entertainment for dancing at bars, clubs, and private parties.

AtOmega

The American War in Vietnam and the attitudes about the Vietnam War in the United States had a tremendous influence on one young Vietnamese musician in particular—Trần Quang Thắng, who is known in Ho Chi Minh City as "Rocky." Born in Saigon in 1965, Rocky was the leader and head spokesperson for rock music in Ho Chi Minh City during the 1990s. In 1996, he explained his feelings to Jenny Lipman, who wrote the following about him and his band, AtOmega:

HCM City rockers AtOmega see [rock music] as a positive revolutionary influence. "Rock music helped bring an end to the American war [i.e. the Vietnam War, because he is speaking from America's perspective] in Việt Nam," explained the band's lead vocalist and rhythm guitarist "Rocky" Quang Thang. "Songs about peace, love and freedom in [the United States during] the 1960s and 70s influenced a generation of Americans and helped change their minds about their government's involvement in Việt Nam." (1996)

In a rather interesting reversal of how I expected his interview to read, Rocky credits American rock in the United States as being the catalyst that ended the American War, not Vietnamese rock in Vietnam. Rocky knows a lot about the United States and its popular music, because most of his family moved there after the war. He chose to remain in Vietnam, however, because he loves his country, as he continued to explain to Lipman: "Some people say the US is paradise or that France is paradise. I say Vietnam can be paradise. Anything is possible here. Happiness comes from your heart, not from the place where you live" (ibid.)

After teaching himself how to play the guitar and read Western musical notation, Rocky formed the rock band AtOmega (also written as Atomega) in 1993 with four colleagues on lead guitar, keyboards, electric bass, and drums. Rocky is the lead singer, the rhythm guitarist, and the main composer for the group, which also plays cover tunes by such classic rock/metal bands as Metallica, Nirvana, the Rolling Stones, Steppenwolf, and others. His love of loud guitar musicians has caused critics to call him a "metal head," a characterization he likes, as Lipman writes: "To [Rocky], the word [metal head] does not just refer to someone who loves loud guitar music. 'To have a metal mind is to have a strong mind with no fear, a cold and clear-thinking mind. I want a cold mind and a hot heart, not the other way around', he said" (ibid.). Perhaps as an expression of his "hot heart," most of Rocky's songs are about children, the dreams of youth, nature, and peace (*VNN*, September 16, 1996).

AtOmega's first CD, and the first rock CD ever recorded in Vietnam, is *Đất Mẹ* (Motherland), which was released in 1996 to great enthusiasm:

> The popular rock group Atomega, [sic] is the first rock music band to release its own album in Việt Nam. Their debut album, "Motherland," has created a stir among HCM City rock fans. "It's given a boost to rock music, which is still a novelty in this city," enthused [sic] Hai Yen, a student at the HCM City University. The band, founded a few years ago, is made up of . . . five musicians, all in their thirties, [who] are true free spirits. They're crazy about rock music and they cherish the "wandering life" of performers. One youngster, grooving at the Youth Club, tried to explain. "The five musicians on the stage, each has his own private and weird habits while performing—and I love them!" . . . No

matter where they choose to play, this band is met with excitement. In his characteristic low growl, which mesmerizes his fans, Quang Thang [Rocky] explains, "With rock music we live as we are, without any ostentation." (ibid)

Quang Thắng and his AtOmega rock band have not made a CD since *Motherland*, due to the high cost of CD production and to the popularity of younger rock bands, such as Bức Tường (The Wall), Ánh Sáng (The Light), Da Vàng (Yellow Skin), and other successful heavy metal groups from Hanoi and Ho Chi Minh City. In the early 2000s, however, "Motherland" and several other tracks from AtOmega's original CD were republished on a CD featuring Saigon rock bands.

An article from 2004, written as a conversation between a Vietnamese boy (Don) and his foreign guest, summarizes AtOmega and the affect the band has had on many Vietnamese youth:

> Atomega . . . is arguably one of Viet Nam's most successful metal bands. Don explained that after the release of their first album, "Motherland," they became the first Vietnamese rockers to distribute a record. Even though "Motherland" was half cover songs of foreign artists, it set an important precedent for Vietnamese rock. "Motherland was kind of a shock to rock fans," Don said. "It led Vietnamese rock into the future. When I was fifteen years old, I used to listen to these guys all the time!" Atomega started the set with their album's namesake track.
>
> "Motherland," it turns out, is something of a patriotic anthem. Still, I wondered how the lead singer, Quang Thắng, who looked like a Vietnamese Carlos Santana and sounded like Jim Morrison, could pull off a patriotic anthem with a look that seemed so borrowed. "A lot of their songs mention the daily life of the people," Don said. "That's the difference between Vietnamese pop and rock. Rock talks about the larger things in society. It talks about the shoe-shine boy, about the dream of a peaceful world." (*VNN*, November 8, 2004)

These references to a "patriotic anthem," the "daily life of the people," and "larger things in society," are reminiscent of Street's insistence that rock *is* political, even though rock's lyrics may not always be overtly so (1986).

In the late 2000s Rocky continues to play gigs in Ho Chi Minh City with his band, and occasionally they play at rock festivals in Hanoi. The "Motherland" mother band of Vietnamese rock is still very active.

Bức Tường (The Wall)

The Hanoi hard rock/heavy metal band, Bức Tường, known as The Wall in English, was probably the most famous rock band in Vietnam in the early 2000s (they disbanded in 2006). Under the leadership of singer, guitarist, and songwriter, Trần Lập, Bức Tường was in existence as a professional band since 1998, although Trần Lập first began the group in late 1994 and early 1995 to play for university students in Hanoi. British music critic Dan Kirk (2004) writes the following about The Wall's formation: "The Wall formed in March 1995, when five plucky young students met at the Hanoi Construction University. Finding they had a similar penchant for power tools and hard rock, forming a band seemed like a better idea than building bridges." All the band members studied architecture and have held jobs as architects while playing in their band.

In 2004 Bức Tường was chosen to represent Vietnam at the second annual World Peace Music Awards (WPMA) held in Ho Chi Minh City (the first WPMA was held in 2003 in Bali, Indonesia). The 5-hour show was held on June 19, 2004, and was "televised to 40 countries to an audience of more than two billion people, a figure that . . . set a new Guinness World Record. The theme of this year's event, Life of Peace, [was] dedicated to great musicians who contributed to peace during their lifetime" (April 28, 2004).

Bức Tường owes a part of its tremendous success to the fact that it was one of the first heavy metal or hard rock groups in Hanoi. More importantly, the band's leader, Trần Lập, learned how to bridge the two realms of traditionalism and modernism—the politics of remembering and the economics of forgetting—by cleverly incorporating social issues and national events into Bức Tường's concert programs, and traditional and sentimental elements into the band's musical interpretations (see Concluding Thoughts). Rather than forgetting about the American war, Trần Lập remembers it and also encourages the youthful crowd not to forget it by including sonic reminders in the band's concerts, such as the noise of a military helicopter in one of the songs. This is an ingenious musical effort to bridge traditional and contemporary ideas in a city (Hanoi) where success and survival in the arts is dependent on such a bridge. Likewise, he remembered the national tragedy of the 2002 fire in the Blue Club in Ho Chi Minh City (see Chapter 6), where many young people lost their lives or were injured; this was just another strategy that Trần Lập employed with great success, probably done unconsciously out of love rather than consciously for gain.

Bức Tường's first CD album, *Tâm Hồn Của Đá* (*The Soul of Rock* in one translation, and *Stone Spirit* in another), led to a large live show by the same name in Hanoi in 2002, which 8,000 young people attended, and which was voted the "Show of the Year" (*VNN*, April 22, 2003). Although *The Soul of Rock* sold nearly 10,000 copies in its first year, some young rockaphiles criticized it for not being hard enough, as Trần Lập explained (*VNN*, November 6, 2002): "You know, fans have been telling us that they thought the first album was too light, that they wanted something harder. . . . When we started out we wanted to make easier, more accessible music." This led to their 2002 concert, what Lập and critics have called "hard rock revolution."

Their second album, titled *Vô Hình* (Invisible), "sold 4,000 copies during its first four weeks on sale in Hà Nội" (*VNN*, September 23, 2003) and more than 10,000 throughout the country "in its first month of release, a record for a rock music CD in Việt Nam" (*VNN*, April 22, 2004). In their second CD, Bức Tường makes a point of including slow and sentimental songs that have Vietnamese aesthetic qualities into their repertoire, as Trần Lập explains (*VNN*, April 22, 2004): "Our goal is to compose and perform rock songs which combine the styles of East and West, blending traditional and modern tunes." One of Trần Lập's best-known songs in that style is "Trường Ca Đất Việt" (A Vietnam Epic Song), which fuses Western and traditional Vietnamese musical elements. Another song, "Bài ca sông Hồng" (Red River Song), included in their *Invisible* CD, begins with a traditional Vietnamese plucked lute, the northern *đàn nguyệt* (pers. com. with Nguyễn Đạt and Nguyễn T. Phong), playing an open fifth interval. The open fifth is then played on the electric guitar and expanded into the typical heavy metal power chord, complete with the distortion that musicologist Robert Walser associates with heavy metal music (1993:2).

Their most recent and third CD, *Magnet*, came out in October 2004. It is a mixture of heavy metal mixed with Vietnamese folk music, as explained in the *Việt Nam News*: "Magnet, according to lead singer Trần Lập [will] leave you transfixed with a fusion of Vietnamese folk tunes and legends put to driving rock music. 'A magnet attracts and pulls you towards it with magnetism. It is the same with rock music. And that is what our latest album promises', says Trần Lập of The Wall. . . ." (October 19, 2004).

As Trần Lập leads his group even more into the folk music past and heavy metal present, he himself explains that it is done with a purpose in mind:

> "Prosperity means nothing if people do not protect and help each other in times of difficulty. . . . The new album is our most satisfactory project. It is the essence of our thoughts, feelings and technique developed over ten years. We have experimented with modern sound mixing methods and highlighted social themes through traditional folk music and modern rock." (ibid.)

As in their earlier albums, Trần Lập again borrows from Vietnamese epics and austere places:

> And the message comes woven in epic tales, as in [the song] "Dau Vet Nghiet Nga" (Severe Vestiges) about the Co Loa ancient citadel and the love of Mỹ Chau and Trong Thuy, set to a rising metal symphony. "The song has an epic scale. It is about the travails of an innocent girl in love who falls into disgrace," says Lap. While "Chuyen Tinh Thuy Than" (Water-Spirit Love) adapts the legend Son Tinh—Thuy

Tinh (The Mountain Genie and the Water Genie), "Ra Khoi" (Going Offshore) uses the jolly and exuberant sounds of Nam Bo's (Southern region) chantey. (ibid.)

One fan raved about The Wall: "The band has introduced me to a completely new style of Vietnamese rock music. They are different from most bands and singers. That's why I like them so much" (*VNN*, April 22, 2004). With their 2004 album, The Wall has made a unique and very successful effort to bridge the modernity of present musical expressions with musical references to the past of Vietnamese traditional folk music and folk legends.

During October 2004, Bức Tường embarked on a tour of Vietnam; it was the first Vietnamese rock band ever to tour the country. The nationwide tour was called "9+" for a reason, according to Trần Lập: "We have spent much time and passion in preparing for the tour. We may not be the perfect 10. We are just 9+. But, we will try our best to entertain and contribute to national music" (*VNN*, October 19, 2004). Sponsored by Honda, a large sign, visible in every shot of Trần Lập, reads "Honda, The Power of Dreams." Although the advertisement refers to Honda's Dream motorbike, which is the dream of every Vietnamese teenager, it can also refer to the power of rock to escape reality.

Bức Tường played their last concert in December 2006, after which they disbanded, "Rock'n'roll veterans lay final brick in The Wall") (*VNN*, December 1, 2006. Whether or not the band's musicians will continue and even evolve throughout the twenty-first century depends on their image among Vietnam's teenagers, who figuratively maintain their youth while the members of Bức Tường age. At the peak of their popularity, Kirk wrote in 2004 that "The Wall can smile smug with a decade of stage action under their middle-aged belts." Because of their many successes, their tremendous talent, and the fact that they were able to very wisely traverse the Popular Music Continuum between traditional and contemporary styles, The Wall will probably be remembered in Vietnam like The Grateful Dead are in the United States.

Bức Tường has had its critics, however, such as one of the members of Buratinox, a younger rock band from Hanoi, who explained the following about The Wall to an anonymous interviewer:

When I asked [members of the rock band Buratinox] which Vietnamese bands they like, Kien blurted out a name and laughed under his breath. Ry A slapped Kien on the knee. I asked for a translation. "He said The Wall, but he was just joking," Don said. . . ."The Wall is a bunch of very good musicians, but they are not truly into rock and roll," Don said, taking a long drag from his cigarette. "The Wall is music for people who want to make the switch from pop to rock, so they are more like pop music. When you do like that, it's like someone else

owns your music. That's not rock. Rock is about your own passion."
(*VNN*, November 8, 2004)

The Buratinox musicians are referring to the fairly conservative and sanitized style of heavy metal played by Bức Tường, which can perhaps be
referred to as classic metal rather than progressive metal.

Ánh Sáng (The Light)

Ánh Sáng, a youthful thrash metal band known in English as The Light,
was called Hanoi's favorite heavy metal band in 2003 (*VNN*, November
29, 2003), and in October of the same year their style was said to be "a
combination of heavy metal and traditional savage [sic] music from Tây
Nguyên (Central Highlands)" (*VNN*, October 27, 2004). They began in
the 1990s as a student rock band in Hanoi.

I had the opportunity to hear Ánh Sáng and a number of other Vietnamese rock bands in an outdoor concert, Rock Ba Miền in Hanoi on the
evening of May 8, 2004. "The first Rock Ba Miền show will gather rock
bands from HCM City, Đà Nẵng and Hà Nội. As the name suggests, the
bands will represent the north, central and south regions" (*VNN*, May 7,
2004, "Hà Nội bands scream let there be rock"). Fans, mostly young Vietnamese in their late teens and early twenties, rocked until about midnight
on a warm evening in the outdoor venue on the northern shore of Hanoi's
largest lake, Hồ Tây or West Lake (see Chapter 8). The event could have
been an outdoor rock concert just about anywhere in America or Europe,
complete with moshing in front of the elevated stage, and plenty of head
banging. The Light particularly impressed me, with singing by Trần Hà in
the style of the late Kurt Cobain and extremely original improvisatory lead
guitar work.

The Light published a CD, *Giấc Mơ Hoang Tàn* (Of Ruined Dreams)
in 2003; surprisingly, their Vietnamese name, Ánh Sáng, does not appear
anywhere in the album. The layout of the album cover and the way the
band's name, The Light, is written with diagonal letters, are identical to
how Metallica presents their name on their album covers. The listing of
musicians on the back cover of *Giấc Mơ Hoang Tàn* features a different
lead singer than the one in the May 2004 concert—Anh Tuấn (Nguyễn Anh
Tuấn), who was formerly the songwriter and lead singer with the Green
Ants pop-rock band. Tuấn sings three compositions in English, whose lyrics are in the album's liner notes, with credit given only to The Light, rather
than Anh Tuấn. Because of their important social content, the lyrics of
these three songs are discussed in Chapter 5.

Once again, the improvisatory lead guitar solos in all of these examples,
like the guitar solos in performances by Bức Tường, Da Vàng, and other
top-notch Vietnamese rock groups I have heard, are exciting, innovative,
and moving. They display impeccable craftsmanship and technique. Dustin

Roasa explains how this craftsmanship comes about and is developed in Vietnamese rock music:

> [I]n Vietnam . . . bands tend to stress craft over originality and formalism over abandon. Hearing a Vietnamese rocker talk at length about the hours he spends honing his skills can sound strange to Westerners, who are brought up with the belief that great music is made in fits of primal inspiration and is not to be sullied by virtuosity. For a Vietnamese musician, though, the approach makes sense: when confronted with an unfamiliar art form, the best way to overcome any self-perceived lack of cultural authenticity is to spend hours alone in the bedroom, practicing until it all sounds and looks just right. (Roasa 2005:11)

I have heard this same argument with regard to Japanese musicians playing salsa, blues, or other non-Japanese musical forms, and I don't believe it to be accurate, at least in the twenty-first century. Also, I know of American jazz musicians who spend hours transcribing Charlie Parker solos and then "improvising" on them during jazz concerts. My belief is that creativity and technique are about equal in importance. It is also my belief that the lead guitarists with both The Wall and The Light rock bands are as "primal" in their creative inspiration and as technical with their craftsmanship as any Western rock guitarists I have ever heard. This view is also contrary to that of Australian economist and musician Adam Fforde who writes: "Since many Vietnamese musicians are classically trained, the path [i.e. 'to devise a product that can compete with those already in existence'] will probably require technical proficiency, which is likely to result in a certain stifling of creativity" (2003:54). Vietnamese music has always been technically proficient and creative. What makes Vietnamese popular music (especially that performed by rock guitarists) Vietnamese, however, is another question that I attempt to answer in the conclusion to this chapter.

Da Vàng (Yellow Skin)

The popular music group known as Da Vàng (Yellow Skin or Yellow Complexion), sometimes called a rock band and other times a pop band by the *Việt Nam News* in the 1990s, was called "the most popular metal-rock band in Viet Nam" in 2004 (*VNN*, October 27, 2004). Nguyễn Đạt (see Figure 7.3), the band's founder, leader, songwriter, lead guitarist, and lead singer explained the flip-flopping of the terminology as follows:

> "Pop-rock is just the word that the newspaper used. The public doesn't understand the term heavy metal, and the news media have to use words the public understands. Da Vàng has always been a rock band. Before 1990 we played only heavy metal, but now we play progressive metal" (personal interview, August 1, 2005).

The Rock Fan Club Web site (http://www.rockfanclub.org/home/) gives 1989 as Da Vàng's birthdate, but the band's official Web site gives 1990 as their startup date: "We started in 1990 with Nguyen Dat (vocal, guitar & songs writing), Hoang Tuan (guitar), Le Quang (bass) and Le Minh (drums). The current line-up are [*sic*]: Nguyen Dat (Vocal & Guitar), Hoang Tuan (Guitar), Vo Dinh (Bass) and Minh Duc (Drums)" (www.davang.com; lack of diacritics and English language irregularities are in the original).

In 2005 Nguyễn Đạt explained to me that he prefers the term "progressive metal" because he is interested in incorporating traditional Vietnamese musical instruments into his style of music: "you can mix local instruments into progressive metal, but you cannot do that in heavy metal." Even as early as 1992, just after their successful appearance at Ho Chi Minh City's first Pop-Rock Festival in March,1992, at Ky Hoa Park, Nguyễn Đạt explained Da Vàng's approach to rock: "We're trying to apply a new style of rock featuring local music to attract a wider audience" (*VNN*, April 7, 1997). Again in 2000 Nguyễn Đạt explained that they were trying to develop a unique sound that would set them apart from other bands: "We try to play a new style of rock featuring Vietnamese music to widen our appeal" (*VNN*, February 16, 2000). To accomplish his goal, Đạt is learning how to play the *ghi-ta* (from guitar or *guitare* in French), the main stringed instrument in *cải lương* (renovated opera, see Chapter 1). As soon as he becomes proficient on it, he will play it with Da Vàng, (personal interview, August 1, 2005). He is concerned, however, that it may not be accepted by the youth because even though "you can mix it, it may be hard to listen to" for young people who are not familiar with *cải lương* music. Meanwhile, although he occasionally makes use of traditional scales during his improvised guitar solos, his improvisational style is very much in a Western heavy metal vein. Just as Rocky and AtOmega did with "Motherland," Đạt also writes and performs songs about Vietnam, hoping that approach will also make his and Da Vàng's style uniquely Vietnamese. In Chapter 5, I discuss a number of his songs that pertain to world social issues and Vietnamese history.

I attended a rock and pop-rock concert in Ho Chi Minh City in May 2004 that featured Da Vàng, two Vietnamese pop-rock groups—Trio 666 (girl band) and MTV (boy band)—and BTR, a Bulgarian rock band. Da Vàng was advertised as a heavy metal band, and their style was much more contemporary and experimental than their recordings from the early and mid 1990s (hence, Đạt's use of the term "progressive metal"). I believe that if Đạt achieves his goal of incorporating traditional Vietnamese musical instruments into his rock palette and continues to improvise using Vietnamese scales and other glocalized ideas, Da Vàng will move high on the arc of culturation for a Vietnamese rock band.

Buratinox

One of the newest bands in Hanoi in 2004, Buratinox incorporates even more traditional music into their style than Bức Tường or Da Vàng do. This is largely because the band's lead singer, Y Ga Ry A, belongs to the Ê Đê minority group from the Central Highlands of Vietnam, as explained in the following story:

> The third act to hit the stage was a youthful and energetic "Buratinox". As Buratinox began to play, Don began to tap his knee with the beat. "Do you hear that?" he asked. "That's the rhythm from Tây Nguyên (Central Highlands) traditional music. The lead singer is an ethnic minority of the Ê Đê group." Indeed, the sing-songy vocals and upbeat staccato seemed different from the other musicians' drawn-out interference. Y Ga Ry A, the band's frontman, minced about the stage and wailed nearly to the point of yodeling. Don continued to tap his knee. "This is the new trend in Vietnamese rock, bringing traditional rhythms or instruments [in]to rock songs," he said. "It just comes from a love for the country." While most of the bands seemed to use the same heavy riffs and high-pitched wails as that of Metallica or Panterra, the sounds, rhythms and attitudes [of Buratinox] were beginning to sound more and more distinctly Vietnamese. (*VNN*, November 8, 2004)

With their self-proclaimed and audience-understood emphasis on Vietnamization (or culturation), Buratinox offers a new color in Vietnam's rock music palette. This is not reflected in the band's name, Buratinox," however, which is taken from the Italian "Pinocchio" children's story, "Buratino"

> "Was it the didactic nature of the story that appealed to them—the lesson against lying? Or was it some sort of metaphor for themselves, their relationships, or even for Viet Nam as a nation? No. . . . They [simply] liked the story because it was familiar to them and reminded them of their childhoods. Their name, it seemed, had only meant to soothe and comfort in the way only a children's story can." (ibid.)

Other members of Buratinox include Vũ Hà on lead guitar, Nam Thang on bass, and Trung Kien on drums (not the same person as the Ho Chi Minh City pianist, pop singer, and Vice-Minister of Culture and Information). Although the band members are inspired to incorporate traditional Vietnamese rhythms into their music, and in their lyrics they address Vietnamese culture "because we love the country," they admit that their major musical influences are Deep Purple and Kiss (ibid.).

CONCLUDING THOUGHTS ABOUT ROCK AND HEAVY METAL IN VIETNAM

How did rock and heavy metal become so popular among Vietnam's youth since the mid 1990s and especially into the 2000s? What, stylistically,

has caused its popularity? Are bands such as AtOmega, Bức Tường, Ánh
Sáng, Da Vàng, and others purely contemporary, or are they somewhere on
the Popular Music Continuum between the traditional and contemporary
styles? Will Shaw describes Bức Tường and one of their evening concerts in
2002 at Hanoi's Giảng Võ Exhibition Center in succinct detail, touching
upon several important issues:

> [W]ith half an hour to go before The Wall appear on stage, tickets are
> changing hands for up to three times the expected price. . . . [I]n the
> media hype leading up to the show they were described as "the big-
> gest and best band in Viet Nam," and their fans have turned out en
> masse to see it proved at The Wall's biggest concert yet. Sponsorship
> has played a key roll [*sic*] in tonight's performance, and giant mobile
> phone banners adorn the walls of the packed auditorium. However, as
> the master of ceremonies appears on stage to thank Sony Ericsson he
> is all but drowned out. The bright young things of Hanoi clearly have
> their minds on other matters. The Wall's fans are an eclectic bunch;
> straggle haired metal men decked out in leather jackets and earrings
> stand along side the capital's professional elite, fresh from the office,
> sporting carefully buffed loafers and tucked in shirts.
>
> As the main lights dip, search lights scour the hall amidst the boom
> of gothic Casio chords; suddenly the lights are up, and there they
> are. . . . The Wall cut quite a sight. There may be something slightly
> dated about their brand of Van Halen style glam racketeering, but why
> not? It's certainly not a detail that bothers their fans, who know almost
> all the songs word for word. As the band pump out their Vietnamese
> hard rock hits, water bottles whiz through the air and girls are hauled
> up on their boyfriends' shoulders.
>
> With every ten minutes that passes the hysteria rises another pitch.
> With their Guns 'N' Roses [sic] style stage show, The Wall have
> clearly been heavily influenced by Western pop culture. Nevertheless,
> a five minute chopper blade sample breaking in half way through the
> gig indicates that the band have been just as influenced by their own
> national history. A further dimension of gravity is introduced when
> lead singer Trần Lập dedicates a moment's silence to those who died
> in this month's fire in Ho Chi Minh City. But the melancholy moment
> doesn't last long. Soon enough the axe wielding stars are huddled
> back round center stage, shoulders hunched up over their star shaped
> guitars.
>
> Meanwhile the teenagers in the crowd are head banging as if it was
> going to be outlawed tomorrow and one by one, shirts are coming off.
> However, Hà Nội's parental community has nothing to worry about;
> security guards carrying formidable looking batons are patrolling the
> hall in large numbers, and despite the high spirits, it's clear that noth-
> ing is going to be allowed to get too out of hand.

Outside the hall, the fans are still buzzing, although there is the occasional note of cynicism. The band claim all the songs are their own, but one fan tells me "it all sounded a bit familiar—it was like listening to a 'best of heavy metal' show." Such niggling issues aside, the show was unquestionably a storming success. As one teenage girl declares before jumping into the nearest available taxi, "that was the best—the best!" (2002)

Although he is writing about Bức Tường, Shaw's characterization of a rock performance event can be seen as an overview of other rock concerts in Hanoi, Ho Chi Minh City, and perhaps other Vietnamese urban areas in the 2000s. Shaw makes several statements that suggest attributes of a continuum spanning two opposite concepts—remembering the past and forgetting the past. Though the former concept is unique to Bức Tường, the latter is representative of most of the heavy metal groups in Vietnam: musical style, demeanor, approach to winning the crowd, the crowd's demeanor, crowd control by the police, and the demeanor of the sponsors.

Bức Tường's remembering the past characteristics were discussed in the section on Bức Tường, and they are briefly mentioned again for emphasis: Trần Lập's reference to the helicopter from the American War period and the mourning of the deaths in the fire at the Blue Club in Ho Chi Minh City. Although these were very brief occurrences that broke the heavy metal mood of the concert for just several seconds, they are significant examples of memory politics and show Bức Tường's concern for Vietnamese mass culture. They are also examples that "say it like it is," which is a characteristic of heavy metal in America, especially of Guns N' Roses (Charlton 2003:247).

The "forgetting the past" qualities during Bức Tường's 2002 concert were greater in number, and they include the following attributes (paraphrasing Shaw's words):

1. Van Halen style glam racketeering
2. Guns N' Roses style stage show
3. Like listening to a 'best of heavy metal' show
4. Heavily influenced by Western pop culture
5. Sponsorship played a key role in the performance
6. Master of ceremonies drowned out as he appears on stage to thank the sponsor
7. Teenagers in the crowd are head banging as if it was going to be outlawed tomorrow
8. One by one, the teenagers in the crowd take their shirts off

With regard to the "forgetting the past" attributes, 1 through 4 are the most obviously contemporary, as they represent the heavy metal influences of the West—glam, and the music of Van Halen, Guns N' Roses, and others, as suggested by the "'best of heavy metal' show." Heavy metal rock music is loud and represents youth alternative culture perhaps better than any other music, as Trần Lập said in an interview: "I like rock music. It's exciting and fierce, like us, like young people" (*VNN*, April 22, 2004). Vietnamese rock and metal bands represented a relatively new musical statement in Vietnamese pop culture during the late 1990s and early 2000s, and it remains as the most obvious contemporary expression in music in the new millennium in Vietnam. Vietnamese rock and metal bands fit into Neil Jamieson's metaphorical applications of *yin*[1]: "Much of what I call the *yin* subsystem . . . was perceived to be (in the terms of cybernetic theory) 'noise' in the system, 'flaws' or 'irregularities' that led to tension, confusion, and malfunction in 'the system'. . . ." (1993:15). Indeed, Vietnam's rock and metal music can be interpreted to have "noise" characteristics when contrasted to the Vietnamese government-approved traditional popular music and *nhạc dân tộc cải biên*.

Attribute 5 fits into a contemporary ideology that pertains to the market economy of Vietnam since *đổi mới* in 1985 and especially since the lifting of the U.S. trade embargo in 1994. Hue-Tam Ho Tai suggests this classification in the following analysis: "With Doi Moi, postwar reconstruction has been cast in economic terms. The two heavily masculine sectors, the bureaucracy and the army, are retrenching while the private trading sector, a traditional feminine domain, is expanding" (2001a:182–183). Thus, the obvious presence of a music industry, as seen with the organization of the Hanoi rock concerts, fits into a global ideology that emphasizes money making.

Likewise, attributes 6, 7, and 8 are contemporary aspects of the "*yin* subsystem" because, like attributes 1 through 4, they stress "'irregularities' that [lead] to tension, confusion, and malfunction in 'the system'" (Jamieson 1993:15). Drowning out the master of ceremonies by the crowd's noise creates confusion for some people; head banging—a type of dancing in place that consists of "vigorous nodding to the beat of the music"— is a typical crowd reaction to heavy metal music (Walser 1993:180n3); and removing and waving T-shirts is yet another. Walser continues: "The loudness and intensity of heavy metal music visibly empower fans, whose shouting and headbanging testify to the circulation of energy at concerts. Metal energizes the body, transforming space and social relations" (ibid.:2). These crowd empowerments are indicative of an altered state of consciousness, explains Jamieson, induced by "the photic-driving of flashing colored lights, the sonic-driving of highly amplified electronic keyboards and electric guitars" of the heavy metal music, which is a "physiological transformation . . . sought by people [i.e. Vietnamese youth] who had learned from prestigious foreign exemplars [i.e. MTV and other American media] of an altered state of consciousness that could free them, at least temporarily, from the particular pressures that the *yang* structures of their society in their time inflicted upon them" (1993:330).

It is perhaps particularly noteworthy that this *yin* reaction occurred in the *yang* (i.e. traditional, masculine) stronghold of Hanoi, the seat of Vietnam's communist government, ancient Chinese mandarins, and the "*yang* subsystem" (to continue Jamieson's train of thought).[2] That "the musical expressions and preferences of Vietnam's youth affect and often clash with the communist government's attitudes about music, aesthetics, and morals" (see p. 2, this volume), causes the Hanoi rockers and rock promoters to rock carefully, as Ben Stocking suggests in his succinct analysis of the contemporary popular music situation in Hanoi in 2003:

> The rockers here know that they have to be careful not to take their fun too far, lest they offend the government. They can scream and dance, but any Snoop Dogg verbal outbursts or guitar smashing would be unacceptable. . . . Tran My Trang, an aspiring concert promoter, is careful to consider government sensibilities when she organizes a show. The contract she uses, which is scrutinized by the Culture Ministry, guarantees that the performers won't take off their shirts or swear onstage. "If you have a good relationship with the ministry, you can persuade them," says Trang. . . .

An obvious question comes to mind with regard to Vietnam's rock and heavy metal bands: Where are the female rock and heavy metal bands? In my exhaustive study of Vietnamese news media published in English, only one article mentions a female rock band, and it is only in a photo caption. In the November 8, 2004, issue of *Việt Nam News* there is a photograph of two young ladies in short-sleeved red sweaters and black pants, one playing electric guitar and the other singing, with the caption "Chick Rock: The boys aren't the only ones to be making a noise in the Vietnamese rock scene." Even with that somewhat politically incorrect caption, the author of the article chose to say nothing about the group. The only other discussion I have found about female rock bands in Vietnam is the following Internet article, which was originally published in the *San Jose Mercury News*:

> Nguyễn Yen Thi had a rock 'n' roll fantasy: She'd play the bass in an all-girl band. Here in Vietnam, where ballads about unrequited love and valiant soldiers dominate the airwaves, her vision seemed as far-fetched as a Communist Party-sponsored Ozzy Osbourne concert. But with a little determination and a lot of help from the Internet, the 18-year-old has become part of a small but growing community of young Vietnamese who are bringing rock music to one of its last unconquered frontiers. . . . These days, even the most determined Culture Ministry bureaucrat would have a tough time reining in the rock 'n' roll passions of Thi and her friends. They gather every Saturday afternoon to jam on the tiny patio of a rock-crazy friend, a cozy spot that, like much of Hanoi, is an odd mix of urban and rural, with scruffy chickens clucking

about and industrial waste flowing by in a nearby creek. "We're the first female rock band in Hanoi!" exclaims Nguyễn Thi Thai Thanh, the lead singer in Thi's group, the Halleys, named after Halley's Comet. "Everybody wants to know, 'How can these girls play rock 'n' roll?' They think we are supposed to concentrate on clothes, shopping and boyfriends." With the wiry frame and manic energy of a female Mick Jagger, Thanh revels in smashing such stereotypes. "We want to play rock!" she growls in fluent but heavily accented English. "We want to prove that girls can do everything boys can do!" (Stocking 2003)

Indeed, women have a marginalized status in Vietnam's rock world as instrumentalists, although as soloists or "front people" women frequently sing in rock style. In 2005, when I asked him about female rock bands in Vietnam, an anonymous male rock musician told me: "There are none. In Vietnam the rock bands are all male, because women want to be singers. There are no taboos against it. Women are beautiful, and they don't want to sweat and look like a man." This is similar to the typical "masculinist" attitude toward rock (see Leonard 2007:23–41), and the situation in Vietnam regarding gender roles is not much different than elsewhere in the world, as Mavis Bayton writes: "The world of popular music is highly structured in terms of gender. Traditionally, women . . . [w]hen they have been on stage, on TV, on record, it has nearly always been as singers" (1998:1). Nguyễn Yen Thi's views, previously quoted, represent an anomaly in Vietnam, and a further exploration of the situation of female Vietnamese rock bands warrants a study of its own. It may be a short study, however.

POP-ROCK BANDS

The alternating and merging of rock and pop in Vietnam that occurred in the 1990s was greatly inspired by the first Pop Rock Festival, which was organized in 1991 and held in Ho Chi Minh City in 1992, and by 1996, there were over thirty pop-rock bands in Ho Chi Minh City (*VNN*, April 12, 1996). The *Việt Nam News* was one of the first publications to use the term *Vina-rock* (or *vina rock*, from "*Vi-et na-m rock*") in a story titled "HCM City bands answer call for more Vina-rock" (*VNN*, February 16, 2000) about one of the most successful pop-rock bands from the turn of the century, Những Chàng Trai Sài Gòn (Sài Gòn Boys), formed in 1997 by six young musicians.

POP MUSIC BANDS

Three kinds of pop music ensembles are discussed in this section: boy bands, girl bands, and bands of mixed gender (i.e. boy–girl bands)—all made up of musicians in their teens or early twenties. It is within these emically determined subcategories (i.e. they are used by writers from the *Việt Nam News*) that Vina-pop and other youthful expressions are found. The gender-specific terms are often employed in press information, but size is not always indicated. Boy and girl bands range in size from over seven members to as few as three. Many of Vietnam's top pop bands developed in the 1990s, encouraged by the many festivals and competitions during that decade.

Boy Bands

One of the most popular boy bands at the turn of the century is seven-member Những Người Bạn (Friends, or The Friends), which began as a trio in 1997. How they began, as briefly explained in the following article, gives us an idea about the developmental processes of boy bands:

> One of a growing number of HCM City pop trios, The Friends are a fully professional band with a nation-wide following. Each band member began his performing life singing solo on the HCM City bar circuit, but the three decided to combine their talents after realizing that their goals were essentially similar. As one band member said: "We each found our other performing halves."
>
> The most popular band member is Lam Trường who has a bold, distinctive singing style and a delivery all of his own. Number two, Trung Kiên, joined the band after a promising solo career singing in bars such as the Paloma in the city's Đồng Khởi Street. He was warmly received during last year's Top Hit '97 held at the Phan Đình Sports Club here where he sang, among other songs, the Elton John classic Candle in the Wind. Kiên, who is actually a graduate of HCM City Conservatory's Piano Faculty, decided that his future lay with singing rather than the keyboards. As he said, "And what I have achieved proves that my choice was absolutely right." Xuân Khôi, a graduate from the College of Social Sciences and Humanities, has a minor role in the band, but has nevertheless proven popular with audiences.
>
> The three young men began their association following their appearance in a concert tour last year, headed by one of Việt Nam's most popular singers, Mỹ Linh. From the start they have striven to deliver a quality show and turned down a number of lucrative invitations following their appearance with Mỹ Linh to concentrate instead on rehearsals. (*VNN*, August 8, 1998)

In 1999, when the band was enlarged to seven members, Lam Trường left to pursue a solo career. Trung Kiên also left in 1999 and joined the Ministry of Information and Culture—today he has the governmental status of People's Artist. The well-known bass guitarist (formerly with Da Vàng) and songwriter Le Quân (see Chapter 5) joined the band in the early 2000s. Although The Friends band tries to perform their own compositions, their first CD included four cover tunes in addition to four original compositions (*VNN*, July 26, 1999). Le Quân now writes many of their songs.

Hanoi also has its boy bands, and one of the most popular in the late 1990s was Quả Dưa Hấu (Water Melon), consisting of four men in their early twenties:

> All band members say they are influenced by Western music and sing many English pop songs. However, as Quả Dưa Hấu's lead singer, 25-year-old Bằng Kiều, is quick to point out, "We always try and invest these songs with something of our own. We are not interested in mere impersonation." Kiều, who graduated from Hà Nội Conservatory, says that band members do not have foreign idols and are keen to perform their own material. He said, "We will be playing more of my songs in the future. My compositions focus around the timeless theme of love, although I pay most attention to the melody." Kiều stressed that some of his band's most popular songs were Vietnamese; contemporary songs . . . and traditional tunes. . . . (*VNN*, May 30, 1998)

It is perhaps significant that this band performs songs with Vietnamese nationalistic flavor, because it is a Hanoi band, from the capital city. Few if any of the other pop bands, for example, perform traditional Vietnamese songs. In the early 2000s, Bằng Kiều left the band and immigrated to the United States, where he now lives in California.

A recent boy band from Ho Chi Minh City is 1088, consisting of five youngsters whose fame can be greatly attributed to their corporate sponsor, the Vietnamese Bird Company:

> Before taking the music scene by storm, members of the pop band 1088 were just another bunch of kids who collected posters of their favorite pop stars. Now, they are becoming the new icons to thousands of music fans in HCM City. "We were ourselves fans but now we have fans, thanks to our sponsor who has made our dream come true," said members of the group. . . . According to the five members of 1088, their sponsor encourages them to play pop music which is not simply a copy of Western bands, but has an international and Vietnamese identity. "We will never dominate the concert circuit and the VCD market without our sponsor. Its duty is to be a bridge which connects us to our fans," a member of 1088 stated. (*VNN*, August 1, 2002)

Similar to the Backstreet Boys and 'N Sync because of their dependence on a corporate sponsor,[3] the 1088 band " . . . is just one of the many pop bands/singers that signed a monopoly contract on music shows with the company. 'Our work is to meet and select the best of the young singers. We help talented singers train their voices and perfect performance styles', said a company representative. He pointed out that his company gives its exclusive singers like [the members of] 1088 a nudge to work hard and divide their time equally between practice and performances. 'The young singers work on their vocal technique and dance skills with music specialists from the HCM City Conservatory of Music'."

Vietnam is perhaps unique because of the way its national conservatories assist in the musical training of certain young pop musicians, as if the institutions are responding to the suggestion of Meritorious Artist Mạnh Hà of the National Department of Art and Performance when he explained that the government "creates favorable conditions for traditional music performances, but forgets pop and rock shows" (*VNN*, February 6, 1998). However, by the twenty-first century, many corporate sponsors fund the training of some of their contracted musicians:

> At present, there are several cultural and art companies in HCM City, including Vafaco, Kim Lợi Studio and Hoàng Đỉnh companies, who have trained several young singers and pop bands. "We signed training and performance contracts with four young singers in the last three years . . . ," said a Kim Lợi official. He explained that young singers who have natural ability often need a few years of training before making it to the top. However, he said, not all will be successful on stage. "Investing in young singers is like looking for pearls in the sea." (*VNN*, August 2, 2002)

Although these comments about sponsorship refer to solo singers, pop-rock bands often emerge when three or more solo singers decide they can do better as a boy or girl band. Sponsorship is very important in all situations, especially in twenty-first century Vietnam when performing and recording contracts require large amounts of funds.

Conservatory training showed its effects in the early 2000s with a boy band called AC&M (an abbreviation for "A Cappella and More"), who chose their name because it represents their ambition: "We want to introduce our fans to an unexplored world of music," said one of its members (*VNN*, October 30, 2002). Comprised of Nam Khánh, Đinh Bảo, Thụy Vũ, and Hoàng Bách, AC&M was one of the first groups to capitalize on the Western classical music backgrounds of the individual members by singing a cappella or unaccompanied, as tenor Khánh explained: "While other pop bands and singers prefer to show off their talents with modern orchestras or dance groups, we perform alone on stage. . . . We are giving young people a new taste of music, and we are receiving a lot of support from fans and critics alike" (ibid.). Another aspect of their uniqueness and appeal is the manner in which they borrow from Vietnam's rich folk song tradition, especially songs from northern Vietnam that are themselves sung unaccompanied by groups. AC&M's formation was the brainchild of its founder and leader, Nam Khánh, who won several HTV singing contests in 1999 and as a music conservatory student sang in the chorus with Ánh Tuyết's ATB band, which often features a cappella singing by the mixed group. With his conservatory friends, AC&M was formed. Their philosophy is "to sing traditional songs about love, friendship, family and our nation, as their melodies tend to fit our style of performance" (ibid.), a tradition Khánh also learned from Ánh Tuyết, but a philosophy that is somewhat difficult to sell among the hip-hop, market music, pop, and rock loving youth of Vietnam. "Our fans call us 'the Brave Knights' because we have had to fight so hard to attract the attentions of a youthful audience who are generally more interested in rock and pop," explained Khánh, and "They're totally different—that's why I like them so much," explained one of their fans (ibid.). Nevertheless, when they perform live shows they incorporate as much of a rock and pop music soundscape as most other pop singing groups, thus living up to the "M" ("More") of their name.

The most popular boy band in 2005, however, is MTV, comprised of four young men who dance and sing. "MTV's four members won the heart of fans, particularly young girls by their attractive appearance and dance skills more than their voice. They drive fans crazy with their stage shows," wrote a music critic (*VNN*, February 26, 2004). Vietnamese music critics say MTV copies the American boy band Backstreet Boys; MTV, however, claims they only learn from them (ibid.). MTV has teamed up with the girl band Trio 666 for concerts in Vietnam and tours to foreign countries, such as Thailand and Italy, and much of their success is because their manager, Tuan Khánh, whose fresh and modern vision, which includes hip-hop and other current fads, has won acclaim throughout the country and abroad.

One of the most recent bands is Techno, as explained by music critic Matthew Watters:

> A HCM City-based duo called Techno, featuring the boyish singer Kỳ Phương paired with the sultry Thuy Uyen, are perhaps the finest purveyors of pure dance pop in Viet Nam. Kỳ Phương, in particular, with a distinctive but unaffected singing style and dance moves that would do Michael Jackson proud, is, in fact, a real star, Việt Nam's coolest male singer. (*VNN*, August 7, 2005)

Although based on a male/female duo combination, Techno incorporates other boy musicians in its performances

Girl Bands

At the beginning of the twenty-first century, there are probably more girl bands than boy bands in Vietnam, and the pop music scene in Ho Chi Minh City and Hanoi is "dominated by young female soloists and trios" (*VNN*, July 26, 1999). Characterized by a cuteness factor that is appealing both to Vietnam's female and male youth, girl bands often exploit their sexuality with short skirts, tight pants, or other sexy attire, or their purity with white *áo dái* (school uniforms) or modest dresses.

One of the earliest girl bands was a trio called Ba Con Mèo (Three Cats), comprised of three sisters who "got their name after singing Con Mèo Kháng Chiến (A Resistant Cat) in a 1989 singing competition." In 1996 the group performed at Ho Chi Minh City's Rock and Pop Festival, causing a sensation with their versions of such popular Western songs as "Don't Speak," "Zombie," and "Lemon Tree" (*VNN*, July 30, 1998). Shortly after the Festival, Ba Con Mèo became motivated to perform songs they considered more wholesome and Vietnamese than covers, as a band member explained: "'We want to sing songs suitable to the young', said member Phương Uyên. 'We are Vietnamese so we can only perform in a Vietnamese style'" (*VNN*, March 24, 1997). In the 2000s, Phương Uyên has become a noted songwriter whose songs are widely performed.

Another female trio that attracted attention in the 1990s was Three A's (3A or T.C. 3A); comprised of three sisters from Hanoi whose first names (Ngọc Anh, Minh Anh, and Minh Ánh) begin with the letter A. They also capitalized on their cuteness and an innocent sexuality

> The Three A's have won audiences over with their swinging but gentle and cute style. In each dance step and every note, the Three A's strive for a professional performance. Middle aged viewers may be shocked by the band's bombastic sexy presence in their short skirts, but they can be tender as well. (*VNN*, February 25, 1997)

An accompanying photograph shows the girls wearing modest white dresses rather than short skirts—I call this the *purity factor*, which I see as a variant of the cuteness factor.

A girl band known for its use of white dresses is called Tam Ca Áo Trắng, meaning "Three Girls in White Dresses." The *Việt Nam News* explained why they have that name: "The three singers in the band are sisters, and two of them, Minh Thư and Minh Tú, both aged 22, are twins. The twins, along with their 24-year-old sister, Tuyết Ngân, always perform in white *áo dài*" (March 24, 1997). There is something innately pure about sister bands in Vietnam, it seems, and many Vietnamese girl bands consist of sisters who began performing together as children and teenagers. The Three Girls in White Dresses, for example, performed on the children's television program *Những Bông Hoa Nhỏ* (Little Flowers), adding to their image of purity (ibid.). Minh Thư performs as a solo pop singer in 2005 and has often appeared on HTV's *Qùa Tặng Trái Tim* (Gifts of the Heart) program.

During the late 1990s, there were even more girl bands than before, perhaps inspired by a Hanoi music festival, Discovery 98. One of the girl trios that became popular then was Con Gái, which translates simply as Girls, a name derived from their first song (*VNN*, February 19, 1999). Con Gái's style is described as " . . . gentle and romantic. . . . This three-member all-girl outfit emphasizes their femininity, but not at the expense of appearing soft" (*VNN*, May 30, 1998).

Another girl band from the same time in Hanoi was Tik Tik Tak, which was touted as being "Vietnam's answer to the American group, Spice Girls, because of their playful style and distinctive outfits" (*VNN*, May 30, 1998). Band member Hồng Thúy, however, explained: "We like the Spice Girls because of their energy. They win with their heart and soul. But Tik Tik Tak have never intended to copy them" (ibid.) Although they are not sisters, the members of Tik Tik Tak radiate a sorority sister essence, perhaps because three of the four studied and graduated from the same school, the Hanoi Art College, and the other was trained at the Hanoi Conservatory of Music. There appeared to be a close, youthful, and collegiate camaraderie among the members, as evidenced by their performance attire, which includes white T-shirts, pedal pushers, and tennis shoes.

The most popular girl band in the early 2000s is Ho Chi Minh City-based Trio 666, consisting of Bích Châu, Hoài Giang, and Phương Loan: "Trio 666 have appealed to a broader age group by performing the work of Trịnh Công Sơn and folk songs. 'We choose songs with more difficult melodies, meaningful words and avoid flashy costumes', says Giang. '"We try as many different melodies as possible to improve the range of our voices'" (*VNN*, January 20, 2003). Tuấn Khanh (who wrote Kasim's hit hip-hop tune), manages Trio 666, and his efforts have catapulted them to stardom by broadening their repertoire to include hip-hop and rock: "[Although] Trio 666 . . . has appealed to a broader age group by performing romantic and folk songs[, t]heir style of hip hop and rock is fresh, making a new impression on fans" (*VNN*, February 26, 2004).

Along with MTV, Trio 666 has also toured nationwide and has performed in Thailand and Italy with great success: "Last year, the Italian Rai International Television station filmed Trio 666 for its annual program about Asian music and art" (ibid.). In mid 2005, music critic Matthew Watters wrote the following about the trio:

> A world-class dance pop group, as good as anything Thailand (or Europe) has come up with, is Trio 666, a group of two gorgeous and talented sisters who seem to be perpetually rotating one of their friends in and out of the group's third slot. Trio 666's mix of close, slightly a kilter harmonies and oddball melodies, linked to rock-inflected dance tracks and performed along with hiply [sic] choreographed and tightly-performed dance moves, make them a truly unique article in the creative wasteland of Vietnamese pop. Trio 666 are cool and slick where other Vietnamese acts are amateurish, but their music is surprising and unpredictable. Only marginally popular when they ought to be huge, Trio 666 is the only act in Việt Nam that I could see rising to popularity in foreign music markets like Korea, Japan, and Europe. (*VNN*, August 7)

At the end of 2005, Trio 666 went on tour in France, Japan, South Korea, and China with Les Souris Delingee, a French rock band, with whom they also produced a CD (*VNN*, August 4, 2005).

Similar to the solo pop singer scene in Vietnam, young girl and boy bands proliferate and there is no way to know which ones will become the star bands of tomorrow. Matthew Watters discusses the current trends in 2005:

> More popular but less original [than Trio 666], in seemingly inverse proportions, are Mắt Ngọc, three girls with decent voices but execrable dancing skills whose most recent tracks (and amusingly weird video clips) are obviously influenced by Jolin's work with Jay Chou in Taiwan. Not a bad influence, but still demonstrating a lack of originality. An offshoot group called HAT make[s] admirably credible use of hiphop flourishes and humorous backing vocals by a very fat MC. Their peppy new song Taxi is fine pop, but most of their other music is pretty pallid stuff. Mây Trắng is a similar group with a longer history: four young women who appeal to teenage fans more for their hairstyles and fashion than for their music. They get points, however, for a couple of hilariously self-deprecating video clips. (ibid.)

Girl bands, like boy bands, come and go in Vietnam, as they do in most globalized and market-driven countries. The term *garage band* does not exist in Vietnam (because there are no garages), but the coming together of young people to form a band, make music, and hope to become famous is very common.

Pop Band Professionalism and Originality

Many of Vietnam's boy and girl bands work hard to become professionals, some financially assisted by sponsors and some on their own. With luck, a few bands gain national and international recognition, but more often than not, most disband after a few years. One characteristic the boy and girl bands seem to share is their very young age, as composer Trần Thanh Túng explained: "Before they formed pop groups, they were just children who studied music at the HCM City Conservatory or at Cultural Houses. They shared the same love for music and singing . . . [although] some bands demonstrated that it was possible for singing groups to be successful despite their youth" (*VNN*, March 3, 2001). Girl band members (i.e. singers) often worked as backing vocalists for pop stars, "so that we could get a feel for what it's like to perform on the big stage," said Quỳnh Anh, singer with Mắt Ngọc, a popular girl band whose members were high school students in the 2000s during the height of their popularity (ibid.).

Because of their youth (Vietnamese boy and girl band members are usually teenagers or in their early twenties), many of the songs they prefer to perform are covers of American and other popular European- and African-derived songs.

> Vietnamese [pop] bands have their critics [and these] critics say that Vietnamese pop is simply a copy of its Western counterpart and that it lacks Vietnamese identity . . . , this has not deterred the pop bands, many of which have gained international recognition, and their legion of young fans. These young boys and girls say they will never give up their ways. (*VNN*, May 17, 2001)

Pop musician Lê Minh, a member of the MTV boy band explains, "We are trying to hone our performance and improve our voices. We know we're similar to Western pop bands. But that's not strange or bad. . . . We admire them like all young people over the world. Why shouldn't we follow in their footsteps?" (ibid.). Nevertheless, a commonality that runs through many of the comments by boy and girl band members is that writing their own songs *is* important, as is their musical training.

How does a teenager or young college student professional pop musician balance his or her time between performance and school? The same article provides some comments from several teenage musicians:

> "We are not children who love music. We are singers and we have to work hard to divide our time equally between our schooling and performance careers," says Quỳnh Anh, a member of the Mắt Ngọc. Mắt Ngọc and Mây Trắng [girl band] have written a number of well-known songs for teenage audiences and plan to pursue careers in music. Their members are currently studying for final examinations at high school. "We will improve our vocal music and dance skills in the HCM City Conservatory," said [a member of] Mây Trắng. (ibid.)

Many band members succumb to the pressures of professionalism: the road trips, the long hours in rehearsal, the difficulties without sponsorship, and the low pay. Others give up band life to pursue careers as solo pop singers, an equally difficult endeavor, but one that can be more successful because it builds on the professional band experiences. In other instances, solo pop singers give up and new bands appear. In the early 2000s, for example, many bands folded, and new ones appeared, some with unique styles:

> The musical landscape continues to change, and the dominance of solo performers is giving way to bands. However, music fans were shocked last year when members of the groups 1088, Ba Con Mèo (Three Cats), Áo Trang (Long White Dress) and Mây Trắng (White Cloud) called it quits. However, fans who prefer the harmonies of groups were sated by the emergence of the new [girl] band Trio 666 . . . [and the] boy band

. . . [which] has brought an unfamiliar style to Vietnamese stages: a cappella. . . . As the Vietnamese music industry diversifies and grows, music lovers can expect even more intriguing developments in 2003. (*VNN*, January 19–26, 2003)

Although the *a cappella* style, which appeared in Vietnam during the early years of the twenty-first century, copies bands from America and England (such as the Backstreet Boys), Vietnam has several traditional *a cappella* vocal styles (such as *quan họ*) from its central and northern highlands that inspired AC&M to create their unique style.

One technique employed by most boy and girl bands is dance, which is also often a copy of similar styles from America and England. Individual or synchronized choreographed movements by the members of a band are common with pop and popular music groups in many regions of the world, and the incorporation of live dancers (i.e. dance troupes) into a live boy or girl band show or video grew in popularity in the early 2000s. This did not meet with approval from the critics, who have often felt it distracts from the musical talents of the musicians, as seen by the title of the article "Will live dance kill the pop scene?" (*VNN*, November 15, 2001). Because this phenomenon occurs most often in live shows, it is discussed in Chapter 5.

Hanoi and Ho Chi Minh City are the two most important cities for pop music in Vietnam; the latter is considered "the promised land for musicians and singers, with boisterous audiences flocking to shows in the cosmopolitan hub" (*VNN*, January 25, 2002). Nevertheless, pop music bands and their singers from Ho Chi Minh City often go north to Hanoi during the winter months, not to experience cooler weather but to win acclaim among the youth in Hanoi, whom the southern musicians see as tough critics:

[T]he HCM City-based The Bells . . . band, comprising two women and one man, came to Hà Nội at Christmas and found a warm reception in the chilly capital. They are not alone. Dan Trường and Thanh Thảo turned down contracts in HCM City to perform thousands of kilometers north at live shows in Hà Nội's parks. "I knew I'd face a challenge in the capital," says Dan Trường. "Hanoians have very high standards for their music, and I wasn't sure whether they'd accept me. But I tried to relax and sing the way I would in HCM City. Most of the southern singers are young and there's nothing we like better than a challenge." Dan Trường says at first he was worried that the time up north might lose him some of his southern fans. "But now I have a few more new fans." Many HCM City singers have received instant acclaim in Hà Nội. Their fashionable costumes, strong stage presence and foreign-style music have been an overnight success. Hanoians are particularly fond of love songs composed by young musicians Đức Trí and Phương Uyên. But one music critic isn't convinced, saying that while HCM City singers are skilled and professional their voices are often too soft for northern ears."(ibid.)

The northern Vietnamese predilection for loud singing, compared to softer singing in southern Vietnam, is perhaps derived from the traditional form of northern chamber music singing known as *ca trù*. This and other traditional forms were known in Hanoi, and their existence today, albeit slight, is part of a traditional music revival that has gained some popularity among the more politicized youth of Hanoi.

STUDENT AND OTHER AMATEUR POP BANDS

Many of the recent (since ca. 1995) professional pop bands in Vietnam began as student pop bands from the urban universities or colleges in Hanoi or Ho Chi Minh City. The student pop band movement grew out of a yearly amateur singing competition for university students known as "Unplugged Music Contest" (after the MTV event), which was first held in 1994 in Ho Chi Minh City (see Chapter 8). All participants in the Vietnamese Unplugged Music Contest, which continues to this day, must compose and sing their own songs in English; the best songs are determined by a panel of Vietnamese and American judges. Over sixty bands compete each year, and most of them do not continue as professionals, although some individuals may find stardom:

> Many vocalists and songwriters have become well-known after these "Unplugged" concert contests, mesmerizing the young audience, although few dreamed of becoming professional singers and musicians. "After graduating, many students who are veteran members leave their bands," said Anh Tuấn, a [former] Green Ants songwriter. "We're hoping students can form a pop music club so that we'll have a place to give performances outside of our college," said Triệu Yên, a student jazz singer. (*VNN*, March 20, 1997)

In 1997, a professional video was made of four winning bands—Green Ants (Kien Xanh), Blue Waves, Bright Sea, and Southern Winds—placing them on par with professional pop bands (ibid.).

During the summer months, water parks are favorite venues for performances by amateur high-school student bands. Generally on Sunday mornings, boy, girl, and mixed bands perform to the encouragement of their high-school peers (Figure 4.1). On July 14, 2002, I attended a high school student pop band competition at Dàmsen Water Park in Ho Chi Minh City at the invitation of Pearl, the mother of a young keyboardist and member of a boy band. For several hours, bands played three or four tunes each to the approval of cheering fans consisting of parents, other family members, friends, and classmates. The latter vigorously waved happy faces and hearts during performances by their favorite bands (Figure 4.2). All performers were very conservatively dressed in white shirts/blouses and black pants/skirts—there was no hip-hop attire, except in the audience. As representatives of metropolitan high schools, appropriate, respectful, and uniform dress was the norm. Such emphasis on high school student dress code conformity (uniformity) and the use of the Vietnamese language for the lyrics, were the only characteristics that identified these groups as Vietnamese. The music they performed was mainstream pop-rock—American style. I captured some of the flavor of the event in my fieldnotes:

> This is a rock band contest featuring local high schools in Ho Chi Minh City: three bubble gum style bands and one that alternates bubble gum and rock. Pearl's son played keyboard in the last and best group. The first band's singers used rather stilted and silly choreography. The last band did more and the bass player jumped up several times. A cheering group of kids in the audience was cute, holding up big hearts for girl singers and a mixed variety of happy faces for boy singers, as well as girl singers. The crowd was very enthusiastic. The venue was the water park section of Dâmsen Park. It began early, about 9:30 or 10:00 am on Sunday. The crowd was a very good size, and it was good clean fun for families.

Figure 4.1   An amateur girl band performing at a contest in Dâmsen Water Park in Ho Chi Minh City, July 14, 2002. Photograph by Dale A. Olsen.

Figure 4.2   A multitude of teenage and preteen fans support their favorite amateur pop music band at a contest held at Dàmsen Water Park in Ho Chi Minh City,
July 14, 2002. Holding and waving smiley faces and hearts, and dressing in clothes
resembling the American flag, are commonplace. Photograph by Dale A. Olsen.

CONCLUSION: GOVERNMENTAL CONSTRUCTIVE
CRITICISM AND "VIETNAMESENESS"

In 1998, about two years before the terms vina-rock and vina-pop were
being used, an interesting critique featuring a dialogue of mostly governmental music officials from Hanoi, government-named "meritorious"
musicians, and other musicians and music critics appeared in the *Việt Nam
News*. Because the contributors suggest several ideas and make important
observations that relate to government policy, I include excerpts from the
article in the next paragraphs, followed by my interpretations. I read some
of these dialogues from the *Việt Nam News* to one of Vietnam's best-
known rock musicians, and that is when he warned me with the words
already mentioned in Chapter 1: "Listen to the panel; when they talk in the
newspaper, it's not the truth" (pers. com. with Musician 1, July 13, 2002,
Ho Chi Minh City). Nevertheless, their opinions seem important to this
study, and they have inspired me to make the following interpretations, as
I attempt to put them into context.

Musician Phạm Tuyên:

One typical feature of the [contemporary popular music] phenomenon is the excitement that such music performance evokes. But the young people should be given more information to help them understand pop and rock music better. Young music bands should be encouraged to compose Vietnamese pop and rock songs, not just mimic foreign ones.

Associate Doctor Vũ Tự Lân (Việt Nam Musicians' Association):

Pop and rock is a strong and modern music style. Its acceptance, however, is open to question. We should understand the essence of pop and rock to receive things that are suited to our national identity. The mass media plays an important role in helping people understand music styles. (*VNN*, February 6, 1998)

One of the main ideas expressed and suggested by the above commentators is that the youthful members of pop rock bands should compose their own songs and not imitate foreign music, meaning that "national identity" should be strived for. It seems to me, however, that musician Phạm Tuyên and Associate Doctor Vũ Tự Lân are unaware of the motivations that have inspired many songs by AtOmega, Da Vàng, Sài Gòn Boys, The Wall, The Light, and others. It also seems they are unaware of the *Việt Nam News* articles that appeared in the early and mid 1990s about the desires of several bands to develop a national expression through their music.

Meritorious Artist Mạnh Hà (Department of Art and Performance):

Not enough attention is given to assessment and criticism of music. Therefore, many music shows of low quality backed by heavy advertising have been staged. Young people, students in particular, prefer listening to foreign music programs [rather] than Vietnamese ones. One reason is that the art and technique of presentation of foreign shows is much higher than local ones. The State creates favorable conditions for traditional music performances, but forgets pop and rock shows. One concern is that "modified" music has an adverse effect on the music taste and lifestyle of young people.

Reporter Huyền Thanh (Music Lovers' Club of the Voice of Việt Nam):

Students still behave badly in some music shows, and need to be educated on the correct ways to express appreciation.

Two other ideas stressed throughout the dialogue are the commentators' beliefs in the "low quality" of the music and the "bad behavior" of the young people in attendance at pop rock concerts. These impressions clearly seem to be derived from a generation gap and inspired by the elitist attitudes of the music officials and artists. The commentators also infer that the youthful musicians and their audience are ignorant of music and should be given "more information" about it. I am tempted to ask, how knowledgeable are the music critics and official music administrators themselves, about the various forms of *nhac trẻ*, including rock, heavy metal, and other forms?

> Deputy General Secretary of Youth Union of the Science and Humanities University, Thảo Vân:
>
> It is a good sign that many students attend pop and rock shows and can sing many foreign songs. This means that music appreciation of young people has widened. But they also do not forget traditional music. One question is: Do we have many good songs to meet the increasing demands of young people? We should not only criticize young people for their behavior in some pop and rock shows and forget the responsibility of the organizers. For example, VNĐ 15,000 is not a small amount of money for students. And they will be the losers when the amount is spent on a low-quality music show. Students expect that there will be shows of better quality in the future.

> Musician Minh Châu (Deputy director of Hà Nội Youth's Culture House):
>
> Young people in the cities of Hà Nội and HCM warmly welcome pop and rock shows. Some of them are knowledgeable and attend performances to enjoy the music, but there are others who just use the shows to meet and have a good time. It is necessary to provide education on music and culture for young people. The Youth union and mass media have an important role to play in providing this.

In contrast to the other panel members, Thảo Vân finds value in pop and rock music, foreign as well as national, because those genres help youth develop an appreciation for music in general by giving them the opportunity to sing along. Likewise, musician Minh Châu, who has nearly continuous contact with young people as director of Hanoi's Youth Culture House, credits youth for their knowledge of music, although he does point out that some of the young people are just out for a good time. He suggests that both the government, through the Youth Union, and the media should do more to promote music education among the youth.

Finally, some of the commentators are critical of the music promoters—the real money makers—who often support musical events just because they are profitable. Like the pop and rock music industry throughout the globalized world, the middle men often become wealthy from the talents of performing musicians.

With the advent of pop music that developed after 1997, and especially the numerous boy and girl bands that became popular, the above commentators would probably even have more critical words because of the overwhelming foreign influences that exist in the 2000s.

What is Vietnamese about Vietnam's popular music in the first decade of the twenty-first century? Specifically, vis-à-vis this chapter, is there a Vietnameseness about Vietnam's rock, pop-rock, and pop bands; and if so, how is it evident? It seems that only among two of Vietnam's rock bands— Bức Tường and Buratinox—has there been an attempt made to be uniquely Vietnamese. However, there are many bands in Vietnam that do not make the national newsprint, except for brief mention. For example, in an article about a rock band contest in Hanoi (see Chapter 7), a band called Bầu Khí Quyển (Atmosphere) that plays a "unique southern style rock" from Ho Chi Minh City is mentioned but not discussed, a Hanoi rock band Ngọn Lửa Nhỏ (Small Fire) is said to "prefer a style known as Nu-Metal," and Sói Đen (BlackWolf), the only band from central Việt Nam, is also mentioned as being highly anticipated (*VNN*, May 7, 2004). None of these rock bands is ever again mentioned in the English press, and the question of their Vietnameseness must remain unanswered at this time.

Other sources, however, occasionally address the issue. Dustin Roasa, for example, writing about Trí Minh, a young electronic composer and improviser (and writer of pop music) from Hanoi, has the following to say about Vietnameseness:

> Minh has thought a lot about these things. It's unavoidable in a country that has allowed in a flood of new information and ideas while still trying to preserve an essential—yet illusory, some might argue—'Vietnamese-ness'. Much of the discourse comes straight from the top: cultural officials, worried about the loss of national identity in the face of such rapid changes, fill the pages of the country's press with articles about the threat posed by globalization.
>
> For Minh, however, the issue is not so complicated. "A lot of people are saying you have to make Vietnamese music, you have to preserve it. But for me, it's in there already. The sounds, the notes, the way everything moves—it's Vietnamese. It comes naturally. I don't have to force it. Sometimes I try to create something that sounds very Western, but in the end it sounds Vietnamese to me." (2005:11)

Trí Minh, of course, is writing about his own art, and not the recorded and performed output of the many rock and pop-rock bands in Vietnam. Nevertheless, his words are worth considering, because they provide a baseline answer to my question of "What is Vietnamese about it?"

Because of the great variety of styles presented by the diversity of ensemble genres discussed in this chapter, several examples of glocalization, indigenizing the global, culturation, or Vietnamese aesthetic qualities have been discussed. Most of them occur among the rock bands, perhaps because instrumental rock (and its variants), by its avant-garde and progressive nature, is more prone to experimentation than pop or pop-rock music. Rock, according to many popular music scholars, can be political (not by its words but by its music), but in Vietnam rock has an evolutionary path rather than a revolutionary one (Street 1986:66). Street captures what I see as the political power of rock music in Vietnam with the following general observation about rock music:

> The 'political success' of a musical form cannot be judged in the same way that we judge a political movement or government. Its success is determined musically, visually and commercially. Its political impact is marked by the way the music is consumed. Music that works politically is not necessarily music that makes political change its self-consciously ascribed goal . . . [It] cannot change the world. It can, however, alter the ways in which people experience that world; it can upset old images and provide new ones. (174)

As such, rock music is very political in Vietnam. I am reminded of the scene, shown many times in Bức Tường's music video of their 9+ tour in 2004, of the thousands of youngsters in the audience with raised arms, most waving their hands but some forming fists, perhaps in silent protest of something that is not spelled out in the lyrics of the songs. I am also reminded, however, of Honda's advertisement behind Trần Lập that reads "Honda, The Power of Dreams," suggesting that a Dream motorbike can also alter the way a teenager experiences the world.

The next chapter pertains exclusively to Vietnamese songwriters, offering a glimpse at some of the most successful auteurs in Vietnam. I also write about songwriting contests, through which young lyricists hope to help sustain the pop singers of Vietnam and offer them interesting materials to work with. We have seen in Chapter 3 how some of the top divas of Vietnam, namely Hồng Nhung and Thanh Lam, have approached the issue of finding new and original songs to sing. It is certainly a challenging problem for pop and rock singers, and a songwriter/composer can either make or break a star.

5 Vietnamese Songwriters, Social Issues, and Government Persuasion

Vietnam memorializes selected epochs from its past, glorifies its natural beauty, and expresses a desire to exist through song. It is a songwriter's heaven in many ways, because there is so much in its past, present, and future about which to sing—good times and bad. Traditional Vietnamese vocal expressions have included narrative songs (*ca trù*, *hát à đào*, and others), lyrical songs (*nhạc cải lương*, *hát chèo*, *hát tuồng*, *vọng cổ*, and other theatrical forms), declamatory songs (*quan họ* and other folk forms), love songs (*tình ca*, *nhạc trữ tình*, and other romantic songs), and a large variety of ethnic minority and other rural songs. Through songs and singing, the people of Vietnam entertain, celebrate, and define themselves as independent and proud, sensitive and modern, loving and romantic. How much of the content and activity of songwriting in Vietnam is the result of persuasion by the communist government? In this chapter I present biographical sketches of a number of songwriters (i.e. composers—the two terms are used interchangeably), categorized according to the following titles and dates of their activity: The Patriarchal Trilogy (1960–1975); Postwar Period (1975–1995); and Post-Sanctions Period (1995–Present). Additionally, I discuss songwriting contests and lyrics that address particular social issues in Vietnam, analyzing them with regard to government involvement and persuasion.

Frank Gerke and Bui Tuyen, in an Internet essay titled "Popular Music in Vietnam," explain that "In Vietnam's music business it is common practice to name the composer in the same breath as the performer. Frequently composers are feted as the real stars" (1999). Three famous older male composers stand out as Vietnam's patriarchal trilogy before and during the American War (1960–1975): Phạm Duy, Trịnh Công Sơn, and Văn Cao. They are, in the fullest meaning of the term, *auteur-s* of the highest quality because of their outstanding creative talents. Only the last two, however, have had an impact on *nhạc trẻ* up to 2005, and the first will undoubtedly have an impact because of his return to Vietnam in 2005.

In the postwar period until the lifting of sanctions (1975–1995), several songwriters became famous in Vietnam because of their French *chanson* (song) style; and others have attempted to incorporate ethnic minority and traditional musical elements into their songs. The best-known songwriter in the former category is Trần Tiến; the most noteworthy songwriter in the latter category is Nguyễn Cường. More recently, since the lifting of sanctions in 1995, young songwriters have written songs reflecting globalization and other Western ideas, such as gender issues. Perhaps the foremost young songwriter is Trần Lập, the leader, guitarist, singer, and songwriter with Bức Tường (The Wall), the most famous rock band in Vietnam in the early twenty-first century. Trần Lập primarily sings his own songs during performances and recordings, much like the famous songwriters/singers before him. Trần Kim Ngọc is one of Vietnam's most successful female songwriters, and through her songs she honors women and their roles as mothers. It is not unusual, however, that the vast majority of songwriters in Vietnam is male, because that was also the French norm for the *chanson* during the colonial period and beyond (Hawkins 2000:35).

THE PATRIARCHAL TRILOGY (1960–1975)

Many songwriters composed music and lyrics during the period of the American War in Vietnam. Phạm Duy, Văn Cao, and Trịnh Công Sơn stand out because they wrote songs that protested the war. I refer to them as the patriarchal trilogy for the years 1960 to 1975, the major period of the American War, and their activity is important for Vietnamese popular music studies in the twenty-first century. Of the three, Trịnh Công Sơn is the most remembered in Vietnam, and his love songs and sentimental songs are extremely important today, constituting a type of folk revival. Văn Cao is much less known today, although his role was very important in Vietnam, and his compositions form the major thrust of the popular music expressions of numerous pop singers, such as Ánh Tuyết and her followers. Phạm Duy immigrated to the United States shortly after the end of the American War and was remembered in the motherland only by people of his generation, until he permanently returned to Vietnam in 2005 at age 85. During his sojourn in the United States his songs were banned by the Vietnamese government, but today a number of his love and sentimental songs are gaining popularity among Vietnam's pop singers. Reflected by their CD sales, Phạm Duy (in the United States among the Việt kiều), Trịnh Công Sơn (especially in Ho Chi Minh City), and Văn Cao (throughout Vietnam) have secured a special place in the history of Vietnamese songwriting. Because of their return to popularity, the ideologies they espoused during the major periods of their musical careers, and the artistic skills they represent as songwriters, they are included as a prelude to this chapter, discussed in alphabetical order.

Phạm Duy

A prolific composer, singer, and scholar, Phạm Duy (born in Hanoi in 1921) became a refugee and entered the United States via northern Florida in 1975 (I met him within weeks after his arrival because he was being assisted by a church in Tallahassee, where he and his family gave a concert). After living in Pensacola several years, Phạm Duy and his entire family moved to Orange County, California, where he lived until 2005 when he returned to Vietnam. Because of his self-imposed exile and the fact that his music was banned by the Vietnamese government for many years, he and his music are little known to Vietnamese youth in the motherland and are all but forgotten except by the people of his age group. Once again in Vietnam after 30 years, he hopes for a revival of his songs about love and the beauty of his native land.

Phạm Duy began his professional musical career in 1943 as a member of a *cải lương* group that toured the country until 1945 (Wong 2004:97). In 1945 he joined the Việt Minh resistence group in North Vietnam to fight against the French. This is when he made one of his first impacts as a songwriter during Vietnam's war of independence from France. His songs "were taken up by guerrillas, students, and villagers" during that struggle (Fish 1989:398). Disillusioned with communism, however, he left the Việt Minh and North Vietnam in 1955, moving to Saigon where he worked for Radio Saigon (ibid.). Gerke and Bui Tuyen write the following about his early career as a songwriter in Saigon: "[Phạm Duy] composed his original songs under the influence of American examples and thereby decisively contributed to the 'modernization' of traditional folk songs. He turned numerous Vietnamese poems into song and translated many western songs—from hits to ballads—into Vietnamese" (1999). His protest songs, somewhat in the style of Pete Seeger, spoke bitterly of the horrors of war, as the following song text excerpt portrays: "The rain on the leaves is the tears of joy of the girl whose boy returns from the war; the rain on the leaves is the bitter tears when a mother hears her son is no more. . . ." (Phạm Duy 1975:xiii). Yet, Phạm Duy explains that "folk songs must [not only] reflect the past but also hold a mirror to the present," as the above song unfolds and seems to give hope: "The rain on the leaves is the cry that is torn from a baby just born as life is begun; the rain on the leaves is an old couple's love much greater now than when they were young." Indeed, many of Phạm Duy's songs during Vietnam's war-torn years were "heart songs," as Stephen Addiss explains in his Introduction to Phạm Duy's book: "His songs at this time were . . . a kind of modern folk music meant to speak to the hearts of the Vietnamese people" (1975:xvii), as the following song text of "Heart Song—Our Foe" suggests (used with permission):

> Our foe is not a man, for if we kill, who is left to live?
> Our foe has a name and his name is "ism";
> His name is "stupidity," his name is "hatred";
> His name is "fear," his name is "evil ghosts";
> He is no foreigner, he is inside ourselves . . .

Perhaps this kind of song text caused Phạm Duy to be rejected by the Vietnamese government, which was unable to look inside itself. Philip Taylor writes that "The composer Pham Duy was probably the most popular musician in the South before liberation. But the communists really hated him as they said he had betrayed the resistance and fled to the South after 1954" (2001:153).

After thirty years away from Vietnam (with only short visits during that time), Phạm Duy returned to his homeland in 2005 to live out his days, as reported in *Thanhnien News*:

> "I hope to return to Vietnam to live the rest of my life with my children," says Mr. Duy. . . . "I have yearned to return for a very long time and have decided to take a new step in my career. The poem Ve Thoi by Luu Trong Van helped me understand that I do not have much time and if I want to do something, I have to do it right away," says Mr. Duy. . . .
> If allowed to live in Vietnam, the composer says he will "take a trans-Vietnam trip and write songs about the homeland, continue studying folk songs and seek permission to perform." Mr. Duy adds that he also wants to introduce his old and new songs to the people in Vietnam. He is currently seeking permission from Vietnamese authorities to allow nine of his old songs to be performed in Vietnam. The songs include five that he composed during the war against French colonists and four other poetic songs. (February 5, 2005)

Phạm Duy has written over 900 songs about love, social issues, and spirituality. He is the most prolific of Vietnam's patriarchal trilogy composers, and if permitted, many of his songs could become widely performed and recorded by Vietnam's pop singers, much like those of Văn Cao and Trịnh Công Sơn. According to the *Việt Nam News*, some of his songs were soon to be re-released in Vietnam in the early 2000s:

> The pre-war songs of once famous Vietnamese composer Phạm Duy . . . who has been living in the United States for years, are expected to be played inside Viet Nam very soon. The songs include Tinh Ca (Love Song), Nguoi Me Gio Linh (The Gio Linh Mother) and Que Ngheo (Poor Village), which were once popular songs broadcast in Viet Nam during the resistance war against the French." (April 2005)

Công Thắng wrote that the Phuong Nam Culture Company will release those and six other Phạm Duy ballads, which were approved by the Ministry of Information and Culture, in a CD titled *Ngày Trở Về* (The Day of Returning to the Homeland) (*The Saigon Times Daily* August 3, 2005). "Phuong Nam Culture is also looking to get the State's permission to stage a live show of Phạm Duy's popular songs at the end of the year. In addition, the company will work with Phạm Duy to publish his recollections and other songs after those get approved for performance" (ibid.). Thus, Phạm Duy has come full circle, and with his return to his homeland, he hopes to regain his former legacy as one of Vietnam's greatest musical patriarchs.

Văn Cao

Of the same generation and ideological inspiration as Phạm Duy, Nguyễn Văn Cao (1923–1995) came to represent the other side of the coin, because he was venerated by the Vietnamese government, rather than scorned. "Văn Cao has passed away, but the art world of his remains for generation after generation to enjoy immensely and passionately, to love and respect him, a love which is as pure and noble as his soul and music" (Ngô Ngọc Ngũ Long n.d.). Văn Cao was one of the most influential songwriters in twentieth-century Vietnam. A songwriter before and after the 1945 August Revolution, his best-known song, "Tiến Quân Ca" (Marching Song), composed in November 1944, was chosen by President Hồ Chí Minh as the national anthem of the new Vietnam. Ngô Ngọc Ngũ Long writes:

> All the patriotic Vietnamese, from the national defending soldiers to the women operating in the jungles of the Northern Vietnam, the mothers in the Southern Vietnam's resistance area, the political prisoners on Con Dao (Poulo Condor) Island, on Phu Quoc Island, in Tong Nha (the Saigon regime's Police Headquarters), in Phu Loi prison, all sang the song, urging them to keep firm their fighting spirit, braving their lives in the fight against the enemy. . . . Half a century has gone by, but today whenever the song is sung, our gratitude should go to Văn Cao, who wrote such a majestic song for the nation. (ibid.)

It is the love songs of Văn Cao, however, that are inspiring to some of Vietnam's pop singers in the twenty-first century, even though the composer was celibate: "A stream of love songs overflew [*sic*] from the heart of a young man who had never known what love was like, who had never taken the hand of a girl" (ibid.). His love songs are sometimes called heroic–love songs. Pop singers such as Ánh Tuyết, Mỹ Linh, and Bích Hồng have created a renewed interest in them and in Văn Cao's sensitive and nostalgic style, by including his songs in their concerts and CDs. Ngô Ngọc Ngũ Long sums up Văn Cao as an artist:

> Văn Cao was a talented, sensitive man. He had aspirations for success in many artistic areas like music, poetry and painting. His poems explored the inner world of man; his paintings, particularly his illustrations, had a style of [their] own. But whenever we talk about Văn Cao, we talk of his music first. Over the past half of the century, he has been a great composer. (ibid.)

Văn Cao's songs are "approved" by the Vietnamese government, and he has been one of the most influential songwriters during Vietnam's recent formative years. He represents the governmental acceptance end of the patriarchal trilogy continuum; Phạm Duy represents the opposite end of governmental nonacceptance; and the third member, Trịnh Công Sơn, falls into the middle: governmental tolerance, albeit after years of persecution.

Trịnh Công Sơn

Perhaps the most celebrated Vietnamese composer in the twentieth century, Trịnh Công Sơn was born in 1939 in Dac Lac province in the Central Highlands and died in 2001 in Ho Chi Minh City. He was one of the most prolific songwriters in Vietnam, publishing eleven song collections between 1959 and 1975 and composing over 600 songs (*VNN*, April 3, 2001). Trịnh Công Sơn was originally known as an anti-war songwriter and singer, and because of his stance against the American War and his opposition to the communist government that followed in 1975, he was dubbed the Bob Dylan of Vietnam by American folk singer Joan Baez, a comparison that has continued to this day. Today, in Vietnam, however, he is known as a composer of love songs and sentimental songs of destiny.

After the defeat of South Vietnam by the Viet Cong in 1975, Trịnh Công Sơn had the opportunity to go to the United States as a refugee but chose to remain in southern Vietnam, even though most of his family left. Because of his political activity through his music, he was imprisoned in a labor camp by the communist government for four years. On April 2, 2001, however, the Associated Press reported a ten-year imprisonment: "When the war ended, most of Sơn's family fled overseas, but he decided to stay. He was equally unpopular with the new communist government for his songs about reconciliation and spent 10 years in forced labor 're-education camps' as a result."

Revealing its common penchant for expressing the "official" governmental point of view, the *Việt Nam News* published the following: "Trịnh Công Sơn, born on Feb. 28, 1939 in Central Highlands Dac Lac province and a native of Hue, was one of those composers that mingled naturally with the new life in the country after the liberation of southern Việt Nam in 1975" (April 2, 2001). Perhaps as a "farewell to the past" of its own, the communist government's politics of remembering suddenly became the politics of forgetting, as the official recognition of Trịnh Công Sơn made no reference to the musician's imprisonment and re-education in an article about his funeral:

Two of Ho Chi Minh City's top officials, communist party chief Nguyen Minh Triet and deputy mayor Le Thanh Hai, visited the mortuary Tuesday where the singer's body had lain in state. This was one sign that the communist authorities have at last given a grudging nod of approval to the man they subjected to four years' of re-education on the Lao border after their victory in 1975. Another was that Sơn's death was reported by all the main official dailies Tuesday, including armed forces' mouthpiece Quan Doi Nhan Dan (People's Army), despite his strong pacifist stance during the war. The official media has sought to rehabilitate the singer as one of its own and has made no reference to the time he spent in re-education camps. "The nation will forever remember his song, 'Joining Hands for Solidarity', as the Song of Liberation Day because it was one of several songs played for days on end by Radio Saigon when it was captured by the revolutionary victors," said the English-language Việt Nam News. The paper claimed that, after the communist victory, Sơn had penned a string of classic songs, although the singer told AFP last year that he had "written nothing beautiful" in the decade after 1975 and had not published a single song. ("Thousands pay last respects to Vietnam's 'Bob Dylan,'"Associated Free Press, April 4, 2001)

Tai explains that "Forgetting can . . . be an attempt to keep the past from damaging the present" (2001a:190), and this clearly seems to be the path taken by the Vietnamese communist government.

Jamieson describes Trịnh Công Sơn's role in the protest music movement of the 1960s and 1970s in Vietnam, as he writes: "The intimate but highly complex relationship between American influence and [his] strong *yin* reaction to the war during the late 1960s in the Republic of Vietnam had many dimensions" (1993:326–329). Anti-war songs that gained him the wrath of the South Vietnamese government included "Who's Left Who is Vietnamese?" which includes these powerful lyrics (used with permission):

Open your eyes and look around here.
Who's left who is Vietnamese?
A million people have died.
Open your eyes and turn over the enemy corpses.
Those are Vietnamese faces upon them.
Going over the human corpses,
Whom have we been defeating all these years?

In addition to the *yin* dimension of this kind of anti-war song (according to Jamiesen), Trịnh Công Sơn's songs about "Mother Vietnam weeping for all her children" were other powerful anti-war expressions through music (Tai 2001a:181). His song "Gia Tài Của Mẹ" (Mother's Legacy) from 1969, for example, has lyrics that empower the sorrows of a Vietnamese mother (a metaphor for Vietnam) who has lost her children to war over the centuries (translated by Nguyễn Vu Thành):[1]

A thousand years of Chinese reign.
A hundred years of French domain.

Twenty years fighting brothers each day,
A mother's fate, left for her child,
A mother's fate, a land defiled.

A thousand years of Chinese reign.
A hundred years of French domain.
Twenty years fighting brothers each day,
A mother's fate, bones left to dry,
And graves that fill a mountain high.

Refrain:
Teach your children to speak their minds.
Don't let them forget their kind—
Never forget their kind, from old Viet land.
Mother wait for your kids to come home,
Kids who now so far away roam.
Children of one father, be reconciled.

A thousand years of Chinese reign.
A hundred years of French domain.
Twenty years fighting brothers each day.
A mother's fate, our fields so dead,
And rows of homes in flames so red.

A thousand years of Chinese reign.
A hundred years of French domain.
Twenty years fighting brothers each day.
A mother's fate, her kids half-breeds,
Her kids filled with disloyalty.

To continue with Jamieson's type of interpretation, this song well illustrates the *yang* (male: army and war) / *yin* (female: mother's love) play of opposites that are bridged by the emphasis on remembering in the refrain. Yet, the horrors of war that are made so evident in the last two lines of each verse seem to suggest the forgetting, willed amnesia, or not knowing that characterize many of Vietnam's youth of today.

Another powerful *yin* song that glorifies motherhood and deplores the horrors of war is "Ngủ Đi Con" (Sleep, My Child, also simply Lullaby), which is "about the pain of a mother mourning her soldier son" (Associated Press, April 2, 2001), as evidenced in the following song text (translated by Nguyễn Vu Thành):[1]

Hò ho ho hó ho hò, please sleep, sleep, my child
The child of mum, yellow-skinned
Lulls you, lulls the bullet dyed your wound pink

Twenty years, a band of children went soldiering
Went, not to return, mum's yellow-skinned child
Sleep, my child

Lulls you, lulled you two times
Oh this body was formerly little (and tender)
Mum's belly was full, mum carried (you) on hands
Hò ho ho hó ho hò, why (do you) sleep at (the) age (of) twenty?

Hò ho ho hó ho hò, please sleep, sleep, my child
The child of mum was born
On lips a word of deep grief resounded
Twenty years, a children band grew up
Went to battlefields, the yellow-skinned child of Fairy and Dragon
Sleep, my child

Lulls you, now rolled in dust
Oh which injury carved into your warm skin (deeply)
This bone and flesh mum wearied from dawn till dark (morning and
    evening)
Hò ho ho hó ho hò, why (do you) sleep at (the) age (of) twenty?
Hò ho ho hó ho hò, my child sleep at (the) age (of) twenty
Hò ho ho hó ho hò, why (do you) sleep at (the) age (of) twenty?
Hò ho ho hó ho hò, why (do you) sleep at (the) age (of) twenty?

What could be perceived as a clearer (albeit simplified) translation is provided in the essay "Faces of Remembrance and Forgetting" (used with permission):

She rocks her child, cradling the bullet that turns his wound red.
At twenty, her child went away to [become a] soldier.
And having gone, never came back.
Sleep my child, child of a yellow-skinned mother.
My god, this body once so slight.
Which I, your mother, once carried in my womb,
Which I, your mother, once cradled in my arms,
Why do you sleep at twenty (Tai 2001a:179)

In 1972, "Lullaby" became a hit song in Japan, another country devastated
by war in the twentieth century. The simplified translation of the song's
title, "Lullaby," does not carry the impact of the mother's loss of her son at
the young age of 20 that the literal translation "Sleep, My Child" does. Of
all of Trịnh Công Sơn's songs that glorify motherhood, this one is the most
yin, perhaps, because of its anti-war stance, based not on devastation of
country, but on a mother's loss, which is a metaphor for Vietnam's loss.

Trịnh Công Sơn's music was not performed live in concerts until 1995 in Hanoi, 1996 in Danang, and 1998 in Ho Chi Minh City:

> The [1998] concert [in Ho Chi Minh City], entitled *Những Dấu Chân Không Năm Tháng* (Timeless Footsteps), featured 21 of the most popular love songs written by Trịnh Công Sơn during the past four decades. Now 59 years old, Sơn is Vietnam's master songwriter of melodies related to love and the destiny of human beings. The audience had a golden opportunity to hear Sơn's latest song titled *Tiến Thoái Lưỡng Nan* (Caught in a Dilemma), performed by the composer himself. He wrote the song after recovering from a serious illness last year. (*VNN*, October 13, 1998)

Once again, Vietnam's official English language newspaper presents the government's version of the "truth," that since the revival of Trịnh Công Sơn's music, only his love and destiny songs are performed and published; the others are still banned. The following lyrics of "Như Cánh Vạc Bay" (Like a Flying Heron) are typical of his "approved" songs, in which love and destiny (and despair) are usually intertwined (Trịnh Công Sơn 1998:166–167; translation in original):

> Is light pink as your pink lips?
> Is rain sad as your sad eyes?
> Your hair, tiny hairs,
> Falling down as bobbing waves.
>
> Is wind glad with flying hair?
> Angry clouds asleep on you,
> on your slender shoulders
> like a heron that flies away.
>
> Is light still mad at your lips?
> Is rain still sad in your eyes?
> Once I took you home,
> I knew that was all!
>
> Spring awaits your passing steps.
> Leaves intone your fragrant hands.
> Leaves dry when in wait,
> like man's life which is obscure.
> Where you are, are there all joys?
> Where you are, is sky all blue?
> I feel scores of tears falling down to make a lake.

At the beginning of the twenty-first century and since his death in 2001, Trịnh Công Sơn continues to be the most popular songwriter in Vietnam, and dozens of albums performed by Vietnam's leading pop singers pay tribute to him (and gain their fame) by featuring many of his love and sentimental human destiny songs (but never the anti-war songs).

The songwriter has inspired an entire new generation of Vietnamese and international pop and jazz singers and instrumentalists. In June, 2004, for example, I attended a packed outdoor concert of his music at the Hội Ngộ Club in HCM City's Bình Thạnh district's Bình Quới Tourism Village, performed by Vietnam's best-known jazz musician, saxophonist Trần Mạnh Tuấn, a visiting Australian jazz saxophonist Fulvio Albano, American singer Jeniffer [*sic*] Thomas (*VNN*, June 9, 2004), numerous Vietnamese pop singers, and a smooth jazz backup ensemble (Figure 5.1). Albano explained his love for Trịnh Công Sơn's music: "'I enjoy Sơn and his songs because I've found that Sơn's music is similar to the jazz that I have been involved with. Through his works, I can find new passions and materials to improve my skills'" (ibid.). In addition, on July 9, 2005, the M&Toi popular music listening club featured a program of Trịnh Công Sơn's songs, which were performed by ten singers, including the famous pop stars Kasim Hoàng Vũ, Hồng Nhung, and Cẩm Vân. Literally dozens of CDs of Trịnh Công Sơn's music are now available in CD shops throughout Ho Chi Minh City.

Figure 5.1 An outdoor concert and tribute to Trịnh Công Sơn at Bình Quới Tourism Village in Ho Chi Minh City, June 9, 2004. Italian saxophonist Fulvio Albano (*left*) is one of the guest artists. Note the picture of the songwriter in the upper left hand corner. Photograph by Dale A. Olsen.

As discussed in Chapter 3, a number of Vietnamese pop singers have found the maturity of their expression in the songs of Trịnh Công Sơn: especially Cẩm Vân, Hồng Nhung, Phương Thanh, Mỹ Tam, Mỹ Linh, Kasim, and probably the greatest singer of Trịnh Công Sơn's music, Khánh Ly. The major reason for this is the profundity of his musical style, which allows for a great freedom of expression. Another reason is that his songs are very Vietnamese, precisely because of their freedom of expression, which is basically a rhythmic concept that is similar to the improvisatory nature of some traditional music. Moreover, the melodic content often features fifth and octave leaps that are also characteristic of Vietnamese traditional music. Many Trịnh Công Sơn's songs are between the traditional and contemporary ends of the Popular Music Continuum because of their sentimental nature and the expressions of love and anti-war in their lyrics. Moreover, they are high on the arc of culturation because of their Vietnamese musical traits. Their suitability for jazz interpretation (an American improvisatory concept) reveals both contemporary characteristics and culturation, the latter because some Vietnamese traditional musics also use improvisation.

It remains to be seen if the other members of the patriarchal trilogy, Phạm Duy and Văn Cao, who throughout their careers were similar in spirit and musical output to Trịnh Công Sơn, will acquire similar fame and inspire yet another generation of pop singers and instrumentalists.

POSTWAR PERIOD (1975–1995)

Gerke and Bui Tuyen explain the following about several of the songwriters from the post-American War period, which actually extends into the present as well: "The musicians who reached fame after 1975 have remained to this day firmly anchored in the tradition of the chanson" (1999). As in the period before, American (jazz and popular styles) and other Western influences were also prominent. This was also, however, a period of experimentation by a number of Vietnamese songwriters, who incorporated Vietnamese folk songs and elements of the ethnic minority people of the Central Highlands into their compositions. As such, the popular song movement was somewhat parallel to the movement in traditional music re-creation known as *cải biên* (short for *nhạc dân tộc cải biên*), which attempted to instill elements of national identity and homeland into traditional music.

Four songwriters of the post-American War period stand out as significant (listed chronologically according to their birth dates): Kpa Y Lăng, Bảo Chấn, Nguyễn Cường, and Trần Tiến.

Kpa Y Lăng

Born in 1941, Kpa Y Lăng has a diverse ethnic minority background; his father is Ba Na and his mother is Chăm, two native cultures from highland and coastal central Vietnam, respectively, which have ancient heritages that feature music during ritual and dance contexts. He left his family when he was 13 to study music at the Hanoi Conservatory of Music, and fifty years later (in 2003) he was a researcher at the Vietnam Arts and Culture Research Institute in Ho Chi Minh City. Kpa Y Lăng is included in this section because his songwriting output did not flourish until the late 1990s.

Being somewhat of a self-trained ethnomusicologist in addition to a composer, Kpa Y Lăng returns to his native Tây Nguyên village once a year during the dry season, as he explains: "I miss the windy, hot and dry weather of Tây Nguyên [and] I'm especially happy because I'm called 'già làng *boóc krạ plây*' (village elder) by villagers" (*VNN*, January 14, 2003). The newspaper writer went on to explain the singer's accomplishments in ethnomusicology and composition:

> [Kpa Y Lăng] was the first to discover the country's two first litho-phones [a lithophone is an ancient instrument that is like a loose-keyed marimba, but made with stone slabs for keys], one in Khanh Son and the other in Tuy An in Central Việt Nam. He has composed many songs for ethnic minorities as well as having conducted research on ethnic folk songs and culture in Tây Nguyên. (ibid.)

Kpa Y Lăng is not currently well known as a popular songwriter beyond his use of ethnic minority materials. He is best known as an ethnomusicologist and professor.

Bảo Chấn

Born ca. 1942 in Hanoi, the son of traditional musicians, Bảo Chấn began composing at the age of 16. He did not reach fame until later in his life, a point that he himself feels is unimportant, as he stated in an interview:

> For me categorization by age is out of the question! Composing music can be thought of as a fruit tree growing. Some fruit ripens early, while other fruit ripens later. Some growers harvest the ripe fruit early, but I am among those to record a late crop. I think that at the age of 40–50, a composer's works begin to mature." (*VNN*, January 16, 1999)

Bảo Chấn stated that jazz has been the modern musical form that has most influenced him, and he sees similarities between traditional Vietnamese music and American jazz: "I often think that traditional Vietnamese music has some features like jazz from the US" (ibid.). As a composer of modern music, Bảo Chấn has also noted the importance of technology: "This is a period of music making and song technology which have developed and existed together with the tide of life and advanced technology. At first glance, this phenomenon seems to be flourishing, but in fact, it is a normal part of life" (ibid.). Indeed, technology becomes more and more important for achieving desired tone color variations, especially to attract the younger generation. Bảo Chấn is also a highly skilled mixer, but technology was to become his fall from grace in 2004.

Bảo Chấn reached notable fame with a song titled "Tình Thôi Xót Xa" (Love's No Longer Bitter), which he "composed" in 1991. It became a hit tune in 1992 and continued to be popular when it was repeatedly performed in 1997 by Lam Trường. In April 2004, however, Bảo Chấn was accused of plagiarizing the song from a Japanese composer:

> [Keiko Matsui] recently accused Vietnamese composer Bảo Chấn of copying the tune to her song "Frontier" in his 1992 hit "Tình Thôi Xót Xa." He claims to have written the song earlier in the 1990s, one or two years before Matsui recorded "Frontier". Chấn maintains the song was based on an emotion the two artists must have had in common. Keiko says Chấn picked up the tune after it was recorded with English lyrics as background music for the "Super Mario Brothers" video game. (*VNN*, September 16, 2004)

In an earlier article titled "Chấn apologizes to listeners for copyright violation," both an American song and a Japanese song were given as the sources for Bảo Chấn's hit tune:

> After the Vietnamese Musicians Association (VMA) secretariat issued an official warning to Bảo Chấn for his lack of responsibility, Chấn admitted that he had not composed the song. He said 99 per cent of the song's melody was similar to two songs—"I've Never Been to Me," written by American musician Charlene in 1982, and a Japanese song, "Frontier," written by Keiko Matsui in 1991. The copyright debate began in early April after Japanese music producer Kazu Matsui wrote a letter to the Vietnamese media, alleging that composer Bảo Chấn had copied his wife Keiko's song, "Frontier." "The two versions are exactly the same tune, not only certain sections, but the whole tune is copied," he wrote. The Japanese couple detected the copying after Vietnamese music lovers contacted them. (*VNN*, June 11, 2004)

Bảo Chấn's mixing capabilities and other technological skills tempted him to tweak two foreign songs and call the result his own creation, something that was unethical but not necessarily illegal before the Berne Convention copyright law. The VMA officials believe that Bảo Chấn has spent many years borrowing melodies from other songwriters and blending them into his own creations (ibid.).

Nguyễn Mạnh Cường

Nguyễn Mạnh Cường was born in Hanoi in 1943, but he has lived most of his adult life in Tây Nguyên, studying the music and cultures of many ethnic minority people and composing songs inspired by his experiences. Nguyễn Cường (as he is known) has dedicated himself and his career to creating awareness of Vietnamese indigenous cultures through his modern musical creations, which are mostly in the pop music vein. His music has inspired the development of a special genre called "Tây Nguyên rock," which appeals to many youth of Vietnam because of performances by such famous pop singers as Siu Black, Bonneur Trinh, and Y Moan. Nguyễn Cường's songs often evoke the landscapes and ethnoscapes of the Central Highlands:

> His first song about Tây Nguyên was Nhịp Chiêng Buôn Kơ Siar (The Gong Rhythm of Kơ Siar Village). The song's melody is strong and hot like the Tây Nguyên people, making Cường popular even among the country's soft music fans. With his songs, Cường takes his fans on a highlands trip full of scenes with wild animals, waterfalls, towering trees and springs, and ethnic minority boys and girls working and singing in coffee and corn fields near the mountains. "I feel deeply the wind and sunshine of Tây Nguyên. The land still makes me feel crazy even though I'm familiar with it." (*VNN*, May 2, 2004)

Although his songs do not deal with social issues of Vietnam's ethnic minorities per se, he makes the majority Việt people and others aware of Vietnam's rich ethnic minority heritage and beauty through the process of composing songs that glorify the Bac Bo, Ba Na, Chăm, Ê Đê, Gia Lai, and M'nông. Having them sung by pop singers who are carriers of the ethnic minority traditions helps to perpetuate that awareness.

Thái Bảo explains that Nguyễn Cường's efforts have caused him to be dubbed "the wild man of the forest" (2000), a nickname based solely on the fact that he incorporates Central Highland traditional musical ideas into his popular music compositions. Thái Bảo continues to write how Nguyễn Cường went about immersing himself in the musical and cultural life of Vietnam's indigenous people in the Tây Nguyên:

> [A]fter graduating from the Music Composition Faculty in 1980, Cường returned to the countryside that had inspired a passion within him. He headed for the hills to meet and mix with locals; he studied their cultures and customs and, more importantly, their folk music which covered the spectrum of the Gia Lai people, the M'nông, the Ba Na, the Chăm, and not least, the Ê Đê. He admits, when pressed, that the Ê Đê musical folklore touched him—and deeply. "The Ê Đê have two kinds of songs, ayray and kươt," he explained. "And in one song there is only a

fundamental note, but it has a powerful vitality like the endless words in Khan stories." Cường's songs are attractive, his admirers say, because of their simplicity and their [ability to capture] the traits of Tây Nguyên cultures, while melding with contemporary elements and not neglecting [the composer's] fondness for his new-found home and people. "I have made a blood mixture of two currents of music to compose pieces of music full of vitality," he admits, with a nod to those admirers who have, light-heartedly, dubbed his style Tây Nguyên Rock. (ibid.)

Nguyễn Cường is so familiar with Central Highland culture that indigenous Dac Lac pop singer and Meritorious Artist Y Moan said the following about the songwriter's compositions: "Many of his works are based on folk songs of our ethnic minority groups. He understands our people's lifestyle" (*VNN*, May 2, 2004). Although Cường's creative efforts have occurred several generations later, his musical efforts are analogous to the post-Revolution movement in the visual arts referred to by Hồ Chí Minh as *văn hoá dân tộc* (national culture). He appears to be the only Vietnamese composer of popular music who is the musical equivalent of nationalistic painters who depicted or represented Vietnamese ethnic minority cultures. As such, he is a nationally inspired songwriter, not influenced by the power collective of the communist government, but driven by his own love of the indigenous environment, cultures, and their music and other folkways. That philosophy also places him high in the arc of culturation.

In 2005 Nguyễn Cường changed his style for VTV3's *Con Đường Âm Nhạc* (Road to Music), a program devoted to portraying the careers of famous composers. With his new style, which is based on other types of Vietnamese folk songs, he hopes to remove the stereotype of being a Tây Nguyên composer. His desire is to be a composer for all of Vietnam, as he states: "I do not want to get stuck in just one place when I can extend my arm to hold the whole country" (*VNN*, July 17, 2005).

Trần Tiến

Born in 1947, Trần Tiến, like Nguyễn Cường, has found inspiration from the music of Vietnam's ethnic minorities; two of his songs, for example, are titled "Ngọn lửa cao nguyên" (Flame of the High Plateau) and "Tiếng trống baranưng" (Sound of the Baranưng Drum) (*Việt Nam Cultural Profiles Project* 2004). In addition, however, Trần Tiến writes songs about other geographic regions of Vietnam, about children, the seasons, and much more, including the French chanson style from the French colonial past. Trần Tiến "combines elements of rock, pop, and Vietnamese folk song in his works" (Gerke and Bui Tuyen 1999). One of his most famous songs is "Sắc Màu" (Color), which was recorded by his niece, Trần Thu Hà, as Anh Thư explains:

[F]or pop star Trần Thu Hà, the road to stardom was a long one. . . . Fans thought of her only as the niece of well-known musician Trần Tiến . . . who helped ensure Ha's rise to fame by penning the hit single Sắc Màu (Color). The song turned Hà into the pop star she always dreamed of being. . . . Thousands of new fans bought Sắc Màu, making it one of the biggest hit songs of last year. . . . Romance has always been a popular topic of pop stars past and present. These songs are easier for young people to compose, write and perform. It's not uncommon for singers to make their name from a single love song. Since 1987, romantic songs by composers like Trần Tiến . . . have helped transform the Vietnamese music scene. (2001)

Trần Tiến's songs have been sung by himself and many of Vietnam's top pop singers, and as Nguyễn T. Phong explains, "his songs are very influential among the youth" and people of other age groups in Vietnam (pers. com., 2006). In 2000, for example, he was highly responsible for recording and masterminding an HIV/AIDS awareness CD that reached many people, and in 1997 his song "Last Words" won the first prize in an AIDS-prevention song competition.

POST-SANCTIONS PERIOD (1995 TO PRESENT)

After American President Clinton lifted sanctions in 1994, Vietnamese pop and pop-rock music began to move more rapidly in the direction of modernization (showing technological advancement) and globalization. The following five young songwriters stand out as most influential during this period: Lê Quang, Xuân Phương, Nguyễn Nhật Huy, Trần Kim Ngọc, Trần Lập, and Lê Minh Sơn. They are presented chronologically according to their dates of birth.

Lê Quang

Born in Binh Thuan province in 1968, Lê Quang is one of the most successful pop music composers in Ho Chi Minh City in the early twenty-first century. A bass guitarist, he formerly played and sang with the rock group Da Vàng until 1999, and now plays with the New Friends band, one of the most active groups to accompany pop singers in Ho Chi Minh City in 2005. Moving from rock to pop was an economic decision and was also a way he could have his love songs performed.

Lê Quang is totally self-taught in music. "Where did you learn composition and music?" I asked him: "On the street and through self study," he replied (personal interview, August 2, 2005). The *Việt Nam News* offers more details about the humble and prolific composer:

Returning from military service with no job, Lê Quang originally turned to music for solace but never imagined [it] would become a career. After joining the Da Vàng rock band as a bass guitarist Quang gave everything he had. "Da Vàng created Lê Quang as he is today. Back then it was only music, no profit or fame," he said. "Just passion." Quang only began writing tunes in 1998 when he tried to write Vietnamese lyrics for some Chinese songs. His first song Di Ve Noi Xa (Going Far Away) became an instant classic among young audiences in 1999. Since then Quang has astonishingly composed over 100 songs. "I am happy with what I've achieved in the past 15 years and I plan to continue," he said. (May 10, 2004)

Lê Quang told me in 2005 that he has written more than two-hundred songs, many of which have been sung by the most famous pop singers in Vietnam, such as Mỹ Tâm, Quang Dũng, Thanh Thảo, and others. He describes his style as a combination of traditional and modern rock, and in his lyrics he likes to write about Vietnamese countryside, villages, rivers, trees, historical times in the past, feudalism times, great generals of Vietnam, and so forth. That is not to say, however, that he is interested in the past; he just finds Vietnam's geography and history inspirational. He also likes to write about children as an expression of the future of Vietnam.

Although Lê Quang focuses mostly on the Vietnamese market, he has one song, "We are the Champions," which was commissioned by Pepsi for the SEA (Southeast Asian) Games. Pepsi pays him $1000 each year for the use of the song, which is sung in Vietnamese and English and used for publicity.

Lê Quang is what could be called a "market economy composer" because he composes pop and pop-rock songs that he knows will have great popularity with Vietnam's youth and will sell through their performances by famous pop singers. They are also beautiful, engaging, and meaningful, and above all, in keeping with what the Vietnamese love most about their popular music, they are sentimental. Lê Quang's popularity is a modern-day success story situated in the middle of the Popular Music Continuum.

Xuân Phương

Born in Hanoi in 1973, Xuân Phương studied composition and piano at the National Conservatory of Music in his hometown. Upon graduation in 1999, he began teaching at the army's Arts and Culture College in Hanoi and shortly became known as a film composer: "His two songs, *Mong Ước Kỷ Niệm Xưa* (Remember the Old Memories) from the television film *Xin Hãy Tin Em* (Please Believe Me) and *Lời Ru Tình Mẹ* (Lullaby on Motherhood) from the film *Của Để Dành* (For a Rainy Day) were . . . among [the] favorite songs on radio and television" (*VNN*, March 11, 1999). Xuân

Phương has found inspiration in composing for films, as he reflects back on his 1999 success: "The easy part about composing songs for films was that I was not constrained by the details of the film. I understood the screenplay, and I just expressed the idea I got from each shot. . . . Composing music for films was a good chance for me to channel my inspiration and create songs from it" (ibid.).

It is common in certain Asian countries, such as India and Japan, for pop songs sung by pop singers in films to become hits. In Vietnam, several pop singers have starred in films and some of the songs they performed in their films have made it to the charts. For a film composer's songs to become well known, they also require performance by well-known singers. Xuân Phương's success with his song "Mong Ước Kỷ Niệm Xưa" (Remember the Old Memories), from the television film *Xin Hãy Tin Em*, was largely because it was specifically composed for a particular female pop trio from Hanoi, as he explains: "When I read the screenplay of *Xin Hãy Tin Em*—a story about the lifestyle of a group of female students—I wrote *Mong Ước Kỷ Niệm Xưa* for the 3A Trio" (ibid.). The use of already famous pop musicians in a film almost assures the success of the songs they perform in that film.

Although Xuân Phương also hopes to write songs just to be sung, without having to rely on visual and literary dimensions, he understands why he has been successful through film score composition, as he explains:

> Bringing music to audiences in this way brings more favor than the usual way. Audiences listen to the music while they are watching the scenes, so it is [easy] to win over audiences' hearts. I am lucky that my music has been introduced through films . . . I would also like to bring my music to audiences by inviting singers to perform my works. The most important thing is finding the right singers to perform my songs and the timing of their releases. (*VNN*, March 11, 1999)

Writing music for films will probably never lead to fame and glory for the composer in Vietnam. As Xuân Phương realizes, permanence as a songwriter depends on live performances and subsequent publications via recordings and print, especially given Vietnam's new copyright law of 2004.

Nguyễn Nhật Huy

Born in 1975 in Ca Mau, the southernmost province of Vietnam, Nguyễn Nhật Huy began composing at age 10, claiming that his first musical experiences were his grandmother's lullabies and that she inspired him to compose (*VNN*, September 2, 2001). Huy studied composition at the Ho Chi Minh City Conservatory of Music, although his degrees are in banking and economics from Ho Chi Minh City's Economics University and Banking

Institute, and he has worked as a trained securities trader. "When I was a student, I wanted to work in the stock market. But I changed my mind because I love music more than anything," he explained (ibid.).

In 2001, Nguyễn Nhật Huy won Vietnam's prestigious *Làn Sóng Xanh* (Blue Wave) Award, a recognition by thousands of fans who vote for their favorite songwriter, for his song titled "Love a Stranger": "The performance by Trần Thu Hà's of countryside music *Thương Nho Nguoi Dung*, 'Love a Stranger', won 4000 votes from listeners to the Sunday Blue Wave Radio Voice of HCM City program" [sic] (ibid.). He said: "*Thuong Nhớ Người Dưng* [Love a Stranger] is my favorite song. The Blue Wave Award has encouraged me to permanently pursue music" (ibid.).

Trần Kim Ngọc

Composer Trần Kim Ngọc was born in 1976, and she is one of the very few Vietnamese female songwriters to gain fame in a seemingly male-dominated field. A 1999 graduate in composition from the Hanoi Conservatory of Music, she has been a member of the International Association of Women Musicians (IAWM) since 1995 (*VNN*, March 18, 1999). She has participated in international music events as Vietnam's premier young female composer, taking part in a festival in Köln, Germany, with 49 other female musicians from around the world in which an entire concert consisted of her compositions.

Ngọc began studying piano at the Hanoi Conservatory of Music when she was 8 years old, and continued until she was 15. Her father, renowned composer Trần Ngọc Xương, however, was her first teacher, to whom she owes a great debt (ibid.). She was 19 when her father died, and she composed an instrumental work titled *Phục Hồn* (Summon) to express her love for him. She continued to write works for Western orchestral instruments, and after *Phục Hồn* she wrote "a chamber music concerto titled *Day Thi* (Puberty) expressing her strong belief in a bright future for Việt Nam" (ibid.).

Although best known as a composer of concert music in Western style, Trần Kim Ngọc is also known as a songwriter, writing her first song in 1988 at age 12. She explains: "That song was a present to my teacher on Teachers' Day" (ibid.). She has written dozens of pop songs since then, and her 1998 song *Với M* (With Mother) was chosen as "one of the outstanding items of the second ASEAN Golden Vocalists Festival in Hà Nội [in 1998] when sung by pop star Mỹ Linh, [and] is now one of the nation's favorite modern-day songs" (ibid.).

Trần Lập

I discussed Trần Lập as the lead singer, lead guitarist, music director, and mastermind of the famous Hanoi-based rock group Bức Tường (The Wall) in Chapter 4. However, he will probably be best known as a composer/ songwriter, especially for the songs he composed for his band.

In 2003 Trần Lập was interviewed by Yến Anh (YA), and he (TL) revealed several important things about his role as a composer:

> *YA:* So how do you come up with your songs?
> *TL:* [It all starts] with an idea. Then I link the idea with an event, build up some inspiration, and do some careful research. Then I write the music. But sometimes, I'm not satisfied with my work. Generally speaking, inspiration plays a very important role in my songs. (*VNN*, September 23, 2003)

Trần Lập's inspiration has included Vietnamese social issues, national events and epics, and even the birth of his son. Inspirational issues and events for him include those that are heroic, like the American War; those that are tragic, like the fire, injuries, and deaths in the Blue Club in Ho Chi Minh City; those that are mytho-historic, like legendary stories about Trong Thuy and My Chau; and others, including those that are beautiful. "The few Vietnamese rockers who write their own music and lyrics are careful to make sure that the words are upbeat, not sinister. 'We compose our songs in a different way. . . . Everything is about the beauty of society'" (Stocking 2003).

Although rock music has been around for some time in Vietnam, even a talented songwriter like Trần Lập has not received commissions to write songs, as he explains in the Yen Anh interview:

> *YA:* Some of your songs have been popular on such Vietnamese TV programs as The Dawn for Students 2000 and Road to Glory I and II. Have you been contracted to write songs?
> *TL:* I have never composed a song on contract. But that doesn't mean I never will. I actually hope I will. I think all world-famous composers have written under contract whether it [is] for a movie or an event. Composers who don't receive any contracts, to a certain extent, don't have that much talent to begin with. (*VNN*, September 23, 2003)

For ten years Trần Lập has led, performed in, and composed music for Bức Tường, and the reality is that he has not had the time to compose songs on contract because, like his colleagues in the band, he maintains his job as an architect. "I'm sure there will be a time in the future," Trần Lập explained, when "playing rock 'n' roll can be a real job" (ibid.)

Trần Lập is one of Vietnam's most talented young songwriters of the early twenty-first century. He is a contemporary artist of the highest quality, yet he is a composer who knows the constraints imposed upon musicians by the communist government. As a result, his personal creativity and culturation guide him on his popular musical journey through the traditional environment of Hanoi, the cradle of Vietnamese communism. To borrow from Ben Stocking, Trần Lập rocks—but carefully (2003).

Lê Minh Sơn

Also born in Hanoi in 1975, Lê Minh Sơn is the youngest of the composers chosen for this study. A classically trained guitarist very adept in jazz, he was a precocious child, as he suggested to the "Culture Vulture" interviewer:

> My father gave me my first music lesson when I was three years old. By six, I was learning the guitar and after two years, I enrolled [age 8] at Ha Noi National Conservatory of Music. I wrote my first song at twelve. After graduation, I studied music in France. Although my advisors encouraged me to stay in France for my career, I returned to Viet Nam. I love my homeland and its people, and try to express this in my songs. Although skilled at the guitar, my passion is song-writing. Playing the guitar helps stoke my writing. (*VNN*, September 23, 2004)

Lê Minh Sơn has also been greatly influenced by the folk music of northern Vietnam, which he has carefully researched. Yet, as a composer he does not copy folklore, but writes original compositions that are inspired by his native land and people. The "Culture Vulture" interviewer (CV) asked him (LMS) questions specifically about his inspirational sources as a composer:

> CV: Why did you choose to break the mold and blend folk music with modern styles?
> LMS: I've been writing this way since I was small. I think the style chose me.
> CV: How long does it take you to write a song? What inspires you?
> LMS: It depends. I normally work quickly. I once wrote a song in 20 minutes, although it took my whole life to gather inspiration for it. [The song titled] Trang Khuyet (the Crescent), however, took me 10 years to write. I wrote the first part when I was 17, and only just finished it. I'm not dependent on inspiration. I hate writers who say they wait for inspiration. I think inspiration comes with spontaneous discovery, but also hard work. To write a meaningful song, inspiration and emotion are necessary, but in the end, a writer must use his mind. Professional writers don't wait for inspiration. I've written hundreds of songs. Some people tell me to release them gradually, but I want to capitalize on this new popularity. (ibid.)

Lê Minh Sơn has written songs for many pop singers, especially those from Hanoi. In 2002 one of his students at the Hanoi Arts College, female pop singer Phạm Ngọc Khue (born 1981), won the *Sao Mai* (Morning Star) star search contest with a song he composed. When the "Culture Vulture" interviewer asked her, "Did Lê Minh Sơn, composer of your trademark song Bên Bờ Ao Nhà Mình, shoot you to fame?", she responded:

> You could say that. Sơn also manages our band. I was exposed to folk music at an early age. As a child, my favorite thing to do was sing the northern folk tunes that my mother [had] sung as lullabies. However, it wasn't until I met Sơn that I began to mix my music with Latin and jazz influences. This gave birth to a new me, a Ngọc Khue who was no longer purely a folk singer. Many reviewers praised our band's chemistry, saying my voice suits the music. Others were more effusive and called the song I sang in the final round of Sao Mai something brand new and exciting. (*VNN*, June 25, 2002)

Lê Minh Sơn has been personally recognized for his creativity and was selected as "Musician of the Year 2004 by *Thể Thao Văn Hóa* (Culture & Sport) newspaper. Sơn continues to combine folk and contemporary music [with] support from diva Thanh Lam" (*VNN*, February 28, 2005), for whom he composes and with whom he often performs (Figure 5.2). In late 2004, their combined efforts in the CD *Nang Len* (Sunrise) were recognized in a gala public concert held November 6 at the HCM City Opera House, where they were accompanied by the Vietnam Symphony Orchestra (*VNN*, November 4, 2004). One of the songs performed in the concert, "*Da Trong Chong*" (Turned to Stone), was accompanied by a Vietnamese folk music orchestra; Lê Minh Sơn explained: "I invited two renowned *ken bop* (an instrument used for funerals) artists from the Việt Nam Tuong Theatre to accompany the song" (ibid.). Lê Minh Sơn has also made arrangements of Trịnh Công Sơn's music, as he explained: "Long ago, I dreamed of combining Son's music with 19th century European classical compositions" (ibid.).

With the exposure gained by composing for Thanh Lam and often performing with her on stage as well as on her CDs, Lê Minh Sơn has made a name for himself as Vietnam's most original composer/songwriter in the early twenty-first century. Thanh Lam calls his music very intense (ibid.), and much of that intensity comes from the ideas he has developed from his years of experiencing and learning about the folk and traditional music of northern Vietnam. Lê Minh Sơn is a highly culturated composer of the twenty-first century, just as Nguyễn Cường was of the twentieth, yet his style demonstrates an individuality and originality unlike that of any other songwriter in Vietnam (several of Lê Minh Sơn's recent creations that were composed for Thanh Lam are musically discussed in Chapter 3 in the subsection about Thanh Lam). The "Culture Vulture" asked him, "What's your next project?"

Figure 5.2   Lê Minh Sơn (*right*) accompanying Thanh Lam (*left*) on one of his songs at the M&Tôi popular music listening club in Ho Chi Minh City, July 23, 2005. Photograph by Dale A. Olsen.

to which he responded: "I plan to write a modern opera with 18 songs of four different genres: ca tru (a traditional chamber music), prewar, revolutionary and modern. I will invite a symphony [orchestra] and pop bands to perform it." Lê Minh Sơn may have an even greater career ahead of him.

SONGWRITING CONTESTS

Because there is so much interest in songs and singing in Vietnam, songwriting contests are prevalent and important to the culture of contemporary popular music, not as big business, but as a way of nourishing public awareness. Beginning in the 1990s and through the mid 2000s, however, songwriting contests are mostly sanctioned and controlled by the government. This concurs with Street's analysis, as he writes: "[S]tates, political parties and movements have used (and abused) popular music in pursuit of their own interests and goals. . . . governments . . . have both censored and sponsored popular music in an attempt to manage dissent or create consensus" (1986:9). Songwriting contests are particularly important to the communist government of Vietnam because of its belief in the power of lyrics to educate and motivate the masses.

During the 1990s, a national songwriting competition called "Looking forward to a Better Brighter Tomorrow" was especially popular in Hanoi when Vietnam was developing its market economy and gaining world economic attention. The third contest of that series, which was sponsored by Electrolux, took place on November 13, 1995, and "included more than 200 song entries by both professional and amateur writers. [Fifteen songs won awards, and songs] with various themes such as love, anti-war, AIDS and environmental protection were performed by professional singers from the Youth Theater" (*VNN*, November 15, 1995). The competition, for songwriters between the ages of 15 and 30, formed "part of a UN funded world-wide youth project, the Global Youth Network. This project [was] designed to encourage cultural diversity and international cooperation [by] using music as the uniting factor" (*VNN*, November 12, 1995). Two aspects, in particular, were emphasized in this songwriting competition: youth culture and the importance of song lyrics. The underlying messages hoped to be transmitted through the songs, as determined by the government, were cultural diversity and international cooperation, the reality of particular health and social issues, and the ubiquitous favorite topic of everyone—love.

Noble causes and social issues are of concern to any modern society, and indeed, throughout history and in much of the world, song lyrics have spread news, expressed concerns, educated, motivated, inspired weeping, caused laughter, provoked fighting, and much more. Lyrics, however, are often censored by governments, condemned by religious groups, praised by some, and feared by others. In Vietnam, lyrics are often self-censored by songwriters, because songwriters and performers alike realize that all published and/or performed songs will ultimately require governmental approval. Again, Street explains the following, not specifically about Vietnam, but certainly including it within his analysis: "The censor's concerns seem to be exclusively with the lyrics. . . . The result of such practices is that both the musicians and the industry develop a system of self-censorship. Because lyric sheets have to be submitted in advance, many artists regard it as pointless to attempt to write overtly political songs" (1986:20). The aspect of self-censorship is of utmost importance to the smooth running of Vietnam's music industry. It is also one of the reasons why love is the most common topic for song lyrics; few can argue against or find fault with sentimental love.

LYRICS AND SOCIAL ISSUES

Over forty years ago, Alan P. Merriam rote the following about the importance of studying song texts or lyrics in ethnomusicology: "One of the most obvious sources for the understanding of human behavior in connection with music is the song text" (1964:187). What can we learn about

Vietnam's youth subcultures from the lyrics of their songs? Probably less than one would hope from the actual words, because of the censorship by Vietnam's Ministry of Information and Culture and self-censoring by the songwriters and singers, which have removed most if not all human behavior issues.

The *Việt Nam News* and other newsprint media, however, have occasionally discussed the lyrics of popular songs in articles relating to human and social issues in Vietnam. In the remainder of this chapter, I present some of these discussions and place them into a number of topical categories. In addition, I discuss several Vietnamese popular songs in the rock genre that deal with particular social issues, are sung in English, and have English lyrics included within their CD albums. The song topics I have delineated include the following: war and liberation; love and romance; HIV/AIDS and SARS; sports and the paragames for the disabled; regional/transnational unity; and social solidarity, human character, and change.

Songs about War and Liberation

Although songs about war (both anti- and pro-war) are currently not being composed in Vietnam to the extent they were during the 1960s, because the country is at peace after hundreds of years of foreign domination, they are a part of the politics of memory and form the basic *yang* (to again use Jamieson's idea) musical repertoire that is favored, encouraged, and supported by the communist government and the official music administrators of the Vietnam Musicians' Association. Likewise, songs about liberation and reunification of Vietnam are more nostalgic reminders of past struggles than voices of the present, although the government tries to retain them as a part of the country's collective memory. In the following paragraphs I attempt to demonstrate that element of hegemony as an aspect of memory politics, rather than current reality.

A number of articles in the *Việt Nam News* from the late 1990s glorify past composers of nationalistic and patriotic songs. One such composer is Phan Huỳnh Điểu, called "A giant of Vietnamese Music" by Phung Quốc Thụy, who wrote:

> Phan Huỳnh Điểu is one of the greatest composers of modern Vietnamese music. Fifty-three years ago, Điểu began his career with *Trâu Cau* (The Betel-nut): a song that still remains vivid in the memories of many of his compatriots. During his recent trip to France in 1991, an elderly fan asked the performance organizers to present the song, as she believed his collection would be incomplete without it. So powerful is [this] song of half a century ago. It reminds one of family and home. Moreover, it recalls the national community that has stood so close and unfaltering. With the romantic yet simple rhythms of the song, it penetrates deep into one's heart and soul. Love for music and love for

his nation were consistent themes of Điểu's compositions despite his lack of musical training. (*VNN*, April 13, 1997)

In addition to nationalism and patriotism, Phan Huỳnh Điểu also composed songs about human love, which to him is inseparable from love of country and love for life. In the same article, Phan Quốc Thùy describes several of Điểu's songs from the 1960s, 1970s, and 1980s that show the inseparability of love for life, country, and one another [i.e. individual human love, between man and woman]:

At the beginning of the 1960s, Điểu composed another hit when his *Những ánh sao đêm* (Stars of the Night) was introduced. The most popular song of 1963, it breathed new optimism and love for life: representing the Northern people's feelings during their cause of socialist construction. The wind continued to blow when Điểu [composed] *Hành khúc ngày và đêm* (March of Days and Nights) in 1972.
"Ngày và đêm bên nhau những đêm ngày chiến đấu
Đêm ngày trong chiến đấu anh với em vẫn ở gần nhau"
(Day and night together we fight;
night and day together, you and I are still close).
Moving from a clear fanfare in *Đoàn giải phóng quân* of the olden days, Điểu borrowed more from the Western style of marching songs. However, love remains forever his rhythm.
Also in 1972, Điểu wrote *Bóng cây K'nia* (Shadows of the K'nia tree) after 10 years of selecting the right tunes and notes. This song clearly confirms his hidden talents which were later shown in *Anh ở đầu sông, em cuối sông* (I am at one end of the river, you are at the other [1978]), *Ở hai đầu nỗi nhớ* (At the ends of longing [1983]), *Sợi nhớ, sợi thương* (String of love, string of longing [1978]), etc.
Nguyễn Xuân Khoát, a composer of the time, once called Điểu a "composer of love." In Điểu's songs, love is never unhappy and painful even when it breaks. It is always crystal clear and warm. That's the kind of Vietnamese love. That's the real Phan Huỳnh Điểu. (ibid.)

This short music history lesson published by the *Việt Nam News* is not just propaganda, however, because, like the love songs of Trịnh Công Sơn, the love songs of Phan Huỳnh Điểu are about love of life and the longing brought about by separation caused by war. The longing to be together again with a loved one is emphasized more than individual human love and tenderness when two people are together.

Another composer of war and liberation songs is Huy Du, who also fits into the "*yang* subsystem" (espoused by Jamieson 1993:15) of overt memory politics. During the American War, Huy Du was a colonel in the People's Army of Vietnam and the secretary general of the Vietnam Musicians' Association. "Before that, he was head of Political General

Department's Dance and Song Troupe for more than 10 years" (*VNN*, April 12, 2000). During a concert in Ho Chi Minh City on April 30 (Liberation Day), 2000, Huy Du's songs (mostly marching songs) were featured with great success:

> The audience of mostly war veterans and students was mesmerized by both Du's patriotic songs and those with romantic themes. "Young people like love songs but are also interested in the words of songs written during the war," said retired colonel Du as he interacted with the audience. "Patriotic songs and marches are popular with many young people who have never experienced the hardship of war," said Du. (*VNN*, April 12, 2000)

Contrary to my argument about forgetting (or not knowing) the past among the youth of Vietnam, this verbal picture portrays the youth (whose ages are not given) as patriotic young people who remember the American War and the liberation of Vietnam. It is hyperbole, however, because the truth is that most of them had not been born by 1975. Huy Du, however, explained his feelings to the audience during the performance:

> "Inspired by reality and the people's fighting spirit in the war for national re-unification, we musicians wrote patriotic songs which now represent a period the country went through," said Du, responding to enquiries as to the inspiration for his songs. "During the war, we also dreamed of romance and fell in love but at that time people's love was more serene and it was unique because our relationships were greatly influenced by our love for the fatherland and the people," said 75-year-old Du whose love songs like *Tình Em* (Romance for you), *Hát Nữa Đi Em* (Sing again, my sweetheart) and *Hoa Mộc Miên* (Mộc Miên flower) still appeal to many, both young and old.
>
> "Love songs, with their sentimental lyrics, now dominate the country's popular music scene, but they focus too much on individual feelings and problems, especially loneliness," said Du. "I do not advocate any kind of music—we cannot urge the youth to sing and listen to patriotic songs, but I am concerned about the number of young people who listen to sad songs at home and at bars and clubs. This type of song emphasizes our problems and creates depression rather than uplifting the spirit," Du told his audience. (ibid.)

Once again, love songs, "with their sentimental lyrics," are discussed as having great importance for the Vietnamese youth of the twenty-first century, as in the twentieth. Emphasis on the individual, his/her desires, feelings, and problems, however, are *yin* characteristics according to Jamieson (1993:19), which, to the Vietnamese government, are less-than-desirable attributes.

Songs about Love and Romance

According to the top Vietnamese governmental musical officials, most of the lyrics of pop songs at the turn of the millennium suggest that the Vietnamese youth are lonely and obsessed with love:

> "Music taste has changed. Hà Nội youth now prefer songs of loneliness while love songs dominate HCM City," says People's Artist Nguyễn Văn Thương. "I don't advocate any particular sort of music. But now, many musicians, most of them young, are writing love songs that we can hear everywhere at anytime," Việt Nam Musicians' Association Deputy Secretary General, Hồng Đăng, said. "The music scene is dominated by soft music which is easier for young people to compose, write and perform with romance being the most popular topic," said Đăng.
>
> The common street expression for such music is "cheesy" (uỷ mị), and HCM City fans have taken to writing to newspapers complaining that concerts are dominated by it. "Verses of many songs lack aesthetic, literary or any philosophical meaning," Nguyễn Văn Tỳ, one of Vietnam's most well-known musicians, says. "There are sentences like *Con gái bây giờ hay giả vờ, thích gì vờ* (Girls now like feigning, like pretending . . .)." Ty offers as an example. Singers and the verses they have to sing have become topics of discussion not only with local newspapers but also by the Vietnam Musicians' Association (VNA). (*VNN*, September 9, 1999)

Instead, the governmental officials (i.e. the administrators in the Vietnam Musicians' Association) advocate songs whose texts deal with national construction, as Nguyễn Văn Thương continued to explain: "Music performances seldom feature songs highlighting the task of national construction. Songs about laborers (or ordinary workers) have never been performed at music concerts" (ibid.) Therefore, he advocates the performances of more patriotic songs, although he realizes that such songs lost much of their popularity after 1975 and that young people in 1999 were only children or not even born yet during the American War. Thus, the government's call for nationalistic and patriotic lyrics falls on deaf ears, as the article puts it, and songs about loneliness and love have come to dominate the musical tastes of the youth.

Nevertheless, governmental leaders continue to express their musical ideas and to exert their persuasive verbiage (if not forceful action), as explained in the conclusion of the same article:

> The VMA recently, in cooperation with the Vietnam Labor Federation, launched a song-writing drive focusing on labor and workers. "It's a good initiative. But there are many things needed for a song to become popular with the masses," said VMA's [Deputy Secretary

General, Hồng] Đăng, who is optimistic about the future of Vietnamese music. "VMA now has more than 400 professional musicians and composers, authors of many thousands of songs. If we make a careful selection, we'll have one thousand good songs sufficient for live music performances, radio and television. Only a handful of love songs performed at live concerts should not be considered the whole country's music image." (ibid.)

The "handful of love songs" and their sentimental aesthetics, however, form a musical thread woven throughout the Popular Music Continuum, from the government's traditional desires (nationalistic and patriotic songs) to the upstart contemporary characteristics of the Vietnamese youth (rock and foreign musical expressions). This musical thread of love songs is a tremendous musical force that allows for the past and the present, the communist government and the youth, and the traditional and the contemporary to exist in harmony.

Much of the success of the music thread of love songs is due to the pop singers themselves. Vietnamese musician Phúng Quốc tries to answer the following question posed by a writer for the *Việt Nam News*—"do [the fans] love the words or the singer?":

"Some songs are very lightweight or feature tales of painful romance—usually unrequited. And because pop stars sing the words, their fans identify them with the meaning of the songs," [Phúng Quốc] said.

The words of one fan certainly prove Quốc's point: "I didn't like . . . *E-mail Tình Yêu* (E-mail Love), which was written by young musician Trần Minh Phi. But singer Đan Trường changed my mind, because he sings the song so wonderfully." Romance has always been a popular topic of pop stars past and present. These songs are easier for young people to compose, write and perform. It's not uncommon for singers to make their name from a single love song. . . . [However, m]usicians and singers must be encouraged to write and perform love songs with high artistic values. It's wrong to think you can be the best singer or musician with only a romantic ballad. (May 9, 2001)

Many of the ideas voiced by Vietnamese pop stars as presented in their musical stories in Chapter 3 also emphasize or suggest a significant importance given to songs of romance.

Nevertheless, many of the singers explain that their love songs and lyrics (i.e. poetry) are a continuation of the sentimental songs of the past. John Charlot captures the essence of Vietnamese tenderness with his description of Vietnamese poetry:

Vietnamese poetry is characteristically tender and lyrical, celebrating quiet living and adolescent love. . . . The Vietnamese see themselves as basically poetic: sensitive, open, vulnerable to beauty, and hungry for affection. This poetic character renders them personal, private, even individualistic, anxious to cultivate "the beautiful things in life" in tranquility. (1989: 449)

Even though Hồ Sĩ Khoách complained in 2002 about the youth's greater interest in making money than reading or writing poetry (Lamb 2002:71), many of the Vietnamese contemporary popular songs about love and romance seem to fulfill that innate Vietnamese desire for *duyên* (charm) and sentimentality.

Songs about HIV/AIDS and SARS

Perhaps related to the youth's preference for love songs and even their feelings of loneliness, is the startling epidemic of HIV/AIDS cases in Vietnam. Caused by unprotected sex and heroin addiction, the number of Vietnamese afflicted with the disease is increasing each year, as Rachel Morris reported: "The [Vietnamese] Ministry of Health reports that 56,495 people are known to have HIV in Vietnam, although there is widespread consensus among people working in the field that the real figure is closer to 150,000. Over 60 percent of the known cases are injecting drug users" (*VNN*, December 8, 2002). Stephen McNally writes that the Ministry of Health estimates an increase to 200,000 persons with HIV by 2005, and that over 50 percent will be between the ages of 10 and 24 years old (2003:113).

Efforts have been made by Vietnamese songwriters, pop singers, and the music industry to create awareness of the HIV/AIDS problem and teach the public about prevention. In 2000 a CD featuring songs and advice from a number of Vietnam's pop singers was released by CARE Viet Nam. It was intended to raise public awareness of and especially educate the male population of Vietnam about sexually transmitted diseases (*VNN*, July 3, 2000). Titled *Khát Vọng Tuổi Xuân* (Youth's Desire), the CD was produced by the Phương Nam Film Company in cooperation with singer/songwriter Trần Tiến. The CD features the following ten most popular songs in Vietnam, listed with their performers: "Em Muốn Sống Bên Anh Trọn Đời" (I want to live with you forever) by Siu Black; "Góe Phố Dịu Dàng" (Graceful Street Corners) by the White Dresses Trio; "Hương Ngọc Lan" (Magnolia Fragrance) by Mỹ Linh; "Khát Vọng" (Desire) performed by Thanh Lam; and "Lời Nói Cuối" (Last Words) by Trần Tiến (ibid.). As an instructive CD as well as an entertaining one, it includes talking:

Besides the music, the pop singers talk about using condoms to reduce the risk of AIDS and voice their opinions on sex and HIV. "I got a letter from an HIV sufferer when I was in Tây Nguyên (Central Highlands) on vacation. The letter moved me deeply," Tiến said. The writer said he was in the final stage of AIDS and that he dared not meet his mother or his girl friend for fear that they would reject him. He asked me to write a song to communicate his message: "Don't die young like me." Inspired by the letter, Tiến wrote "Last Words" which won him the first prize in the anti-HIV song competition held in Viet Nam in 1997. (ibid.)

The CD also includes a booklet containing basic information about HIV/AIDS, including the mailing addresses of the advisory and support services for HIV and AIDS victims, as La Long writes: "CARE's 'Men in the Know' program is the first sexual health project by the [CARE] organization aimed specifically at men in Vietnam. The program is funded by the Australian government organization AusAID [Australian Government Agency for International Development]" (*Saigon Times Daily News* July 05, 2000).

Other musical efforts to create public awareness about HIV/AIDS prevention include public performances, such as a 2002 concert in Hanoi titled *Live and Let's Live Together*, affiliated with World AIDS Day, a time of awareness encouraged and supported by the United Nations (*VNN*, November 30, 2002). The concert featured personal stories of HIV victims, with the purpose of ending stigma and discrimination against those carrying the disease, as Laurent Zessler, director of the UNAIDS program in Vietnam, said: "HIV/AIDS-related stigma and discrimination rank among the biggest and most pervasive barriers blocking effective response to the AIDS epidemic. . . . De-stigmatizing HIV/AIDS at all levels of society will encourage more open discussion and a better understanding of how to avoid infection" (ibid.). Several of Vietnam's most famous pop singers performed, and the concert was broadcast nationwide on Vietnam Television.

In November 2003, the World AIDS Day Concert took place in Hanoi as a joint effort with the International Day for Physically Challenged Persons and International Volunteer Day (*VNN*, November 26, 2003). Held in Thống Nhất Park, four Hanoi-based expatriate bands performed—Deputies, Irreflexible, Sound Advice, and Sun Red River—with Vietnamese jazz musician Quyền Văn Minh and singer Quang Vinh. Double billed as *Live and Let Live* and *Voice of Our Own*, the purpose of the concert was twofold: to foster acceptance for people with HIV/AIDS and to create understanding about disabled people and their desire for independence.

Songs about HIV/AIDS are not only about prevention through safe sex; they are also about the need to understand and end discrimination towards those afflicted with the disease. Public awareness is essential in both areas. Perhaps the 2003 approach to meet jointly with two other social awareness groups was an attempt by the HIV/AIDS organization to attract a larger public. Many members of the Vietnamese public, as in most regions of the world where HIV/AIDS has reached epidemic proportions, are afraid of those afflicted with the disease. Dr. Hoàng Thị Tuyết

Minh, the director of Hanoi's Hải Âu Club (a drop-in center for drug users, many of whom have HIV/AIDS, funded by Family Health International), for example, explained that "Many families refuse to let a drug user or an HIV patient live in their house" (*VNN*, December 8, 2002). The musical recordings and public events are efforts to inform and teach the public (primarily other young people) to be accepting of their peers who suffer with the disease.

More recently, Vietnam, like other Asian countries, has had dangerous encounters with SARS. Unlike HIV/AIDS, SARS is not a social issue because it is not attributed to personal or group behavior. Thus, songs have not been composed to encourage prevention measures or to create public awareness but have been composed and sung to honor those who have died of SARS, especially the Italian physician and public health specialist, Dr. Carlo Urbani, who first recognized the illness:

> Urbani was trained as a medical doctor, and worked for the World Health Organization (WHO) as a public health specialist. Urbani diagnosed a mysterious illness in a patient at the French Hospital on February 28, 2003, recognizing the irregularity of the symptoms immediately, and took decisive action. By immediately quarantining the hospital and working with the WHO and the Ministry of Health in Vietnam to put the city under containment control, Urbani saved many innocent lives. A month and a day after his initial diagnosis, Dr. Carlo Urbani passed away from complications from that same mystery illness, SARS. As UN secretary General Kofi Annan said, "It is the cruelest of ironies that he [Urbani] lost his own life to SARS while seeking to safeguard others from the disease." (*VNN*, March 27, 2004)

In honor of his achievements, sacrifice, and death, a memorial concert was organized and presented on March 29, 2004, in the Hanoi Opera House. Famed pop singer, Mỹ Linh, performed twelve songs, including two Italian operatic favorites, "Con Te Partiro" and "O Sole Mio," sung with her daughter in Italian (*VNN*, March 27, 2004).

Songs for Sports and the Paragames for the Disabled

Although sporting activities and events are not social issues in themselves, athletic events for the disabled are. Vietnam calls these *paragames* (also written *para games*), which are similar to the Special Olympics held in the United States. Moreover, when paragames occur as world events, such as the World Cup or the SEA Games, then they become not only social issues but also political ones. The playing of sports is an activity that is highly favored by the Vietnamese government. During its Ninth Congress in 2001, for example, the Communist Party of Vietnam spelled out the value of sports in Article VI.1. (see Chapter 2).

Two songs written by two composers were selected as official songs for the 22nd Southeast Asian Games (SEA) and the ASEAN Paragames II in Hanoi in 2002: "Vì Một Thế Giới Ngày Mai" (For the World of Tomorrow) by Quang Vinh and "Chào Paragames Hà Nội" (Welcome Paragames Hà Nội) by Nguyễn Dỗ:

> Vinh's song celebrates the ability of athletics to encourage peace and friendship through athletics. "No one loves sport more than the young," said Quang Vinh. "They're the most passionate and impartial audiences, and their love for sport encourages them to live and work better. More songs on sport need to be written." . . . Nguyễn Dỗ, a disabled veteran in Hanoi, . . . combines Vietnamese traditional tunes and modern songs. Like Vinh, Dỗ uses simple words that can be easily translated into English. His aim to help spread the word about Vietnam, its people and its disabled, particularly in South East Asia. "We want to share our hardships with Vietnamese and foreign players who have to overcome obstacles to live, work, and play sport," said Nguyễn Dỗ, who runs a small shuttlecock factory that employs . . . wounded soldiers and the disabled. "For players at Paragames II, my song praises the disabled who face many challenges integrating into the community," said the 70-year-old veteran. (*VNN*, August 22, 2003)

Some of the Party's ideas were also echoed by participating musicians at the 22nd SEA Games and the ASEAN Paragames II: "Kỳ Phương, a member of the HCM City-based Techno band, said that . . . he and his friends like to sing 'Vì Một Thế Giới Ngày Mai' and 'Chào Paragames Hà Nội' because the songs, with strong melodies, 'bring faith, hope and energy to everyone'" (ibid.).

Other sporting events in Vietnam also attract songwriters and pop singers who find a particular excitement in sports songs:

> Thousands of football fans were surprised when pop star Mỹ Tâm recently performed the song "Niềm Tin Chiến Thắng" (Believe in the Victory) at the final round of the National U-21 Football Cup at An Giang Province's Long Xuyên Stadium. Created by young musician Lê Quang, the song is one of few on sport activities. "Our fans are getting bored with sentimental songs about loneliness and unrequited love. We now want musicians to write songs based on new topics like sport," he said. [Kỳ] Phương's dream is to be selected to sing "Vì Một Thế Giới Ngày Mai" or "Chào Paragames Hà Nội" before local and foreign audiences. Top singers like Thanh Lam, Hồng Nhung, Trần Thu Hà and Mỹ Tâm are also interested in singing at opening ceremonies of key sporting events in the Southeast region. (ibid.)

Though similar, perhaps, to the Super Bowl and other American football game halftime shows, the desires of the pop singers seem to be less commercial, monetary, self aggrandizing, and sexual (compare with Janet Jackson at the 2004 Super Bowl, for example).

Some insight into a composer's inspiration and motivation to write sport songs can be derived from a 2004 interview with Phó Đức Phương (PDP), Director of the Music Copyright Center and musical director of the ASEAN Paragames II. The interview was conducted by Hương Lan (HL), in his weekly editorial series, titled "Inner Sanctum". In my analysis of Phó Đức Phương's interview, I discuss his philosophy, style, and inspiration, step by step.

> *HL:* [The interviewer recites the song text of "Bài Ca Trên Xe Lăn" (Song Sung in Wheelchairs), performed at the opening ceremony of the second Para Games]
> *We all share sunlight and tropical rain with each other.*
> *We also share tears, smiles of joy and sadness*
> *and the thirst for eternal love . . .*
> *Torch! Burn forever in everybody's heart*
> *so that our aspirations and wishes fly high*
> *up to the twinkling stars over there*
> How on earth did you compose such a beautiful song?
>
> *PDP:* As a matter of fact, I "re-incarnated" myself in the life of a disabled person, immersing myself in their daily struggles. I am very afraid of this physical condition. "Live to love each other." How empty and trite it is for [us] who are able-bodied!
>
> *HL:* What have you found in your journey of re-incarnation?
>
> *PDP:* Equality! Disabled people and non-disabled people are equal: they are equal under sunlight and tropical rains, they are equal in joy and sadness and have an equal thirst for love. In a word, we are equal in this common universe. Therefore, in the face of that boundless equality it does not matter if we are unlucky. I sighed with relief because I had discovered the concept of equality. If there is a truly motivational force to help people with disabilities overcome their sadness, it is the sense of equality. And in deeper analysis, nobody can ascertain whether disabled people are less capable than ordinary people, or vice-versa. (*VNN*, May 2, 2004)

Realizing that it is impossible to make the foreign reality of being disabled his own reality, Phó Đức Phương explains that he immersed himself into the daily struggles of a disabled person, which he calls "reincarnating" himself in that person's life and daily activities. In that state of mind, he explains, he was able to make the subjective realization that all people are equal, in spite of their handicaps.

Hương Lan continued to discuss Phó Đức Phương's *modus operandi*, and delved into the composer's use of Vietnamese traditional music for inspiration, as the interview continues:

HL: The "Song Sung in Wheelchairs" and, in particular, the song sung at the closing ceremony of the Second Para Games revealed an entirely novel Phó Đức Phương; your songs had never been so young and fresh. Was it the first time [you] went beyond ca trù (Vietnamese traditional festival songs), chầu văn (Vietnamese ritual songs) and dân ca quan họ (folk love duets)?

PDP: As a matter of fact I have never had the intention to renovate myself. I come from Bac Ninh, that is why quan họ and ca trù draw deep emotion from me. I certainly wish to empathize with people and be understood, but it is not why I compose songs. We must at first be ourselves though sometimes we feel somewhat lonely.

HL: But if you follow the same path sooner or later you will become uninspired, don't you think?

PDP: Right! We can get stuck in a rut anytime, and folk songs become dated very easily. That is why composing folk music means we have to constantly re-invent ourselves. . . . Whoever sympathizes with us doesn't want to be stuck in the past. To lack creativity and ingenuity is to become an archaeologist. . . .

HL: Do you think that it [composing folk music] could develop into a trend?

PDP: More exactly an orientation for discovery. But even if it does become a trend, it would not be a main path, the one that could win the sympathy of the majority. I believe that besides diversity, there must be some common denominator in arts. (ibid.)

Thus, Phó Đức Phương's use of or inspiration derived from Vietnamese traditional song styles (what he calls folk music) such as *ca trù*, *chầu văn*, and *dân ca quan họ* make him philosophically similar to Nguyễn Cường, who borrowed from the music of Tây Nguyên. Yet, Phó Đức Phương realizes the danger of too closely emulating folk song materials when composing pop music. The use of folk or traditional materials in songwriting must be an inspirational one for developing an original style, rather than being a (re)creative one of imitation, as he suggests in the continuation of the interview:

HL: But in arts there must also be individuality?

PDP: I never want the arts to become something created just to be performed or to prove your intelligence and boldness. We must at first work with our whole mind and heart. We could certainly have our own individuality but we must at the same time be . . . easily understood by everybody. For me, arts are not meant to prove the prominence of our artistic language or thinking but what matters most is our feelings and the way we express them. It's also the same with a song's lyrics. I like to use the most simple words to express what I would like to say. No more and no less! (ibid.)

How does a composer/songwriter like Phó Đức Phương balance his *yang* musical assignment with his *yin* individuality (to use Jamieson's metaphors)? Hương Lan approaches that question as the two men continue to talk:

HL: With such thinking, have you ever felt like you were getting lost in the musical life of today?

PDP: Some worries, yes, but not imperious thoughts. Life balances itself. It is like a current or a top spinning very fast. In order to move, it must have some relative balance, otherwise it would fall. Our musical life continues to develop, doesn't it? In some respects it could have deviated a little. In general, it has been balanced all the time. (ibid.)

Phó Đức Phương's place in Vietnam's songwriting world is unique because he composes by assignment or by order from the government:

HL: You said that you compose just for yourself, but nearly 100 percent of your musical works came from assignments. How do you explain it?

PDP: You are right! Among the songs I have composed so far, very few are borne out of inspiration. But I am a professional composer, so I have to fulfill my programs. Orders are a mark of professionalism. (As a matter of fact, orders are, but the motives are a form of release for me.) I have yet to be inspired to create something without an original direction. (ibid.)

Although he composes by governmental order, Phó Đức Phương is still able to express his personal characteristics even as he honors his government's demands. For him it seems that there cannot be inspiration without an assignment, and then, when a directive is given, his creative individuality emerges. Without that directive or motivation, he considers himself sluggish (ibid.). The concept of composing popular music and writing socially effective lyrics by assignment from the Vietnamese communist government is manifested by competitions for songs about particular issues, of which the paragames for the disabled are included.

Songs about Regional/Transnational Unity

Another sporting event that has motivated songwriters is the Association of South-East Asian Nations (ASEAN), sort of regional, yet transnational, version of the Olympic games. Southeast Asia's unity organization (ASEAN) has an official anthem, which was composed by a Vietnamese composer, Đỗ Hồng Quân, in 1997, when he won the "ASEAN Anthem" competition with the following lyrics:

> For thousands of years, nations live side by side.
> Immense seas, rice fields, mountains, forests.
> Like pearls that shine in the south-eastern sky.
> Like dragons ascending from Asia.
> We are ASEAN.
> We walk hand in hand, shoulder to shoulder.
> We join in the song for the future.
> Live in peace forever.
> Broaden our vision.
> Open wide our arms, embracing new friends.
> With the world. ASEAN.
> Happiness. Prosperity. ASEAN. (*VNN*, June 10, 1997)

Đỗ Hồng Quân, born in Hanoi in 1956, is head of the Composition Department at the Hanoi Conservatory of Music and is also a film composer (ibid.). With the song's words of solidarity, unity, peace, and prosperity, the songwriter looks toward the future rather than the past.

Songs about Social Solidarity, Human Character, and Change

Two popular music songwriters stand out as modern-day poets in Vietnam for their broad-based issue-oriented lyrics: Nguyễn Anh Tuấn and Nguyễn Đạt, both rock musicians who write many of their lyrics in English.

Nguyễn Anh Tuấn

A Hanoi songwriter who is interested in social solidarity is Nguyễn Anh Tuấn, the lead singer with the Hanoi thrash metal band The Light (Ánh Sáng), which was discussed historically and musically in Chapter 4. Prior to his work with The Light, Anh Tuấn sang and played lead guitar with the Sài Gòn Boys and Kien Xanh (Green Ants). In The Light's 2003 recording, *Giấc Mơ Hoang Tàn* (Of Ruined Dreams), Anh Tuấn sings three songs in English. In them he addresses issues relating to social solidarity and human character.

"Let's Boycott Social Evils" (track 3) seems to be directly inspired by the VCP's reports as presented in Chapter 2. Although the English lacks correct syntax, the messages are clear, as the following lyrics demonstrate:

> Never regard yourselves as experienced
> Drug, prostitution, violence and others
> Those make you so proud? You failure

It will destroy your fortune and where life will be driven?
Surely it be you think.

You may never want to be
Life storm has swept you with social colorfulness
But is it nothing good for you to care?
Nothing interesting for you to do?
Don't let your life be drifted.

Let's boycott social evils
Get away from those
Let's boycott social evils
To be the gentles
Let's boycott social evils
Turn back to justice
Let's boycott social evils
Make your society better.

Do something for your life
Make it better to your society
Even though it's small.

These are very uplifting words for a normal (by which I mean nonreligious) heavy metal band, and they represent a *yang* message shrouded in a *yin* delivery. They are as if written by someone from the VCP because of their emphasis on making society better by contributing to it and expressing good behavior, themes preached by Hồ Chí Minh himself.

Similarly, "Believe in Yourselves" (track 6) carries a very positive message in its lyrics, as the following demonstrate:

Don't be credulous on what is said
Don't be gullible in what is done
Things might not be truthful as you catch

Life is different
From what you're expected
It can be destructiveness
Whenever you're hurried.

But never lose your heart
Fortune is the real fact.

Life is not meaningless as you propose
Rely on your heart telling you where to go
Create your own belief to cope things

Success's waiting for you at the end of road.

Don't be credulous on what is said
Don't be gullible in what is done
Things might not be truthful as you catch
Believe in yourselves.

Less about social solidarity and more about meaning in life, these lyrics by Tuấn also suggest a distrust of society, perhaps ("Things might not be [as] truthful as you [think]"). They remind me of the comment from Musician 1 (from a 2002 interview) that newspapers do not speak the truth. Yet, verse three is filled with hope ("Life is not meaningless as you propose"), offering suggestions for how to survive ("Rely on your heart telling you where to go" and "Create your own belief to cope [with] things").

These kinds of hopeful lyrics seem to be an attempt to narrow the yawning generation gap between youth and their elders (their parents and the government officials); yet, the mode of delivery is very hard rock or heavy metal (which The Light calls thrash metal). As if Anh Tuấn understands that generation gap, in the lyrics of "Sea of Fire" (track 5) he seems to ask members of the status quo to feel the rock melodies and enjoy the "crazy" music:

You can see the fire flaring brightly in my eyes.
You can feel the fire burning brightly in my heart
Together we feel rock melodies,
Raging through our hearts and souls.

We should get together
Enjoy this crazy rock music.
You can hate fact
That what we say is true.

Fire
Burning fire
Eyes afire
Souls on fire
Heart's desire
Sea of fire.

All together let's light a fire
A sea of fire, a sea of fire, a sea of fire
Gather together nearer the fire
Feel the heat, feel the beat and desire
Forget the sadness in your heart
Float up on the sea of fire
Sea of fire.

Although the lyrics show concern for the human condition of young people ("Forget the sadness in your heart"), I interpret the words "Sea of fire" to be metaphors for the destruction of the past (like cremation), a cleansing or purification process, a burning passion, modernism, and many others that seem to suggest a new beginning.

Nguyễn Đạt

Another rock composer who is concerned about world issues and expresses his ideas in his songs is Nguyễn Đạt, the founder, director, lead singer, and lead guitarist with Ho Chi Minh City's leading heavy metal band, Da Vàng (see also Chapter 4 and Figure 7.3). I asked Đạt about his inspiration and philosophy as a rock songwriter, and the following is a part of our dialogue:

DO: What is Vietnamese about your songs?

ND: I sing about social situations, about war, by which I mean the history of war within myself. I sing about the environment, which is a part of my personal war, as in the following: "The sea will become fire. The jungle will become empty." The meanings are opposite. For example, a ship makes an oil spill through the water, and the water burns. No trees are left to burn, so that is the "play on words." People say "you make the wrong lyrics." So I explain it to them.

DO: Are you and the music you compose concerned with remembering Vietnam's past?

ND: Vietnam's history is very long, and within its history, people mostly talk about the Vietnam [American] War, which is just a little piece of our history. I want to talk about the past, with some conditions; that is, the good conditions only.

DO: Are you and the music you compose and perform concerned with moving ahead and saying farewell to Vietnam's past?

ND: Yes. I am always concerned about the future.

DO: Does the music you write in any way relate to Vietnamese or world social issues or social change?

ND: Yes, it relates to the environment, anger, forgiveness, traffic jams, and so forth. (personal interview, August 1, 2005)

Nguyễn Đạt's lyrics to the title song of Da Vàng's first CD, *S.O.S.*, which means "Save Our Soul," address one of the greatest social issues of our time: the threat of nuclear war, as his translation into English reveals:

Sittin' on the TV I see many wretches
Listen to the radio you'll know the places on the flame
Stop violence! Don't pull the trigger

Our spoken words are the cry for the peace
Our metal music's crying to cease atomic warfare
S.O.S.
S.O.S.

Listen to the gunfire everyday on the Earth
Surfing the Web we seek cyber peace lovers
Get together: "get out of the war"
Our spoken words are a cry for peace
Our metal music is crying to stop atomic warfare
S.O.S.
S.O.S.

For the children in our world, we're warning about the holocaust
To the new millennium, what can we all do now?
We scream:
S.O.S. Stop the war.
S.O.S. Save the peace
S.O.S. Save Our Soul. . . . .

Another one of Nguyễn Đạt's songs, titled "Circle of Friends," is a joyful song of hope for the future, as his translation into English suggests:

The wind and dust blowing on the road
Cloudy skies tonight and the lonely one walks through the night
You remember when you look for me, don't you?
Now I'm coming home and we will share the same beliefs
In the sunshine, we throw up the sad past
We will hold together and we will come to a future world
In the sunshine, we throw up the sad past
We will hold together and we will come to a future world

We'll fall in love for a thousand years
We'll talk together for a thousand words
I believe you can keep the faith, and he shows us a promised land
We will hold together and we will come to future world
A circle of friends

Whereas rock music lyrics in Western cultures often shift between the rebellious and the risqué, some Vietnamese rock lyrics deal with social issues and have important messages to relay to their listeners. Though the messengers (often grunge and long-haired performers) may appear rebellious and risqué within the norms of the status quo, their messages are usually profound and seemingly sincere.

CONCLUSION: SONG TEXTS AS
MUSICAL WORD PAINTINGS

When the lyrics of Vietnamese pop and rock songs are studied, the following question again comes to mind: What is Vietnamese about Vietnamese pop and rock music, as evidenced by their lyrics? I suggest it is the unabashed sentimentality of the words (as well as the music in many instances) of the former and the seriousness of the message of the latter. Recalling the many ideas presented in this chapter about lyrics (e.g., war, anti-war, liberation, patriotism, homeland, landscapes, environmental protection, motherhood, love between man and woman, HIV/AIDS, tragedy, death), they all express some kind of sentimentality and love of humanity. If this chapter had also included lyrics from red and yellow songs, sentimentality would also be their unifying characteristic. *Nhạc trẻ* songs are popular because they seem to span the breadth of sentimentality.

> I [take] some time to put myself into the pictures in my head. For a song inspired by the Tet holiday, for instance, I imagine people walking through the streets, breathing the special air and the special sounds that can only exist during the New Year. I try to visualize it and interact with my thoughts and then begin playing the music. I flow myself into the music. In a sense it's like painting. (Roasa 2005:11)

Vietnamese song texts are, in fact, musical word paintings in a sense. They express the same sentimentality, tragedy, love, and hope through words and music (to which the words are set) that paintings do through brush and palette—from human interaction with beauty, loss, tragedy, love, family to many other aspects that affect the human psyche and soul. In the words of James Lull, "The point should be clear. Lyrics matter" (1987:157).

There is a paradox created, however, when songwriters write their lyrics in English. Without the use of the Vietnamese language, for example, it becomes difficult to discuss the Vietnameseness of the songs. It is not unusual, however, for rock singer/songwriters outside of English-speaking countries to express themselves in English. Ramet has developed a three-phased structure to explain the development of rock and language use in communist countries:

> [T]he earliest phase was imitative, as the bedazzled local youngsters struggled to master the new idiom. This was followed by a second phase, in which emergent rock 'n' roll bands wrote their own material but always sang in English—the supposed obligatory language of rock 'n' roll. Eventually, a third phase ensued, in which local rock groups

began to sing in their own languages and to develop their own musical styles. (1994:3)

Furthermore, the use of English (the language of the United States and capitalism) in Vietnamese popular music can be interpreted as a mild form of protest. Ramet's characterization of the situation in the Soviet Union has relevance in Vietnam: "Where the lyrics were concerned, the authorities grumbled, in the early stages, because the songs were generally performed in English—which some of them could not understand and which, besides, was the language of the West" (Ramet, Zamascikov, and Bird 1994:192). In the late twentieth century in the former Soviet bloc, English is again the favored language for rock, as singers and bands desire to capture the global market (Ramet 1994:3). This may also be the situation with Vietnamese rock, which always seems to be about a decade behind the West.

The next chapter studies the performance venues for mostly live popular music in Vietnam. As an aspect of musical place, which is a specific locality within a particular region, performance venue analysis pertains to how songwriters, individual singers, and ensembles are able to publicly disseminate their art forms. A study of performance venues also deals with issues of music as commodity versus music as art and mass culture.

6   Performance Venues for (Mostly) Live Popular Music

Place (or locality) "has emerged as a key concept in contemporary popular music studies, picking up on well-established trends in cultural geography and drawing on social anthropological methodology" (Shuker 2005:154). This chapter, however, does not deal with place or locality in the geographic sense of area, nation, or physical region within geographic boundaries, but with performance place (buildings, parks, and other venues) within urban settings. It specifically pertains to popular music entertainment or performance venues and the socio-cultural-political reasons for their being and the types of music taking place within them. The analysis of musical performance venues can be an important measure of identity and memory, and as such, informs the study of Vietnam's popular music as politics. The following essay about a performance venue in Hanoi, for example, is like reading about a monument to the intellectual and romantic past that has been lost to and replaced by the popular culture of the present:

> There's an old building perched on a jetty on one side of the Thiền Quang Lake in Hà Nội's Lenin Park. It is well known to Hanoians old and young alike, and in a way for similar reasons. An old faded sign on the side of the building is the only clue to its former status. It reads: "Ho Chi Minh Youth Union. Hà Nội Culture House for pupils and students." Although it has always fulfilled the function of entertainment center, few who used to go there twenty years [ago] would recognize the atmosphere today. It used to be one of the few night spots for Hà Nội's youth. Evenings of poetry reading, discussion groups, and language classes were common. Parties were held there, and music was popular. It was the center of Hà Nội's student social life. But a lot of time has passed by since the last discussion group was held.
>
> Considered an ideal location right in the heart of Hà Nội, next to a scenic lake and away from the crowds, there was little chance of it escaping the attention of the business community. The old building now echoes to sounds of Western pop and a neon sign spells out the words "Top Disco Club." This must be good news for Hà Nội's youth, you may imagine. There is undoubtedly a shortage of leisure facilities in the

THAT'S RIGHT, FREE ENTRY ALL NIGHT.
HOWEVER, FOR AN EXTRA $10 WE'LL LET
YOU DRINK, DANCE AND MINGLE...

Figure 6.1   Cartoon from the *Việt Nam News*, February 5, 1996 (used with permission).

nation's capital. But there's a problem. It's no longer the meeting place for the city's student community. Few of them could afford the $4 entrance fee, let alone the $5 per hour for the privilege of having a girl to dance with. Drinks at between two and three times their normal cost are a further deterrent to students. So what could have been the ideal place for the young to enjoy has now become the preserve of the rich. But some of the blame has to be placed on the traditional culture houses themselves. It is easy to complain [about] the degradation of cultural life, but the houses did little to help themselves. Perhaps if they had adapted to the new situation and catered for the changing demands of city youth, this situation may never have arisen. (*VNN*, November 11, 1995)

Indeed, as Hanoi and Ho Chi Minh City expand and modernize, old musical and artistic haunts are transformed into modern entertainment venues or disappear altogether. Why does this happen? Why are some performance venues used for one type of music and not another? Why are particular locations chosen for new performance venues? What role does performance venue play in the choice of music performed? What are the relationships, if any, between performance venue and social class? I attempt to answer some of these questions in this chapter.

HISTORICAL PERFORMANCE VENUES

During the French colonial phase of Vietnam's history, French officials built elaborate opera houses in Hanoi and Saigon. They were important venues for classical music, dance, theater, and, of course, opera, all entertainment genres for the European colonial elite. Like many of the Catholic churches also constructed by the French, Vietnamese locals were not allowed inside the buildings. Considered the jewels in the French crown in both colonial cities, after the revolution and expulsion of the French in the 1950s, both opera houses were used for office space and political events for the Vietnamese military. During the 1960s, their names were changed to Municipal Theater, and they were (and still are) used for local musical, dance, and theatrical performances. On rare occasions, the Municipal Theaters in Hanoi and Ho Chi Minh City are used for popular music concerts and other popular music events, especially for visiting artists. Today the structures are again often called opera houses, and they are used primarily for government-sponsored functions, including some "by invitation only" popular music concerts that include government-approved music and performers.

LARGE INDOOR/OUTDOOR COMMUNITY PERFORMANCE VENUES

Large community performance venues in Vietnam include youth entertainment establishments such as youth cultural (or culture) houses with both indoor and outdoor spaces for concerts and cultural/information centers that are endorsed and often supported by the Vietnamese national, regional, or city governments. Rather than commercial establishments, they are understood as locations where Vietnamese youth can be entertained in ways the government deems appropriate.

The youth cultural house concept, which began after reunification of Vietnam in 1975, was of an entertainment setting where youth culture was endorsed and sponsored by the Vietnamese government. According to the essay that began this chapter, however, the Hanoi Culture House was described in 1995 as if it were a thing of the past. By contrast, similar youth cultural houses in Ho Chi Minh City during the same time period have been described as thriving performance venues for culture and sports, and as centers of learning: "More than 6,000 youths attended a musical program held at the Youth Cultural House Monday to celebrate the 65ᵗʰ anniversary of the Ho Chi Minh Communist Youth Union" (*VNN*, March 23, 1996). The venue was the headquarters of the Saigon Student-Pupil Association after the 1975 reunification of Vietnam, and it was converted to the Youth Cultural House for young people a decade or more later:

> Most, 96 per cent of those who attend regularly, are between the ages of 14 and 35, and over half are students. . . . Since 1993, [evening] classes have been held in computers, foreign languages, music, housekeeping, gymnastics, sports and medicine, plus more specialized courses on everything from AIDS prevention to marriage consulting, psychology to Marxist-Leninist theory. (ibid.)

The Youth Cultural House was a center for learning as well as an entertainment venue, and seemed to have met the needs (especially sports) of every young person in Saigon during the 1990s, or so the article would have us believe.

Another one of the large community youth establishments, Hội Quán Trẻ, or Ho Chi Minh City Youth Club, catered to music, rather than sports. It was the performance venue for a large pop music show attended by nearly a thousand young people in 1996:

> Since the HCM City Youth Club (Hội Quán Trẻ) opened its doors five months ago, it has made a name for itself as the in place to rock and roll, putting on gala performances each weekend that bring together more than 30 Vietnamese rock bands. One Sunday morning at the end of July, the Youth Club packed in over 800 cheering fans who came to see Sài Gòn Metal, the latest band to explode on the city's growing music scene. Youngsters in the audience clapped their hands and sang along to lyrics from bands like Guns N' Roses, Queen and Metallica. Such excitement levels are not uncommon at the Youth Club, which charges its weekly shows with rock and roll electricity, generated by well-known local bands like Atomega, Da Vàng (Yellow Complexion), Đen Trắng (Black and White), Sao Sáng (Bright Star), Hy Vọng (Hope) and Rock Alpha.
>
> Popular student bands also put on shows at the Youth Club, including Sóng Xanh (Blue Waves) of the Polytechnic College, Đồng Xanh (Green Field) of the city's Students Association and Morning of HCM City University. (*VNN*, August 19, 1996)

This was one of the first performance venues for large pop music concerts in Vietnam, and it functioned as a place where rock and other pop music genres thrived in the mid to late 1990s. American heavy metal music and performances by Saigon metal bands were the featured sonic delights. Though this seems rather unusual for a country that just twenty years earlier (and even ten years earlier) had preached the evils of Western-influenced rock music, it is relevant that this effort to provide a physical performance place for popular musical modernizing, as it were, occurred in Ho Chi Minh City, Vietnam's modern metropolis and the locale of the country's burgeoning market economy. Moreover, it was happening shortly after American President Bill Clinton removed the U.S. trade embargo on Vietnam, and private businesses were beginning to support seemingly Western causes such as popular culture:

> Tiến Phát, a private business, has invested more than VNĐ 500 million (US$45,000) to build up this music venue and the club's founders want to set up a "Creative Department" to encourage bands to write new songs. Speaking about the club's formation, manager Lê Quang Thuận, said, "We want to help young rock bands to have a place in which to perform and to interact with the audience. Many youths in HCM City like rock music, but they had nowhere to perform and to enjoy rock. The Youth Club is an ideal place for them."
>
> Members of Sài Gòn Metal said, "Coming to the Youth Club means that our wandering performances from provinces from north to south have ended. We now have a place to play." For those in the mood to groove, the HCM City Youth Club is the place to be. (ibid.)

In Ho Chi Minh City during the 2000s, the youth culture house concept continues to flourish as a performance place for music and other youth activities. The Youth Culture House in downtown District 1, just west of the huge Diamond Plaza Shopping Center, for example, is a lively venue for popular music concerts, art shows, sporting activities, and foreign language study. In 2005 I attended an outdoor popular music concert at the Youth Culture House that featured solo pop singers, boy and girl bands, hip-hop dance groups, and Siu Black as the featured attraction. In spite of several heavy downpours of rain, the show continued during periods of calm and mist, as most of the teenage audience members either donned raincoats or squeezed under a large tarp. All the instrumental accompaniments for the singers and dancers were prerecorded. I captured my impressions of this concert venue and performance in the following fieldnotes:

> As I was walking to the Diamond Plaza I came upon an enclosure with buildings and a big concrete court where a concert was advertised for today from 5:30 to 7:30, featuring Siu Black and other singers I thought I would never get to hear in person. I caught a moto [motorbike taxi] back to my hotel to get my recording equipment, and here I sit now, waiting for the performance to begin. It cost only VNĐ 14,000 to get in, which even includes a free CD (actually, the ticket

says VNĐ 7,000, so I guess the "free" CD is another VNĐ 7,000. I've got a good aisle seat and am sitting on two chairs because I don't think one will hold me (the chairs are made from very thin plastic). I forgot my ear plugs, so I hope it won't be killer loud. The place is filling up, and especially the seats with backs like my chair. Behind me are bench seats (actually they are chairs without backs). This entire place seems like a school, and this venue is like a flat stadium—it looks like a basketball court, but there aren't any hoops. In the center is a huge umbrella or tarp—it doesn't look like it will rain, however. It's now 5:45. Most of the audience seems to be made up of teenagers, although there are some people in their 20s. I'm certainly the only foreigner here. There is a nice breeze as it becomes early evening, and now I see rain clouds behind me. I just heard the first microphone check and now the pre-show music has been turned off. It's 5:55 and an unseen person is speaking, testing the PA system. Yes, it's loud! Two hosts (a young man and a young woman) have appeared and the concert is beginning with a dance/singing group of twelve young people in blue and white clothes. The music track is prerecorded and the singers are lip-synching. Next two girls are singing, and it's really loud—thank goodness I have some tissue paper to wad up and stick in my ears. Now a boy in a black suit dances with a school girl, accompanied by boy dancers in white pants and shirts with red ties—this is the cuteness factor, but for boys! The audience hardly claps at all. It is beginning to rain now, and everybody is trying to get under the big umbrella. Luckily, I have my own.

After the rain, Siu Black made her appearance, bringing everyone to their feet, as I continued to write in my fieldnotes after she finished her set:

She was rockin', in spite of the fact that she is no spring chicken. Siu Black really shows her experience, and besides being a great singer, she's a wonderful show woman. Her choices of music were straight-ahead rock and roll, with no ethnic minority gimmicks as she presented in her 'live show' DVD that I have [where she comes on stage riding an elephant].

At this outdoor venue, there was no live band. The combination of live singing to a prerecorded soundtrack, however, was very effective, in spite of its excessive loudness (for me).

Cultural and Information Centers are usually large public buildings with substantial community halls that are common in provincial towns. They are performance venues for the perpetuation of Vietnamese national culture and pride. Chung Quốc Hưng describes a semi-participatory, community musical event in Bình Thuận, north of Ho Chi Minh City in south-central Vietnam:

Aspiring young songsters and chanteuses in the central province of Bình Thuận have found a place to indulge their passion for the art of singing—and they are rolling up in droves. If you pass by Bình Thuận Cultural and Information Center on a Saturday night, don't be surprised if you see thousands of bicycles parked outside. Buy a ticket, go in, and marvel at the capacity crowd in the 4,000-seat center. Most are aged 16–20, and they are all there to soak up the enthusiasm and talent of the area's professional and amateur singers. They come not only from the city of Phan Thiết itself, but also from surrounding areas like Hàm Thuận Nam and Hàm Thuận Bắc.

One spectator named Hồng said he had set off for the center in the early afternoon, to be sure of getting a seat—and maybe even a chance to perform. "I'm dying to get up there on stage," he confided. The singers come on stage one by one, to rapturous applause. Hồng was lucky this time, and got his chance in front of the crowd. But another man sitting near him was as glum as could be. It was the fourth time he'd put his name down to sing, and the fourth time he'd missed out. "I come here almost every Saturday night except when I'm off fishing," he said. Why doesn't he go to the karaoke lounge instead? "The karaoke places are stuffy and they're very expensive. Here, you've got the crowds, the talent—it's so exciting!"

Some people use wily and persuasive means in their efforts to get five minutes in the limelight. They tell the organizers they come from remote areas, and hope that pity will be taken on them. . . . [A]t the Bình Thuận Cultural and Information Center, an official named Võ Hoàng Tuyết Lan proudly told me a story about a Hà Nội girl who had come a few weeks ago. She was in Phan Thiết to take part in a national tae kwondo contest, but heard about the Saturday night sing-along and came to take part. The girl from the big city told Lan she was amazed at the number of people and quality of singing in a town of that size. Lan said the center was hoping to do more than just entertain. Some of the musical programs highlighted folkloric music, or had educational themes. Recently, one concert included information about preventing HIV/AIDS. She said she hoped that the popularity of these nights would convince other provinces to follow Bình Thuận's lead. (2001)

It is difficult to imagine a 4,000 seat hall where music directors or other people in charge let the public sing on stage (if only for five minutes), in addition to coordinating professional singers, amateurs, and instrumentalists. Unlike karaoke clubs (see Chapter 9), the open mic night is not as concerned with making a profit as it is for providing wholesome entertainment for the people, laced with educational, nationalistic, folkloric, and disease (HIV/AIDS) prevention information (see also Chapters 5 and 7).

LARGE COMMERCIAL PERFORMANCE VENUES

Unlike the community performance venues for youth musical entertainment, commercial establishments such as youth clubs, discotheques, dance (electronica such as techno, house, etc.) clubs, and *nhạc trẻ* clubs for teenagers are primarily driven by profit. The *nhạc trẻ* clubs, however, are also motivated to feature pop music, pop singers, and pop dancers.

Laura Menendez, one of my students in 2004, went dancing at the Phương Đông club (known as Liquid Discotheque in English), located in District 1 of Ho Chi Minh City, one evening in 2004 and described her experience in her fieldnotes:

> A local high school student had recommended the place [Liquid Discotheque] to me as being the "best disco in Saigon." Several of the local friends I met later in my trip suggested that we all go out there together one night. We met up on a Thursday night and rode together on motorbikes to the club. Upon entering I saw that it was very similar in set-up to the Rainforest Disco I had attended before: there were many tables surrounding a dance floor that was illuminated by multicolored lights.

I had my own personal experience at a similar but much larger club, the Blue Club in Ho Chi Minh City's District 1, near the Bến Tranh Market on Lê Lợi Street. Located on the second floor of the former International Trade Center building, my fieldnotes describe my age-centric impression of the Blue Club, an experience that will forever remain in my memory:

> Tonight at 10:00 pm, I went to the Blue Club in downtown Ho Chi Minh City. I'm not sure what to call this type of club—disco club, techno club, rave club, or perhaps just dance or night [nite] club. I have never in my life experienced anything like this. It was as futuristic as anything you could ever imagine—blue and green spotlights flashing everywhere over continuous black lights; techno music with the bass so loud and so monotone (it never changed pitch) that my pants legs vibrated and my stomach felt upset; and so many young Vietnamese jammed into one place, like sardines in a can. It was impossible to speak to anyone without cupping your mouth to his or her ear. (July 2002)

On October 29, 2002, the Blue Club and the entire International Trade Center building in which it was housed burned down, killing 60 persons, injuring 70 more, and causing US$2 million in property damage (*VNN*, June 12, 2004). By 2005 the club had reopened with a new and somewhat historically metaphorical (hopefully not prophetic) name—Volcano.

Discotheque and *dance club* seem to be the most common English terms used in Vietnam to describe these electronica performance venues. Dancing takes place to music provided by CD technology, featuring remix, very high volume, reverberation, repetition, and very loud bass—all sonic mind-altering characteristics. I was unable to analyze the music performed at this dance club, and because there are so many variants of dance music in America and Europe, I cannot make valid comparisons. Will Straw, for example, writes the following about the diversity of dance club music in general:

> At one level, dance music culture is highly polycentric, in that it is characterized by the simultaneous existence of large numbers of local or regional styles—Detroit 'techno' music, Miami 'bass' styles, Los Angeles 'swingbeat', etc. . . . A comfortable, stable international diversity may rarely be observed. (1997:501)

Straw's delineation of the many kinds of dance music during the 1980s (his article first appeared in 1991) in America and England may be relevant to Vietnam's dance music styles in the 2000s, as Vietnam is about a decade behind the West regarding popular culture.

Unfortunately, loud music is not the only mind-altering agent found at such large commercial entertainment locations, as the following excerpts from the *Việt Nam News* suggest:

> Recently, there has been an increase in the number of young people caught using ecstasy in nightclubs, restaurants and hotels. (*VNN*, June 27, 2005)
>
> Phuong Kieu Vi [not her real name] was unaware of the risks she was taking when she first tried drugs at the age of 16. She simply wanted to enhance the pleasure of dancing, she said, and "those small pink pills make your dancing 'hot'." Vi . . . didn't find it alarming to use drugs. If anything, it wasn't uncommon for other people in the night-club to pop pills, gyrate rapidly and yell wildly. After a while, Vi not only used ecstasy to dance but [also] to stimulate her sexual desire. (Written by Hong Thuy, *VNN*, April 5, 2004)

Drug use is a problem in Vietnam, and it is a social issue that is occasionally dealt with by songwriters, especially as it relates to HIV/AIDS (see Chapter 5 and McNally 2003).

Vietnamese youth seem to enjoy dancing at these performance venues, as the following article "Dancing the night away in HCMC" suggests:

> HCM City now has about 40 discotheques and scores of dancing halls inside cultural houses crowded every night with youths looking to dance the night away. With their modern sound and light systems, places such as Deelight, Đêm Mầu Hồng (Pink Night), Thái Sơn, Samson, and the

Rex, to name a few, pack in the crowds. Maxim's, and discotheques at hotels like the Sài Gòn Star, the Century and the New World are frequented primarily by foreigners because of their high prices.

Many youths save their money to go dancing. However, according to oriental traditions, many parents do not want their children, particularly their daughters, to go out dancing. "We don't want to spoil them," one mother of a 17 year-old girl said. Thanh Yến, a student at HCM City's Technical College said, "My parents do not want me to go dancing. But without it my life is so dull."

HCM City's young people take their dancing seriously. Many of them even study dance. Minh Trang, 23, is taking a dance class at the Youth Cultural House. "I think that people of this modern time must know how to dance," she said. One professional choreographer put it this way: "Dancing cannot be omitted from the cultural activities of people. We must commend the owners of the dancing halls for contributing to our culture." (*VNN*, February 3, 1997)

Although this article emphasizes the importance of dancing among Vietnam's youth, my impression of the dancing styles at the Blue Club was that it was neither unusual, interesting, nor artistic. Compared to dancing styles associated with Latino music in Florida, or even contemporary disco in the United States, I found the Vietnamese dancing at the Blue Club to be very conservative. It consisted of very little body movement, with heads slightly bobbing up and down. In fact, when I first walked into the area along the dance floor, I thought people were sitting down because there was no movement. After a few minutes sitting behind the techno artists (i.e. the DJs), I realized that the people in the middle space of the club were dancing. My observations seem consistent with Straw's analysis of dancing styles at American and British dance clubs: "Among a [dance] club's clientèle, . . . distinctions take shape around the degree to which people dance within disciplined parameters (as opposed to cutting loose). . . ." (1997:500).

In my fieldnotes written after the evening at the Blue Club, I described other aspects of the event and gave my impressions of the technology and the people:

A young lady found us bar stools, and it was there, the farthest away from the loudspeakers, that my pants legs shook with each bass vibration. After about ten minutes I suggested to Tom [an American musician colleague who went with me] that we wander around the place to observe the behavior of the participants, watch the dancers, and get a general feel for the event. We watched some rather uninteresting dancers on the upper level: one had flashing fingernails and several others had flashing rods in their hands. Then we wandered down to the main level along the main dance floor with its hundreds of strobe lights and flashing green and blue spotlights to another bar (no drinks were served there) situated immediately behind the performing artists (DJs)—about four young Vietnamese guys who were manipulating the soundboards, computers, CD players, and other electronic gadgetry. There were even several cases of vinyl recordings stashed there. It was very interesting to watch the mediated music manipulators, who were artists in their own right. From our new vantage point, the music was bearable, but I cannot imagine the decibels just in front of the speakers where the main dance floor is. Periodically, fake smoke shot up from the floor and green and blue spots alternated with white flickers at appropriate times to coincide with the music.

It is the combination of all the above—loud music emphasizing repetitive bass, flashing colored lights, fake smoke, flickering white lights—that make the appellation dance/house/techno/trance club perhaps the best name for this kind of large commercial entertainment venue.

A smaller dance club that is very diverse in its entertainment offerings is the Tiếng Tơ Đồng, also known as Queen Bee Night Club, across from the Rex Hotel in District 1 (Saigon) of Ho Chi Minh City. As a poster in the doorway to the establishment advertises, a variety of dancing opportunities await a highly enticed foreign clientele—hence the poster in English and Vietnamese (Figure 6.2). Beginning at 8:00 every night, the Queen Bee offers disco dancing on the third floor to DJ-created spinning or scratching technology (see picture in lower right-hand corner of poster), karaoke rooms (see Chapter 9) and a lounge bar on the second floor, and sit-down listening to Vietnamese popular music singers with a live band on the first floor. I wrote the following fieldnotes on the day I first encountered the club on May 27, 2004:

> I happened upon the Tiếng Tơ Đồng club, which is across from the Rex Hotel. When I walked in the foyer I realized that the space is also the site of the famous Queen Bee Night Club, which is on the third floor. The popular music listening club is on the first floor, and a karaoke bar is on the second. Nobody was around so I walked into the first floor club. It has a very large stage with a lot of equipment set up. The audience seats are almost theater style, but with little tables in front of them, and all the seats face the stage. It is a perfect venue for live performances, and the stage is also set up for a live band.

Moreover, the club features free admission for women on ladies night (Tuesdays), other free admission opportunities advertised are a happy hour and hip-hop music (it doesn't say when, but the poster suggests that hip-hop music is during happy hour).

Single Vietnamese women seeking (foreign as well as wealthy Vietnamese) men are often commonplace at such commercial entertainment locations. The following article characterizes some of the women (and the evils

Figure 6.2 Poster at the entrance to the Queen Bee Night Club (Tiếng Tơ Đồng) in downtown Saigon. Photograph by Dale A. Olsen, 2004.

of their smoking habits) found in such establishments, as the author writes specifically about the Queen Bee Night Club:

Vietnamese girls in short and sophisticated dresses, and smartly dressed men, push one another to get a place on the dance floor. "I find this place somewhat like a night-club in Hong Kong," comments a Singaporean man, "You can see a large number of girls smoking here. I don't understand why they are taking up the habit, while in our country smoking is banned in public places and frowned upon. "In my mind," the distraught man continued, "Vietnamese girls are gentle, soft, kind and well-behaved. They shouldn't destroy their good reputation with the filthy habit [of smoking]."

The increasingly visible number of young girls smoking here says something about the crafty ability of tobacco companies to [focus] their advertising towards young women, and they are aided by sultry Hollywood actresses such as Sharon Stone playing the roles of smoking, sophisticated women. Girls in a group with their eyes fixed towards the dance floor eagerly await the late night slow dances and love songs. With the loud music, people can hardly exchange words. "Hi!" shouts a Vietnamese man to a girl in a black mini skirt. (*VNN*, February 5, 1996)

At the Queen Bee and other large commercial entertainment establishments in Vietnam, loud music and smoking go hand in hand. The above author singles out young girls who smoke, not young boys, but the smoking habit is the concern of the author. It is true that very little has or is being done to ban or limit smoking anywhere in Vietnam, except on tour buses and airplanes (and in some restaurants in Ho Chi Minh City in 2005), and the image of smoking with being cool, sexy, or wealthy (i.e. a member of the market economy) is certainly reinforced by Hollywood stars, other entertainment icons, and the tobacco industry. In addition, it is an addiction, and little is done in Vietnam to help people cope with tobacco dependency (it is not a social issue in Vietnam, as HIV/AIDS is, for example [see Chapter 5]).

Two other kinds of clubs cater to Vietnamese teenagers rather than young adult youth: *hội quán trẻ* (youth) and *nhạc trẻ* (youth music) clubs. *Hội quán trẻ* (also used as the name for a club; see p. 176) clubs often feature live musicians, and in the 1990s they were the premier performance venues for Vietnamese rock and roll bands. I never saw a *hội quán trẻ* club advertised in Ho Chi Minh City, but *nhạc trẻ* clubs are quite common in downtown Saigon. Rather than featuring generic *nhạc trẻ* music (i.e. crooner style), they are similar to the disco clubs already described, because they have flashing colored spotlights and extremely loud disco music; but they are different because they feature several dancers displayed on small circular stages and occasional on-stage pop singers accompanied by live musicians. *Nhạc trẻ* clubs cater more to sitting than dancing, and they appeal more to young teenage Vietnamese people, rather than to young adults in their twenties and thirties who prefer the dance clubs and popular music listening clubs (discussed in the next section). In Ho Chi Minh City, *nhạc trẻ* clubs open in the midmorning and continue early into the next morning, whereas the dance clubs are open only during the evenings until the wee hours of the mornings. Most of the generic *nhạc trẻ* pop singers appear in the evening, as they make their rounds from one *nhạc trẻ* club and *phòng trà ca nhạc* club (see next section) to another. This is, in fact, one of the major ways Vietnamese pop singer wannabes have of making themselves known to the young Vietnamese public.

The similarity between *nhạc trẻ* clubs and dance clubs is striking, nevertheless, as I wrote in my fieldnotes on July 20, 2002, about the Café Nhạc Trẻ 008 in downtown Saigon:

> I walked into this club expecting to find a coffee house atmosphere. Instead, I was surprised to find an ambience similar to the Blue Club, with very loud techno music, but with three female dancers on round stages in the middle of the club, much like a strip club, but they had their clothes on. Behind them was a stage with a drum set on it, but no live musicians at 3:00 pm. Like the Blue Club, blue spotlights were flashing and moving all over, and the place was illuminated only by a black light, making the white shirts of the kids a shade of brilliant glowing blue. Nobody was dancing except for the three girls. All the clientele were sitting at round tables, talking to the accompaniment of the extremely loud music.

The commonalities are extremely loud mediated music, flashing spotlights, and black lights; the dissimilarities are public dancing versus no public dancing. Another similarity between *nhạc trẻ* clubs and dance clubs is the profit-making motif based on drink sales, as I explained in my fieldnotes written about each experience:

Café Nhạc Trẻ 008 (July 20, 2002): The manager or someone in a leadership role tried to get me to sit down at the bar and order beer or wine. This was after several girls were unsuccessful in getting me to sit down. I just wanted to observe, however, and told the man I was just going to stand and look for a while. He finally walked away, realizing he couldn't force me to sit down.

Blue Club (July 11, 2002): At the entrance to the club, the people at the ticket counter did not charge us the usual VNĐ 60,000 cover charge, for some reason. We think they figured we were there looking for some of the girls, and they would get their money that way. Or, they probably charged us foreign prices for the drinks. We were directed up a slight level to a bar, where we each ordered a Corona beer, priced at VNĐ 60,000 apiece (US$4), American prices.

Tom pointed out to me that in the space behind us, which was probably the quietest place in the club, wealthy people were pouring a very expensive cognac as if it were water. He knew the Vietnamese price for that stuff—over a hundred US dollars a bottle. We determined that the young adults that attend these places are probably quite wealthy, and they probably all speak English.

What does the Vietnamese Communist Party think about loud music, smoking, and other activity at these large commercial popular music performance venues? I reflected on that after my experience at the Blue Club, as I wrote in my fieldnotes:

> The communist government probably does not like this type of performance event, but in a metropolis like Ho Chi Minh City, which is trying to keep up with the other major Asian cities, it is impossible to do anything about it. This is where it's at; this is the future; this is the economics of forgetting at work; this is globalization in its mediated glory.

When I wrote those thoughts I did not know about the smoking ban in Singapore. Nevertheless, Singapore is perhaps an anomaly because of its strict laws, and what takes place in the large commercial pop music and dance performance venues in Ho Chi Minh City is probably the norm throughout Asia.

POPULAR MUSIC LISTENING CLUBS

What I call a *popular music listening club* is known as *phòng trà ca nhạc* (literally, music and song tea room) in Vietnamese. These places are commercial performance venues that differ from the establishments described above because they are smaller, do not feature dancing, and are sit-down clubs (Figure 6.3) devoted to the art of listening to live musical performances. The selling of drinks (but not tea) at relatively high prices is secondary to listening, although waitresses are always present to take your order. In 2004, for example, I sat at a small table for several hours with only one beer and was never pressured to purchase another; similarly, in 2005 I ordered one lemonade or iced coffee and was never pressured to purchase more. Usually, however, an over-30 crowd (i.e. a mature audience) pays above average prices for several alcoholic drinks throughout an evening. In addition, there is always a cover charge, but not an entrance fee. Rather than dancing or drinking, the popular music listening club audience comes to hear Vietnam's top popular music singers and wannabes, and in the process fans become transfixed by the music's power (although there are always exceptions when some people talk or drink too much, and their behavior disrupts the ambience). Though no contemporary popular music performances in Vietnam are political to the extent of accompanying political manifestos, inspiring collective action, or overtly opposing the government, the performances at *phòng trà ca nhạc* clubs are political in that they provide escape for the audience, as suggested by

John Street: "Pop's inability to change the world is compensated for by its ability to articulate and alter our perceptions of that world, and perhaps more importantly, to give a glimpse of other, better worlds" (1986:166). Likewise, "Pop . . . can . . . alter the ways in which people experience that world" (ibid.:174). More than at any other public establishments where I attended performances of popular music in Vietnam, the audience members at the popular music listening clubs were seemingly entranced by the music and transported to other worlds. "This was where the music found its power" (ibid.:171).

Each star performs for approximately thirty minutes to an hour (often to prerecorded music) about two hours after numerous lesser-known singers have sung four songs each (usually accompanied by a house band). The typical evening's famous pop singer, whose name and picture has been on the marquee for a week outside the building, usually makes her or his appearance around 10:30 or 11:00 PM. After her or his half-hour to one-hour presentation, everyone leaves and the establishment closes.

The *Việt Nam News* also refers to these performance venues as lounge rooms, bars, cafes, and night clubs, as explained in the following article:

Figure 6.3   ATB popular music listening club west of the Bến Tranh Market in Ho Chi Minh City, District 1. The establishment is owned by Ánh Tuyết and was formerly a theater for *hát bội*, traditional Vietnamese drama. Photograph by Dale A. Olsen, 2005.

[M]any people are shunning larger venues—choosing instead smaller spots like bars, cafes and night clubs. "Some people say clubs aren't suitable for serious music shows. I don't think so," said singer Thu Phương. "I don't care where I am. The best stage for a singer is anywhere with an audience."

Fellow performers Thanh Lam, Hồng Nhung and Bằng Kiều are winning over audiences at small shows throughout the city. "In bars and cafes we only perform soft, romantic songs," said a regular singer at the ATB Club. "Here, we feel like we are singing for our best friends." In the dimly-lit and cozy atmosphere of the ATB, audiences can enjoy renditions of *Hoài Cảm*, or Nostalgia, by Cung Tiến, *Thiên Thai*, or Paradise, and *Suối Mơ*, Dream Stream, by Văn Cao.

"Other light songs are seldom performed at big shows because they are not suited to overwhelming distortion from electric guitars and the pounding of drums," said ATB's owner and singer Ánh Tuyết. "Unlike theatres like Hòa Bình and Bến Thành, audiences here feel close to singers. We share feelings at bars and clubs," said Tuyết.

Romantic music is most popular at clubs such as Tiếng Tơ Đồng on Đồng Khởi Street, Đồng Dao on Nguyễn Huệ, and M&Tôi on Lê Duẩn where customers are seen as more mature and middle-aged. (August 28, 2001)

Several years later, the *Việt Nam News* again described the smaller and more intimate performance venues in an article titled "Small venues hot spots in HCMC City," which is vaguely similar to the article written two years before:

Live music is alive and well in HCM City, however most music fans prefer more intimate venues rather than big events. Some years ago, small venues did not exist. Now, HCM City's night life is transformed by bars, cafes and night clubs. Owners of such spots try to attract more customers by paying top-dollar for outrageous decorations and well-known singers. In the dim light and cozy atmosphere of clubs like ATB, Tiếng Tơ Đồng and Đồng Dao, audiences can relax to the gentle sounds of romantic favorites like *Suối Mơ* (Dream Stream) by Văn Cao, *Tình Nghệ Sỹ* (Artist's Love) by Đoàn Chuẩn, and *Hoài Cảm* (Memory) by Cung Tiến. Mature customers seem to prefer the resident band at the Thiên Hà Café in District 1. They only play songs by the late composer Trịnh Công Sơn.

Former Hanoians like to reminisce at the Hà Nội & I Café where the owner from northern Vietnam sings every night. His repertoire includes songs like Hà Nội Đêm Trở Gió (A Windy Night in Hà Nội), Hà Nội Mùa Lá Bay (The Season of Leaves Falling in Hà Nội) and Chị Tôi (My Sister). These softer songs are seldom performed at big live concerts because they are not suited for the crushing, distorted chords of electric guitars and throb of beating drums. (November 13, 2003)

Figure 6.4   The stage of the M&Tôi popular music listening club on Lê Duẩn Street in downtown Ho Chi Minh City, District 1, showing one of the featured female singers and two backup musicians. Photograph by Dale A. Olsen, 2004.

Both these articles describe specifically named popular music listening clubs, such as ATB, Đồng Dao, M&Tôi, and others. Although the articles stress the intimate nature and quiet atmosphere of the clubs, especially when compared to the larger performance venues preferred by Vietnamese teenagers and other youth who prefer rock and techno music for dancing and socializing, the popular music listening clubs I attended were usually very loud. As the photograph in Figure 6.4 shows, electric guitars, electric bass, several electronic keyboards, and drum set are included as part of the M&Tôi popular music listening club house band accompaniment for the individual singers, and the overall amplification is extreme. The ATB popular music listening club seen in Figure 6.5, on the other hand, is not as loud as the other clubs. Although all the accompanying instruments in the ATB club are amplified, some of the performances have an unplugged feel about them, thus creating a more intimate soundscape (or one could say ATB's technoscape is less severe than the other clubs).

Another major characteristic of the popular music listening clubs is that the preferred repertoire is romantic music (*tình ca*) and other sentimental songs (*nhạc trẻ*)—the preferred music of the majority of Vietnam's popular music singers. Ballads and other crooner-type songs by such famous songwriters as Trịnh Công Sơn and Văn Cao are highly preferred

Figure 6.5 Ánh Tuyết performing on the stage of her popular music listening club, ATB, in Ho Chi Minh City. Photograph by Dale A. Olsen, 2005.

by established singers; younger divas perform covers as well as original songs. Some of the top pop stars, such as Mỹ Tâm and Kasim, perform only original songs to previously recorded soundtracks, and the hip-hop inclined pop singers, such as Kasim, Mỹ Tâm, and Thanh Thảo, often perform with dancers.

Of all the popular music listening clubs, Ánh Tuyết's ATB (Figure 6.5) most attempts to create an atmosphere of old Vietnam, as I explain in my fieldnotes from an evening's performance:

> The ATB theater is very impressive inside and outside. In short, it reminds me of the movie set for The Quiet American. A Charlie Chaplin silent movie is being projected on the backdrop of the stage—sort of a nice touch and probably symbolic of the better times from Vietnam's past. The movie's kind of violent in a "nice" sort of way, like Vietnam's peaceful yet violent past, as it were. I've actually read about Vietnam yearning for its peaceful past, even though it has had almost constant wars and other conflicts for centuries. This is a beautiful theater inside—lots of Hoi An lanterns; water art; huge vases; a big fan with a picture of Văn Cao on it; sculptured bonsai here and there. A soft saxophone playing in the background has now stopped and the curtain has been pulled. Let the evening begin! (August 4, 2005)

How did the evening proceed? What kind of music was performed at this "shrine" of music past and present, with its many reminders of traditional Vietnam? Once again, my fieldnotes capture the moment (or the hours) of a live evening's performance:

> It's 8:35 p.m., and the ATB choir and band open the show. The choir consists of six girls and five boys, arranged 3+5+3 on the stage, with the band behind them, divided into two halves. The band includes bongo and conga drums, trap set, 1 guitar, electric bass, and 2 keyboards. There are no more than 50 people attending the show at this time.
>
> After the opening act, a young, pretty announcer introduces the first singer: a young man wearing a Western suit who sings a slow ballad. Behind him a picture of a bridge is projected on the large backdrop screen. For his second song he sings another ballad, a cover from the United States—an "oldie"—perhaps an Italian song. Actually, this is a Perry Como or Dean Martin tune that I recognize; it is sung, however, in Vietnamese. More Vietnamese scenery is projected on the big screen.
>
> The pretty announcer comes out again and introduces a young lady wearing a tight red dress. Accompanied by a young man playing an amplified acoustic guitar while sitting on a stool, the female singer performs a ballad. Now she sits on a stool and plays guitar as well. It's another ballad (yawn!). She's good though. The young man plays Spanish style guitar music, with a descending tetrachord in the interlude. It's great guitar playing with a very authentic-sounding flamenco flavor.
>
> The announcer comes out again, followed by the band and four of the choir boys dressed in black pants, wide belts, and white long-sleeve shirts with rolled-up sleeves—the uniform! They sing a ballad, of course, accompanied by congas and bongos.
>
> The announcer introduces another attractive girl singer who sings . . . a ballad. The keyboard imitates a traditional instrument, and the tune sounds like a Trịnh Công Sơn piece—it has that type of melody. For her second song she sings another ballad. Most of the pictures that are projected appear to be from the Da Lat area.
>
> The announcer introduces a young man in a suit. Oh, a ballad. Another Da Lat scene—a waterfall—is projected. Hmmm, another ballad. Just about everyone in the theater is intently listening, EXCEPT the people just behind me, who are very loud—I seem to attract such people. It's also getting smoky in here. There are probably between 65 to 70 people in attendance now.
>
> The announcer introduces an older lady, probably in her 40s. She reminds me of Cẩm Vân, a soprano, but it's not. She sings, what else?—a ballad. For her second song, however, she sings a type of a tango, the variation of the evening. The crowd loves it, and she receives the most applause so far tonight.

The announcer introduces a young man—the boy I talked to this afternoon while waiting for Ánh Tuyết, hours before the show. He told me he won an HTV singing competition last year. He sings a ballad with a beat, accompanied by a cool sax sound played on the keyboard. For his second song he sings another ballad with a type of reedy *sáo* melody. This is an interesting piece because of the Vietnamese traditional instrument sound. Now the song becomes a march. Projected on the back screen are photographs are of the Nha Trang beach with palm trees.

A girl singer follows, who sings a ballad. The synthesizer imitates the same single reed instrument again. The picture being projected is of Halong Bay.

Now she sings an upbeat ballad, while the projected pictures are of one of the little lakes in Hanoi, or it may be Halong Bay from the shore; it's hard to tell, but it's a pretty scenery shot. Another young female singer joins the group and she sings yet another ballad—a very slow waltz, which includes a faster second part in duple meter. She sings another ballad, but is now accompanied by three backup girl singers, seated on the stairs on stage. All of this music is the closest to Japanese *enka* (popular musical genre) I have heard in Vietnam. I don't recognize anything Vietnamese about it, contrary to what Ánh Tuyết and Nguyen Anh Chin told me this afternoon. Now the projected scenery is from the mountains in Sapa.

Six girls wearing yellow *áo dài* are now singing—they make up the female section of the house choir. It's now 10:25 PM, and another boy singer is on stage, singing another ballad, followed by—yup!—another ballad, this one a cover tune sung in French. I NEED AN INTERMISSION!

Now it's 10:30 and Ánh Tuyết, the hostess, owner, and the star, finally comes on stage, accompanied by terrible microphone squeals. She begins her act with a slow ballad, accompanied by Nguyen Anh Chin on the piano and the six girl choir. Now she sings a blues ballad, accompanied by piano. "What's Vietnamese about this piece?" I ask myself. The audience is very attentive, although some continue to talk. Now she sings a ballad with the full choir. As she sits on the stage, terrible microphone feedback is created. The band has returned, and now she sings a Strauss waltz. "What is Vietnamese about that?" I again ask myself. The full ATB band (instruments and choir) now do a traditional Vietnamese-sounding introduction, with the synthesizer imitating traditional instruments. I guess that is as Vietnamese as the evening will be. A kind of march follows the introduction, or perhaps it is meant to be a type of polka. It is obviously a pre-1970s song, her final one of the evening. (ATB Club, August 4, 2005)

If nothing else, my fieldnotes emphasize the great love the Vietnamese have for slow ballads. Relative to this chapter, however, they also suggest the use of a musical soundscape that matches the décorscape of the ATB theater, with just enough Vietnamese elements to make it slightly exotic. However, the exoticism has a definite prewar flavor, both visually and musically; this is, in fact, Ánh Tuyết's objective.

COFFEE HOUSES, CAFÉS, AND HOTEL LOUNGES

Sometimes referred to as *pop shops* according to writer Quế Anh, coffee houses, cafés, and hotel lounges are small performance venues that cater to quiet listening and light gastronomic delights, such as coffee, drinks, and snacks. As one of the world's largest coffee producers, Vietnam has only recently developed the coffee house as a gathering place. Quế Anh colorfully describes the coffee house scene in Hanoi:

> Is it a revival of Paris' left bank? The second coming of the Beats' Greenwich Village? Not quite, but with over 30 coffee houses, and undoubtedly more on the way, Hanoi is quickly establishing itself as Vietnam's contemporary vanguard of a decidedly Western tradition—combining coffee and music.
>
> Most of the city's coffee houses are concentrated downtown. Many of them started as standard cafes or restaurants, then realized they could attract more customers by playing live music. Some hire a capella singers, some hire six-piece jazz ensembles, and some hire just about anyone willing to go on stage and entertain a room full of diners.
>
> One of the leaders of this new pack of cafés is Quyen Van Minh's jazz club, where expats and young Vietnamese alike come to enjoy both the tunes and the tastes. It is not a new thing to give musical performances at restaurants and bars. But Hanoi's new breed of coffee houses use music purely as a lure to get customers in the door, not as an atmospheric accompaniment to a meal.
>
> With different shops come different styles, different tastes and different clientele. The shops in Truong Dinh, Thanh Xuan and Pho Vong could be classified as the popular clubs, or "pop shops," as far as the drinks and singers are concerned. Mainstream, populist, lively and welcoming, these shops are noisier because of their popularity with young people. But noise to some is music to others.
>
> Luxury shops are air-conditioned, often with better locations and interior decorations, such as Ho Guom Xanh, 157 Shop, Coi Nguon, Hollywood, Fashion Café and Paloma. The newer coffee houses offer more spacious stages, creating more space for diners to shake off some calories on the dance floor after dinner, and offering places for amateur singers to croon away with hopes of making it big.
>
> With both business and bass booming, there is no doubt that Hanoi's coffee house craze will be around for a while yet. The question remaining is, will the coffee? (*VNN*, n.d.)

Though Quế Anh's description seems to cover a wide gamut of performance venues, some with jazz bands, dancing, and dinner, the venues included here are smaller than the others, and as the author suggests, the primarily coffee and food establishment owners "realized they could attract more customers by playing live music." Thus, the primary purpose of these "pop shops" is gastronomic rather than musical.

Another function of some of the coffee house, café, and hotel lounge performance venues is to give the public an opportunity to perform as amateur singers. As such, the establishments are similar to karaoke bars (see Chapter 9), but with live rather than mediated accompaniment for amateur singers and other wannabes. Many of these performance venues also feature chamber music and/or jazz performances. One such establishment in Ho Chi Minh City that features the former is Gió Bắc coffee house on the northwest corner of the contemporary-looking Cong Truong Quoc Te plaza/traffic circle in District 2, just west of Notre Dame Cathedral; another that features jazz (in all its combo manifestations, including jazz/pop) is the lounge in the Sofitel Plaza Hotel on Lê Duẩn street. Several nights a week during the summer of 2005 I played with the combo, performing jazz standards and popular music, including bossa novas, Beatles tunes, and American popular songs from the 1940s through the 1960s.

BOWLING ALLEYS AND INTERNET CAFÉS

Like coffee houses, bowling alleys are a Western phenomenon recently introduced into Vietnam's large cities. Unlike them, however, musical entertainment is mediated rather than live. Nevertheless, they have become popular entertainment venues for Vietnam's youth, as suggested in the following article (*VNN*, August 26, 2002): "The youth social scene in HCM City has long revolved around coffee shop culture, but a new venue is poised to become the young person's next hangout of choice—the bowling alley has arrived in the south, and its popularity is booming. . . . 'Visit a bowling alley and you can listen to music, meet beautiful people and put your worries behind you. You can laugh and cry out at the top of your voice while playing [the] game. It's great' [said a customer]." The bowling alleys I visited in Ho Chi Minh City in 2002, 2004, and 2005 featured pop music as noisy background sonic wallpaper. Usually situated on the top floors of department stores (such as Diamond Plaza in downtown Saigon), bowling alley complexes blast out the same recorded pop music everywhere—in the bowling alleys themselves, the pool room, the game room, and even into Colonel Sanders' Kentucky Fried Chicken and other fast food restaurants.

The passive music making that goes on at bowling alleys also occurs in some deluxe Internet cafés (such as Internet World in 2002, now out of business), either individually from an Internet terminal or from large television screens that generally display MTV or Asian MTV during operating hours. Internet establishments are among the fastest growing venues for mediated music in Vietnam, although most of the music is heard through headphones.

CONCERT HALLS AND THEATERS

Large halls referred to as theaters (or theatres) in the newsprint are often huge concert halls, because they are rarely used for theatrical performances. In Ho Chi Minh City there are a number of very large ultramodern halls, such as Bến Thành Theater and Hòa Bình Theater, which are used for pop music concerts and other music events. The Bến Thành Theater is a large glass structure crowded into an area with other public buildings. It is used for dramatic presentations for children as well for as a variety of pop music activities. The Hòa Bình Theater (Figure 6.6), by contrast, is a large contemporary edifice that is situated in a major location in Ho Chi Minh City's District 10, next to the Việt Nam Quốc Tự Buddhist temple and the Kỳ Hòa Park. As sort of a shrine to music, modern art depicting various kinds of music adorn the façade and the landscaping in front of the building (Figure 6.7).

Figure 6.6   Hòa Bình Theater in Ho Chi Minh City, which is situated next to the Việt Nam Quốc Tự Buddhist temple in District 10. Photograph by Dale A. Olsen, 2002.

Figure 6.7 Musical pop art on the façade of the Hòa Bình Theater in Ho Chi Minh City. Photograph by Dale A. Olsen, 2002.

STADIUMS AND ARENAS

In Vietnam, stadiums and arenas exist for either sporting events or rock and pop-rock concerts, but not usually for both. Stadiums are primarily used as music venues, although there have been large concerts presented occasionally at sports arenas as well, such as the concert by the German singer/dancer Boney M, who performed at the Phan Đình Phùng Sports Arena in Ho Chi Minh City in 1995 (*VNN*, January 6, 1995).

One of the most popular music stadiums in Ho Chi Minh City is Lan Anh Stadium in District 3. A rather small structure as stadiums go, Lan Anh Stadium is mostly covered to keep out the rain. In the athletic portion of the stadium, folding chairs facing a large stage are set up for pop and rock concerts. Huge speaker systems that fill the complex with sound during concerts are set up. Even in the last row of the bleachers, at the farthest possible spot from the stage, the music during a concert by Da Vàng in 2004 was so loud that my ear plugs once again served me well (see Figure 7.3).

PARKS

Not all parks in Vietnam are performance venues for pop music concerts, but several cater to the musical tastes of young people. During the summer months, water parks are important locations for free competitive performances by high-school and other student pop-rock bands, and inexpensive performances for students by well-known pop singers. The most notable parks in Ho Chi Minh City are Đầm Sen in District 11 (which has already been described in Chapter 6, relative to a high-school pop-rock band competition), Suoi Tien in District 9, and Kỳ Hòa in District 10. In Hanoi, a popular venue is Hồ Tây water park on the southern shore of West Lake (this has already been described in Chapter 6, as it pertained to a rock concert in Hanoi).

CONCLUSION: PERFORMANCE PLACE AS COMMODITY, LEISURE, IDEOLOGY, AND POWER

Entertainment or performance venues in Vietnam are mainstream popular music establishments, for the most part. There are, for example, few if any alternative and casual performance venues where experimental bands can perform, such as the "live houses" in Japan, Taiwan, and elsewhere (Sekine 2007:210).

Except for the large government-supported community performance venues discussed at the beginning of this chapter, the primary raison d'être of all the other performance venues is to make money, in spite of the various cultural and moral reasons sometimes given for their existence. Simon Frith discusses leisure and its various meanings in his article titled "Formalism, Realism and Leisure": " . . . the moral approach to leisure is complemented (and sometimes opposed) by commercial entrepreneurs churning out 'escapist' cultural commodities with reference not to their content but to their profitability" (1997:172). The cartoon near the beginning of this chapter (Figure 6.1) visually and comically points out the profitability and price gouging that seem to rule at most commercial popular music performance venues in Vietnam, and the accompanying article discusses the overpricing of drinks at a dance club known as Queen Bee in 1996, "Dancing away dollars over a simple orange juice"):

> People with a weak heart [*sic*] should be forewarned before entering the "Queen Bee" club at night. First encounters can be startling. One of the attractions of the club is free entrance. But after settling in, an unpriced drink menu is brought out. The receipt that later arrives quenches one's curiosity: VNĐ 70,000 (nearly US$7) for an orange juice. "It is not expensive," says a security man. "The difference here is we don't charge our customers entrance tickets. We tack on a little bit extra for the drinks. "The first drink it is VNĐ 70,000, but after the second, the rate is normal," he adds.
>
> One of the most popular dancing clubs in the city, "Queen Bee" is almost always full of revelers. On New Year's Eve, there was no room to move, as was the case at several other popular clubs. "I prefer the 'Queen Bee'," says Khai, a regular. "This place is for everyone, not just

for the rich. As you can see, the majority are Vietnamese," he adds. The official opening time of the club is from 7:00 PM, but people arrive fashionably late at 11:00 PM and normally stay until 2:00 AM. The club's atmosphere is whipped-up by loud music, mostly rap, hip hop, and techno, supported by four Vietnamese girls and two Singaporean men singing and dancing new moves the whole night on stage. (*VNN*, February 5, 1996

I experienced the same price gouging for a beer at the Blue Club in 2002 (although it was an imported Mexican Corona). Though the admission was free for my friend and me (but not for others, it appeared), it was likely assumed that we would spend the equivalent of about twenty dollars for drinks, a lot of money for an evening out in Vietnam, especially for the Vietnamese. Likewise, at the popular music listening clubs where a cover is charged, the price for a drink of any kind is considerably higher than at most restaurants.

What does the fact that these performance venues are predominantly commercial tell us about music and dance as commodity, leisure, and ideology in Vietnam? According to Frith, "[their] commodity form can't be denied . . . , but the problem is to what extent [their] commercial function determines [their] cultural meaning" (1997:166). Subcultural theorists argue that "meanings are created out of commodities" (ibid.), but such an argument would place Vietnam's large commercial performance venues (where most of the music is mediated) into the same category as the popular music listening clubs (where most of the music is live), and that creates a false relationship between what could be termed "the pleasure of mass culture" and "[t]he pleasure of art" (Frith citing Theodor Adorno, ibid.:165). It is not my purpose to argue that dance music (trance, disco, house, etc.) performed at dancing clubs is "mass culture" and popular music (*tình ca*, *nhạc trẻ*, etc.) performed at popular music listening clubs is "art," but they are both commodities, and their performance venues are venues for leisure activity. However, I have argued that the large commercial performance venues create an entrancing atmosphere by virtue of the amplitude (loudness) and repetitiveness of its music, whereas the popular music listening clubs create an entrancing atmosphere by virtue of the *duyên* (sweetness or charm) of its music (in spite of its high amplitude, especially of the bass). Adorno identifies a similar dichotomy, as Frith explains:

This subjection of creativity to commodity form . . . was made possible, according to Adorno, by the technology of mass production, and he explained the popularity of mass music in psychological terms: the pleasure of mass culture is the pleasure of a particular kind of consumption—a passive, endlessly repeated confirmation of the world-as-it-is. The pleasure of art, in contrast, is the pleasure of imagination and involves an engagement with the world-as-it-could-be. (ibid.)

I see this as true, when applied to the performance venues termed dancing clubs and listening clubs. The "consumption" with regard to the former, however, is alcohol (and perhaps ecstasy and other drugs), which definitely emphasize the "world-as-it-is," whereas the sentimental ballad-like songs of the latter, and their *duyên*, emphasize the "world-as-it-could be," or the world-as-it-once-was (e.g., prewar songs at the ATB club).

Additionally, there is no question that both (in fact, all) types of popular music performance venues are sonic (and visual) places for the creation of power, as Street suggested: "[Popular music's] power is the power to delight: the ability to draw people together and to find a common resonance in their private feelings" (1986:223). The many types of venues in Vietnam just go about creating power in different ways.

At the beginning of this chapter I asked another question that is important for understanding popular music performance venues in Vietnam: What are the relationships, if any, between performance venue and social class? Straw, with regard to places of musical activity in America and Britain, makes the following correlation between performance venues and social class:

> These sites [he is referring to "the schoolyard, the urban dance club, the radio format"], themselves shaped by their place within the contemporary metropolis and aligned with populations along the lines of class and taste, provide the conditions of possibility of alliances between musical styles and affective links between dispersed geographical places. (1997:504)

With regard to the placement of performance venues and their alignment with particular populations in Ho Chi Minh City, I find there is little correlation. Vietnamese cities are motorbike cultures, and it costs little and takes very little time to go anywhere within the confines of urban areas. The fact that the most overpriced club venues (because of cover charges and prices for drinks and food) are in Saigon (i.e. District 1) rather than in outlying areas of Ho Chi Minh City (i.e. the other districts), however, is an important factor, but only because the heart of the city is where most global kinds of entertainment takes place. The heart of the city is also where the markets, the bus stations, and other necessary attributes for the smooth functioning of an urban area are located. Large rock concerts are typically not in the downtown areas of cities because the water parks and stadiums are not located downtown.

The next chapter studies some of the musical shows, festivals, competitions, and other musical events that take place in the diverse performance venues of Vietnam. Without actual events, performance venues (unless they feature mediated music) are lifeless structures and places, devoid of context and human significance. With actual events, however, artistic dissemination is possible within their confines.

7 Disseminating Popular Music
Pop and Rock Music Concerts, Festivals, and Shows

Large-scale popular music concerts, festivals, and shows are grouped together in this chapter because they are essentially the same type of event; the words concert, festival, and show are used interchangeably in the *Việt Nam News* and in other Vietnamese English language publications, including advertisements (posters, newspaper announcements, fliers, etc.). As we have seen in Chapter 6, large live events in Vietnam are held in concert halls and theaters, arenas and stadiums, public parks and water parks, school grounds and other sites that can accommodate large crowds. I see these large-scale popular music events as having the following four purposes or reasons for their occurrence (in alphabetical order): aesthetic, economic, ideological, and personal. These purposes are so thoroughly mixed, however, that it is difficult if not impossible to determine which is most important. By *aesthetic purpose* I mean entertainment quality, which is mostly a value judgment. The *economic purpose*, however, can be measured by dividing it into two subcategories: for profit and for free. Furthermore, profit can be measured in terms of money earned or lost. By *ideological purpose* I refer to charitable versus noncharitable events. Finally, I see the *personal purpose* as incorporating at least two basic ideas: the career enhancement of the performer(s) and a ritualistic *performance high* for the performer. These four categories are quite arbitrary, and the first and last (aesthetic and personal) are found in all of them in various degrees. Indeed, as Roy Shuker writes: "Concerts are a ritual for both performers and their audience" 2003:205), meaning that the aesthetic and personal reasons for their being are part of what Mantle Hood calls "the untalkables of music" because they cannot be scientifically measured (1982:307–310). Therefore, in this chapter I analyze large-scale concerts, shows, and festivals from the points of view of my middle two parameters, as placed within the following subheadings: Pop Music for Profit/Pop Music for Free; Shows as Competitions; Pop and Rock Concert Tours; and Pop Music Shows for Charity. The following paragraphs include my analyses of many popular music (mostly pop and rock music) events that occurred between 1992 and 2005; they are studied chronologically. In addition, I analyze the popular music events in terms of the politics of remembering and the economics of forgetting.

POP MUSIC FOR PROFIT/POP MUSIC FOR FREE

Large pop and rock music events in Vietnam have occurred since the early 1990s. Although at first the musicians did not receive much money for their participation, performing at a large-scale event was considered an honor and a step towards possible stardom. Furthermore, crowd satisfaction, then as now, led to a musician's personal satisfaction as an artist and entertainer. Nevertheless, large sums of money were always spent by event organizers or sponsors, as Dân Anh writes:

> Music impresarios spend heavily, buying sound and light systems and advertising. They pay pop stars like Mỹ Linh, Thanh Lam, Hồng Nhung, Phương Thanh and Lam Trương handsomely to perform at their concerts. The Babi Culture and Trading Company spent almost VNĐ 500 million [US$36,000] to produce Mot Thoang Việt Nam (A Glimpse of Việt Nam) at the Bến Thành Theater. Organizers spent almost VNĐ 1.5 billion [US$108,000] for Nhip Tim Cua Da. "Advertising fees account for a large part of our costs," says entrepreneur Phuoc Sang who organized Nhip Tim Cua Da. Sang spent almost VNĐ 150 million [US$10,800] advertising. Production costs might be high but organizers still make profits from ticket sales and sponsors who want their names displayed at performances. The demand for entertainment is increasing. Show business profits are expected to go higher and the shows become more competitive in the future with excellent opportunities for impresarios. (1999)

This article (the only one of its kind to give expense details of an event) can serve as a standard for the cost of putting on a concert, festival, or show in Vietnam (in 2005, however, they were much more expensive). Other articles, especially those about charitable concerts, often discuss overall earnings.

The first Pop-Rock Festival in Vietnam took place March 2, 1992, in Ho Chi Minh City (*VNN*, March 4, 1992). Lasting several days, altogether more than twenty pop-rock bands from Ho Chi Minh City participated, and approximately one-thousand people attended the opening performance alone. This was a unique event because it was cosponsored by two government supported agencies: the Youth Cultural House (where it was held) and the Labor Cultural House. This recognition by the communist government is one of the reasons I have chosen this festival to be the approximate starting date of my study. Not only did it have an impact similar to that of Woodstock's in the United States because of the relatively large number of young people who participated both actively and passively, but it also legitimized the contemporary expressions of pop-rock music in the eyes of the traditionally minded establishment.

Newspaper coverage of Vietnamese pop-rock concerts did not occur again in the *Việt Nam News* until April 1, 1997, and in a 1999 article, Dân Anh suggests that concerts featuring Vietnamese musicians were not common during that interim period, as he writes:

> Vietnamese songs and their singers are winning the hearts of fans who once preferred western music. An industry that began to grow in Việt Nam about three years ago [1996], when international promoters organized successful expensive-to-attend shows in Hà Nội and HCM City featuring such world renowned singers as Sting and Leo Sayer, has given way to home-grown stars and their music. Now shows featuring Vietnamese pop singers attract thousands of fans. (*VNN*, July 7, 1999)

One of these "home-grown" concerts occurred on March 26 and 27, 1997, when over 10,000 young people attended two pop-rock performances in the Kỳ Hòa Park in Ho Chi Minh City. Called *Coca-Cola Pop Rock '97*, the event took place after Clinton's visit to Vietnam, which resulted in the lifting of the U.S. trade embargo. Coca-Cola was one of the first big businesses from the United States to open a branch in Vietnam, and because of its corporate sponsorship, tickets were very inexpensive for the general public at only VNĐ 4000 and 2000 (approximately US$.40 and .20 in 1997) and were free for college students (*VNN*, April 1, 1997). Eight pop-rock bands performed, including the well-known groups Da Vàng and Kien Xanh (Green Ants).

In the fall of 1997, a new concert series for students called *Đêm Tr* (Youth Night) was organized in Ho Chi Minh City at the Bến Thành Theater. The brainchild of Nguyễn Trọng Hiếu, a former rock guitarist with the Sóng Xanh (Blue Waves) student rock group, the first *Đêm Trẻ* concert attracted 3000 young people (*VNN*, November 10, 1997). The series, cosponsored by Maybe Line, Nippon Paint, and Tiger Beer, included one concert each month for a year. As many as fourteen bands participated, including student groups as well as professional ones.

Although the *Đêm Trẻ* pop-rock concerts featured bands rather than pop singers per se, many of Vietnam's pop music stars performed at a concert titled *Thì Thầm Mùa Xuân* (Whispers of Spring), also known as *Top Hits* concert, which was held at the Bến Thành Theater in April 1998 (*VNN*, March 6, 1998). In complete contrast to the pop-rock concerts held in the same theater, tickets for this event sold on the black market for as much as VNĐ 400,000 (ca. US$40 apiece, one-hundred times more than the *Đêm Trẻ* tickets); average tickets, however, sold for VNĐ 60,000 and 80,000 each (about US$6 and $8, respectively). Some of the performers included Thu Phương, Lam Trường, and other pop music idols.

The *Top Hits* concert was too expensive for most of Vietnam's young people, but government-sponsored concerts in Ho Chi Minh City's Cultural House, Cultural Park, Worker's Palace, the Bến Thành Theater, and other venues, were held in 1998 at very low prices—some were even free. One concert series was described as follows:

> The YCH [Youth Cultural House] music program Introducing New Songs attracts large crowds each Sunday morning with the latest hits, while offering the chance to interact with the musicians. "The program creates a successful link between the musicians and the fans," said one YCH promoter. "Apart from this, they offer both relaxation and entertainment to the audiences." "Most people who come to this program are students or young workers," he added. Many say the atmosphere at these concerts is one of intimacy and youthfulness, more so than at any professional programs. The wit and unexpected questions raised by young audiences during banter with the musicians are usually interesting, and sometimes musicians find it hard to give suitable answers. At least two musicians are introduced each Sunday. At one such YCH meeting with the audience, musician Nguyễn Duc Trung could only smile and remained tongue-tied when a young woman told him that he was handsome. (*VNN* 4, 1999, #DSC00115)

The youth culture house concert concept (see Chapter 6) creates a close connection with and builds rapport between musical artists and young people (students and young workers) in Vietnam. At the same time, the youth culture house administration can regulate who the performers are and what type of music is performed. According to various newsprint articles, however, the music is wide-ranging: from red songs (*nhạc đỏ*) to pop, from folk dance to (undoubtedly censored) hip-hop, and from amateur student bands to well-known professional ensembles.

Another series of free concerts were sponsored by two municipal organizations in Ho Chi Minh City in 2002:

> Struggling students are often deprived of seeing their favorite music groups live because of high ticket prices. But now the music is coming straight to them—for free. Two HCM City organizations, the HCM City Student Association (HAS) and the HCM City Student Support Center (HSSC), have created a program that will bring pop singers to universities and dormitories around the city. . . ."We hope that it will give us a feast of happiness and passion after our days of hard studying," said one student from HCM City National University. (*VNN* 4, 1999, #DSC00115)

One of the musicians performing in a band called KTX explained that "his band will sing songs in praise of love, friendship, family and, of course, country" (ibid.). Although he speaks as if he is quoting directly from the "Political Report of the Central Committee to the National Congress of the Communist Party" (see Chapter 2), the KTX band was important for introducing Vietnamese pop music to students who had been saturated with Western pop. Moreover, the HAS and HSSC are both government-supported student help associations.

In June 2005, what may have been one of the most costly free concerts in Vietnam took place at the Victoria Hotel and Resort complex in the Mekong Delta. It featured Vietnamese pop music diva Thanh Lam accompanied by Ho Chi Minh City's MTV band and the French punk rock band, La Souris Deglinguee (LSD), also known as The Busted Mouse in English. "The concert [was] free to people who live along the Mekong River near the Victoria Hotels and Resorts, as part of Victoria's 10th anniversary in Việt Nam" (*VNN*, June 10, 2005). No information was published about the cost of the concert; however, it was not a charitable event, and Thanh Lam and LSD are expensive entertainers under normal circumstances.

These newsprint stories about concerts, festivals, and shows for profit or for free probably represent only a handful of the events that have taken place in Vietnam since 1992. They demonstrate, nevertheless, that Vietnamese artists, entrepreneurs, musicians, politicians, and others, for the most part created a balance between profit making and the lack of profit in the 1990s and early 2000s. With a few exceptions (such as the very expensive *Whispers of Spring* or *Top Hits* concert held at the Bến Thành Theater in April 1998), it seems that the musicians and gatekeepers have been able to keep the public and student masses as their primary concern by making Vietnamese pop music affordable to them because of government and/or corporate sponsorship. In this case, a paradox is created in that the politics of remembering is also the economics of remembering because of the high cost of production and near zero profit, and the remembering is not of the past but of the present. The government and/or corporate sponsors have funded elaborate concerts that are inexpensive for the public; they are primarily for students, and their objectives are to encourage praise of country, family, friendship, and love, as the KTX band member explained above. Added to these objectives is praise of singing, which is encouraged at the governmental level by its support of competitions.

SHOWS AS COMPETITIONS

Singing contests are very popular in Vietnam, as they are in Japan and, more recently, in Great Britain and the United States. The first competition to be mentioned in the *Việt Nam News* is called the *Collegiate Music Competition Unplugged*, which began in Ho Chi Minh City in 1994 (*VNN*, April 15, 1997). Held annually, it is sponsored by the city's College of Social Sciences and Humanities. According to its rules, original compositions must be sung in English, and "The competition aims to encourage creativity among students while providing them with a 'playground' and . . . healthy extracurricular activities" (ibid.), the latter additional factors relating to the government's objectives to encourage friendship, love, and other desired values. Paradoxically, however, the requirement to sing in English strengthens the cultural influences of globalization (or Americanization). Regarding the musical attributes of the *Collegiate Music Competition Unplugged*, nothing is mentioned in the press about the fact that the term "unplugged" was coined in the United States for a series of concerts organized by MTV "where artists perform without any electronic amplifications or enhancement to showcase their natural musical talents" (Banks 1997:304).[1] Judging from a photograph in the *Việt Nam News*, musicians played acoustic guitars into microphones, and no electric guitars were used (June 13, 1997). All of these characteristics suggest that this competition is a bridge between the politics of remembering and the economics of forgetting, or, as if on a continuum, it is somewhere in the middle. Remembering is seen with the emphases on values; forgetting is seen with the emphases on singing in English and the adoption (or adaptation) of an American system of musical delivery (i.e. being unplugged).

The majority of the singing competitions are sponsored by two television stations in Vietnam, HTV (Ho Chi Minh City Television) and VTV (Việt Nam Television), which have an active role in the dissemination of values because both companies are owned and administered by the government.

HTV hosted a singing contest in 1998 in which the winner received VNĐ 12 million, approximately US$850 in 1998 (*VNN*, December 19, 1998). "More than 1,800 youths between the ages of 16 and 30 from all over the country competed in the two-month-long contest. Twelve were selected as finalists at a public performance held on Tuesday at the city's Municipal Theater. The singing contest, an annual event, was first organized in 1991 with 800 performers and has continued to attract many entrants" (ibid.).

In 1999, VTV held a singing contest in which the winner was awarded VNĐ 15 million, nearly US$1000 (*VNN*, December 10, 1999). There were more than one thousand young singers who entered the competition, and fifty-seven were chosen as finalists.

In 2001, HTV hosted a singing and pop band contest called *Pop Music and Youngsters Festival*, in which two ethnic minority singers from Tây Nguyên shared the first prize of VNĐ 20 million, nearly US$1,500 (*VNN*, September 20, 2001). About the *Festival*, the Secretary General (a governmental position) of Ho Chi Minh City's Musicians' Association, stated: "The festival aims to discover talented new bands and encourage their musical pursuits. We hope the competition will enable amateur pop bands to develop and grow" (ibid.). In the 2002 *Pop Music and Youngsters Festival*, Đồng Đôi (Teammates), a pop band from Hanoi, won the top awards (*VNN*, May 25, 2002). Đồng Đôi, from the Vietnamese Army's Song and Dance School, also won for the best original song titled "Nhớ Về Tuổi Thơ" (Childhood Memories). Paraphrasing himself, the same Secretary General of the Musicians' Association in Ho Chi Minh City said, "We hope the festival will help amateur musical talents to develop and grow" (ibid.).

The biggest and most important televised song competition is Việt Nam Television's biennial star search contest, *Sao Mai* (Morning Star), which began in 1997 and was expanded, improved, and renamed in 2004 as *Sao Mai–Điểm Hẹn* (Morning Star–A Destination). It is a major event that includes thousands of contestants, thousands of live attendees, and millions of television viewers, much like American Idol in the United States.

What these newsprint vignettes tell us about pop song festivals as competitions is that they are all supported by official government organizations, such as universities and television companies. Private enterprises often take part as cosponsors, although the governmental agencies set the rules. These official agencies, all the way up to the *Sao Mai–Điểm Hẹn* star search contest, realize the importance of nurturing pop music development among Vietnam's youth, seemingly without restrictions until the 2005 requirements stated for the *Sao Mai–Điểm Hẹn* competition. It is perhaps also noteworthy that the winning Đồng Đôi pop band from the Army's Song and Dance School won with their original song, "Childhood Memories." How far childhood memories are from the politics of remembering is perhaps open to discussion. It may be coincidental or not that Đồng Đôi won all top honors in 2002.

In addition to live competitions for pop singers, Vietnam also supports contests for rock bands, especially in the 2000s. Most of them occur in Hanoi, which paradoxically is the center for rock activity in Vietnam, especially through the efforts of two rock advocacy groups, Hà Nội Rock Club and Rock Vision Working Group (the paradox is that rock is very contemporary and Hanoi, the capital of Vietnam, is very traditional). The following news article appeared a day before the 2004 rock award ceremony and show *Rock Ba Miền* was held outdoors in the Hồ Tây (West Lake) Water Park:

> A live rock show and award ceremony will be held tomorrow in Hà Nội as the best rock bands from all over the country let their hair down and rock out. Rock fans in the capital can catch the show Rock Ba Miền at Hồ Tây Water Park.
>
> Vietnamese rock has been gaining popularity since the first major outdoor Việt Rock Concert last year in Giảng Võ Stadium in Hà Nội. The first Rock Ba Miền show will gather rock bands from HCM City, Đà Nẵng and Hà Nội. As the name suggests, the bands will represent the north, central and south regions. Joint-promoters Hà Nội Rock Club and Rock Vision Working Group plan the show to continue annually.
>
> The list of nominees for best rock dude includes Trần Lập from Bức Tường (The Wall) and Trần Hà of Ánh Sáng (The Light). Up for best rock band in the land award are Da Vàng (Yellow Skin), Atomega, Ánh Sáng (The Light), The Wall and Thủy Triều Đỏ (Red Tide). "We plan

to present awards for young talented rock bands; the best Vietnamese Rock album and the best Vietnamese rock song next year," said
Nguyễn Tuấn Thành, one of the chief organizers.

All the bands will be performing their own material, a great opportunity for bands like HCM's Bầu Khí Quyển (Atmosphere) performing their unique southern style rock for the first time in the northern
capital. The Light, a seasoned Hà Nội band keen on thrash metal, will
raise the curtain with five songs. Also performing, fellow Hanoians
Thủy Triều Đỏ are considered the young hopefuls who have been making waves in rock circles over the last two years. Yet another Hà Nội
rock band, Ngọn Lửa Nhỏ (Small Fire), prefer a style known as Nu-
Metal, exemplified by their newest songs Ngổn Ngang (Jumble) and
Ảo Giác (Illusion). One of the most widely anticipated acts will be Sói
Đen (BlackWolf), the only band from central Việt Nam. (*VNN*, May 7,
2004, "Hà Nội bands scream let there be rock")

This article is very informative for the number of rock bands discussed,
most of them never described again in the press. The number of rock bands
mentioned from Hanoi verifies my point that Vietnam's political capital is
also the Vietnam's rock capital.

In addition to *Rock Ba Miền*, an amateur rock band festival and competition is held annually in December at the same venue in Hanoi, as the
following article explains:

The Rock Music Festival 2004 will rock Hà Nội's West Lake Water
Park on Saturday night, promoting a music trend that has been gaining
popularity with youth in Việt Nam. Heads will bang to eight amateur rock groups selected to perform by the Hà Nội Culture and Information Department and mostly made up of Vietnamese students and
members of Hà Nội's resident expat community.

Bands to perform include 50/50, Kurga, Dark Age, 69 ERS, 7 Days,
Final Stage, Lazy Buddha, and Lives Together. The festival, organized
by Việt Nam Advertising and Entertainment Company and sponsored
by Kim Dinh Trading Ltd, is offering 17 awards worth VNĐ 12 million
(US$800) for the best bands. (*VNN*, December 11, 2004)

Tickets for this event cost VNĐ 25,000 (about US$1.60), and the gate
clearly did not cover the awards totaling US$13,600 (i.e. US$800 X 17
awards). The article reveals the Kim Dinh Trading Company (representing
economic globalization) as the sponsor, and also mentions the role of the
Ministry of Information and Culture in the selection (i.e. censoring) of the
songs to be performed. It was about this time (i.e. 2004) that sponsors also
took a role in the selection of music to be performed, adding to the effects
of censorship. It is significant, perhaps, that *The Rock Music Festival 2004*
was for student and expatriate rock bands only, two groups of people over

which the government has firm control (both university admissions and foreign visas are government controlled).

POP CONCERT TOURS

David Naggar writes, "No one except major stars makes any real money touring. For everyone else, touring is done primarily to help promote record sales" (2000–2004:115). He continues with these vignettes: " . . . she took six 18-wheelers, and four busses to transport her people and props. . . . she had one bus just for security guards, and another bus just for shoes!" (116). These are not Vietnamese pop stars, but Cher and Janet Jackson, respectively, on tour in the United States. Proportions such as these, by contrast, do not exist in Vietnam and probably never will. Contemporary popular music concert tours in Vietnam are very recent and rare (although national *cai lương* tours were very common from the 1920s until the mid 1950s; Pham Duy and Canh Thân toured the country singing *nhac cai cach* or reformed music in 1944–1945; and the Ban Hợp Ca Thăng Long went on a national tour in 1953). The first contemporary popular music tours were not documented by the *Việt Nam News*, however, until 1997:

> There's a boom in famous local singers launching solo performance tours throughout Vietnam. Subsequent to the first such tour, pop star Thanh Lam's swing through Hà Nội, HCM City and Việt city. Hồng Nhung, one of the most heralded singers in Vietnam, fixed late December to mid-January for her own tour. Mỹ Linh, the 22-year-old singer who has won the hearts of thousands of young people, has just announced a tour starting January 6. Such a solo tour is a good opportunity for singers whose talent has matured and who are particularly well prepared. They need to watch their step because Vietnam's promoters are not clearly up to the demands of the profession as yet. (*VNN*, December 22, 1997)

Three tours by three female pop stars on separate occasions do not really signify a "boom," but the three are the top-selling popular culture icons in Vietnam, and their tours generally coincide with the marketing of their CDs. No details have been published about their promoters, sponsors, or how the tours were funded, but the point of the article is that the singers themselves are way ahead of the gatekeepers.

Several years later, female pop singer Hồng Hanh made a two-city tour (one actually, because she is from Ho Chi Minh City), including Ho Chi Minh City and Hanoi, which was "entirely self-funded—a first for Việt Nam. 'My husband and I have invested our efforts and own money into this program', Hanh says" (*VNN*, September 21, 1999). That same year Ánh Tuyết did a concert tour that included Hanoi, Danang, Hoi An, and

Ho Chi Minh City, and in 2000 Lam Trường and Phuong Tranh did a joint tour of Vietnam's largest cities (*VNN*, October 25, 1999).

Why bother to tour in a relatively small country like Vietnam with just a handful of large cities? Phương Thanh explained it this way: "Truong and I will regret if we don't organize our concerts when we still have large audiences and before our popularity wanes" (ibid.) Indeed, with Vietnam's fan base getting younger and the *Sao Mai–Điểm Hẹn* competition turning out new heartthrobs each year, the expense and hassle of major city tours, which means renting large theaters or music stadiums, is not usually worth the trouble. Instead, many Ho Chi Minh City recording artists travel to Hanoi and other large cities to perform in the smaller popular music clubs, and vice versa for Hanoi pop singers. The following story, which appeared in 2001, relates to both large-scale and intimate concerts performed by touring and/or local pop stars:

> Could the country's music scene's glory days be over? That's what is being asked as organizers refuse to back big concerts—except those receiving sponsorship from bigger commercial companies. "The more we've invested in big shows, the more we've lost," said one promoter who organized many successful concerts in HCM City and nearby provinces in recent years. "We've had to calculate carefully and cut expenses to the minimum," he said. "That means our shows became less interesting. And we lost audiences." ... While giant venues like Hòa Bình and Bến Thành theaters offer less [sic] live-shows, many fans are going to bars, cafes and night clubs. The owners of such small entertainment venues are optimistic. "Attracting a few hundred customers a night isn't difficult," one said. "We can relax in the cozy atmosphere of a small night-club," said a fan. (*VNN*, November 5, 2001)

The situation with solo pop singers is different than with rock bands, because the former can travel and give shows accompanied by their pre-recorded sound tracks, or they can put together excellent programs with house bands. Rock bands, however, require heavy equipment and large crews and do not often tour, although Ho Chi Minh City bands occasionally play shows in Hanoi and elsewhere with local rock bands and vice versa. The first Vietnamese rock band to make a nationwide tour was Bức Tường (The Wall) in 2004.

POP MUSIC SHOWS FOR CHARITY

There are many worthy causes in Vietnam, and there are many pop musicians who give up their time and provide their talents for charity. Why are Vietnamese pop singers willing to do concerts for charity? Pop star Phương Thanh explains her reason to an interviewer for Inner Sanctum:

As a person of the public I have to perform my obligation towards society, and share the love they reserve for me. A singer, an artist, is a beautiful image among the audience. If we do charity with all our hearts, the results will be very good. In the future the audience will not remember my name as a singer, but they will remember an artist who knows how to share with and help others. (*VNN*, April 4, 2004)

Hồng Nhung is another pop star who has expressed her philosophy about helping others, explaining that her willingness is "prompted by her own difficult childhood and a path to fame that was uneven" (*VNN*, July 18, 1999). She has also been one of the most generous of Vietnam's pop singers. In 1999, she donated all of her earnings from a four-night concert, totaling VNĐ 200 million (US$14,300), to a charitable cause. Her aim, besides providing entertainment, is "the setting of goals and delivering of messages for the social good," she explained (ibid.).

Many pop music shows for charity are organized by Vietnamese agencies in conjunction with the United Nations and other international, as well as national, organizations. Others are purely national efforts. In the following paragraphs I have organized Vietnam's pop music shows for charity during the ten-year period between 1995 and 2005 into the following six categories: Children, Agent Orange Victims, Diseases, National Disasters, Scholarships for Needy Students, and General Hardships. There are probably many more worthy causes that have inspired pop music shows for charity in Vietnam, but these are the only ones documented in the *Việt Nam News*.

Children

The International Day of the Child inspired a series of charity concerts in 1996 titled *More than Music*, organized by UNICEF, the UN World Food Program, and the Việt Nam National Fund for Children. The concerts were intended "to raise public awareness and funding for Việt Nam's street children, disabled children, ethnic minority children in remote areas and other needy youngsters." The money was used to set up "scholarships for poor children with high scholastic achievements, family and community-based rehabilitation of disabled children, compassion homes for street children and a revolving credit scheme to assist integration of street children into their communities" (*VNN*, May 27, 1996). One 1996 concert featured Dutch-Indonesian musician Daniel Sahuleka, French musician Patrick David, Vietnamese pop singer Mỹ Linh, and modern dancer Lê Văn, all of whom donated their services. In addition, a number of street children performed a composition written for them.

In 2000, pop singer Lam Trường, accompanied by two bands (The Friends from Ho Chi Minh City and Brothers from Hanoi), performed two concerts for street children at Lan Anh Stadium in Ho Chi Minh City.

Three years later, in 2004, a number of pop singers and dancers from Ho Chi Minh City performed a benefit concert

> at the Hòa Bình Theater to raise funds for rural children born with facial deformities. Organized by the HCM City Culture and Information Department's Support Fund for Poor Patients and Prudential Insurance Company, the event—titled For Children's Eyes and Smiles—also encourages supporting underprivileged children through charity activities. (*VNN*, April 16, 2004)

These are only three concerts that have occurred every fourth year since 1996, and there were certainly many others that did not make it into the *Việt Nam News*. Helping children to survive the many calamities that can befall them, from homelessness, lack of education, Agent Orange sickness (unique to Vietnam), and many others, is a concern of the United Nations (UNESCO), other world organizations, and the Vietnamese government. There are no newsprint stories in English, however, about benefit concerts for the approximately fifty-thousand homeless and rejected *hapa*, Amerasian children of American fathers and Vietnamese mothers, during the ten years after the American War, because there was no effort by the Vietnamese to help them until their exodus to the United States in the 1980s (see Phương Thảo's stories in Chapter 3).

Agent Orange Victims

Many of the pop music shows for charity are to help people suffering from the effects of Agent Orange dioxin poisoning: "According to the World Health Organization, 2 million Vietnamese live with disabilities because of the spread of Agent Orange defoliant during the American War. Approximately 450,000 of them are children, and most live in rural and remote regions" (*VNN*, February 19, 2004). Even in 2004, the horrors of the American War linger, and the tragedy is increased when the victims were not even born until decades after the War ended. Called *The Kind Heart Concert*, a musical show was held in Ho Chi Minh City's Opera House on November 2003 for children suffering from the disabling effects of Agent Orange. Organized by the local Association for Disabled Children and the Municipal People's Committee, the show was additionally sponsored by Tenamyd Pharmaceuticals of Canada and other companies. It featured such singers as Cẩm Vân, Hồng Nhung, Phương Thảo, Quang Linh, and others, a veritable "who's who" of pop singers in Ho Chi Minh City. A similarly named show for child victims of Agent Orange took place at Hanoi's Municipal Theater (the former Opera House) on February 2004. It was also organized by national agencies, such as the Organization for Children with Disabilities, and featured many singers and musicians of all ages, including pop stars Mỹ Linh and Thanh Lam.

Similar pop shows for charity have been organized for all living victims of Agent Orange, not only the children. In 1997, for example, a concert titled *Dòng Thời Gian 1* (Course of Time 1) featured songs written during the American War, and in 1998 *Dòng Thời Gian 2* featured songs written after 1995; both concerts were held in Ho Chi Minh City and included such pop singers as Ánh Tuyết, Bằng Kiều, Lam Trường, and Thu Phương (*VNN*, July 28, 1998).

An event was held in Ho Chi Minh City in September 2004 for victims of Agent Orange; it featured several hundred musicians and artists. Titled Đêm Trắng (Sleepless Night), the event lasted an entire Saturday and included the selling of art works and crafts, a photographic auction, and musical performances, including new songs composed especially for Agent Orange victims (*VNN*, September 20, 2004).

Diseases

The first charity pop music shows devoted to HIV/AIDS awareness in Vietnam were held in Hanoi in November and December of 1997 in conjunction with the World AIDS Day on December 1. The series was the grand finale of an earlier "song writing contest on HIV/AIDS awareness and education. The contest, which was launched in early October, attracted 366 participants singing 431 songs; with four of the performers carrying the HIV virus" (*VNN*, November 27, 1997). The concert series was repeated in Ho Chi Minh City a week later, and the entire series was "supported by Vietnam Youth Union, National AIDS Committee, health and education volunteers, and United Nation[s] organizations like UNDP, WHO, UNICEF, UNFPA and UNESCO" (ibid.).

Dengue fever is a disease that particularly threatened children in the late 1990s in Vietnam. In 1999 Hồng Nhung performed a series of four concerts titled *Lullaby 99* that were dedicated to children and the eradication of dengue fever through prevention, as Nguyễn Thị Minh Thái wrote:

> [Hồng Nhung's] effort was intended to prevent [dengue fever] because prevention is better than treatment. Nhung asks all adults to ensure that their children sleep under mosquito nets; to spray against mosquitoes and not to store water in their houses for too long or allow it to gather where mosquitoes can breed. She also expresses her sympathy for the families of children who have died from dengue fever. She says 90 percent of child victims are from southern Việt Nam where the rainy season continues for most of the year. (*VNN*, July 18, 1999)

This was a concert that earned over US$14,000 for Vietnam's dengue fever eradication program, and it was the first ever pop show (let alone a series of four shows) for charity performed by a single artist. "Nhung's audiences say that her generosity has made them much more aware of the disease. It has also made them realize that she has a golden heart" (ibid.).

Severe Acute Respiratory Syndrome (SARS) eradication has been another worthy cause for charitable pop music shows in Vietnam. In 2004, Dr. Carlo Urbani, an Italian physician, first discovered the disease and soon after died from it himself. His successor, Carlo Scialdone, in conjunction with the United Nations International (UNIS) in Hanoi, organized charity pop music shows in 2004 and 2005 that featured pop singer Mỹ Linh; the shows were to commemorate Dr. Urbani's work with SARS and other diseases in rural Vietnam.

National Disasters

One of the most frequent and devastating national disasters in Vietnam is flooding, especially in the Mekong River (Cuu Long in Vietnamese) Delta region of southern Vietnam. During heavy rains, the Mekong River Delta is often subjected to floods that leave hundreds of thousand inhabitants homeless. Held only when such a disaster occurs and the need arises, flood-aid concerts usually take place in Ho Chi Minh City. In September 1999, and again in October 2001, benefit concerts raised several hundred million VNĐ. The funds were donated to flood victims in Ho Chi Minh City through Vietnam's Department of Culture and Information program known as Sponsor for Poor Patients. The 1999 concert featured a lineup of a half-dozen pop stars, several boy and girl bands, and four comedians (*VNN*, September 16, 1999). The 2001 benefit concert featured Ánh Tuyết and ATB, her 36-member band (*VNN*, October 29, 2001).

In 2005, pop singer Mỹ Linh performed a charity show with the Brothers boy band in Hanoi for the benefit of Malaysian tsunami victims (*VNN*, January 28, 2005), another flood disaster, although Vietnam was not affected by the tsunami.

Scholarships for Needy Students

Although scholarship help for financially disadvantaged students does not seem to be as much of a worthy cause for charitable pop concerts as those for the disabled, diseased, and destitute, a program known as the Nguyễn Thái Bình Scholarship Program supports outstanding students in financial need. Held annually in conjunction with a fashion show since 1991, the event is called *Duyên Dang Việt Nam* (Vietnamese Charm). The *Thanh Nien* (Young People) newspaper organizes the show and distributes the scholarship funds: "Over the past five years, the fund has granted scholarships, worth VNĐ 1 million each, to nearly 1,300 outstanding students from universities and high schools nationwide. The fund's managers are hoping to raise enough money for about 260 scholarships this academic year" (*VNN*, May 21, 2002). A secondary function of *Vietnamese Charm* is to invite Việt kiều pop singers to participate, as Mỹ Duyên writes:

> Vietnamese Charm will also give local and overseas Vietnamese singers and actors an opportunity to display their talents, including Jimmii Nguyễn, Thanh Ha and Trizzie Phuong Trinh. [Vietnamese nationals such as] Mỹ Linh, Quang Linh, Hồng Nhung, Thanh Lam, Lam Trường and Dan Trường will perform popular melodies and traditional favorite songs. Young singer and composer, Jimmii Nguyễn, will bring to the program some of his latest songs, including Thinking of You and Feelings of the Expatriate. "Through these songs, I want to share with other expatriates my feelings and experiences about the homeland and birthplace," Nguyễn said. Nguyễn also agreed to donate his own earnings for the show to the scholarship fund for needy students. (*VNN*, April 3, 2000)

Not only bringing in a valuable source of income for the scholarship fund, the Việt kiều pop singers (most of whom were very young children when they left Vietnam with their parents ca. 1975) may also help to remove any animosities that perhaps still exist between national and overseas Vietnamese people in Vietnam.

General Hardships

This is a difficult category to define, but the *Việt Nam News* published several articles about three kinds of benefits that can best be interpreted as being held for general hardships, such as securing funding for gratitude houses and helping poor people. In the fall of 1998, "Pop singers from all over the country played to a full house at HCM City's 2,000-seat Hòa Bình Theater last weekend, during a concert to raise funds for gratitude houses" (*VNN*, October 13, 1998). Nothing else is explained about the purpose of the benefit concert or what a gratitude house is; rather, the article goes into detail about the program, which "featured 21 of the most popular love songs written by Trịnh Công Sơn during the past four decades" (ibid.). It was also the first concert of his music in Ho Chi Minh City, according to the article.

Pop music charitable shows for helping poor people are also not defined well, except for one article that mentions a benefit concert for eye operations for the poor. That information appears in a short paragraph about flood-aid concerts:

> Jointly organized by the Municipal Service of Culture and Information, Phuoc Sang Trade and Entertainment Company and HCM City Sponsor for the Poor Patients, the concerts expect to raise at least VNĐ 100 million—half of which will be donated to residents of flood hit provinces.

The rest will be given to the project *Sight for the Poor Blind* to pay for a series of eye operations next year. (*VNN*, September 16, 1999)

VNĐ 50 million would have equaled approximately US$3500 in 1999, which would not go far towards eye operations in nonsocialist countries. The project *Sight for the Poor Blind* is one of several administered by the Ho Chi Minh City Sponsor for Poor Patients.

In Hanoi, a similar charity concert is held annually for poor people on New Year's Eve (January 31, which is not the traditional Vietnamese new year's celebration known as Tet). Called the *Nối Vòng Tay Lớn* (Joining Arms in Great Circle) concert and hosted by the Hanoi Cultural Friendship Palace, the fund-raising organization is called For the Sake of Poor People Fund. In 2002, the concert raised more than VNĐ 6 billion (about US$400,000) (*VNN*, December 26, 2003). Ho Chi Minh City was also involved in the same concert, and the two were linked by simultaneous live television broadcasts. Performers in the concerts included Mỹ Linh, Mỹ Tâm, Phương Thanh, Lam Trường, Siu Black, Poong Thiết, Ngọc Bảo, and 8-year-old Xuân Mai.

What conclusions can be made about pop music shows for charity in Vietnam? The most obvious is that the Vietnamese have a great desire to help their fellow citizens who are victims of human and natural disasters and others who suffer for other reasons. From the communist government down to the people, that desire seems to be strong. However, I cannot explain why I see poor beggars on the streets of Hanoi and Ho Chi Minh City, many without limbs and others apparently suffering from Agent Orange illness or other diseases affecting the skin. Musical conclusions are easier for me to make. Along with doing a general good (i.e. helping society) by supporting charities with their money, the psychological support of pop singers for the many social causes is also very important. By believing and supporting a cause, for example, the fan base of the pop stars may also support the cause, and this is often more important than money because it represents an ideological change. Pop stars in Vietnam (as elsewhere in the world) are trendsetters and their persuasive powers are often greater than those of parents, teachers, and certainly government officials. In addition to being able to exert a power of persuasion, pop singers also receive a great deal of glory for their willingness to sacrifice their earnings. Not only are they able to present a caring, loving, and humanistic side of themselves, the newsprint articles in the *Việt Nam News* always present glowing descriptions of the artists (these are all metaphors for the government, undoubtedly). In fact, the articles rarely say much about the benefit or charity itself; instead they go into detail about the singers' lives and accomplishments, which everybody already knows but likes to be reminded of. Perhaps that is good *Việt Nam News* journalism (i.e. writing what the readership enjoys reading); nevertheless, the glory is certainly advantageous to the singers, which they richly deserve.

CHOREOGRAPHED DANCERS, SMOKE, FIRE, AND OTHER STAGE EFFECTS

Vietnamese popular music shows follow the Western model that includes extramusical stage effects. Boy and girl band shows, for example, feature elaborate dance choreography, both with extra dancers and by the featured artist(s) as well, and rock and pop music shows include heavy usage of on-stage smoke effects and, less often, fire (pyrotechniques). These are fairly recent developments in Vietnam, however, and newsprint articles about them in English do not appear before 2000.

By 2000, there were twenty professional dance troupes in Ho Chi Minh City that provided choreography for live shows, television broadcasts, or music videos of popular music. Huỳnh Hòa Bình explained, however, that there are still not enough dancers for all the musical productions:

> Organizers of concerts and special events where dancers are needed sometimes have to turn to amateurs, finding them at dance clubs, cultural clubs and aerobic classes. These amateur dancers are usually between the ages of 16 and 23. Although many have been dancing for as long as eight years, members of the art circle are concerned about the quality of their performances. They say that without professional choreography they often appear lacking in style and synchronization. (2000)

Many of the dance routines that accompany live musical performances are imitations of trendy dance styles seen on foreign television and music videos. This has led to criticism, and in 2001, the government became somewhat involved:

> Bored audiences complain—regularly—that dancers accompanying singers usually imitate or base their performances on what is trendy in other countries. Now the cultural dilution has received semi-official recognition and was raised at a meeting between the public, representatives of the municipal Culture and Information Department and the city's branch of the Việt Nam Dancers' Association. "Without professional choreographic training, these dancers often appear lacking in style and synchronization," said Meritorious Artist Kim Tiến. "Excessive use of accompanying dances may hurt the music in the end," Tiến said. "Singers will become less confident when they perform without the dancers." People's Artist Việt Cường, says the problem might rest with choreographers. "Dances accompanying singers make performances livelier, but many choreographers have invested neither the time nor the effort in training dancers," he said. "And that hurts the performances." (*VNN*, September 16, 1999)

Most of the professional choreographers in Ho Chi Minh City are themselves former dancers who have turned to choreographing dance groups to fill the demand.

During the summer of 2005, I attended an outdoor youth concert at the Youth Culture House in Ho Chi Minh City that featured dancers in about half of the acts. Some dancers were very conservative (without abrupt movements), as can only be suggested by Figure 7.1. Other dancers demonstrated contemporary and energetic hip-hop movements, including break dancing, as seen in Figure 7.2. I found that the many instances of break dancing at the 2005 show were little more than male exhibition dances, almost similar to Brazilian *capoeira* movements without the martial art aspect (i.e. combat moves, especially between two people), and they had little or no relationship to the music. Another similarity that came to my mind was Chinese acrobatics—movements for display of physical coordination and strength, rather than enhancement or interpretation of musical performance. Indeed, in my opinion, movement without heeding or recognizing the musical beats or melodic nuances verges on acrobatics rather than dance.

Fake smoke and real fire are used in some rock concerts (Figure 7.3): the former is also common on many popular music stages, coupled with laser or other light show effects. Both the Đồng Dao and M&Tôi popular music listening clubs, for example, make wide use of fake smoke and laser lights, benign but impressive stage effects. The larger disco and dance clubs make heavy use of laser lights, and pyrotechnics are relegated to outdoor rock

Figure 7.1 Conservative dancers at pop-rock concert at the Youth Culture House in Ho Chi Minh City. Photograph by Dale A. Olsen, 2005.

Figure 7.2   Hip-hop dancers at pop-rock concert at the Youth Culture House in Ho Chi Minh City. Photograph by Dale A. Olsen, 2005.

Figure 7.3   Spot lights and fake smoke during a rock concert with Da Vàng at Lan Anh Stadium in Ho Chi Minh City. Nguyễn Đạt is the lead guitarist in the middle. Photograph by Dale A. Olsen, 2004.

concerts. As such, all these effects are very similar to popular music stage effects in professional club or show settings throughout the modern urbanized world.

CONCLUSION: THE FUTURE OF POP MUSIC SHOWS IN 21ST CENTURY VIETNAM

Large-scale live concerts, festivals, and shows have become less popular in Vietnam in the twenty-first century than they were in the late 1990s, whereas music videos (on VCD or DVD) for home use are more popular (see Chapter 8). There are a number of reasons for this, including expense, lack of sponsorship, popularity of television shows, and lack of original music performed at live events. Perhaps Vietnam in the twenty-first century is following the trend of the rest of Asia where, "With some exceptions, concerts are not a successful aspect of the music business," according to Sekine (2007:210).

Production expense is the biggest factor in the reduction of popular music shows in Vietnam, as the following article explains:

> The country's music scene seems to be starting to run out of steam. Tuổi Trẻ (Youth) newspaper inquired about the reasons behind [near] empty concert halls. Are music lovers simply not informed about the musical events taking place or are the shows not up to fans' expectations? . . . One certainty is that live shows require money. An artist working in the field estimated that even VNĐ 500 million is not enough to organize an original show. . . . Singer Tuấn Hưng's concert cost about VNĐ 400 million and has made him a debtor of the Music Love Company. (*VNN*, May 31, 2003)

Related to expense is the increasing lack of sponsorship, and many shows have been cancelled because they did not have sponsors (*VNN*, August 17, 2004). Truong Thi Thu Dung, director of the Rang Dong Music Tapes and Dics Center and (occasional) organizer of large concerts, said: "Without sponsors, music organizers can not put on big concerts with just the profits from ticket sales" (ibid.).

The popularity of television shows and the greater availability of VCDs and DVD of live shows have also kept would-be concert goers in their homes. Thanh Liem, owner of HCM City-based Tieng To Dong music club in Ho Chi Minh City explained: "With various kinds of TV music shows, audiences can stay at home and watch their favorite acts, instead of going out to live concerts" (*VNN*, August 17, 2004). His club's patronage dropped 40 percent in 2004.

Another concern expressed by some fans is a lack of originality on the part of songwriters and songs chosen to be sung by pop stars. Many pop singers "sing the same songs that made them pop stars some years ago, [and they] lack the new material necessary to sustain audiences," said a fan (ibid.).

Are there more profound reasons for this decline of live popular music shows in Vietnam during the first decade of the twenty-first century? It may be a sign of change in that the government's attitudes towards its politics of remembering are being replaced by the economics of forgetting. Or, perhaps, it is just the economic reality that live shows are too expensive for the government to support, as it did in the 1990s. It is probably a mixture of both.

As Vietnam continues on its path of economic growth as a communist country, its music industry (which the government controls) also grows. Everything that songwriters, composers, singers, band members, and other creative musicians do constitutes a large part of Vietnam's music industry. Neither creators of lyrics or music nor artistic performers or ensembles work without the hopes of mediated dissemination of their art (via audio recordings, music videos, and other technological means) and making money in the process. The next chapter discusses popular music dissemination in Vietnam via audio and visual recordings, and the role such dissemination plays in the politics of remembering and the economics of forgetting.

8   Disseminating Popular Music
Audio and Video Recordings

Without the dissemination of popular music via personal audio and visual carriers, such as audio cassette tapes and compact discs and music video cassette tapes and compact discs, there would be no music industry in Vietnam beyond live shows (which are on the wane, as concluded in the last chapter). Issues and narratives that pertain to the production and use of these musical artifacts tell us much about Vietnam's economic and technological growth during the last decade of the twentieth century and into the twenty-first century, including the role of piracy and use (and abuse) of copyright.

Vietnam did not have the means to record its own contemporary popular music with professional studio quality sound equipment until well into the mid 1990s, let alone to manufacture (i.e. make copies) and distribute such products. How Vietnam's recording production industry developed and continues to grow in the realm of the "three sectors of the recording industry [recording the originals, making copies, and the distribution of copies]" (Laing 1998:337) is, therefore, a recent story. It begins with the production of audio cassette tapes, followed by video cassettes. CD production became the next market commodity, followed by VCD and later, DVD production.

AUDIO CASSETTE AND CD PRODUCTION OF POPULAR MUSIC

Audio cassette production began in Vietnam in the late 1960s and early 1970s, existing concurrently with 33 1/3 rpm Long Play vinyl records (1960s–1980s) and reel-to-reel tapes (1960s–1970s), replacing 45 rpm recordings in the 1960s, which replaced 78 rpm records that were produced from the 1930s until the 1950s. Audio cassette production continued well into the 2000s, and Ho Chi Minh City at one time had eleven cassette production and distribution companies that disseminated Vietnamese music, mostly recordings of folk songs; love songs by composers such as Văn Cao, Trịnh Công Sơn, and others; children's music; *cheo* opera music; *cải lương* renovated theater music; and other traditional popular musics. Also included in the Vietnamese cassette culture was the distribution of contraband recordings of *nhạc vàng*—music composed and sung by Việt kiều in America, Australia, and France, which the *Việt Nam News* described as "poor quality overseas Vietnamese sentimental music" (August 19, 1996). In June, 2004, I visited Dalat in the central highlands, where CD shops were selling hundreds of very high-quality pirated *nhạc vàng* CDs recorded in California, even though it is illegal to sell them and own them in Vietnam (Vang Bao Thuy, pers. com., June 7, 2004). A large number of the *nhạc vàng* CDs I saw for sale were interpretations of songs composed by Phạm Duy (see Chapter 5).

Equally popular with the Vietnamese youth in the mid 1990s were pirated cassette tapes of international pop music recordings that were copied illegally without hesitation: "Cassette producers are . . . keenly tuned in to copying updated international music. They are fully aware that a majority of their customers are young people" (*VNN*, August 19, 1996). Also in Dalat and other provincial cities, pirated cassette audio tapes of international pop music were still being sold in 2004.

Audio compact discs began to increase in popularity beginning in approximately 1992, and prices for an original, nonpirated CD were to VNĐ 500,000 each in 1992 (*VNN*, May 23, 1997), which was a lot of money then (approximately US$50). By 1997 their prices had dropped to between VNĐ 150,000 to 180,000 (about US$10) for a genuine CD. Pirated CDs copied in China and smuggled into Vietnam soon became popular at a fraction of the cost of the original products. By 1997 pirated CDs had almost completely replaced audio cassette tapes in major urban areas, although the date may be even earlier: "Chinese-made bootlegs, available for about VNĐ 25,000 a disc, have allowed CDs to completely replace tapes in most households. And although the bootlegs brought other problems with them—tax evasion, copyright violations—they gave young people easy access to western music" (ibid.).

The majority of the Chinese pirated CDs were copied from CDs of American and European pop singers and bands. After President Clinton removed the United States trade embargo in 1994, the Vietnamese economy improved, making it possible for clubs, restaurants, bars, and many family households in large urban areas to purchase CD players.

Driven by the huge market of pirated pop music compact discs produced in China and the increasing demand for local Vietnamese music during the decades after *đổi mới*, several state-operated audio companies (namely Saigon Audio in Ho Chi Minh City and Hồ Gươm Audio in Hanoi) made plans to purchase sophisticated audio recording and editing equipment from Europe. Contacts were made with audio recording companies in Belgium, England, France, and Germany (*VNN*, October 1, 1995). Negotiations for the purchase of very professional quality equipment, however, broke down because of the high cost and the difficult economic times in

Vietnam for its struggling music industry. Nghiêm Trọng Cường, director of Hồ Gươm Audio, optimistically explained, however, that "If we are to import a CD recording system, we will be able to produce as many as 4 million CDs a year" (ibid.). In 1995, however, Vietnam's CD-purchasing public was still small: "The domestic market can consume only 1 million CDs a year," explained Cường, thus balancing his visionary enthusiasm with marketing reality—Vietnam could not support such a market at that time. Nevertheless, this was an important phenomenon whereby technology began to shape politics. By attempting to enter, and thereby dominate, the CD-producing wing of Vietnam's music industry, the government could more easily control the contents of the products.

The pirated pop music CDs made in China and distributed illegally in Vietnam, however, seemed to satisfy Vietnamese consumers for the moment. Even *nhạc vàng* (also known as V-pop) music and love songs recorded in France or the United States by Vietnamese immigrant musicians were almost immediately reproduced illegally in China and sold in Vietnam at the fraction of their European or American prices.

The state-operated Saigon Audio and Hồ Gươm Audio music companies made another attempt to produce CDs in Vietnam in 1995 by recording them in-country and having them burned (i.e. copied from the master) in Korea; one-thousand copies were made at a time. The program was not successful, however, for at least two reasons: the Korean-made CDs were still three times more expensive than pirated Chinese CDs, and the government-chosen musical selections had little appeal to the Vietnamese youth:

> "No one is willing to buy a CD which records just marching songs written by northern Vietnamese wartime composers" . . . [and] there were instances of having to include at least one song written or favored by someone who has political influence . . . , writes Nguyễn Trí Bình (*VNN*, October 1, 1995).

Nguyễn Trí Bình continues to explain the following about Vietnam's unique dilemma in his article titled "Vietnam wants to cut its own discs":

> Among the many images of Vietnam that are immortalized in various art forms and artifacts—conical hats bent low reaping corn [or planting rice], the farmer with a plough, the street vendor with a shoulder pole with baskets on either side—the boy on the buffalo with the flute is perhaps the most romantic, symbolizing the country's agricultural dominance and its musical traditions.
>
> Vietnamese are musically inclined. Even the otherwise very shy folk in the countryside sing songs in karaoke parlors with gay abandon. All shops selling musical cassettes and compact discs (CDs) are crowded, live music shows are packed to full capacity and cassette and CD players

have really caught on in the urban markets. [However, the] CD market here is dominated by pirated products from China. . . . Now, local firms want to get in on the act. Vietnam's audio companies aim at having their own compact disc recording studios in an attempt to corner at least 20 percent of the domestic CD market. (ibid.)

By August 1996, however, Vietnam was still contracting with foreign audio companies to burn and copy recordings made in Vietnam. Although locally produced CDs did exist, the government imposed a 30 percent tax on each CD made in Vietnam. Thus, locally made CDs could still not compete with pirated Chinese imports (*VNN*, August 19, 1996).

Saigon Audio finally purchased CD production equipment in late 1996, and in early 1997 it began producing CDs. Because of local control and a rise in number and quality of young Vietnamese pop singers, boy bands, and girl bands, "the quality and quantity of locally made CD's improve[d] considerably" (*VNN*, December 11, 1997). Moreover, the locally produced CDs were considerably lower in price than legally imported CDs and were only slightly higher in price than Chinese pirated discs. Now local pop musicians from Ho Chi Minh City and Hanoi were able to make themselves better known by recording covers and original songs in Vietnam. Part of the success of this new program was an increase in national pride, perhaps influenced by Vietnam's continued growth in the free market. The following article creates an optimistic picture:

Vietnamese music on Vietnamese-made compact discs (CDs) is growing in popularity despite the deluge of international CDs on the market, most of which are imported illegally. Domestically-produced CDs were a rare sight in shops until a few months ago, and those available were not selling well.

Music lovers have had a change of heart, however, as production and the sale of Vietnamese music CDs [have] soared. At CD shops on Nguyễn Thi Minh Khai Street the new trend in music is evident. In the past the majority of customers at these shops wanted to hear the international top ten; they are now asking for albums off the Vietnamese charts. International stars like Mariah Carey, Celine Dion and Tony Braxton, and young male bands like Boyz II Men and Back Street Boys were only a short while ago the top choice for many. But talent from Vietnam, especially vocalists like Hồng Nhung, Lam Trường and Mỹ Linh, now top the sales charts.

Noting the change in tastes, the Saigon Audio-Video Enterprise has begun to produce more CDs featuring traditional Vietnamese music from different parts of the country. One fan of Vietnamese music said that while musical ability and the quality of local CDs does not always match up to international music, she prefers locally-made discs because she can relate to the music and unique styles of the singers.

"Vietnamese songs stir up feelings of pride about my homeland and people," she says. (*VNN*, September 24, 1998)

This may be just hyperbole from the state-owned newspaper, but the majority of the CDs I found for sale in stores between 2002 and 2005 were nationally produced recordings by Vietnamese singers.

The CDs that were the most popular with youthful Vietnamese consumers were *singles* recorded by individual pop singers (a single in this sense means a single singer). Moreover, each single is based on the marketing device of selecting one particular song that the singer and her/his fans have specified is the singer's hit song; this has been determined mostly through crowd reaction at public performances in schools, clubs, and other performance venues.

The first Vietnamese recorded and produced CD was *Giã Từ Dĩ Vãng* (Farewell to the Past), a single by female pop singer Phương Thanh in 1998 (see Chapter 3). It, like many other CD singles that followed, contains only three songs, with the title track the best-known of the lot. Many singles have been sold since *Farewell to the Past*, but "the format has hardly brought about a revolution in the local music industry" (*VNN*, June 27, 2002). Although less expensive than a complete CD album, many consumers find VNĐ 20,000 (about US$1.34 in 2002) too much to pay for only three songs (a one-CD album with about eighteen songs costs between VNĐ 35,000 and 50,000, about US$2.34 and US$3.39 in 2002). Although these prices are extremely low by USA (and European) standards, a locally pirated one-CD album fetched between VNĐ 7,000 and 12,000 (US$.47 and .80) during the same time period.

CD singles are often more problematic to produce than one-CD albums because "[f]or a CD single to be successful and make a profit, the record company must invest a lot of money in an eye-catching cover—sometimes twice as much as a full-length CD," explained Huỳnh Tiết, the director of Bến Thành Audio and Video Center (*VNN*, June 27, 2002). Nevertheless, according to the same article, "CD singles have the benefit of being cheaper and faster to produce than a full-length album." As the reporter concludes, youthful consumers will ultimately determine the future of Vietnamese pop music CD singles recorded and produced in Vietnam by the Vietnamese.

Another format produced in Vietnam that is extremely popular in CD stores is the one- to three-CD album featuring a number of Vietnamese pop singers and bands in a potpourri of greatest hits and/or covers of American and European pop tunes. Often such albums appear in several volumes, titled appropriately *Top Hits*; *Top Hits '97* (or any other year); *Nhạc trẻ Sài Gòn*; *The Best of* [name of singer]; and others. The album *Top Hits '97*, produced in 1997 by VAFACO Productions in Ho Chi Minh City, includes ten covers originally performed by the Backstreet Boys, the Bee Gees, Elton John, and Madonna. Four well-known Vietnamese pop singers (Mỹ Linh, Trung Kiên, Thu Phương, and Huy MC) perform such famous tunes as

"Now and Forever," "When You Tell Me that You Love Me," "Don't Cry for Me, Argentina," "Candle in the Wind," "Get Down, "Save the Best for Last," and others. Sung in Vietnamese, except for the first words of the refrain to "Get Down," the album also includes printed song texts in Vietnamese for the first four songs in the list.

Special CD albums are produced each year for the Christmas/New Year season; though not a traditional Vietnamese holiday period, the end of December through January 1 is a commercially popular time of year in Vietnam's cities. Holiday albums are not usually about the American/European festive season per se (although some are about the secular aspect of Christmas) but they are about making money: "Viet Nam's top singers have been in top gear at recording studios in recent months in a bid to complete albums in time for Christmas and New Year and make new waves with young audiences for the upcoming festive season" (*VNN*, October 13, 2003). Referred to as a "lucrative end-of-year market," pop singers work hard to release their new CDs.

Slow, romantic, ballads are the most popular songs for the holiday market, as the Popular Music Continuum that spans traditional and contemporary soundscapes is reinforced by another set of dichotomies, the Christmas holiday as a commercial venture and the desire for national unity and togetherness, as suggested by pop singer Hồng Nhung in the same article: "I learned a lot after the release of my last album *Một Ngày Mới* (A New Day) four months ago, and I understand the most important thing that music fans look for in an album, is that the singer shares their feelings as if they are a close friend" (ibid.).

The tripartite production process of recording, burning or copying, and distributing CDs was in full bloom in Ho Chi Minh City in 2005, with generally magnificent products at low prices compared to world market values for similar merchandise. In Vietnam, the CD has taken "its place as a symbol and example of Western-style modernity alongside Levis, McDonalds and Coca Cola" (Laing 1998:341). This contemporary characteristic of technological growth within the music industry at large is an important step in the economics of forgetting, as Vietnam's popular music stars are artistically and technologically on equal footing with other world artists.

MUSIC VIDEO CASSETTE, VCD, AND DVD PRODUCTION OF POPULAR MUSIC

Video cassette recording and production began in 1993 when the HCM City Television Service Company made music videos in its studio of singers/songwriters Cẩm Vân and Nhã Phương performing their own songs. These first music videos were titled respectively *Tiếng Hát Cẩm Vân* (Songs performed by Cẩm Vân) and *Tiếng Hát Nhã Phương* (Songs Performed by Nhã Phương). Several years later came the release of *Saigon Young Music*, a music video compilation of *nhạc trẻ* by local pop singers.

In the early stages of Vietnamese video cassette production, vocalists and bands mostly recorded covers, which was not received well by music critics:

> Few of the bands recorded on the new video tape have built up strong followings because they mainly reproduce world famous songs and music from internationally famous groups such as the Beatles, Pink Floyd and the Bee Gees. They fail to create something new in words and melodies. Their most common mistake has been to abuse the original western style while trying to compose Vietnamese songs. The composers lean so much towards foreign word expression that their music becomes too clumsy and difficult to establish their own distinctive style. Unique style and constant new creations are of most importance for any band trying to make a name for itself. (*VNN*, July 24, 1997)

Nevertheless, the new music video format brought well-known and unknown local pop singers and bands into Vietnamese homes, whereas before such entertainment was only available live or in audio cassette format.

The local video recordings of in-country Vietnamese pop musicians also served to create an awareness of local, as opposed to foreign, talent: "Once only interested in foreign music, consumers have warmed up to the wide variety of locally made products. 'I like to buy Vietnamese video music cassettes, especially mixed programs with songs, dances and short comedies', one customer said" (*VNN*, December 11, 1996). Variety of programming created more interest and higher sales than purely pop music shows. Especially popular were video cassettes of children's music, such as *Cả Nhà Thương Nhau* (Mutual Love Among Family Members), which sold 40,000 copies in 1996 (ibid.). In addition, songs by famous wartime and postwar composers such as Văn Cao and Trịnh Công Sơn were popular, and were also big sellers among visiting Việt kiều, who purchased them, took them back to their diasporic communities in Australia, France, and the United States, and made multiple copies for friends and sometimes to sell in the overseas black market. This latter breach of transnational commerce ethics provoked some of the first concerns about copyright infringement in Vietnam: "'Copyright is our prime concern. Many of our most popular programs are copied cheaply and sold for less', said Phan Thị Mộng Thúy, Director of Phương Nam Film. Some producers who want to recover capital quickly have sold their original programs to music companies run by Vietnamese living abroad" (ibid.).

By 1997, several budding young filmmakers found more job opportunities making music videos than art or documentary films, resulting in a new focus for music videos—beautiful images of scenery (not the singers) rather than drab studio shots. "Today, Vietnam's video makers are applying the poetry of the cinema to musical forms. They earn a living, and they are also making albums come to life through vivid images that are true to the essence of the lyrics" (*VNN*, October 2, 1997). Since 1998, Dương Minh

Long has emerged as one of Vietnam's leading music videographers, and his first creation, titled *Ru Tình* (Lullaby to Love), featured songs by Trịnh Công Sơn:

> Each of the pictures for the 10 songs in the video, all performed by Trinh Vĩnh Trinh, Sơn's sister, was taken in different localities in the country, from the attractive old quarters in Hà Nội, to [the] immense sand hills in Phan Thiết and forest regions in the Central Highlands province of Đắc Lắc. (*VNN*, January 17, 1998)

Dương Minh Long has also produced beautiful landscape videography for music videos featuring Mỹ Linh and other Vietnamese stars.

Vietnam is indeed a beautiful place for landscape, seascape, and other visual "scapes" suitable for the sentimental and often nationalistic lyrics of its youth music. In 2002, while visiting a Chăm tower archaeological site near Phan Thiết, I observed a film crew shooting scenery for a music video among the ancient, impressive, and exotic ruins (Figure 8.1). Indeed, the Chăm towers scattered throughout the southern region of Vietnam between Phan Thiết and Nha Trang create a powerful image of Vietnam's ancient Champa Kingdom. Image is important in Vietnam's music videos, but creating an "image" in Vietnam's music video industry refers to landscape, setting, set, and other visual ideas, and not as much to creating the image of the individual pop singer or featured musician(s). Vietnamese pop music artists, themselves, are responsible for creating their own image in the process. This is unlike the music video industry in the United States, for example, where "record companies use videos . . . to help develop their artists . . . establish and cultivate a certain image. . . ." (Banks 1997:296). In Vietnam, pop artists are also responsible for funding their own story line music videos (as opposed to live show music videos).

Although dozens of Vietnamese popular music singers have made music video clips, those by Thanh Thảo and Mỹ Tâm are representative, and the following brief descriptions characterize most of Vietnam's story line music videos. Titled *Sự Thật Một Tình Yêu* (Single Stories of Spotless Love) and subtitled *Album Thanh Thảo / Mỹ Tâm*, the jointly published video album is labeled VCD Ca Nhạc 1182. My version is probably a pirated copy (it is difficult to tell).

Many of Thanh Thảo's videos portray sanitized images of Vietnam and Vietnamese youth subcultures that are unrealistic because the poverty and congestion are removed. Some are filmed in Dalat, one of Vietnam's most beautiful towns, nestled in the central highlands and graced by many waterfalls and lakes. Dalat was also the French colonial gem of southern Vietnam and, because of its beauty and cool weather, was a getaway spot for writers, artists, and politicians. It is the perfect setting for music videos. In Thanh Thảo's Dalat video clip, *"Anh Muốn Nói Yêu Em"* ("I [boy] want to say I love you [girl]"), mostly exotic or luxurious props are used,

Figure 8.1 A film crew photographing scenery for a music video among Chăm ruins near Phan Thiết, Vietnam, in June, 2002. Photograph by Dale A. Olsen.

such as beautiful young peasant girls carrying fruit and vegetables across their shoulders on horizontal poles, rather than elderly ladies; a gentle old man with an Uncle Ho beard; fancy ten-speed bicycles; expensive Honda Dream motorbikes; black boots; luxurious cars; old historical buildings or new ornate ones; and so forth. The common people, their houses, one-speed bicycles, or old motorbikes are seldom seen. This is not the real Vietnam, but the Vietnam of make believe and travel brochures! The vocal and instrumental recordings are done in the studio, and the lip-synching in the videos is never accurate. Although professional quality is absent, the images, nevertheless, are beautiful and the singing is excellent.

Many of Mỹ Tâm's story line music videos, on the other hand, are filmed in Hong Kong and remind me of Jackie Chan movies. In her video clip titled "Có Phải Ta Chia Tay" (Should We Be Separated?), Mỹ Tâm and her accomplices appear as superheroes who seem to spend half of their time running through city streets in chase scenes (the villains are always running between two innocent people rather than around them, usually knocking them down in the process), through subway stations, across tops of buildings, and down other paths—the action is also reminiscent of James Bond movies. There is no need for lip-synching in Mỹ Tâm's action videos because her rather incongruous slow ballads function as unemotional narratives over the action (her singing is not shown to be coming from her mouth while she functions as a living action doll in the drama). This technique makes the professional quality of her videos easier to evaluate, because the studio recordings are excellent, the filming is well done (albeit trite), and the entertainment factor is successful (if you like Jackie Chan style film action and Mỹ Tâm's singing). These superhero music clips are obviously expensive to produce, but Mỹ Tâm has the required capital as one of the wealthiest pop singers in Vietnam.

Video clips of live performances or live shows are usually funded by the sponsors of the shows, whose names are generally displayed all over the set (on the walls, floors, and banners). Some live shows, as they are called, feature elaborate sets and dozens of dancers; others, such as Bức Tường's (The Wall's) 9+ tour in 2004 (which was made into a music video), feature very little advertising. Some live shows have story lines, such as *Búp Bê Đẹp Xinh* (The Beautiful Doll), performed in 2002 by Thanh Thảo at *Lam Anh* stadium in Ho Chi Minh City. Made into a karaoke-type DVD and VCD (released in 2003), *Búp Bê Đẹp Xinh*'s story line or plot includes "a theme of a whimsical fantasy world filled with toys for children" (*VNN*, August 30, 2002). Moving from scenes that portray Thanh Thảo in child-like innocence as "the beautiful doll," to a cowgirl, to the latest hip-hopper, the show features dancers dressed as horses, Spiderman, robots, and other pop symbols. "I want to have an abstract and modern theme for my music show that will attract young audiences," said the show's director, Huỳnh Phúc Diễn (ibid.). One of the songs from the video breaks away from the childlike innocence of the "the beautiful doll" as Thanh Thảo sings: "I'm no longer a little girl. My burning lips could be kissed . . ." (translation by Phong Nguyen). Indeed, "the beautiful doll" grows up, perhaps heightening the show's appeal to young audiences of the post-teenybopper stage.

In the early 2000s, Vietnam began producing music video VCDs and DVDs of studio-recorded performances and live performances at concerts. The quality of many of these first laser technology video discs produced in Vietnam was poor, with rough fade-outs, abrupt juxtapositions and transitions of material, and inconsistent themes. In just a few years, however, the quality improved greatly. Many of the laser disc music videos of shows include a karaoke version of the performance in addition to a straight documentation of the event—usually the karaoke version is a DVD and the other is a VCD. Just about all of the music video VCDs and DVDs also exist in pirated versions that cost less than the equivalent of two dollars, compared to the original packages priced about twice as much. The piracy of Vietnam's own video and audio materials by the Vietnamese themselves has become a great problem for artists, entrepreneurs, and others in the music industry.

Without the support of MTV and other transnational music television enterprises until 2005, Vietnam's music video industry had nowhere to go beyond home sales, karaoke clubs, and local television air play. By late

2004, however, Vietnam's music industry began to explore MTV Asia and MTV Southeast Asia, and Vietnam itself began to develop its own home-grown MTV, which was a part of the VTV (Vietnam Television) national television network. If deals can be made, music television viewers within and outside Vietnam will be rewarded with the entertaining music and dance of the likes of Mỹ Tâm, Thanh Thảo, Kasim Hoàng Vũ, and other popular young music stars.

POPULAR MUSIC AUDIO AND VIDEO PIRACY

The pirating or illegal copying, manufacturing, and selling of audio and video materials at extremely low prices began in 1991 with Chinese copies of mostly American and other European-derived pop music (*VNN*, March 23, 1995). Originally in 1991, when Chinese pirated CDs first appeared in Hanoi, a single disc cost as much as VNĐ 40,000 (roughly US$4.00); in a few months, however, the price came down to approximately VNĐ 15,000. "Shoppers for pirated CD's . . . included many foreign backpackers who are attracted not only by cheap prices but also by the variety of music. As soon as a new release was made in Western countries, Chinese manufacturers would have such music copied overnight" (ibid.). The pirated foreign recordings, which continued to flood the tourist areas of major Vietnamese cities in 2005, include the latest pop music stars, jazz artists, European classics, and basically anything that sells to tourists.

Often, however, the inexpensive pirated CDs are of very poor quality, as the following published anecdote makes clear:

> Two months ago the director of a company in Hanoi received a newly released double CD set of Richard Clayderman as a present from his daughter living in Sydney, Australia. He gave her a call telling her [that] though he highly appreciated her gift, she had better not buy anymore CD's like that in Sydney because such double CD sets were available in Hanoi and cost only VNĐ 40,000, or about eight times less than the original CD set. The director, [however,] who runs a factory making products for export, seemed to pay no heed to product quality. The Chinese-made CD's with pianist Richard Clayderman available in Hanoi are poorly presented, with several misprints on the disks. (*VNN*, January 17, 1998)

In 2005, over ten years after that incident, the same problems existed, as a consumer explained about the poor quality of illegally made CDs: "'some of them can only be used several times before they break. . . . Even some turned out blank or have fewer songs than on the playlist'. Vietnamese people often say 'cua re la cua oi' . . . [you get what you pay for]" (*VNN*, March 6, 2005). Such characteristics as misprints in the printed narratives, song lists, and credits, unplayable or inferior audio and video, and so on, are common occurrences in all pirated audio and video compact discs in Vietnam.

The legal selling of recorded music on the Internet began in 2005 with Vietnam's first government-approved online music selling Web site (www. nhacso.net), which was a joint project of the Financing and Promoting Technology Company and the Viet Nam Music Copyright Center (*VNN*, June 08, 2005). With over seven-million Internet users in Vietnam, the market is huge, and at VNĐ 1000 to 2000 (US$. 06 to .12), the fee is reasonable. The director of the Center said "We are determined to stop music copyright violations [although we] expect many difficulties" (ibid.).

VIETNAM'S COPYRIGHT LAWS

Although Vietnam has had copyright laws since the 1960s, many loopholes kept CD producers and show organizers from having to pay composers and songwriters for the use of their creations (*VNN*, May 3, 2000). It was not until 1994 that Vietnam had an official governmental ordinance that somewhat protected composers, songwriters, and authors, giving them control over their own intellectual property: "The law covers plays, broadcasts, videos, photographs, plastic art, architecture, maps, books of all kinds, and many other works" (*VNN*, December 17, 1994). It also pertained to the fair use of and royalty payments to composers for songs performed during pop music concerts. As before, however, the law was difficult to enforce, and it did not address international concerns.

On October 26, 2002, Vietnam joined the Berne Convention when Decision 332 was signed by President Trần Đức Lương: "Decision 332 [is/was] an international agreement on the protection of [world] copyrights in science and arts publications" (*VNN*, August 20, 2002). The other signatories, however, were only the United States and Switzerland. Nevertheless, the new international law secured the protection of foreign intellectual property from piracy and unauthorized performance and publication in Vietnam, and likewise, Vietnamese intellectual property in the United States and Switzerland. The administration and enforcement of the law was in the hands of three organizations: the Vietnam Music Copyright Protection Center, Vietnam Recording Industry Association, and Vietnamese Literary Copyright Center, the latter a branch of the Vietnam Writers' Association (*VNN*, November 4, 2004).

In 2004, the situation improved but problems still existed. For example, a small fine (the fine cap was VNĐ 100 million [US$6,426]) was charged per performance violation of copyright, but because that amount was much less than the profit made, offenses continued. "To minimize violations, [offenders] have to be charged a fine similar to the value and scale of the violation," stated Lê Kiều, chief inspector of the Ministry of Science and Technology (*VNN*, July 27, 2004). Moreover, there were not enough inspectors within the Ministry to police intellectual property rights violations (ibid.).

On October 26, 2004, Vietnam finally signed an expanded version of the Berne Convention that includes most countries in the world. Since then, the artists with money and professional backing adhere to the rules of the Berne Convention. Mỹ Tâm, for example, purchased copyrights for several foreign songs in 2005, becoming the first pop singer in Vietnam to do so (*VNN*, March 22, 2005). By purchasing the rights to record "Cançáo do Mar," a Portuguese language pop song performed by Sarah Brightman and "My Lover," a Japanese ballad—both songs appeared on her CD titled *Mỹ Tâm's Album Volume 4*—Mỹ Tâm set the precedent for paying (a) mechanical royalties for the right to record (and translate) foreign songs and (b) performing royalties for the right to perform them. Normally, in the United States, mechanical royalty fees are paid by the recording company and performing royalties are paid by the performing venues, such as Internet web broadcasters, nightclubs, restaurants, radio and television stations, and others (Naggar 2000–2004:73). Because of the newness of the laws in Vietnam, however, Mỹ Tâm's organization (she and her team of managers, directors, etc.) paid the fees. The adherence to world copyright laws will become more commonplace in Vietnam as the twenty-first century progresses. Without the proper policing (inspectors, higher costs for violations, etc.), however, infractions will undoubtedly occur for some time within the daily (and nightly) life of Vietnam's music industry.

On November 1, 2004, performing covers in concert became illegal in Vietnam. Famous pop singers and lesser-known wannabes initially felt the constraints of the Bern Convention copyright law more than rock bands did, because the latter have often performed more original songs than covers, as Le Vu Hu Don explains: "I think it will hurt pop musicians more, [because they] play more covers than rock and roll musicians. They often translate them into Vietnamese, but they're still covers" (*VNN*, November 8, 2004). Indeed, pop singers are very accustomed to performing at popular music listening clubs where singing covers is the norm, whereas stadium and arena rock bands (as opposed to those that play clubs and private parties), which need larger (usually outdoor) venues to perform in because of their equipment, personnel, and loud volume, prefer to play original songs (which is also their selling point). So far, the international copyright law does not affect body language, dress, or on-stage dance styles, which for rock bands in Vietnam will probably always be copies of the behaviors of foreign musicians and bands.

CONCLUSION: ECONOMICS AND MUSIC TECHNOLOGY

The terms *music industry* and *music business* are almost oxymorons in Vietnam because, as we have seen, gatekeepers and middlemen have little to do in the production and dissemination of popular music. In the words of Negus (1996:66), "the idea of coming in between, or of intermediary action" on the part of a second party, such as recording companies, has not played much of a role in Vietnam. It also seems to me that for most musicians anywhere in the world, the act of reducing music purely to a money-making venture runs contrary to the musicians' art. Nevertheless, the reality is that someone is making or will make money from the artistic outputs of musicians. Performing musicians in Vietnam, perhaps because of Vietnam's centuries of domination by royal courts, Chinese mandarins, French colonists, American advisors, and communist bureaucrats, did not have much control over the money-making aspects of music making until the country entered the modern world of commerce and market economics after *đổi mới* in 1985. Even twenty years later, the reduction of music to a purely money-making venture has not yet happened.

When CD recording and production reaches the state of perfection it has in America, Europe, Japan, and other technologically advanced countries, and when the Berne Convention copyright laws take total effect, the cost of purchasing CDs may skyrocket beyond the ability of most Vietnamese people to purchase them. Will this force piracy to continue? Will it allow inferior recordings to proliferate? I think it will lead to more singers, musicians, and songwriters writing their own original songs, which the Vietnamese public will learn to treasure (as they are now treasuring the songs of Trịnh Công Sơn, for example), thus eliminating a reliance on foreign material. When more songs and recordings of the musical quality of Thanh Lam's and Hồng Nhung's recent CDs appear, those that I have placed at the top of the Arc of Culturation, the world may begin to pay royalties to Vietnam. Thus the Berne Convention will be a financial boon rather than a burden.

As Vietnam enters the technological age of the twenty-first century, its use of mediated musical and other art forms and its inevitable further development of them will increase. One of the biggest arenas for mediated music transmission in Vietnam in the early 2000s is karaoke, which is an important phenomenon of mediated and live music fusion. Karaoke, however, offers few rewards for Vietnam's popular music artists, because much of the music young people enjoy singing in bars to the accompaniment of prerecorded audio tracks, is not national music. A greater problem, however, is social rather than musical. Studied in the next chapter, karaoke establishments are struggling to survive the communist government's crackdown on what it considers to be "places of ill repute"—meaning, the government believes them to be breeding grounds for drug use and illicit sex.

9 Vietnamese Karaoke
Place, Pleasure, Politics, and Profit

Karaoke is the act of singing to a prerecorded accompaniment. Originally developed in Kobe, Japan, in the early 1970s, the term *karaoke* comes from two Japanese terms—*karappu* (*kara* for short), meaning empty, and *okerestu* (*oke* for short), meaning orchestra (a word borrowed from English). Literally then, karaoke means empty orchestra, although it can be more precisely glossed as "instant empty vocal track with recorded orchestra accompaniment and superimposed text; just add hot singer." The point and analogy I want to make is that karaoke is not empty at all. Just as instant coffee is not coffee until you add hot water, karaoke does not exist until you add a person (or several people) who enjoy singing for aesthetic pleasure. Therefore, the process of singing is just as important as the end result. In Vietnam, karaoke is driven by the pop star syndrome, where the singer *karaokes* (used as a verb) to be a pop music star for a few minutes or to gain valuable experience singing with an accompaniment on her or his bumpy road to stardom. Anh Thư explains the latter phenomenon: "At night, [the aspiring young pop music star wannabe] sings in cafes or karaoke bars, treating it as practice for the time when he breaks through into the country's pop music scene" (2003). Therefore, karaoking (or karaokeing) is taken very seriously. Also, in Vietnam, government officials don't trust it for political reasons; entrepreneurs and hostesses need it for profit making; and young people, families, and businessmen enjoy experiencing it for diversion and socializing.

In Japan, since its inception in the 1970s, karaoke developed via a number of technologies: from audio tape, video cassette, laser disc, digital video disc (DVD), video compact disc (VCD), IC chips for computer playback possibilities, and cable TV. All provided opportunities for an individual to sing along to an accompaniment of prerecorded music. In Vietnam, most of the recent developments of video cassette, DVD, VCD, and computer technologies are found.

Karaoke permanently came to Vietnam fairly late—not until the late 1980s or early 1990s, after *đổi mới* and when Vietnamese technology in Ho Chi Minh City was finally advanced enough to record and mass produce empty vocal tracks with orchestral accompaniment and superimposed Vietnamese

Figure 9.1   A cartoon from the *Việt Nam News*, February 9, 1996 (used with permission).

texts on VCDs. Thus, early karaoke in Vietnam was essentially pirate karaoke (Ōtake and Hosokawa 2001:185). Karaoke video tapes came from Japan or China before they were produced in Vietnam, but they were in Japanese or Chinese so were of little use to the Vietnamese because they could not read those languages. In the 2000s, many Vietnamese pop songs of extremely high quality are recorded by leading pop singers and mass produced and sold on DVDs for very reasonable prices (VNĐ 30,000 or US$2 in July, 2002). Sometimes labeled as MTV, they are music videos on compact laser discs and have nothing to do with MTV (although they may be associated with song contests from VTV or Vietnamese television, especially VTV3).

In addition to mediated accompaniment, live bands have occasionally accompanied singers for contests and shows, and the phenomenon is still called karaoke, even though nothing is empty at all. The emptiness comes from the fact that the singers practice and learn the songs in the traditional karaoke manner, either in bars, clubs, rooms, or at home, with prerecorded technology.

The history of karaoke in Vietnam is filled with interesting developments, and as the cartoon in Figure 9.1 suggests (from *VNN*, February 9, 1996), karaoke has not always appealed to every Vietnamese person. It is, by and large, an urban middle-class commercial phenomenon, although it is slowly gaining popularity in rural areas, and even among the mountain minority groups, because so many Vietnamese people love to sing.

HISTORY OF KARAOKE IN VIETNAM

Karaoke was little known in Vietnam until it became possible to manufacture empty vocal track media with superimposed words in Vietnamese. In the early 1990s the situation changed, and by 1994 karaoke was very popular, especially in Ho Chi Minh City. In their article, "Karaoking Saigon" (notice how the word is used as a verb in the title), Patrick Raszelenberg and Trịnh Trí Ninh describe the excitement about karaoke:

> Karaoke is everywhere in Ho Chi Minh City, from Marsian luxury hotels and spiffy little establishments downtown to tiny bars in hidden backyards and alleyways in the residential quarters. At Karaoke Village on Yersin, Co Giang, De Tham and Nguyen Trai streets in the 1st district, you can sing along for 5–6000 *dong*/hour (50 US cents).
>
> Also in the 1st district, the Cau Ong Lanh market boasts thirty karaoke rooms right in the middle of the market stands. Some women, instead of buying food for their families, would come here to spend their money singing away.
>
> In the 3rd district, dozens of karaoke rooms offer their services from 8 AM to late at night ignoring their neighbor's rest hours. Karaoke is booming in several poorer areas as well, like the 8th district, where an hour of yelling and hollering strips you of no more than 4000 *dong*.
>
> According to a bar owner on Yersin street, most of the customers are students on vacation. At the markets, the regular ones are young idlers killing time irking bystanders with the distorted sound of their Meistersinger voices transporting the screeching howls resembling early 20th century gramophones into the somber, tranquil delta nights. (*VNN*, July 31, 1994)

With their clever writing, it is difficult to know whether Raszelenberg and Ninh are supportive of karaoke or not. Although they use "karaoking" in their title, they seem to equate the process with "yelling," "hollering," "screeching," and "howling" in their narrative. In 1994 karaoke was still new and exotic in Vietnam, inspiring all kinds of opinions.

By 2000, karaoke was still popular in Ho Chi Minh City, as expressed in the following article, "HCM City sings its heart out":

> It seems as if a whole metropolis is alive with song. Karaoke fever has swept Viet Nam's second city. "How can I live without karaoke?" asked a vendor in HCMC City's Tan Dinh market, echoing the sentiments of

a growing number of city-dwellers. . . ."Most people in this city love music, therefore they love karaoke. Just by following the words on a video screen, any person can become a karaoke singer," the owner of a karaoke club in Nguyen Dinh Chieu Street, said. (*VNN*, November 10, 2000)

Karaoke-ing is democratic music making because anyone can participate. This is significant in a communist country such as Vietnam. Not only is karaoke democratic, it is the epitome of big (music) business. However, it is not so much the economics of forgetting; it is more just plain money making economics. Nevertheless, it is escapism, and similar to what Street wrote about rock, it helps people alter the way they experience their world (1986:66).

KARAOKE VENUES AND SITUATIONS

Several kinds of karaoke venues and situations developed in Vietnam during the 1990s, which one writer calls "different types of karaoke services" (*VNN*, November 10, 2000). I prefer the terms *venues* and *situations*, because some venues exist for particular situations, and some of the situations are within the same venue. Although the *Việt Nam News* is neither clear nor consistent about the venues and situations of karaoke, their most common terms for the venues are *bar, club, parlor, room*, and *shop*. The two terms I use for situations are *hát với nhau* (sing with others) and karaoke *ôm* (cuddle or hugging karaoke). Ōtake and Hosokawa refer to these as "'high' karaoke and 'low' karaoke" (ibid.).

The following article presents another idea about the variety of karaoke venues and situations and the lack of clarity that distinguishes between them. Here the distinction between venues that pertains to "high" and "low" karaoke are based on economics rather than situation:

So popular has [karaoke] become that there are now nearly 800 businesses licensed to run karaoke services in HCM City. . . . They range from poorly-equipped, stuffy rooms in quiet alleys to big clubs with the latest equipment in noisy streets. Even well-known hotels such as the Sai Gon Star have opened karaoke rooms to attract more customers. . . . [The owner of a karaoke club] said different types of karaoke services attract different kinds of customers. "Prices are pretty low—about VNĐ 10,000 an hour during the day and double that in the evening—so my karaoke club draws people who don't have that much money, such as students, workers and officials," he said. (*VNN*, November 10, 2000)

Indeed, the contrast between expensive and inexpensive venues for karaoke is high. "Just a few blocks from gorgeous karaoke restaurants with large

TV screen[s] under chandeliers, one finds illegal karaoke rooms operating in ordinary private houses" (ibid.). With them come "different types of karaoke services" (mentioned above), which could refer to the technology of the audio/visual playback systems, or to a variety of human services, from foods and beverages to extracurricular cuddling.

The wording *hát với nhau* is not used in the *Việt Nam News*, although it is the term that appears most often on bar marquees. "Sing with others," the literal translation of *hát với nhau*, usually refers to clubs, bars, and restaurants, but it can also mean a karaoke room. The clubs, bars, and restaurants are public, but karaoke rooms are private. Karaoke *ôm* can also occur in a private room, sometimes referred to as "parlor" in the news print. Hence, there is confusion with the English terms.

Kayla Price, one of my American students in 2002, writes the following about her experiences with a *hát với nhau* karaoke music bar in Ho Chi Minh City in 2002:

> *Hát với nhau* . . . is distinct from the other varieties of karaoke because it is done in a public setting and singers are subject to losing face in front of the audience as opposed to singing in a small private situation where there is not such pressure. *Hát với nhau* is perhaps the variety of karaoke most similar to that practiced in the United States because it involves an audience. Yet unlike American karaoke, *hát với nhau* is performed seriously and with an air of professionalism. (n.d.)

About another karaoke bar in the beach town of Vũng Tàu, Price writes the following:

> The small karaoke bar proudly displayed the words *hát với nhau* on its window alongside the name of the bar. We were eagerly greeted at the door and directed to a small table towards the back of the long skinny room. There were a few other patrons at the bar, but no one had begun singing karaoke yet, as the night was still rather young. There was a small basket of karaoke request slips on our table along with a pen and a thick book of English language songs, which an inquiry revealed to be the only songs sung in this particular bar. This karaoke venue was different [from the bar in Ho Chi Minh City described above], by the fact that the microphone was cordless instead of mounted on a microphone stand on stage. Thus, it was passed around from patron to patron, enabling them to remain in their seats as they sang. Whereas the other karaoke establishments catered to a mainly Vietnamese-speaking audience, this particular bar was devoted exclusively to English language songs. (n.d.)

Though one establishment will slightly differ from another, two relevant points about *hát với nhau* made by Price are the seriousness of the singing by the patrons and the importance of not losing face as a singer.

Karaoke rooms, by contrast, are designed more for fun without the pressure, as the following article explains:

"The karaoke room is like a private world that allows you to sing your favorite songs and chat with your friends or relatives," said . . . the manager of [a] karaoke club in [Ho Chi Minh City]. His club is one of the best-known in the city. With its modern décor and selection of the latest national and international karaoke CDs, the . . . club attracts many young people and businessmen. Like other luxury karaoke clubs, . . . [it] features English, Chinese, Japanese and Korean songs in addition to Vietnamese favorites. "My family likes to relax with karaoke each weekend. We have to pay at least double what we would have to pay in more humble places, but we are very happy there," one frequent . . . client said. (*VNN*, November 10, 2000)

A karaoke room is characterized by a space like a large living room, big enough for a family with children, or group of friends, to sit down in and sing without inhibition. Sarah Scarborough, another one of my 2002 American students, captures the spirit of a typical karaoke room in the following narrative:

Ly Ly Karaoke is the name of a particular establishment in Ho Chi Minh City that is an example of a "karaoke room." This particular place consists of a bright green walled room filled with paintings of people singing and who seem to be beckoning customers towards a staircase leading to a private karaoke room. The customers' final destination is a rather large room that includes white tile floors, a bathroom with a built-in bathtub, and a very noticeable, rather large, and colorful sofa that lines one entire wall. The sofa is colored in three layers of blues, greens, and pinks, which seem to fit the rest of the décor. In the middle of the room is a table with white tablecloth draped over its top; two microphones, books and a remote control are placed within arm's reach on the table. Straight ahead from the sofa is a twenty-inch color television set with a digital component beneath it. The TV set is placed high enough that while relaxing on the sofa, one can view the screen from any position. Tam instructs us on how to work the karaoke remote control while we flip through the book to find our favorite song. "Just look through the book and enter the digits that go with the song, it's easy to find some song," she said; "don't worry if you no sing well, I will start first and then you start." As the Vietnamese song begins to play and the words are put across the bottom of the screen, we begin to sing along with Tam. Since we don't know the language we can only sing the last words of the song: "ngay, la, da." We were the backup singers, and Tam just laughed. This particular karaoke room stays open all night and we were surprised to notice that once we left around 5 AM, we could hear other people singing in the room next door. (n.d.)

The term karaoke *ôm* does not appear on the marquee of an establishment. Therefore, it is not an official business. A typical karaoke *ôm* venue is similar to a karaoke room, but the difference is the possible outcome of sexual favors (i.e. more than hugging, with an additional fee) with a hostess—hence, the term "*ôm*." Brian Elms, another one of my American students in 2002, describes his experience at a cuddle karaoke room in Ho Chi Minh City:

We were led to the rear of the club into a private karaoke room, which was self-contained. An octagonal bar with a diameter of around 15 feet was at the room's center. One wall housed a large karaoke screen and stereo system. Furthest from the entrance was a row of tinted windows facing the street, while directly opposite was a two-way mirror facing the dance floor for the viewing pleasure of the occupants. Multicolored, kaleidoscopic patterns were painted on the ceiling, giving the room a '70s technicolor dreamcoat feel. Little did I know that I had inadvertently stumbled upon the infamous karaoke *ôm* form of entertainment. For the first hour we were at the club we consumed copious amounts of Chivas Regal on the rocks. The service was, as usual, extraordinary. We were outnumbered two-to-one by the bartenders and wait staff. After several rounds of scotch to loosen-up, the karaoke began. The music began with a duet of the Righteous Brother's, "You've Lost That Loving Feeling," followed by a string of Chinese "bubble-gum" type songs. Everyone seemed to be a bit more excited than before. Even the bartender was grinning from ear to ear while signaling with his index finger at a side door. One of the managers led a group of scantily clad women in a line in front of where we were sitting. Michael strolled in front of the women from one end of the line to the other, as if he were imitating Patton in an old newsreel. Michael and Waydee selected women, who remained with the two for the rest of the evening. On the taxi-ride back [to our hotel], Michael explained to me that you pay a flat-fee for both the room and unlimited drinks, as well as the [non sexual] services of the women. The women are paid to swoon and caress the customers. They participate in the karaoke by singing or encouraging the patrons to sing with enthusiastic cheers and clapping. They all double as prostitutes for the right price. (n.d.)

Another term appearing in English newsprint in Vietnam for karaoke entertainment is *private household*, although this kind of venue is not explained at any length except by Patrick Raszelenberg and Trịnh Trí Ninh in their article, "Private households active in the karaoke business":

It is estimated that [the] Binh Thanh district presently has some 108 private households active in the karaoke business. Most of these rooms are air-conditioned, thus attracting a fair number of customers. One young man who is a regular customer remarked: "Air-con karaoke is expensive but the places are nicer and service is friendlier. It's totally alright to bring your girlfriend along, too." Prices are ranging from 20,000 to 40,000 *dong*/hour and people are allowed to choose the songs of their liking. (*VNN*, July 31, 1994)

They continue and explain about high-end karaoke venues, as a contrast to the private home karaoke venues. The pirated video cassette culture karaoke is replaced by sophisticated computer chip karaoke, as they write:

> The days when karaoke with video cassette tapes dominated these ACK (air-con karaoke) places are long gone. Even CDs are inferior to IC chips, each chip containing 300 songs. At the moment, CAVS-4000 with IC chips (US$2,379) are the most popular ones at these high-class karaoke establishments.
>
> Luxury karaoke with private, air-con'd [*sic*] and noise proof rooms, computerized song control and hostesses is also becoming more popular. The Caesar in the 5th district counts 29 private karaoke rooms, the Ben Nghe club nine and the Hoa Binh theater eight. Each of these places recruits hostesses according to external appearance no matter how cacophonous their vocal chords vibrate. They're there to keep the business going, not to enthrall [you with] a Puccini interpretation resembling Mirella Ereni. (ibid.)

Negative opinions have mushroomed about all forms of karaoke since the mid 1990s. At first attitudes about karaoke were very favorable (because it was new), but later attitudes became mixed. Some young people love it, whereas older people, including government officials and others in power, barely tolerate it and some even strongly disapprove of it. The negative attitudes, which are predictably voluminous in the *Việt Nam News*, vary from musical dislikes to moral concerns, and often distinctions are not made between *hát với nhau* and karaoke *ôm*, or between the venues.

VIETNAMESE ATTITUDES TOWARDS KARAOKE

Musical disapproval with *hát với nhau* is based mostly on the inability of certain performers to render songs in a professional way. In 2000, for example, one disapproving male was quoted in the *Việt Nam News* (November 10): "'I hear many of my favorite songs completely massacred by people with terrible voices', grumbled one man who lives near a karaoke business." Nevertheless, the freedom to be able to sing in public, however terrible one's voice may be, is also a part of the democratic nature of karaoke.

Karaoke has led to rowdy behavior (also part of its democratic nature, perhaps), as Raszelenberg and Ninh continue to explain:

> There's nothing wrong with karaoke but these places have become the site of numerous quarrels and punch-ups. At the same time, Vietnam doesn't produce enough karaoke songs to meet people's needs. Most tapes are brought in from abroad. Surely many of us have heard the lamenting canto of young kids "performing" at a karaoke place next door: "I am alone, so allooouuhne . . . Even in love I still feel alooane. . . ." (*VNN*, July 31, 1994)

Quarrels and fighting at karaoke venues are probably the result of an over-consumption of alcohol rather than poorly performed music.

Morality and subversion, however, are of greater concern for particular individuals and the government as a whole. In 1992, for example, an article titled "Karaoke should be put back on right track" was published; it deplored the immoral and reactionary outside influences that karaoke has brought to Vietnam:

> [W]hat is causing concern to the public here is the perverse form Karaoke has taken on: the playing of illegally imported video-cassettes with obscene views and with songs of reactionary contents composed under the former Saigon regime. . . . At a hotel in Hanoi, karaoke equipment is delivered to private rooms for a visitor to enjoy it with his partner with greater comforts. At some other cafes and restaurants in the city, karaoke with smuggled video-cassettes showing obscenity, violence and horror movies is offered almost publicly. The police office of HMC City has arrested Tran Xuan Vinh, owner of a shop renting a total of 19 video-cassette-recorders and 500 video-cassettes with obscene and reactionary contents. In a word, karaoke has deviated far from its original idea as sound, pleasant pastime to become an immoral activity undertaken for profits only. (*VNN*, November 3, 1992)

By 1996, what was now referred to as karaoke *ôm* was raising eyebrows because of its association with what some called pornography, as suggested in the article "Youth hurt by exposure to pornography":

> The free market has only intensified the desire among youth to experience "modern" culture like karaoke and video. But the healthy entertainment brought by these devices also triggers many dangerous trends. . . . *Bia ôm* and karaoke *ôm* venues, featuring beer and karaoke plus "hugging" have spread very quickly and pollute the city's living and cultural environment. . . . As a result of these many so-called

"cultural activities," social morality has degraded day by day. The damage to tradition and cultural identity are increasingly evident everywhere. . . . Recently, the HCM City People's Committee issued Decision 59/CT/UB to step up the fight against pornography and other behavior that violates accepted cultural norms. Organizations and offices from 18 districts have cooperated in these efforts.

In Hanoi, video and karaoke shops are now being forced to register officially as part of the nation-wide campaign against anti-social practices. Both video and karaoke shops are awaiting instruction, as more concrete information is still being examined by the Hanoi Culture and Information Service. (*VNN*, January 9, 1996)

Similar to a family karaoke room, but frequented only by men with their Vietnamese female hostesses, what was becoming known as karaoke *ôm* began to evoke governmental disapproval. In February of the same year, a very detailed article titled "Karaoke bars offer more than romantic tunes in Vietnam" was published, and it painted a clear picture about morality issues and the ways government was going to handle cuddle karaoke with its decree 87CP[1]:

It offers the public the entertainment of warbling popular tunes to pre-recorded music, but in many karaoke parlors in Vietnam, it was not only romantic tunes but romance itself that was offered, until recently.

When it arrived in Vietnam a few years ago, karaoke was an instant hit among all sections of the population, and parlors mushroomed all over the place. A service industry rife with other commercial possibilities such as selling more liquor and food, especially the former, it was not long before what was initially a family and friends affair grew into "coffee, tea and/or me" affairs. The new range of services included glamorous hostesses, who, apart from serving refreshments, could also be counted on to sing and provide companionship.

This in turn spawned a whole network of providers whose service fees were included in the price-lists. In the VNĐ 30,000 that is charged for a can of beer, for example, was included "cyclo and reception" overheads. Commission for cyclo drivers was reportedly VNĐ 2,000 per can of beer consumed by customers brought by him, or 10 per cent of the total bill. The "reception" fee referred to the waitresses who earn VNĐ 1,000 per can of beer sold, and who exhort the clients to consume more, "cheering" the clients on.

The lot of the waitresses is pitiable, though they are the main profit earners for their bosses. Young (usually under 30) and attractive, they have to pay between VNĐ 200,000—500,000 as broker's fees to get the job. The bosses "help" them with this amount, and other expenses for cosmetics and clothes at interest rates of 20 and 25 percent per month. The repayment takes a long time, and at the end, most of the time, all they have earned is some gaudy clothes that can only be used in bars. Those who want to escape have to face the mafiaesque system and its consequences. Sometimes, these women also have to face the wrath of enraged spouses who hold them responsible for their husband's misdemeanor.

But karaoke parlors have come under the purview of the government decree 87CP on investigation and eradication of social evils issued by the Prime Minister. Under the decree that came into effect on the day it was issued, December 12, 1995, among the requirements for a karaoke parlor are [the following]:

— Over 20 square meter area for a karaoke room.
— More than 10 lumens lighting in the karaoke room.
— Clear glass windows that outsiders can look through.
— Karaoke tapes should be on the approved circulation list.

Investigations will regularly be carried out by the Ministry of Information and Culture, To Quan Mau, an official of the Standing Directorate of the decree 87CP told *Việt Nam News*. Any parlor that does not observe the conditions will be fined and have its license revoked, Mau added. (*VNN*, February 9, 1996)

The governmental decree 87CP seemed to have had little effect on the proliferation of karaoke *ôm* parlors, however, and in 2002 and 2004 cuddle karaoke was still going strong.

In December 2002, another governmental document "ordered karaoke bars adjacent to diplomatic and Government offices, schools, clinics and religious places . . . to either move away or shut down" (*VNN*, December 21, 2002). The establishments had until February 20, 2003, to comply or lose their operating licenses. The karaoke debate continued into 2003 and beyond. In July 2003, reporter To Phan (TP) interviewed the Culture and Information Minister, Phạm Quang Nghị (PQN), and asked him about karaoke and moral issues:

TP: The fact is that karaoke shops, bars and discotheques have become venues for prostitution, drug abuse and debauchery that degrade the national character. So how should your ministry and the cultural and information industry respond?

PQN: Karaoke, bar and discotheque are among the stimulating cultural activities. They are necessary to the people's needs for entertainment but should maintain Vietnamese cultural identity. The ministry is planning to limit the development of false cultural forms. It has asked culture and information department directors to investigate karaoke shops, bars and discotheques and close those [which] violate the law. However, it's just a plan. The truth is that entertainment licenses are granted by the Planning and Investment Ministry in accordance with the Business Law. It helps cause duplication and management disharmony. (*VNN*, July 10, 2003)

The Minister responded as someone who seems to enjoy karaoke himself, calling it one of Vietnam's "stimulating cultural activities . . . necessary to the people's needs for entertainment." Nevertheless, it can be detrimental to "proper" values, as he suggests when he says that it does not "maintain Vietnamese cultural identity" and is a "false cultural form."

The issue of "cultural identity" is not clarified by the Culture and Information Minister, and what he probably means is "Vietnamese standards of proper morality," as suggested in the 1996 *Political Report of the Central Committee (Seventh Tenure) to the Eighth National Congress of the Communist Party of Vietnam*. In Section V of Part III, subtitled "To Build an Advanced Culture with Profound National Identity," for example, the following is stated (I have categorized this as I.A.1. in Chapter 2, endnote 1): "The central task in the fields of culture, literature and arts is to help shape the Vietnamese person in terms of thinking, behavior, morality, feelings, and lifestyle." Because the Communist Party has not specifically determined what proper (or improper) morality is, and the Minister has not explained what he means by his terms, however, this is simply a paper tiger issue. Cultural identity is a slippery concept to begin with (as are the concepts of "false" or "true" cultural forms), especially as an aspect of internal nationalism (i.e. within the motherland, as opposed to external nationalism among diasporic or overseas subcultures). To emphasize my point, in 1997, though still concerned about moral degradation because of karaoke, the socialist government of Vietnam developed a response of "if you can't beat 'em, join 'em" by sponsoring an official karaoke contest, as explained in the following newspaper article, "Uncle Ho brings revolution to karaoke in Vietnam":

> Hanoi's Culture and Information Department, a fierce opponent of the "social evils" spawned by karaoke, has softened its stand to mark the 107th birthday of Vietnam's late president and nationalist leader, Ho Chi Minh. The *Lao Dong* newspaper said on Saturday that an official karaoke contest would be held in central Hanoi from May 25–30. Anything goes in the capital's ubiquitous karaoke bars, from the Beatles and Vietnamese folk songs to prostitution and drug abuse. But next week's official sing-along will have a special theme: "Uncle Ho and the Revolution." (*VNN*, May 17, 1997)

It is noteworthy that with its concern about the "social evils" of karaoke, the government took a different approach: to attempt to control karaoke by instigating an official karaoke contest. Building upon the tremendous political power of music as a propaganda tool, the government approved of karaoke for nearly a week, and Hồ Chí Minh's 107th birthday was celebrated in a unique way. With its politics of remembering, the government realized, perhaps, that official sanctioned events are easier to control than unregulated ones.

KARAOKE AS AN INDUSTRY IN VIETNAM

Many of the attitudes about the evils of karaoke cited above also relate to the one characteristic that is of primary importance to any market economy—profit. The numerous karaoke narratives suggest that karaoke is good business in Vietnam, especially in the large urban areas. Business and profit, however, come in many shapes and forms, and I see two large categories existing: *business* (meaning little business) and *industry* (meaning big business). I distinguish between the two because of the differences in expenditure and profit involved with karaoke. For example, an evening in a family karaoke room does not cost much for participants if alcohol and food are not overly consumed; therefore, profit is slight—this is the *business* of karaoke. By contrast, more money is expended and profits are greater with high-tech karaoke, that is, when technology includes the design and manufacturing of playback equipment, the production of playback materials, and the recording of personal CDs of karaoke costumers—this constitutes the *industry* of karaoke. I will discuss only the last one: the recording of personal compact discs for karaoke customers.

Recording studios specializing in karaoke music make high profits in Vietnam, and many wealthy Vietnamese urbanites enjoy owning CDs of themselves sounding like pop singers. A karaoke singer can be a star on stage for a few minutes, but with your own CD, you can be a star forever.

Based on a technology that originated in Japan, the recording studio equipment in Ho Chi Minh City for making an individual CD is also Japanese. For that reason, equipment is expensive and recording sessions can be costly, catering mostly to wealthy Vietnamese:

> Tuấn Anh, who honed his music industry skills while studying in Australia, set up the A2Z recording studio in District 1 [in Ho Chi Minh City] with VNĐ 500 million [about US$33,000] worth of equipment. "My recording studio is filled with the most modern equipment in the city. Some singers and bands also like to record here," he says. A2Z charges VNĐ 99,000 [US$6.60] per hour for singers and VNĐ 90,000 [US$6.00] to record the results on CD. . . . [C]ustomers can choose from Vietnamese, English, French, and even Chinese songs. "Our customers choose their favorite songs from a list. Then they have 15 minutes free of charge to practice following the lead of our technicians. When they feel ready, we begin to record their voice. My technicians and I mix the CD." (*VNN*, June 23, 2001)

Recording studios such as A2Z are very professional and can record ensembles as well as individuals. Smaller studios are also found, and by the summer of 2002, dozens of digital studios had sprung up in Ho Chi Minh City (e.g., Born To Sing, Nice, Viết Tân, and Bến Thành) to meet the demand of singers who wished to record their own voices with prerecorded sound track.

Wealthy Vietnamese can also purchase home equipment to make amateur private recordings, according to the article, "Vanity studios take karaoke to new heights in HCM City":

> Unlike professional studios that cost between $20,000 and $25,000 to open, an amateur recording studio only needs about $3,000–$5,000 to buy a computer with a soundcard, amplifiers, speakers, headphones and microphones. Using specialized software, the studio can adjust the singer's voice to make it sound like a professional. The studios are becoming money-making machines for their owners, who are often songwriters, musicians or singers themselves. Some of the smaller studios are challenging the bigger players by recording background music for performances, musical backing for poems, or dubbing for the advertising industry. Studio staff can also be hired as mixers for all kinds of events. Some studios are trying to edge out their competition by offering 50 per cent discounts to professional singers, and 30 per cent to students. Twenty per cent discounts are also available to people who pay with credit from the Asia Commercial Bank. (*VNN*, July 9, 2002)

Vietnamese youth and even families find the possibility of making a CD intriguing, and being a good singer is not necessarily a requirement, as one studio owner explained: "You don't have to be a professional singer to record an album anymore. . . . Just try to do your best—our technician knows how to make your voice sound more beautiful" (ibid.). A customer is led into a soundproof room in the studio where he/she is provided with headphones that transmits the instrumental accompaniment and a karaoke screen that displays the lyrics of the chosen song. Added to the cost of VNĐ 100,000 (US$6.67) an hour is an additional charge of VNĐ 200,000 (US$13.33) for recording and mixing the album. "Extra copies of the CD cost more, and are available in a range of formats: 30-minute videos cost VNĐ 55,000, minidiscs are VNĐ 55,000 and CD-ROMs are VNĐ 22,000. The prices vary little between studios" (*VNN*, July 10, 2002).

It is not unusual for an amateur singer to spend up to VNĐ 3 million [US$200] over several recording sessions to make the finished product, complete with an artistically designed CD cover. Nevertheless, the expense is worth it to some Vietnamese upper-class urbanites, as explained by a young medical doctor in Ho Chi Minh City: "I had the most wonderful time of my life. . . . I sat there with a microphone in my face in a modern recording studio. I'm not a singer, but I recorded my voice just like professionals do" (*VNN*, June 23, 2001).

Diệp Bảo Chánh, the manager of the Sài Gòn Star recording studio in Ho Chi Minh City explained that recording CDs is popular with families as well as with the youth: "Occasionally, a family will come in to record an album featuring the voices of all their family members, from grandparents to grandchildren" (*VNN*, July 9, 2002).

His studio is so popular that many customers repeatedly make CDs of themselves."One client has set the record by making 10 albums here, but most customers only make about three or four CDs," said a studio technician (ibid.). Professional songwriters in addition to karaoke lovers also make use of studios such as Sài Gòn Star, finding them to be a relatively inexpensive way to make multiple CD copies of their songs for distribution.

Some of the karaoke clubs in Ho Chi Minh City will also record their customers and provide them with CDs of their performances for comparatively little money. Costing only VNĐ 15,000 [US$1.00] an hour for singing, VNĐ 30,000 [US$2.00] for the recording process, plus a little more for the finished product, the price is right, but the quality is not usually very good, as one singer explained: "Recording at karaoke clubs is like playing a game of chance. . . . Most voices aren't strong enough for singing, and many famous songs sung terrible sound like murder" (*VNN*, June 23, 2001). Nevertheless, owning a CD of oneself singing and being able to play it for friends is an aspect of great pride and enjoyment for many Vietnamese, and the audio quality is not that important to them.

The recording of CDs of one's singing, and especially recordings of family members, are examples of the "technology of memory," according to Marita Sturken (1997:12). The CDs (or videos) themselves, as material objects, can be thought of as *artifacts of memory*, especially as they are passed along to children and grandchildren years after they were recorded. Karaoke, however, is still most popular as a living process with live singers on stage.

KARAOKE AND THE LAW

In 2004, the Vietnamese communist government, through its Ministry of Information and Culture, officially announced a drafted regulation stating that karaoke bars in Vietnam would be banned by January 1, 2005. It claimed that karaoke bars were "fronts for brothels and drug dens," according to its survey, which found 80 percent of Vietnam's karaoke businesses guilty of harboring such illegal activities (*VNN*, March 14, 2004).

Negative reactions from Vietnamese citizens from many walks of life to the possible banning of karaoke, were strong in the early 2000s, as Thu Hà suggests in his column, "Talk around Town":

Feeling relaxed after an hour of singing at the Ngọc Huyền Karaoke Bar in Hà Nội, Hoàng Mai, 25, and her three friends worry what they will do if karaoke is banned. Mai isn't the only one to worry. Many people, from youths to the middle-aged, urban to rural residents, professionals to manual laborers, are becoming increasingly concerned about where to go for recreation if karaoke parlors are forced out of business. . . .

The draft law has already been sternly rebuked by many of the country's karaoke lovers. "With only a handful of recreational forms available, karaoke is an exciting activity, especially for the youth," said Anh Tuấn [not the same rock musician discussed earlier], who works for a German owned firm. Besides reading books, watching movies or listening to music at home, the 27-year-old Hanoian says he, his friends and relatives like to sing at karaoke bars to relax after a long day's work at a high pressure job. "Despite my awful voice, at karaoke parlors I can loudly belt out my favorite songs effectively clearing away my sadness and multiplying my happiness," Mai said.

Students, who are still dependent on their parents for money, enjoy karaoke for its economic value. "It is more expensive to meet friends at coffee bars than karaoke parlors where it costs only a few thousand *dong*," said Phạm Huyên, a third year university student in HCM City. Despite being able to afford a karaoke machine, many Vietnamese prefer to go to karaoke parlors than to sing at home. "I am not as enthusiastic when I sing at home because I like having many friends around when I sing. My house is not large enough to contain many people and besides, I don't want to disturb my neighbors," Võ Thị Ngọc Loan, an employee at the Southern Bảo Việt Life Insurance Company said. . . . [It is] difficult for the general public, especially the youth, to imagine the day they and their friends will not be able to relax and sing at their favorite karaoke bar. (ibid.)

Public attitudes towards karaoke are indeed mixed throughout Vietnam, as suggested above. Official attitudes are also varied.

What is unclear about the proposed decree is whether all karaoke establishments will be targeted, or only those that allow undesirable activities to occur within their walls. As of March 2005, karaoke bars in Vietnam had still not been banned, although some were raided, with the consequence of discovering illegal drugs and sex rings:

One hundred and one people tested positive for illegal recreational drugs following a raid on a Binh Thanh District karaoke parlor by HCM City Police on Wednesday morning. At 4 AM, Police . . . found 148 drugged men and women, aged 16 to 30-years-old. The people found at the establishment were taken to the Police station where urine tests were conducted. A search of the karaoke parlor and the suspects' belongings helped Binh Thanh Police identify and seize more than 30 synthetic Ecstasy pills and five bags of Katalme, a type of high-quality heroin that is inhaled. Police also found underwear and used condoms littering the 13 rooms of the karaoke bar. . . .

Neighbors said most visitors to the karaoke bars were from affluent families and drive expensive motorbikes. They added the bars operate all night long and create disturbances in the area. According to [the] deputy chief of the Police Department in Binh Thanh District, the drug users were released by police after their urine tests. [He] said his department has informed the drug users' local authorities to work out measures to give them strict punishments. (*VNN*, March 11, 2005)

This suggests that the punishment for using illegal drugs may not be severe in Vietnam, but the opposite is true for selling such drugs, and public executions of drug dealers is common: "Nine defendants involved in a drug trafficking ring . . . will face the firing squad as a result of sentences handed down by an appeals court of the HCM City People's Court on Wednesday" (*VNN*, June 19, 2004).

The attitudes of other public officials, economists, and businessmen are to go after the evils of drug use and prostitution, rather than the establishments where such evils may take place. Phạm Chi Lan, a member of the Prime Minister's research board, for example, states: "Violations do happen, but the penalties should be applied directly to the violators, not to every business person. If the culture and information managers are so worried about how to deal with karaoke services, they should try to find other means of doing so" (*VNN*, February 27, 2004). Likewise, economist Lê Đăng Doanh states:

> I don't think we should mix up our goals with our means. If the goal is to deal with prostitution, it should be achieved using means other than a ban on karaoke parlors. . . . I believe there are many other ways to deal with people who hide illegal businesses at the back of karaoke parlors. Karaoke services should not be banned. (ibid.)

A Ho Chi Minh City businessman and owner of a karaoke parlor in District 3 likewise expressed concern: "Why should we have to close our business when we are operating in accordance with the Government's rulings? I know that some karaoke parlors are a front for illegal business, but it is obvious that the Government's loose management is to blame. Why doesn't the Government take more effective actions to wipe out these social evils?"(ibid.) Lê Anh Tuyền, the Legal Department director of the Ministry of Information and Culture, provides the main reason behind the proposed ban: "Article 6 of the Enterprise Law bans any business that goes against the nation's culture and customs or negatively affects national security and defense" (ibid.) This rationale goes directly back to the concerns of the 1996 and 2001 *Reports* of the Communist Party, as discussed in Chapter 2, and suggests that the banning of particular karaoke businesses that front unpatriotic activities is legal, whereas the banning of all of them is not.

An additional problem that may affect the future of karaoke in Vietnam is the country's new copyright law as adopted with the Berne Convention, which requires karaoke bars to pay royalties for the use of copyrighted songs. In the following interview, Đại Đoàn Kết [DDK] from the *Great Solidarity* newspaper interviewed Lương Nguyên [LN], deputy director of the Vietnam Music Copyright Center:

DDK: Karaoke bars will now have to pay royalties for copyrighted music they play. How will this be implemented, especially as many believe copyrights can only be enforced by the music's producer?

LN: When putting together music, the producers will have paid for the copyright of the song they wish to use, and casual listeners have nothing to worry about. However, if they use these musical products for business purposes, it's different . . . In line with this, company owners should pay for music broadcast on airplanes, buses, tourism sites and karaoke bars. The first karaoke bars that agreed to pay for copyrights are those in the northern province of Ha Tay. The province's Music Copyright Center and Department of Culture and Information have co-operated to make it fair for the businesses and the songs' authors.

DDK: How will these fees be collected?

LN: We have a fixed price for copyright fees. For example, we will collect VNĐ 750,000 [US$50] from each karaoke room per year for lowland provinces. The price will be lower for mountainous provinces. The highest price is VNĐ 15,000 [US$1] per karaoke room per day, a total of over VNĐ 5 million [US$333.33] a year, collected from first-class bars in big cities.

DDK: How will the composers be paid?

LN: The provinces' departments of culture and information have a list of songs used in their karaoke bars. In this case, we will divide the fee equally among all songs. Although it is only a small sum of money, we must collect it to assure fairness for all.

DDK: How much money has your center collected from these bars?

LN: Up to now, we have collected nearly VNĐ 80 million [US$5333.33]. We also began collecting in Ha Giang, Lang Son and Vinh Phuc. Owners and managers in some mountainous areas like Ha Giang have great respect for copyright laws. However in Ha Noi, nearly 500 karaoke bars are still out of our reach. We are working with the city's People's Committee and the Department of Culture and Information on this problem. (*VNN*, August 8, 2005)

Though these fees seem slight relative to United States dollar amounts, the additional costs will undoubtedly be absorbed by the singers. The above

Figure 9.2   A cartoon by Trịnh Lập, from the *Việt Nam News*, March 14, 2004 (used with permission).

interview does not address the question of foreign covers, as Luong Nguyen's answer to the final question ("Whose songs are the most frequently used?") suggests: "The musicians whose songs were regularly used are Văn Cao, Trịnh Công Sơn, Phạm Tuyên and Trần Tiến." If karaoke is allowed to continue, the copyright issue should not be a concern, unless the cost of singing foreign covers requires a higher royalty payment.

CONCLUSION: THE DEMOCRACY OF MUSIC MAKING

Karaoke, which is the world's greatest public display of individual singing by people who are untrained in the art of singing, is a powerful force in the free world and is a struggling phenomenon in Vietnam. Karaoke symbolizes the democracy of music making, as I suggested above, and this is the key to its popularity around the world. This musical democracy is perhaps also one of the main reasons karaoke is anathema to the communist government. Karaoke in Vietnam seems to have little to do with the politics of remembering and more to do with the economics of forgetting, in spite of Nguyễn Xuân An's opinion that it is a vehicle for the singing and popularizing of revolutionary songs. However, karaoke as memory politics and cultural identity are present with the video imagery of place that is so prevalent, even though it is more of an imagined place of romance and tranquility. In Vietnam, karaoke has also been a way to remember the past through foreign covers, and soon (with the country's new copyright laws) it may symbolize the past of foreign covers. That economic reason, in fact, may be the real reason for karaoke's decline in Vietnam, and the high cost of purchasing legal audio/visual clips to which the public will want to sing along may cause it to have its microphone cable cut, as shown in Trịnh Lập's drawing in Figure 9.2.

10 Conclusion
The Politics and Economics of Popular Music in Vietnam

In this book I have presented a glimpse at what popular music in Vietnam was like between 1990 and 2005, where it came from, who its major actors were, how it was perceived and controlled by the communist government, and how it was shaped by Vietnam's market economy and influenced by globalization. In 2005 I asked Hồng Nhung what she thinks pop music in Vietnam will be doing in the next five years. She said, "I think it will be zooming in a zillion directions. That is very Vietnamese. Everybody does things differently." "It's sort of like how the Vietnamese youth drive their motorbikes on the streets, in every which direction," I responded. The metaphor is appropriate, I believe, because memory politics and market economics have caused many forms of popular music to exist together on a type of popular music continuum in Vietnam and have caused all kinds of popular music to be heard almost any place and at any time. Indeed, while walking down the CD market street (Huynh Thuc Khang) in Ho Chi Minh City, I often experienced sonic jams, just as I experienced motorbike traffic jams while riding on a *moto* (motorbike taxi).

Luke Peereboom, the manager of Catwalk Disco in Ho Chi Minh City, stated in 1996 that "Music is the universal language of peace and friendship and the Vietnamese youth appreciate different kinds of music from all over the world" (*VNN*, January 19). He was specifically referring to music inspired by African-influenced popular music genres from the Caribbean and other regions (the article is titled "Afro rhythms rock HCM City's hipsters") and to his new show, *Cool Black Sounds*. However, Peereboom also characterized the Vietnamese youth as having "increasingly sophisticated tastes and international vision. . . ." Although perhaps overemphasizing the government's (i.e. the government-controlled music industry) and media's interest in globalization and perhaps even reconciliation (i.e. "peace and friendship" after years of conflict), Peereboom's statement is worth unpacking because of the power it attributes to music.

Is music like a magical charm (*duyên*) or an opiate that can create peace and friendship in a country, a culture, an individual, a relationship? According to Felix Soh, writing in the Singapore *Straits Times*, music is akin to Karl Marx's idea of religion as the opiate of the masses, because (he believes) it functions in the same way (article published in *VNN*, July 27, 1999). Music may have the power to create peace and friendship, perhaps, but only if the music genres allowed to be expressed are what the hegemonic forces consider to be peaceful musics. In Vietnam, these peaceful musics, as we have seen, include a number of expressions on the Popular Music Continuum, including many of the genres, such as rock, heavy metal, and hip-hop, which are often watered down by the Vietnamese musicians themselves, perhaps because of self-censorship or to give them the *duyên* or charm that the Vietnamese consider essential. The most peaceful are the songs that constitute the musical thread I have called love songs.

THE POLITICS OF POPULAR MUSIC IN VIETNAM

As I have shown with my "Arc of Culturation" or "Vietnamization" analyses of particular creations by some Vietnamese songwriters and singers (especially those of Nguyễn Cường, Lê Minh Sơn, Hồng Nhung, and Thanh Lam), it appears that what is a farewell to the past is not an erasure of the musical pasts that pertain to Vietnam itself, but a respect for and revival of them for the purposes of creativity and personal growth. These creations and philosophies support the adage that there cannot be a future without a past.

Ramet considers a respect for and revival of the past (she is referring to folk idioms, which are a kind of past) to be the fourth phase of musical development and creativity in communist countries (1994:3), although she writes the following with reference to rock (rather than folk idioms) in Soviet Europe during the 1990s: "more recently, there have been clear signs of a fourth phase, characterized by the turn to local and exotic folk idioms for material. . . ." Within this "fourth phase" there is what I perceive to be a potential danger, however, if politics gets involved in the development of popular music. In Vietnam, this danger is the manufacturing and marketing of musical nostalgia. Vietnam's music industry can learn from what has taken place in Vietnam's tourism industry. Although the two industries cannot perhaps be logically compared because of the tangible characteristics of the former (history, geography, etc.) and the intangible or abstract nature of the latter (sound, rhythm, love, etc.), both are influenced by memory and patrimony, both are driven by money and the market, and both are loosely controlled by communist gatekeepers at local levels (the Vietnamese government delegates authority over both tourism and music). The parallels are striking, and the following narrative of the tourism industry in Vietnam is worth hearing as an analogy.

Laurel B. Kennedy and Mary Rose Williams, in their article "The Past without the Pain," explain how in 1990 the Vietnamese government, after requesting a market analysis of tourism by foreign image makers, decided that Vietnam must be "re-script[ed] in the popular consciousness . . . [and that Vietnam's] tourist industry needed to tell a new story of Vietnam to potential travelers" (2001:136). The resulting re-presentation of Vietnam's story through tourism is what Kennedy and Williams call "a vision of a sweet past, . . . [the] manufacture of nostalgia, . . . [and] The Past without the Pain [the title of the article]" (137). Government-approved tourist packages provide tourists "with an experience of the country very distant from the experience of the people of Vietnam. It is instead a construction of Vietnam—its history, its culture, its people—designed for Westerners, through their own eyes" (157). They continue:

> Far from promoting understanding of the Vietnamese people, their valorous history, their culture and way of life, the tourist industry invites foreigners to experience Vietnam from the position of dominance and control that Westerners appeared to lose forever at Dien Bien Phu [where the Vietnamese defeated the French] in 1954 and in Saigon in 1975. (159)

And finally, "Vietnam's past is selectively reconstructed to appeal to Westerners or, perhaps more accurately, to marketers' ideas of Westerners and their interests. (160)

A parallel situation has already occurred with Vietnam's renovated and partially imagined neotraditional music (see Arana 1994 and 1999), especially as it is performed at many tourist venues in Vietnam. The possibility of something similar happening in Vietnam's music industry with regard to popular music is also taking place with, for example, the music revival of Trịnh Công Sơn's songs of the past without the pain (meaning that only his love songs are allowed to be performed), the sanitized heavy metal of The Wall (i.e. sung without many references to social issues), rapping about love rather than social problems by Kasim and other pop singers, and countless other examples discussed in this book. Both the governmental controls on Vietnam's tourism and music industries (especially karaoke) are forms of censorship, which exist mostly for political and cultural reasons.

I have no doubt that Vietnam's leaders and its people want their country to move forward and come into its own as a cultural and economic force in Asia and the rest of the world in the twenty-first century. It is not an isolationistic country which lives in the past, but (I have found from personal experience) it is a forgiving and hopeful one that looks toward the future. Vietnam's popular music is becoming an important cultural and economic voice in the country's progress. It will even become more important in the world market if Vietnam says farewell to its past and present policies of historical, cultural, and political censorship of music and other modes of communication, some of which have existed since colonial times (Taylor 2003:153, fn. 10) and grown exponentially since 1975. "[If] we impede music, we inhibit our ability to be fully human" (Nuzum 2004:153)—these are important words for twenty-first century Vietnam and the world.

THE ECONOMICS OF POPULAR MUSIC IN VIETNAM

A particular facet of popular music in Vietnam involves a handful of pop singers who are interested in becoming stars on MTV, throughout Asia and the rest of the world. Kasim and Mỹ Tâm are especially noteworthy in this regard, as the former has expressed his desire to become a globally known pop singer, and the latter has already performed with American superstars. Several of Vietnam's boy bands and girl bands, such as MTV and Trio 666, have made successful tours to foreign countries, and The Wall set its sights on MTV Asia before it disbanded in December 2006.

Beyond the aspirations and successes of a few pop stars and bands in Vietnam (as I have discussed in Chapters 3 and 4), the youth in general make a connection between contemporary popular music, globalization, making money, learning English, and *not* thinking about the past. The high attendance of teenagers at rock and pop/rock concerts in public places and at youth culture houses (as discussed in Chapters 6 and 7) attests to the importance of contemporary popular music in their lives. Although Street was probably thinking of rebellious change when he explained that rock has the power to "upset old images and provide new ones" (1986:66; see Chapter 4), in Vietnam those new images are not about rebellion against the government or social change, but are almost always about the youth's desires to be modern, financially successful, own Honda Dream motorbikes, and listen to pop music on the Internet. The singing of *nhạc trẻ* songs and other ballads at karaoke bars, clubs, and houses (see Chapter 9) and the listening to and viewing of music videos that distort reality (see Chapter 8), are not only activities that fulfill a love for singing among Vietnam's youth, but they are also powerful agents for forgetting the past—or at least covering it up—and imagining the future.

Notes

NOTES TO CHAPTER 1

1. The official Web site (www.davang.com) of Da Vàng (a rock group in Ho Chi Minh City) mentions that the first Pop-Rock Festival took place in 1991 at the Youth Culture House in Saigon, where they won second place for the "best band." This festival, held on a different date and at a different venue than the Pop-Rock Festival described by the *Việt Nam News*, may have been precursor to the official first Pop-Rock Festival of 1992.
2. The Reporters Without Borders group lists the following countries as the ten worst, from first to tenth: North Korea, Cuba, Burma, Turkmenistan, Eritrea, China, Vietnam, Nepal, Saudi Arabia, and Iran (*BBC News*, October 26, 2004).

NOTES TO CHAPTER 2

1. The 1996 reports were translated and published as supplements in the *Việt Nam News* on April 10 and June 29. The original reports do not clearly make the divisions I have made in the outline formats, and as my paraphrases read, there are references to culture and the arts in several of the topics that I have labeled something else. In the first report, for example, I.A.1. speaks about the arts but only as they relate to the shaping the character of an individual. Likewise, II.B.1. speaks of artistic heritage as it relates to allegiance to the state (nationalism), and II.C.1. addresses the arts and ethnic diversity. Indeed, all of the points in the four topics overlap somehow as they relate to expressive culture. Another example is IV.B.1., refers to "the intrusion of noxious cultures," which is a major concern for the government as particular types of foreign music enter Vietnam, along with other foreign influences resulting from globalization. Therefore, all the points in the outlines are very important, as the Reports spell out the thought processes of Vietnam's Communist Party towards expressive culture and proper individual and group behavior. The relevance for popular culture, however, has to be inferred.
2. These are the ways the term *culture* is used in the first and second *Political Reports of the Central Committee (Seventh Tenure) to the Eighth National Congress of the Communist Party of Vietnam* (VNN, Supplements, April 10 and June 29, 1996) and the *Second Report of the Central Committee Eighth National Congress of the Communist Party of Vietnam* (VNN, April

20, Supplement, 2001): advanced characters of culture; advanced culture; allocations for culture; cultural activities; cultural build-up; cultural centers; cultural creations; cultural development; cultural enjoyment; cultural heritage; cultural identity; cultural products; cultural relics; cultural values; culture as spiritual foundation of society; cultured families; cultured life; deep infusion of culture into each and every community; elements of culture; field of culture; heighten culturality; humankind's cultural quintessence; intangible cultural heritage; integrating culture; international cultural exchanges; introduce Vietnamese culture; noxious cultures; pornographic cultures; profane cultures; public cultural facilities; traditional cultural values; Vietnamese culture; Village of Ethnicities' Cultures.

NOTES TO CHAPTER 3

1. According to Shuker (2005:121–122), as a marketing device, recording companies and CD stores have developed "metagenres, which are rather loose amalgams of various styles (e.g., alternative rock, world music)" to simplify the categorization process.
2. From the following Web site (no longer on line): http://www.click2vietartists. net/html/singer_anhtuyet/index.htm
3. From the following Web site (no longer on line): http://www.asianweek.com/ 2000_05_04/ae_phuongthao.html
4. From the following Web site (no longer on line): http://www.click2vietartists. net/html/singer_phuongthaongocle/index.htm
5. From the following Web site (no longer on line): http://www.click2vietartists. net/html/ singer_thanhlam/.
6. From the following Web site (no longer on line): http://www.visualqui.com/ index.php?cat=8&paged=3.
7. From the following Web site (no longer on line): http://www.limsi.fr/Recherche/ CIG/ehongnhung.htm.
8. From the following Web site (no longer on line): http://www.cinemusic.net/ reviews/2003/ quiet_american.html.
9. From the following Web site: http://www.pbs.org/vietnampassage/perspectives/perspectives.music.html.
10. From the following Web site (no longer on line): http://www.nhandan.org. vn/english/20030205/index.html. Nhan Dan (http://www.nhandan.org.vn/ vietnamese/index.htm and in English at http://www.nhandan.org.vn/english/today/) is "The central organ of the Communist Party of Vietnam."
11. From the following Web site (no longer on line): http://www.vnstyle.vdc.com. vn/myhomeland/vietnamincloseup/chitiet.cfm?ID_Tin=756&CM=tb_VN_ closeup.
12. *Ả đào* is chamber music from northern Vietnam, according to Mark McLeod and Nguyễn Thi Dieu, who describe one of the most famous types, *hát ả đào* (2001:173): Hát ả đào, or 'the singing of songstresses', rooted in the traditional society of the North, evolved from ceremonial music to . . . music of entertainment. It puts to song classical poems chosen for their beauty or specially written by the listeners and performed by talented songstresses accompanying themselves with percussion instruments. (2001:173)
13. From the following Web site (no longer on line): http://www.undp.org.vn/ mlist/ develvn/122002/post12.htm.
14. Y Moan has been a source of inspiration for younger ethnic minority pop singers and musicians: Những Người Bạn Lang Bian (Friends of Lang Bian)

is the name of a pop band founded by Krăjăn Plin and Krăjăn Dick, two singers of the Lạch ethnic minority . . . a branch of [the] K'Ho ethnic minority,
[who] live in the Lang Bian mountainous area of the Tây Nguyên. "I started
dreaming of founding a band of my own, like Y Moan's, three years ago,"
Plin says. "I want to introduce our ethnic minority music to visitors to Lang
Bian". The eight-member group performs Lạch folk songs and pop rock written by Plin and Dick. The pop rock they play is influenced by the minority's
own folk music. (*VNN*, April 14, 1999)

NOTES TO CHAPTER 4

1. The theory or concept of *yin* and *yang* (*âm* and *dương* in Vietnamese) is
   most commonly understood as a concept of balance (of opposites) originally
   espoused by the ancient Chinese sage popularly known as Confucius (Kung
   Fu-tzu, ca. 551–479 B.C.), as published in his *I Ching* (Book of Changes).
   Writing about Vietnam, Neil Jamieson (whose model I find intriguing and
   logical) takes what he refers to as a neo-Confucianist approach in explaining
   yin and *yang*: "The traditional Vietnamese worldview constituted an all-
   encompassing cosmological scheme based on *yin* and *yang*, conceived as two
   primordial forces from which everything else in the universe was created"
   (1993:11). Furthermore, Schuyler Cammann explains that the old Chinese
   concept "of two basic forces in nature—contrasted rather than opposed"—is
   ideally "kept in perfect balance" (1985:215). For such opposites or contrasting entities to function properly, there must be a balance, as Jamieson (ibid.)
   continues to explain: "In all things, when a proper balance was maintained
   between *yin* and *yang*, harmony was maintained and beneficent outcomes
   were assured." Therefore, the bipolar system of *yin* and *yang* must have a
   workable bridge to be successful. This provides the rational for my Popular
   Music Continuum (see Chapter 1).
2. As Jamieson uses the term "*yin* subsystem" to refer to "irregularities" of
   the status quo (1993:11), I will occasionally adapt his idea and use the term
   "*yang* subsystem" to refer to the communist government's ideological basis
   (which I also call the status quo ["regularities," as it were], hegemony, and
   traditional thought). In this way I try to keep the Traditional Popular Music
   to Contemporary Popular Music Contiuum relevant to other cultural (and
   political) ideas.
3. Until this article about the boyband 1088 appeared in 2002, sponsorship in
   Vietnam seemed to refer only to financial support given by a corporation to
   bring about shows and other performance opportunities, in return for the
   right to use on-stage and other advertising of corporate products. This article
   seems to suggest that sponsorship in twenty-first century Vietnam has begun
   to mirror sponsorship in the United States, which includes more control of
   musicians via training and, ultimately, musical style.

NOTES TO CHAPTER 5

1. http://www.comp.nus.edu.sg/~nguyenvu/Artists/TC_Sơn/VT_Music_
   TCSon_forum.htm (no longer on line).

NOTES TO CHAPTER 7

1. The acoustic MTV concerts were a response to the lip-synching scandal and lawsuit against Milli Vanilli for their deception during concerts (and on music video).

NOTES TO CHAPTER 9

1. The 1995 decree 87CP is translated as follows: "Enhancing the management of cultural activities and cultural services, increasing the elimination of serious social evils" (McNally 2003:121, fn7). Regulations about karaoke rooms (one of the serious social evils) were established in February 1996 (ibid.:114).

Glossary

ả đào—Chamber music from northern Vietnam (see also *hát ả đào*).

áo dài—A long dress for women.

cải lương—Renovated theater, short for *hát cải lương*

ca trù—Traditional festival songs, also referred to as northern Vietnamese chamber music with vocal texts.

chầu văn—Ritual songs.

dàn bầu—A plucked single string (monochord) chordophone.

dân ca—Romantic or modernized folk songs.

dân ca quan họ—Folk love duets.

đàn dáy—A plucked lute chordophone.

dân tộc—Nationality, nation, or national, a concept advocated by President Hồ Chí Minh. See also its variants, *tính dân tộc* and *văn hoá dân tộc*.

đàn tranh—A plucked zither chordophone, similar to the Chinese zheng.

đổi mới—Changing for the new, new way, or renovation. Vietnam's open-door policy, generally said to have been instigated in 1985 (some sources say 1986).

đàn nguyệt—A plucked lute chordophone with three strings.

duyên—Charm, perhaps from the French *duen*.

hát ả đào—Singing of songstresses, rooted in the traditional culture of northern Vietnam and evolving from ceremonial music to become entertainment music based on classical poems chosen for their beauty or specially written by the listeners; it is performed by talented songstresses accompanying themselves with percussion instruments.

hát chèo—Lyrical songs.

hát ru—Lullabies

hát tuồng—Lyrical songs.

hát với nhau—Karaoke sung for fun in clubs, bars, restaurants, and other public places.

hội quán trẻ—Youth club that often features live musicians.

hò—Work songs.

karaoke ôm—Hugging or cuddle karaoke; karaoke with a hostess, which can include sexual favors for an additional fee.

nhạc cải lương—Music (i.e. songs) derived from *hát cải lương* (renovated theater) and other theatrical genres.

nhạc dân tộc cải biên—Reformed/improved/renovated national music or neotraditional music sanctioned by the government.

nhạc đỏ—Red music, a colloquial term for *nhạc cach mạng* (revolutionary music), which are songs that venerate revolution, war, and victory from Vietnam's past.

nhạc hoa—Cantonese pop music, songs influenced by Cantopop.

nhạc nhẹ—Light music, a term for love songs in a light rock style.

nhạc sến—Cheesy music, a derisive term for *nhac quê hương*, a song style that consists of weepy love songs popular in Vietnam before 1975. The style is similar to market music.

nhạc thị trường—Market music, a musical style intended for and loved by the Vietnamese lower classes that always has to do with love, lost love, and weeping.

nhạc tiền chiến—Prewar music, meaning pre-American War and often pre-Indochina War against the French; in other words, pre-revolutionary music.

nhạc trẻ—Youth music, a particular ballad-like music sung in a crooner style.

nhạc trữ tình—Lyrical music.

nhạc vang—Blue music, sentimental songs of the Việt kiều or overseas Vietnamese, often based on the song style of prewar music.

phòng trà ca nhạc—Music and song tea room, referred to as popular music listening club.

quan họ—Declamatory songs.

red songs—See *nhạc đỏ*.

Sao Mai–Điểm Hẹn—Star search contest.

sáo trúc—A horizontal or transverse flute aerophone.

tiền chiến—Prewar, meaning the pre-revolutionary period in Vietnamese history.

tieu—A vertical end-blown notch flute aerophone.

tình ca—Love songs.

tính dân tộc—National character, a concept advocated by President Hồ Chí Minh.

tỳ bà—A plucked lute chordophone with four strings, similar to the Chinese *pipa*.

văn hoá dân tộc—National culture, a concept advocated by President Hồ Chí Minh.

vọng cổ—Lyrical songs.

Bibliography

Addis, Stephen. 1975. "Introduction." In *Musics of Vietnam*, by Phạm Duy, edited by Dale R. Whiteside. Carbondale: Southern Illinois University Press.

Anh Thu. 2000. "Against all odds." *Việt Nam News* (January 23–30).

———. 2001. "Local top hits help make stars of aspiring pop singers." *Việt Nam News* (May 9).

———. 2003. "Karaoke bar or major star—the difference is who's behind you." *Việt Nam News* (April 5).

———. 2004a. "Young singers hit big time." *Việt Nam News* (January 4).

———. 2004b. "Entertainers tear hair out over new rules on rad styles." *Việt Nam News* (July 31).

Appadurai, Arjun, ed. 2001a. *Globalization*. Durham, NC: Duke University Press.

———. 2001b. "The globalization of archaeology and heritage: A discussion with Arjun Appadurai." *Journal of Social Archaeology* 1/1: 35–49.

Arana, Miranda. 1994. "Modernized Vietnamese traditional music and its impact on musical sensibility." *Nhac Viet* (Spring & Fall).

———. 1999. *Neotraditional Music in Vietnam*. Kent, Ohio: The International Association for Research in Vietnamese Music.

Banks, Jack. 1997. "Video in the machine: The incorporation of music video into the recording industry." *Popular Music* 16/3: 293–309 (Oct.).

Bayton, Mavis. 1998. *Frock Rock: Women Performing Popular Music*. Oxford, UK: Oxford University Press.

BBC News. 2004. "Press 'least free' in Asia, Cuba." UK Edition. October 26.

Blackburn, Philip. 1993. "Voices of Vietnam." http://www.rootsworld.com/rw/feature/vietnam.html

Blackburn, Philip and Jan Dodd. 2000. "Vietnam." In *World Music. The Rough Guide, Volume 2: Latin and North America, Caribbean, India, Asia and Pacific*, edited by Simon Broughton and Mark Ellingham, 462–469. London: Rough Guides.

Cammann, Schuyler. 1985. "Some Early Chinese symbols of duality." *History of Religions* 24/3: 215–254 (February).

Charlot, John. 1989. "Vietnamese cinema: The power of the past." *The Journal of American Folklore* 102/406: 442–452 (Oct.–Dec.).

Charlton, Katherine. 2003. *Rock Music Styles: A History*. Fourth edition. New York: McGraw-Hill.

Chung Quốc Hưng. 2001. "Would-be pop stars throng open mic night in Bình Thuận community hall." *Việt Nam News* (May 20).

"CPV [Communist Party of Vietnam] Central Committee's Political Report." 2001. Supplement, *Việt Nam News* (April 20): 1-15.

Da Ly. 2001. "HCM City music scene attracts Hà Nội singers." *Việt Nam News* (July 28).

Dân Anh. 1999. "Bootleg CDs, videos and films might be worrying domestic pro-
ducers but live performances of popular Vietnamese music is thriving." *Việt
Nam News* (July 7).
Drummond, Lisa B. W. and Mandy Thomas, eds. 2003. *Consuming Urban Cul-
ture in Contemporary Vietnam.* London: RoutledgeCurzon
Đức Ngọc. 1998. "Pop star Thanh a big hit." *Việt Nam News*, December 26.
Elms, Brian. N.d. "The role of Vietnamese women in two disparate forms of enter-
tainment." Unpublished paper (for MUS 3934r, The Florida State University,
Summer Program in Vietnam, June 2002).
Fahey, Stephanie. 1998. "Vietnam's women in the renovation era." In *Gender and
Power in Affluent Asia*, edited by Krishna Sen and Maila Stivens, 222–249.
London: Routledge.
Feld, Steven. 2001. "A sweet lullaby for world music." In *Globalization*, edited by
Arjun Appadurai, 189–216. Durham, NC: Duke University Press.
Fetherstone, Mike, Scott M. Lash, and Roland Robertson, eds. 1995. *Global
Modernities.* London: Sage.
Fforde, Adam. 2003. "Vietnam—culture and economy: Dyed-in-the-wool tigers?"
In *Consuming Urban Culture in Contemporary Vietnam*, edited by Lisa B. W.
Drummond and Mandy Thomas, 35–59. London: RoutledgeCurzon.
Fish, Lydia M. 1989. "General Edward G. Lansdale and the folksongs of Ameri-
cans in the Vietnam War." *The Journal of American Folklore* 102/406: 390–
411 (Oct.–Dec.).
Frith, Simon. 1997. "Formalism, realism and leisure: The case of punk." In *The
Subcultures Reader*, edited by Ken Gelder and Sarah Thornton, 163–174. Lon-
don: Routledge.
Frith, Simon, Will Straw, and John Street, eds. 2001. *The Cambridge Companion
to Pop and Rock.* Cambridge, UK: Cambridge University Press.
Garofalo, Reebee, ed. 1992. *Rockin' the Boat.* Boston: South End Press.
———. 2007. "Pop goes to war, 2001–2004: U.S. popular music after 9/11." In
Music in the Post-9/11 World, edited by Jonathan Ritter and J. Martin Daugh-
try, 3–26. New York and London: Routledge.
Gelder, Ken and Sarah Thornton, eds. 1997. *The Subcultures Reader.* London:
Routledge.
Gerke, Frank and Bui Tuyen. 1999. "Popular music in Vietnam." *Vietnam-Culture
A Panorama with Images, Texts, Sounds and More.* Internet webpage. http://
archiv.hkw.de/english/culture/1999/vietnam/ezine/popmusik.html
Gibbs, Jason. 1998. "Nhac Tien Chien: The Origins of Vietnamese Popular Song."
Things Asian. http://www.thingsasian.com/stories-photos/1211
———. 2005. "Vietnam." In *Continuum Encyclopedia of Popular Music of the
World, Volume V: Asia and Oceania*, edited by John Shepherd, David Horn,
and Dave Laing, 221–29. London: Continuum.
Hamm, Charles. 1995. *Putting Popular Music in its Place.* Cambridge, UK: Cam-
bridge University Press.
Hawkins, Peter. 2000. *Chanson: The French Singer-Songwriter from Aristide Bru-
ant to the Present Day.* Aldershot, Hampshire, England: Ashgate Publishing.
Hood, Mantle. 1982. *The Ethnomusicologist.* New Edition. Kent, OH: The Kent
State University Press.
Huỳnh Hòa Bình. 2000. "Dance fever hits HCM City." *Việt Nam News* (April
8).
Jamieson, Neil L. 1993. *Understanding Vietnam.* Berkeley: University of Califor-
nia Press.
Kellner, Douglas. N.d. "Globalization and the postmodern turn." http://www.
gseis.ucla. edu/courses/ed253a/dk/GLOBPM.htm [no longer available]

Kennedy, Laurel B. and Mary Rose Williams. 2001. "The past without the pain: The manufacture of nostalgia in Vietnam's tourism industry." In *The Country of Memory: Remaking the Past in Late Socialist Vietnam*, edited by Hue-Tam Ho Tai, 135–163. Berkeley: University of California Press.

Kerkvliet, Benedict J. Tria. 2003. "Authorities and the people: An analysis of state–society relations in Vietnam." In *Postwar Vietnam: Dynamics of a Transforming Society*, edited by Hy V. Luong, 27–53. Singapore: Institute of Southeast Asian Studies.

Kim Thinh. 1995. "Traditional values undermined in Vietnam." *Việt Nam News* (December 27).

Kirk, Dan. 2004. VietNamNet, October 28, 2004 (http://english.vietnamnet.vn/service/printversion?article_id=538322) [no longer available]

Korpe, Marie, ed. 2004. *Shoot the Singer! Music Censorship Today*. London: Zed Books.

Kourtova, Plamena. N.d. "Indigenizing the Global: Popular music as culture in post-communist Bulgaria. Paper presented at the PCAS/ACAS Annual Conference, Savannah, Georgia (October, 2006).

Laing, Dave. 1998. "Knockin' on China's door." In *Popular Music: Intercultural Interpretations*, edited by Toru Mitsui, 337–342. Papers of the 9th biennial Conference of the International Association for the Study of Popular Music (IASPM), held in Kanazawa, Japan, July 1997. Kanazawa: Graduate Program in Music, Kanazawa University.

Lamb, David. 2002. *Vietnam, Now*. New York: Public Affairs.

Le Duan. 1976. *This Nation and Socialism are One* (translated by Tran van Dinh). New York: Vanguard Books.

Leonard, Marion. 2007. *Gender in the Music Industry: Rock, Discourse and Girl Power*. Aldershot, Hampshire, England: Ashgate Publishing.

Lipman, Jenny. 1996. "Rockers take root in HCMC." *Việt Nam News*, May 9.

Lull, James. 1987. "Listeners' communicative uses of popular music." In *Popular Music and Communication*, edited by James Lull, 140–174. Newbury Park, CA: Sage Publications.

———, ed. 1987. *Popular Music and Communication*. Newbury Park, CA: Sage Publications.

Luong, Hy Van, ed. 2003. *Postwar Vietnam: Dynamics of a Transforming Society*. Singapore: Institute of Southeast Asian Studies.

———. 2003. "Gender relations: Ideologies, kinship practices, and political economy." In *Postwar Vietnam: Dynamics of a Transforming Society*, edited by Hy V. Luong, 201–223. Singapore: Institute of Southeast Asian Studies.

Maga, Timothy P. 2000. *The Complete Idiot's Guide to the Vietnam War*. Indianapolis: Alpha Books.

Mai Hong. 1995. "Traditional music in changing times." *Việt Nam News* (November 5).

Manuel, Peter. 1988. *Popular Musics of the Non-Western World: An Introductory Survey*. New York: Oxford University Press.

Marr, David and Stanley Rosen. 1998. "Chinese and Vietnamese youth in the 1990s." *The China Journal* 40: 145–172 (July, *Special Issue: Transforming Asian Socialism. China and Vietnam Compared*).

McLeod, Mark W. and Nguyen Thi Dieu. 2001. *Culture and Customs of Vietnam*. Westport, Connecticut: Greenwood Press.

McNally, Stephen. 2003. "*Bia om* and karaoke: HIV and everyday life in urban Vietnam." In *Consuming Urban Culture in Contemporary Vietnam*, edited by Lisa B. W. Drummond and Mandy Thomas, 110–112. London: Routledge-Curzon.

McVeigh, Brian. 2000. *Wearing Ideology: State, Schooling, and Self-Presentation in Japan.* Oxford, U.K.: Berg Publishing.

Menendez, Laura. N.d. "Blending in, to the night life of Southeast Asia: An ethnographic exploration." Unpublished paper (for MUS 3934r, The Florida State University, Summer Program in Vietnam, June 2004).

Merriam, Alan P. 1964. *The Anthropology of Music.* Evanston, Illinois: Northwestern University Press.

Milioto, Jennifer. 1998. "Women in Japanese popular music: Setting the subcultural scene." In *Popular Music: Intercultural Interpretations*, edited by Toru Mitsui, 485–498. Papers of the 9th biennial Conference of the International Association for the Study of Popular Music (IASPM), held in Kanazawa, Japan, July 1997. Kanazawa: Graduate Program in Music, Kanazawa University.

Miller, Terry E. 1991. "Music and theater in Saigon—1970: An American soldier's observations revisted." In *New Perspectives on Vietnamese Music: Six Essays*, edited by Phong T. Nguyễn, 21–35. New Haven, CT: Council on Southeast Asian Studies, Yale Center for International Studies.

Miller, Terry E. and Phong T. Nguyễn. 1992. "Music in Ho Chi Minh City and Southern Vietnam, Summer 1991." *Nhac Viet: The Journal of Vietnamese Music* 1/1: 21–42.

Minh Hiền. 1997. "Everything's looking rosy for Hồng Nhung." *Việt Nam News*, May 15.

Mitsui, Toru, ed. 1998. *Popular Music: Intercultural Interpretations.* Papers of the 9th biennial Conference of the International Association for the Study of Popular Music (IASPM), held in Kanazawa, Japan, July 1997. Kanazawa: Graduate Program in Music, Kanazawa University.

Naggar, David. 2000–2004. *The Music Business (Explained in Plain English).* San Francisco, CA: DaJé Publishing.

Negus, Keith. 1996. *Popular Music in Theory.* Hanover, NH: University Press of New England.

Ngô Ngọc Ngũ Long. n.d. http://www.nhandan.org.vn/english/today/culture.html

Nguyễn Hùng and Mai Phương. 2002. "Audiences in thrall of Mỹ Tâm's power." *Việt Nam News* (March 10).

Nguyễn, Phong T., ed. 1991. *New Perspectives on Vietnamese Music: Six Essays.* New Haven, CT: Council on Southeast Asian Studies, Yale Center for International Studies.

———. 1998. "Vietnam." In *The Garland Encyclopedia of World Music, Vol. 4, Southeast Asia*, edited by Terry E. Miller and Sean Williams, 444–517. New York: Garland.

Nuzum, Eric. 2004. "Crash into me, baby: America's implicit music censorship since 11 September." In *Shoot the Singer! Music Censorship Today*, edited by Marie Korpe, 149–159. London: Zed Books.

Olsen, Dale A. 2000. "Globalization, culturation, and transculturation in American music: From cultural pop to transcultural art." In *Reflections on American Music: The Twentieth Century and the New Millennium*, edited by James R. Heintze and Michael Saffle. Monographs & Bibliographies in American Music Series, The College Music Society. New York: Pendragon Press.

———. 2001. *Music of El Dorado: The Ethnomusicology of Ancient Andean Cultures.* Gainesville: University Press of Florida.

———. 2004. *The Chrysanthemum and the Song: Music, Memory, and Identity in the South American Japanese Diaspora.* Gainesville: University Press of Florida. New World Diasporas Series.

Onishi, Koji. 1998. "Shibuya-Kei (Shibuya Sound) and globalization." In *Popular Music: Intercultural Interpretations*, edited by Toru Mitsui, 480–484. Papers of the 9th biennial Conference of the International Association for the Study of Popular Music (IASPM), held in Kanazawa, Japan, July 1997. Kanazawa: Graduate Program in Music, Kanazawa University.

Ōtake, Akiko and Shūhei Hosokawa. 2001. "Karaoke in East Asia: Modernization, Japanization, or Asianization?" In *Karaoke around the World: Global Technology, Local Singing*, edited by Tōru Mitsui and Shūhei Hosokawa, 178–201. London: Routledge.

Perris, Arnold. 1985. *Music as Propaganda: Art to Persuade, Art to Control.* Westport, Conn.: Greenwood Press.

Phạm Duy. 1975. *Musics of Vietnam.* Edited by Dale R. Whiteside, with an Introduction by Stephen Addiss. Carbondale: Southern Illinois University Press.

Phạm Thị Thu Thủy. 2003. "Thanh slows pace to boost enjoyment." *Việt Nam News* (May 31).

"Political Report of the Central Committee (VII Tenure) to the VIIIth National Congress of the Communist Party of Vietnam," in Supplement, *Viet Nam News* [sic] (April 10, 1996): 1-6.

Price, Kayla. N.d. "The public face of karaoke: *Hat Voi Nhau* in Vietnam." Unpublished paper (for MUS 3934r, The Florida State University, Summer Program in Vietnam, June 2002).

Ramet, Sabrina Petra, ed. 1994. *Rocking the State: Rock Music and Politics in Eastern Europe and Russia.* Boulder, CO: Westview Press.

Ramet, Sabrina Petra, Sergei Zamascikov, and Robert Bird. 1994. "The Soviet rock scene." In *Rocking the State: Rock Music and Politics in Eastern Europe and Russia*, edited by Sabrina Petra Ramet, 181–218. Boulder, CO: Westview Press.

Redhead, Steve. 1990. *The end-of-the-century party. Youth and pop towards 2000.* Manchester, U.K.: Manchester University Press.

Reyes Schramm, Adelaida. 1991. "From refugee to immigrant: The music of Vietnamese in the New York–New Jersey metropolitan area. In *New Perspectives on Vietnamese Music*, edited by Phong Nguyen, 91–102. New Haven, CT: Yale Center for International and Area Studies.

Roasa, Dustin. 2005. "The art of noise." *Timeout*: 9–11 (July 4–10).

Robertson, Roland. 1995. "Glocalization: Time–space and homogeneity–heterogeneity." In *Global Modernities*, edited by M. Fetherstone, S. Lash and Roland Robertson, 27–44. London: Sage.

Rock Fan Club. http://www.rockfanclub.org.

Sahlins, Marshall. 2000. "The return of the event, again." In *Culture in Practice: Selected Essays*, 293–352. New York: Zone Books.

Scarborough, Sarah. N.d. "If these walls could talk: An American's view on Vietnamese karaoke." Unpublished paper (for MUS 3934r, Ethnographic Fieldwork in Music, The Florida State University, Summer Program in Vietnam, June 2002).

Sekine, Naoki. 2007. "The music business in Asia." In *The Global Music Industry: Three Perspectives*, edited by Arthur Bernstein, Naoki Sekine, and Dick Weissman, 199–263. New York and London: Routledge.

Shaw, Will. 2002. "Lasers blazing, The Wall take Hà Nội." *Việt Nam News* (November 11).

Shuker, Roy. 2003. *Understanding Popular Music.* 2nd ed. London: Routledge.

———. 2005. *Popular Music. The Key Concepts.* 2nd ed. London: Routledge.

Song Ngan. 2003. "Budding pop star on the rise." *Việt Nam News* (January 11).

Soucy, Alexander. 2003. "Pilgrims and pleasure-seekers." In *Consuming Urban Culture in Contemporary Vietnam*, edited by Lisa B. W. Drummond and Mandy Thomas, 125–137. London: RoutledgeCurzon.

Stock, Cheryl. 2003. "*Doi moi* and the crisis in Vietnamese dance." In *Consuming Urban Culture in Contemporary Vietnam*, edited by Lisa B. W. Drummond and Mandy Thomas, 219–240. London: RoutledgeCurzon.

Stocking, Ben. 2003. "Vietnam rocks—carefully." Knight Ridder Newspapers, from the San Jose [California] *Mercury News*. Posted on the Internet, Feb. 28, 2003, at http://www.aberdeennews.com/mld/kentucky/news/world/ 5285100.htm and also at http://www.bayarea.com/mld/mercurynews [no longer available].

Straw, Will. 1997. "Communities and scenes in popular music." In *The Subcultures Reader*, edited by Ken Gelder and Sarah Thornton, 494–505. London: Routledge.

Street, John. 1986. *Rebel Rock: The Politics of Popular Music*. Oxford, UK: Basil Blackwell, Ltd.

Sturken, Marita. 1997. *Tangled Memories: The Vietnam War, the AIDS Epidemic, and the Politics of Remembering*. Berkeley: University of California Press.

Tai, Hue-Tam Ho, ed. 2001. *The Country of Memory: Remaking the Past in Late Socialist Vietnam*. Berkeley: University of California Press.

———. 2001a. "Faces of remembrance and forgetting." In *The Country of Memory: Remaking the Past in Late Socialist Vietnam*, edited by Hue-Tam Ho Tai, 167–195. Berkeley: University of California Press.

———. 2001b. "Introduction: Situating memory." In *The Country of Memory: Remaking the Past in Late Socialist Vietnam*, edited by Hue-Tam Ho Tai, 1–17. Berkeley: University of California Press.

Taylor, Nora A. 2001. "Framing the national spirit: Viewing and reviewing painting under the revolution." In *The Country of Memory: Remaking the Past in Late Socialist Vietnam*, edited by Hue-Tam Ho Tai, 109–134. Berkeley: University of California Press.

Taylor, Philip. 2001. *Fragments of the Present: Searching for Modernity in Vietnam's South*. Honolulu: University of Hawai'i Press.

———. 2003. "Digesting reform: Opera and cultural identity in Ho Chi Minh City." In *Consuming Urban Culture in Contemporary Vietnam*, edited by Lisa B. W. Drummond and Mandy Thomas, 138–154. London: RoutledgeCurzon.

———. 2004. *Goddess on the Rise: Pilgrimage and Popular Religion in Vietnam*. Honolulu: University of Hawai'i Press.

Thái Bảo. 2000. "A wild man tames with gentle songs." *Việt Nam News* (December 17).

"The Communist Party of Vietnam, The Eighth National Congress (An unofficial translation of the main body of the address made by General Secretary Do Muoi at the opening of the congress)," in Extra, *Việt Nam News* (June 29, 1996): 1-3./*/74104141555554071

Thomas, Mandy and Lisa B. W. Drummond. 2003. "Introduction." In *Consuming Urban Culture in Contemporary Vietnam*. London: RoutledgeCurzon.

Tiger Translate. 2007–2008. Vietnam Brewery Limited. http://www.tigermusic. com.vn/home.php

Trần Minh Phi. 1999. "Husband-and-wife duos wow music fans." *Việt Nam News* (July 28).

———. 2000. "High flying songbirds are all a-flutter. *Việt Nam News* (May 28).

Trịnh Công Sơn. 1998. *Trịnh Công Sơn: Tuyển Tập, Những Bài Ca Không Năm Tháng*. Hue: Nha Xuat Ban Am Nhac, Nguyen Van Vinh Advertising Co.

Việt Nam Cultural Profiles Project. 2004. "Popular music" (last updated August 7). British Council Viet Nam, http://www.culturalprofiles.org.uk/Visiting_ Arts/Directories/Overview/-13.html

Truyện cổ tích Việt Nam. Vietnamese Legends and Folk Tales. 2001. Hanoi: Thế Giới Publishers.

Việt Nam News. 1992, 1994–2006. Hanoi and Ho Chi Minh City. Việt Nam News Agency.

Việt Nam News Online. Hanoi and Ho Chi Minh City. Việt Nam News Agency http://vietnamnews.vnanet.vn/

Vo Van Kiet. 1981. "The cultural and ideological front in Ho Chi Minh City." *Vietnamese Studies* 69: 130–150.

Walser, Robert. 1993. *Running with the Devil: Power, Gender, and Madness in Heavy Metal Music.* Hanover, NH: Wesleyan University Press.

Whiteley, Sheila. 2000. *Women and Popular Music: Sexuality, Identity and Subjectivity.* London: Routledge.

Witzleben, J. Lawrence. 1998. "Localism, nationalism, and transnationalism in pre-postcolonial Hong Kong popular song." In *Popular Music: Intercultural Interpretations*, edited by Toru Mitsui, 469–475. Papers of the 9th biennial Conference of the International Association for the Study of Popular Music (IASPM), held in Kanazawa, Japan, July 1997. Kanazawa: Graduate Program in Music, Kanazawa University.

———. 1999. "Cantopop and Mandapop in pre-postcolonial Hong Kong: Identity negotiation in the performances of Anita Mui Yim-Fong." *Popular Music* 18/2: 241–258 (May).

Wong, Deborah. 1994. "I want the microphone": Mass mediation and agency in Asian-American popular music." *The Drama Review* 38/3: 152–167 (Fall).

———. 2004. *Speak it Louder: Asian Americans Making Music.* New York: Routledge.

Young, Stephen B. 1979. "Vietnamese Marxism: Transition in elite ideology." *Asian Survey* 19/8: 770–779 (August).

Index